Writing Communities

A Text with Readings

Writing Communities

A Text with Readings

Stephen Parks

Syracuse University

bedford/st.martin's
Macmillan Learning
Boston | New York

For Bedford/St. Martin's

Vice President, Editorial, Macmillan Learning Humanities: Edwin Hill
Editorial Director, English: Karen S. Henry
Senior Publisher for Composition, Business and Technical Writing, Developmental Writing:
  Leasa Burton
Executive Editor: John E. Sullivan
Developmental Editor: Alicia Young
Senior Production Editor: Kerri A. Cardone
Media Producer: Rand Thomas
Senior Production Supervisor: Lisa McDowell
Marketing Manager: Joy Fisher Williams
Copy Editor: Kathleen Lafferty
Indexer: Jake Kawatski, Live Oaks Indexing
Photo Researcher: Sheri Blaney
Permissions Editor: Elaine Kosta
Senior Art Director: Anna Palchik
Text Design: Lisa Buckley Design
Cover Design: William Boardman
Cover Photo: Hill Street Studios/Eric Raptosh/Getty Images
Composition: Jouve
Printing and Binding: LSC Communications

Manufactured in the United States of America.

1   0   9   8   7   6
f   e   d   c   b   a

For information, write: Bedford/St. Martin's, 75 Arlington Street, Boston, MA 02116
  (617-399-4000)

ISBN 978-1-4576-6742-8 (Student Edition)
ISBN 978-1-319-07821-8 (Instructor's Edition)

Acknowledgments

Text acknowledgments and copyrights appear at the back of the book on pages 427–36, which constitute an extension of the copyright page. Art acknowledgments and copyrights appear on the same page as the art selections they cover.

Contents

8 Writing Place: Mapping Yourself onto Local, National, and International Communities   249

9 Writing Networks: Creating Links Online and Offline   302

Preface for Instructors

Textbooks are rarely considered to be personal statements of belief, and certainly not by the students who must do the work textbooks require. Yet woven into the advice, assignments, and readings of *Writing Communities* is a belief not only in the power of academic writing when linked to community need but also in the work of entry-level college writing classes.

This is a hard-earned belief. It is the product of my attending college during a recession that wiped out the steel industry in Pittsburgh in the 1980s. It is the product of having seen this generation lose its economic foothold in the middle class, witnessed adults reduced to long-term unemployment, and watched families break under the pressures of poverty. But more than that, this belief is premised on having seen many communities draw upon a history of common support and of common vision to rebuild futures for themselves and their children.

For me, this common support took the form of ensuring that not only could I attend college, but I could afford to graduate. It meant additional support during the long years of graduate school, years that resulted in my becoming a professor of rhetoric and composition — a field that I never even knew existed until I got to college. And this support resulted in my eventually teaching the very courses that had ensured my own academic success.

Ultimately, it was the field of rhetoric and composition's commitment to creating entry-level writing classes designed for working-class students, marginalized students, and students who needed additional support to succeed, that afforded me the skills I needed to graduate. Freshman writing helped me to understand what the university meant by "academic discourse." It explained the need for sources, evidence, and thesis statements. And it was both longtime and new friends in undergraduate and graduate school who reminded me that an education that separates you from your community is a limiting and damaging process. Ultimately, my writing courses taught me that you should support the community that supports you.

It was out of this belief that I began to create writing courses that connect students to their neighborhoods and the course syllabus to the community. I did this in an effort to draw together knowledgeable people regardless of their "degrees" to work on issues such as education, housing, and cultural justice. It was out of this context that my students began to see how coming to the university did not mean leaving behind all they valued in their home communities. Out of this work, perhaps, they also began to see how a freshman writing course could supply them with a map to navigate the terrain of the university not just as an exit from economic instability but also as means to return home as an ally for those still struggling.

I have intentionally included many examples of these students' work in the pages of *Writing Communities* in the form of writing prompts, short essays, interviews, and extended stories. Their work speaks to the belief in education, of the power of freshman writing, and of the need to give back on the way up. Their work is inspirational, providing examples of what can emerge from college writing courses.

I understand that textbooks are not by nature statements of personal belief. Textbooks can, however, enable students to begin their own personal educational journey. Such was the case with me, and I hope this textbook enables a similar journey for your students.

The Structure of *Writing Communities*

Writing Communities is organized into two parts: Part One: Reading and Writing Communities and Part Two: Collaboration and Publishing. Each part opens with instructional chapters that provide students background in the concepts they need to succeed at academic writing and community-engaged work. The latter sections of Parts One and Part Two are comprised of thematic reading chapters that offer diverse selections ranging from personal narratives and poetry to essays and academic scholarship. Each reading chapter ends with a series of *Writing with Communities* projects that provide a set of extended assignments, usually for groups, designed to enable the students to enact the concepts of the book with activities focused on on- or off-campus projects. (These features are discussed in greater depth on pages xvii–xviii.)

Part One: Reading and Writing Communities

The first half of the text provides the conceptual framework for students to understand the connection between academic writing and community writing. This part shows students the connection between the essential academic literacy skills taught in writing courses and the seemingly extra skills that community writing can provide. It is the premise of this book that learning how to blend these two sets of skills together will best prepare students for whatever writing they may undertake in the future, including any projects they complete with community partners.

Chapter 1, Reading Strategies and Intellectual Communities, opens with a piece of community writing focused on how a resident helps a couple lost in her neighborhood. That story is used to pose the questions of not only who is an intellectual but also what it means to read a situation from the position of a member of that intellectual community. Drawing on the work of Antonio Gramsci, the chapter sets forth definitions of *traditional* and *organic intellectuals*, which then go on to serve as organizing terms for the difference between academic and community intellectuals. This chapter highlights the different reading strategies of each intellectual community as well as the power of bringing such strategies into dialogue.

Chapter 2, Academic and Community Discourse, also begins with a piece of community writing, this one focused on a Latina student who frames her education as learning how to exist within two different language communities: English and Spanish. That piece becomes a metaphor to talk about how different discourse communities frame research topics, develop research strategies, and develop writing that draws forth more conversations. Again, the goal of this chapter is to have students position themselves as collaborative members of a community.

Following this section are two chapters of readings aimed at enabling students to both solidify and expand their understanding of the concepts discussed in the first two chapters.

Chapter 3, Writing Education: Moving from Home to College Communities, presents excerpts of readings by "recognized scholars" Antonio Gramsci, David Bartholomae, Andrew Delbanco, and Harry Boyte and Elizabeth Hollander. It also includes community and student authors who contributed to a community publication called *Pro(se)letartiets*, which emerged from a partnership between Syracuse University and the United Kingdom–based Federation of Worker Writers and Community Publishers. These readings are designed to engage students in understanding the role of college, recognizing the insights of different types of intellectuals, and figuring out what that recognition means in practice in classrooms, educational programs, and institutional missions.

Chapter 4, Writing Classrooms: Discovering Writing within Classroom Communities, offers readings by Gerald Graff, Carmen Kynard, and Christopher Wilkey that move students from the "university" to the "classroom" — in particular, the writing classroom. These readings pose "academic writing" as a topic worthy of intellectual debate, the value and intent of which are not finalized. The goal of this chapter is to give students the opportunity to consider the relationship of academic writing to a series of communities, ultimately seeing its workings as complex and in need of constant negotiation.

Part Two: Collaboration and Publishing

Part Two expands on the discussions in Part One by connecting them to the concrete practices of community partnership work, including strategies such as how to develop writing prompts, support writing groups, develop ongoing community organizations, and create publications. This emphasis on pragmatic skills grows out of my experience working with students, whom I have often found enter partnership work unsure of its purpose, their role, and whether they possess the skills to succeed. Part Two helps to demystify the process and provide them with tried-and-true tools that can be used in this work.

Chapter 5, Community Partnerships, acts as a direct pivot into the partnership work. It draws on earlier arguments to suggest that the first act of collaboration is for students to understand the neighborhood students are about to enter. The chapter emphasizes that students respect the neighborhood where they'll be working, prompting them to research the community and gain knowledge of its needs and values. A workshop model, the "Story of Self," provides a strategy for working with the community partner to develop short personal stories about why everyone is involved in the project.

Chapter 6, Establishing Community Writing Groups, continues the focus on practical skills, covering everything from how to write useful writing prompts to the mechanics of creating writing groups. To begin to connect the skills discussed, showing how they work best when integrated into a common project, this chapter also introduces a narrative case study of Adams College—a fictional school that tells the story of how one community project grew into a sustained partnership.

Chapter 7, Community Events and Community Publishing, follows a similar structure to Chapter 6, continuing the narrative of Adams College. Here the story of the growth of a college/community partnership details how to set up community events such as forums and open mic nights as well as how to turn the writing produced from such partnerships into publications.

At this point, the book moves back to chapters of readings.

Chapter 8, Writing Place: Mapping Yourself onto Local, National, and International Communities, introduces the concept of mapping to ask students to consider how the possibility equal partnership is only realized through concerted effort. The chapter contains readings by Nedra Reynolds, Paula Mathieu, and Jesús Villicaña López. These readings explore how the insights and voices of community intellectuals are often not included in local policy matters. The chapter then moves to pose a series of strategies to counter this challenge.

Chapter 9, Writing Networks: Creating Links Online and Offline, begins with a story by a Libyan democratic activist to highlight the utopian aspects that are associated with digital culture. The readings that follow both expand upon that possible utopia as well as ask students to consider how such euphoria might be tempered. To this end, the chapter contains essays by Nicholas Christakis and James Fowler, James Paul Gee and Elisabeth Hayes, Matt Mason, and WikiLeaks .org to explore how networks, both in-person and online, enable collaboration.

Chapter 10, Writing Identity: Moving in and across Boundaries, focuses on the ways in which body image is a cultural construct, one that is often limiting and in need of transgression if a person is on the margins of power. To support this conversation, there are essay by four authors: Wesley Yang, Stacey Waite, Gloria Anzaldúa, and Jonathan Alexander.

Features of *Writing Communities*

A variety of writing assignments and sequences facilitate complete engagement with the text and support critical thinking and analytical writing.

Checkpoints throughout the text ask students to reflect on—and write about—how the instruction of the text relates to their own background and community values. **Rundown** boxes at the end of each instructional chapter offer bulleted summations of the material in the chapter, and **Discussion Question and Activities** ask students to engage with each other to analyze the concepts of the text.

Four kinds of post-reading questions prompt students to relate the selections to the larger discussions of the text. **Reading** questions provide students guidance on which key terms or concepts need to be studied to fully understand the reading. **Inquiring** questions provide common activities and discussion questions designed to help students relate a reading's relationship to the thematic topic of the chapter. **Composing** questions provide the opportunity for students to respond in writing (print or digital) to the reading, often asking them to do research based on their campus or surrounding community. Finally, **Connecting** questions ask students to draw connections and comparisons among the authors in the chapter. An appendix of **Key Terms** also helps students to gain a richer sense of the concepts deployed throughout the book.

Each reading chapter also concludes with six **Writing with Communities** projects (thirty in total, numbered sequentially throughout the text). These projects consist of sets of extended assignments, usually group-oriented, that enable students to blend the conceptual framework of book instruction with on-campus and off-campus activities, projects, and publications. The Writing with Communities projects draw together different themes and concepts from the readings and ask students to engage in collaborative research as well as conversation. However, these projects can also serve as a launching point for the specific work of a community project that might be part of your class. For instance, projects that provide a framework to produce a particular type of publication can be applied to the specific group with which you are working; audio projects focused on an off-campus issue that utilizes audio and online strategies can also be adopted for a campus issue facing your students. In that way, the skills of a specific project are transferable to your exact need. I would strongly suggest reviewing these projects in conjunction with the readings ahead of time and assessing which might be suitable for your particular class and community partnership. Students will likely have opinions on which projects they would most like to undertake.

Acknowledgments

The essential theme in this book is collaboration, and I have certainly been blessed to have been supported by a wonderful community in creating this book. This community began with my closest friend and ally, Jim Seitz, who first convinced me that the time was right to take on such work. It expanded to include wonderful friends and editors at Bedford/St. Martin's: Leasa Burton, senior publisher, and John Sullivan, executive editor for readers, whose patience as I worked to find a format that reflected the ethical vision of my community partners was humbling. And truly, this specific community could not have functioned and reached it goals without the steady leadership of Alicia Young, who really deserves to be listed as co-author of this book given her consistent attention to the sentences and concepts that fill the pages.

I also need to recognize important individuals who were part of my community prior to—and hopefully long after—*Writing Communities*. Lori Shorr has been a North Star for all of my work, consistently demonstrating what moral judgment and deep collaboration entail. Sadie Shorr-Parks's writing has modeled for me the need to pay attention to each word; Eliot Shorr-Parks has consistently pointed out the need to imagine the real student in the real classroom; and Aaron Moss has enacted a moral vision for the powerless that echoes across these pages. And Jude Shorr-Parks consistently demonstrates that kindness is the most fundamental element in any learning situation.

I must also mention those who early in my career helped me understand what the composition and rhetoric classroom could mean to those to whom I was most committed: the diverse community of working-class students. It began with the Basic Writing Committee chaired by Jim Seitz, moved to a lifelong collaboration with Eli Goldblatt, and expanded to include colleagues such as Ira Shor, Paula Mathieu, Adam Banks, Ellen Cushman, Elaine Richardson, Cristina Kirklighter, Donald Lazere, Deborah Mutnick, Nick Pollard, Shannon Carter, and Linda Adler-Kassner. My time at Syracuse University has been the most rewarding intellectual experience of my life. For that I am grateful to all my colleagues, but Eileen Schell and John Burdick deserve particular thanks for consistent and often hard-fought commitment to creating a university focused on social justice and equity. I truly admire their work.

I also want to acknowledge Jess Pauszek, Romeo Garcia, Ben Kuebrich, Tamara Issak Bassam, Vani Kannan, Jason Luther, Telsha Curry, and Vincent Portillo. I met them when they were graduate students, but to my thinking, they represent how the next generation of scholars will continue to expand our field's commitment to issues and ideas that transcend the narrow confines of an increasingly "traditional" discipline and pedagogical vision.

Of course, none of this would have been possible without the many community writers and activists who allowed me to be part of their important political work. While their names are throughout all the New City Community Press publications (newcitycommunitypress.com), I want to specifically thank Mark Lyons and Mother Earth—the ethical tent poles on whose vision important community publishing work has been done.

In another life, I have also been fortunate to be a publisher. This means I have witnessed all the hidden labor that makes it possible for you to hold this book. And so I save my final thanks for those individuals on whom this whole enterprise depends: Assistant editor Jennifer Prince saw to innumerable details along the way. Kerri Cardone, senior production editor, also helped with countless important details and suggestions. Kathleen Lafferty, copyeditor, tightened the prose and offered many important suggestions. Thanks also to Elaine Kosta and Kalina Ingham, who cleared text permissions; Billy Boardman, who designed the cover; Lisa Buckley, who is responsible for the wonderful interior design; and Sheri Blaney and Martha Friedman, who oversaw and secured permission for the images in this book.

I have also had the good fortune to be a journal editor and have learned the value of insights offered by critically minded reviewers. So I want to acknowledge the following professors and scholars who offered criticism, praise, and detailed recommendations as I developed *Writing Communities*, for which I owe them many thanks: Hannah Ashley, West Chester University; Jeanne Bohannon, Kennesaw State University; Kathy Cain, Merrimack College; Kaitlin Clinnin, Ohio State University; Chip Dunkin, University of Mississippi; Karen Forgette, University of Mississippi; Eli Goldblatt, Temple University; Beth Gulley, Johnson County Community College; Tobi Jacobi, Colorado State; Barbara Jaffe, El Camino College; Ed Jones, Seton Hall University; Jacqueline Kerr, University of Tennessee Knoxville; Cristina Kirklighter, Texas A&M University; Travis Rountree, University of Louisville; Rachael Wendler Shah, University of Nebraska Lincoln.

A final thanks to Kristen Krause and Kristi Johnson—my friends, my allies, and, really, just truly great people.

Steve Parks
Associate Professor of Writing, Syracuse University

Get the Most Out of Your Course with *Writing Communities*

Bedford/St. Martin's offers resources and format choices that help you and your students get even more out of your book and course. To learn more about or to order any of the following products, contact your Bedford/St. Martin's sales representative, e-mail sales support (**sales_support@bfwpub.com**), or visit the Web site at **macmillanlearning.com**.

Select Value Packages

Add value to your text by packaging one of the following resources with *Writing Communities*. To learn more about package options for any of the following products, contact your Bedford/St. Martin's sales representative or visit **macmillanlearning.com**.

Writer's Help 2.0 is a powerful online writing resource that helps students find answers whether they are searching for writing advice on their own or as part of an assignment.

- **Smart search:** Built on research with more than 1,600 student writers, the smart search in *Writer's Help* provides reliable results even when students use novice terms, such as *flow* and *unstuck*.

- **Trusted content from our best-selling handbooks:** Choose *Writer's Help 2.0, Hacker Version,* or *Writer's Help 2.0, Lunsford Version,* and ensure that students have clear advice and examples for all of their writing questions.

- **Adaptive exercises that engage students:** *Writer's Help* includes *Learning-Curve*, game-like online quizzing that adapts to what students already know and helps them focus on what they need to learn.

Student access is packaged with *Writing Communities* at a significant discount. Order ISBN 978-1-319-11810-5 for *Writer's Help 2.0, Hacker Version,* or ISBN 978-1-319-11811-2 for *Writer's Help 2.0, Lunsford Version,* to ensure your students have easy access to online writing support. Students who rent a book or buy a used book can purchase access to *Writer's Help 2.0* at **macmillanhighered .com/writershelp2**.

Instructors may request free access by registering as an instructor at **macmillanhighered.com/writershelp2**.

For technical support, visit **macmillanhighered.com/getsupport**.

***Portfolio Keeping*, Third Edition, by Nedra Reynolds and Elizabeth Davis**, provides all the information students need to use the portfolio method successfully in a writing course. *Portfolio Teaching*, a companion guide for instructors, provides the practical information instructors and writing program administrators need to use the portfolio method successfully in a writing course. To order *Portfolio Keeping* packaged with this text, contact your sales representative for a package ISBN.

Instructor Resources

macmillanlearning.com

You have a lot to do in your course. Bedford/St. Martin's wants to make it easy for you to find the support you need—and to get it quickly.

Resources for Teaching Writing Communities is available as a PDF that can be downloaded from the Bedford/St. Martin's online catalog. In addition to chapter overviews and teaching tips, the instructor's manual includes sample syllabi, correlations to the Council of Writing Program Administrators' Outcomes Statement, and classroom activities.

Teaching Central offers the entire list of Bedford/St. Martin's print and online professional resources in one place. You'll find landmark reference works, sourcebooks on pedagogical issues, award-winning collections, and practical advice for the classroom—all free for instructors. Visit **macmillanlearning.com /teachingcentral**.

Join Our Community!

At Bedford, providing support to teachers and their students who choose our books and digital tools is our first priority. The Bedford/St. Martin's English Community is now our home for professional resources, featuring Bedford *Bits*, our popular blog offering new ideas for the composition classroom and composition teachers. Connect and converse with a growing team of Bedford authors and top scholars who blog on *Bits*: Barclay Barrios, Steve Bernhardt, Susan Bernstein, Traci Gardner, Elizabeth Losh, Andrea Lunsford, Jack Solomon, Elizabeth Wardle, and Donna Winchell, among others.

In addition, you'll find an expanding collection of resources that support your teaching. Download titles from our professional resource series to support your teaching, review projects in the pipeline, sign up for professional development webinars, start a discussion, ask a question, and follow your favorite members.

Visit **community.macmillan.com** to join the conversation with your fellow teachers.

A Letter to Students: A Teacher's Assignment

For the first "assignment" in this textbook, I have tasked myself with the following writing prompt which requires me, the writing teacher, to explain to you, the student, the goals of this book.

Writing Prompt: "Why College Writing?"

Write a short essay explaining the goals of an entry-level college writing course, the course typically called "Freshman Composition." Be sure to address the questions students typically ask: Why must I take this course? What is academic writing? Why

are there required readings in the course? How will what I learn translate to other courses and to life beyond my college? What purpose does such a course serve? In writing your response, remember to avoid overwrought jargon and cliché. Imagine that you are addressing real students about to take a real course. How can you explain the value of the course? How can you explain why it will be worth their time and effort?

Lori Shorr

I assigned myself this task because it is not enough to simply write a textbook—to assume that the connections among the assignments, the readings, and the goals of a college student will be self-evident. In fact, I can remember taking a required writing course during my first years in college, one where the professor made the mistake of assuming that we students understood what was happening in the course. We didn't. And because we didn't, it was a very long and confusing semester.

What I learned from that experience was being mysterious about the inner logic of a course results in indifference. It's like playing a game where only the referee knows the rules. Eventually someone will earn points, but more often than not, they will have no real idea how it occurred or how to make it happen again. It is a frustrating experience.

This kind of arrangement strikes me as unfair. I have always felt that teachers need to be very clear about how a course will work, how it will teach students the necessary skills to write effectively in college, and how it will fit into the broader picture of a student's college education. Moreover, I also want to show you how what you learn from this book and in a writing course can be useful to you *after* college.

The purpose of this book is to help you learn how to link the ideas in your classroom with local efforts to improve your community. As you work through this textbook, I will ask you to imagine that everyone is an intellectual—not just the teachers standing in front of your class, but the neighbors standing next to you in the grocery store line. Everyone has lessons to teach us. Everyone is a potential ally. In fact, this book will make the argument that by learning how to combine academic and community knowledge, college writing, and everyday speech, you will gain the necessary skills to not only to succeed in your college writing courses but also to advocate for change in your local community, in your region, and in your country. This is why the focus of this book is on writing *communities*.

Since these are some pretty big claims I'm making, I'd like to offer a little further explanation as we begin our time together.

Entering the Academic Community

There is a myth that entry-level writing courses are for students who *can't* write. This is untrue. Not only can every college student write, but every student also brings a critical sensibility to her or his writing. The real issue is linking these already-possessed skills to the demands of college. Entry-level writing courses are designed to teach you how to connect your existing skills to essential college writing strategies.

And the need for such a course is straightforward. You are entering a new community. Almost no one would expect to enter a community for the first time and immediately understand all its workings: it would take time to learn all the rules. Likewise, you should also not expect to fully understand college writing as you begin college and learn its rules. You are in an entry-level writing course not because of a deficit in your writing (though good writers are always imagining how they might improve their craft). You are in an entry-level writing course because you are an entry-level student, learning the specific goals and expectations of the academic community you have just entered — and the coin of the realm in this community is academic writing.

Academic writing is the term given to the common strategies developed by college-based researchers to answer questions within their particular fields of inquiry (think history, biology, business, and so forth). Of course, the best researchers also push against accepted beliefs, discover new knowledge, and, consequently, create new writing strategies to represent this knowledge. In that way, academic writing is always in flux, yet it will almost always have certain characteristics.

Academic writing is an argument based upon previous arguments. Academic writers use the insights of others to develop new insights. For that reason, most academic writing emerges from a community that is researching a particular set of concerns — for instance, historians studying the reasons for World War II. This being the case, academic writing can usually be recognized by an abundance of footnotes and extended bibliographies, which acknowledge the scholars and writers to whom new writers are responding. (You will see that many the readings in this text have abundant notes and references, which you can find beginning on page 427.)

Academic writing explores key terms and produces new knowledge. Every community has its own way of speaking. Academic writers use key terms from their research communities as entryways into particular topics but then revise the terms to take on new meanings or interpretations. This book, for instance, will use terms such as *organic intellectual* and *community* in a particular way to support a particular discussion.

Academic writing is always open to debate and critique. Members of academic communities are generally argumentative. For this reason, it's uncommon that any given piece of writing is ever seen as the final statement on a subject; rather, every piece of writing is used as a launching point for further exploration. In essence, academic writers believe we can always learn more and owe it to our community to try.

In fact, you should imagine this book as part of an academic conversation by a community of scholars on the meaning of the terms *community*, *intellectuals*, and *academic writing*. As you read this book, you will be asked to adopt many of the habits of these scholars. For this reason, you might track the use of these terms, seeing how they grow and develop throughout the chapters. In doing so, you will be preparing yourself to offer your own insights into what these terms might mean and the conversations they might enable. In this way, like academic writers, you will be asked to create new knowledge about the topics being discussed.

To learn academic writing strategies, you will need to read extensively. As noted above, academic writing emerges out of conversations within academic communities. Assigned readings in writing classes are attempts to represent the work of that community. By engaging with the readings assigned in class, you learn the conventions of that conversation and gain enough expertise to begin to join in.

As you begin this work, you should also note that academic writing does not subscribe to one particular format. Instead, academic writing represents a set of attitudes and strategies that can be tweaked to fit different academic conversations. This is why the specifics of academic writing might be different in history or in biology and why the same terms typically might not cross over from nuclear physics to literature. And this is why there is no single class that can prepare you for every type of writing done in college, but why an entry-level course can teach how to think critically and respond thoughtfully regardless of what kind of question you are answering or for what audience you are writing.

Staying Connected to Your Home Community

At the outset of the work before us, it is important to remember that you do not leave your home community or your values behind when you begin college. Rather, you bring your own values and insights with you as you enter the classroom.

We all come from somewhere: a rural town, a suburban tract, or, perhaps, a sprawling city. These places have formed our values, our ways of understanding the world. It was these places that we were first tested, that we made the small and large decisions that have formed our identity. For some of us, these tests might have been primarily personal, such as defending a friend or standing with a family member. For others, these tests might have come through collective action, such as taking part in a community rally or speaking out in a public forum. At each of these moments our internal moral compass acted as a guide through the uncertain terrain of daily life.

College can be understood as another such test—another moment when your values are brought into dialogue with a diverse range of individuals, ideas, and collective efforts. It is another moment when you are asked to make public decisions about your personal beliefs. As noted earlier in this letter, when you enter college, you will be asked to imagine yourself as part of a new community. Stepping into a college classroom presents the challenge of bringing your past into the present, drawing the values of your home community—your own experiences—into conversation with the demands of the academy. And it is at this moment students often experience competing demands inside and outside of the classroom.

Yet in some ways, college is a more dramatic example of a basic fact: We are always living in the midst of change, always framing our identity in relationship to new ways of speaking and acting. If we think about our own communities, we will see that their boundaries are always changing: New residents bring new languages, religions, and traditions. Local businesses bring new ways of eating, entertaining, and representing ourselves. National debates over marriage, human rights, and immigration affect our immediate friendships and community alliances.

A community is also much more than just a geographic space. Social media sites such as Facebook and Instagram have expanded the terrain upon which we interact with friends—indeed, virtual communities such as *Second Life* or *Minecraft* allow us to conduct entire "lives" online. Digital and real-life communities can even interact, such as with kickstarter.com, to build hybrid spaces dedicated to producing material change in the "real world." *Community*, then, stands not only for physical terrain but also for the personal and virtual networks that overlay, transcend, and exist within earth-based boundaries.

If you want to stay true to yourself and to your community, the question becomes how to draw the insights learned at home into partnership with the lessons learned at college, to work toward creating a vital and productive community.

Linking Communities

As noted earlier, you will be asked to work with a set of terms in this book (*intellectual*, *community*, and so forth), and the assignments you complete will help you to see how you might use such terms to develop collaborations with other students and with community members. And if you learn how writing can generate such alliances, you can begin to think about how to build a bridge between your home community and your college community. You can position yourself as a writer who works to bring your values into conversations with others in order to form new possibilities.

It is at these moments that you can begin to recognize the potential power of writing. While writers cannot control the ultimate reception of their work, they can strategize about how it will be distributed across local, regional, and national channels. Writers can take on the difficult task of adopting accepted terms, using these terms within arguments and styles designed to reach a particular community, and work to develop persuasive invitations for other people to join the conversation. Think about the term *justice*. The definition of justice as generated in a philosophy class might not fully explain justice in your home community, nor might either definition equate with justice as defined by your family. The best definition of justice, would be that which draws these different meanings together—one that you could create. In this way, effective writers not only navigate existing academic terrain but also provide a compass through which others can join their journey.

Your writing, then, can help people from different communities discover a common set of values and beliefs and initiate new conversations—conversations that can prompt real change.

Community Publishing

If the goal is to blend college and community insights, fusing both together for the purpose of being active community members, it is important to do so in a way that provides multiple methods for testing how such work might gain a public audience.

For many students, active engagement with writing does not move beyond the classroom—the circulation of their work stops at their instructor. There is certainly value in such work; as I mentioned earlier, understanding the requirements of academic writing is a crucial skill to succeed at college, and such work will be a component of the work this book asks you to do. It is, however, only one example of the power of writing.

Community publishing has been a traditional venue through which individuals and organizations have circulated their ideas and concerns. These publications are often multimodal, blending such formats as chapbooks, blogs, audio recordings, and e-books to get their message out. Indeed, if you were to study such publications, you would see how the materials chosen for the publication and the distribution avenues reveal who the author(s) imagine as a valuable audience, who might be worthwhile to connect with as potential allies. Such publications also show that it is not only the words that have meaning but also the format in which those words travel—whether in a journal, a zine, a blog, or a national newspaper.

As you move forward in your study of writing, it will be equally important to study and engage in the central role of community publishing. It is in the act of publishing that the value contained within your words takes on a public form. It is a moment where your intellectual labors become a material artifact that can circulate within your community and beyond. For this reason, this book also addresses the important role of community publishing in any writing project.

Final Thoughts

The essence of this letter boils down to an important question: Can a college composition course enable students to enact this vision and practice of writing? And, in essence, this question represents a new chapter in higher education—it speaks to the fact that your generation is being asked to imagine the university as a place where you become a public citizen.

Such a statement might seem at odds with popular media accounts, which often frame millennial college students as spoiled slackers who are unwilling to leave home. Yet your generation has witnessed (and fought) two wars in response to 9/11, the worst act of violent aggression against the United States since Pearl Harbor. It has suffered from and worked to solve the greatest economic crisis since the Great Depression. And it has been active in the largest civil rights struggle since the 1960s. Members of your generation have undertaken active roles in their communities and larger public conversations. As such, members of this generation both demand and require an education that links the skills of a strong university education to a sense of a larger public good.

The university itself has also changed in response to political challenges. Over the past thirty years, amid intense national debates, public policy has placed stronger emphasis on community-based volunteerism and nonprofit programming as a means to address social needs. There has been a de-emphasis on federal intervention. Facing strong criticism for remaining an "ivory tower" in the midst of such changes, universities have had to redefine their role as public institutions. To this end, students, classrooms, and programs are being asked to imagine how academic knowledge can be applied to contexts outside of the confines of a campus. Today, crossing over the threshold of a classroom now often also means stepping into the community in which those classrooms exist.

It would be nice to imagine that this public mission has created a context in which a student or community member's home knowledge could become a resource. Too often, however, students are asked to deploy classroom-based theories *on* a community instead of working *with* a community to produce new knowledge that can transform daily life. Such practices imagine the university as the home of intellectuals and the community as recipients of those intellectuals' insights.

Yet we all know that communities are rich with intellectuals. The elderly woman who sits on her stoop, sharing her historical knowledge with the next generation, is an educator. The mechanic who understands the need for more jobs for young adults is an organizer. The single parent educating his or her children in public schools is an advocate for literacy rights. Indeed, political philosopher Antonio Gramsci once claimed that everyone is an intellectual. In doing so, he was arguing that in every human activity there is a component that demands intellectual insight and from which an intellectual vision of the world can be created. In this sense, we are all intellectuals, all community-builders.

The difficulty facing universities is how to support the community's own intellectual sense of purpose, its desire for change, as well as support the work of educating students. The answer lies in Gramsci's insight: Everyone is an intellectual. For if everyone is an intellectual, then everyone can also be a teacher. And under the right circumstances, partnership work can bring all these intellectuals together (students, faculty, and community members), blending existing knowledge and new insights to create solutions and possibilities for local communities. For such partnership work to happen ethically, for it to be a true partnership, there must be an expansion of our sense of who can teach and from whom we can learn.

A famous teacher, Paulo Friere, named such moments *conscientization*: the moment when the critical insights of all involved move beyond simple student/ teacher dynamic and become a space of genuine problem solving, calling on the skills and knowledge of everyone involved to be part of a collective solution. In this way, expanding the classroom to include community intellectuals ideally not only broadens the number of individuals from whom a student can learn; it also enables the student to become a teacher, someone whose insights about language and community can be part of an organized effort to improve the lives of those within and around the classroom. The ultimate goal for this book is to show you how to create a space of genuine problem-solving, engagement, and understanding that allows for all of these voices, all of these intellectuals to come together as part of a collective solution. Classrooms can begin to show new ways in which writing and power can interact to produce local change. And it is this idea of a larger civic identity—that fleeting glance into the full complexity of taking your voice public—that marks the work of the modern university.

You enter the university classroom with your own values and your own intellectual insights. You blend the insights of the academy and your community with the hopes that this fusion will produce not only new frames through which to build our individual lives, but to build a better collective future for the streets in which we will make our home. In the process, you reinvent the possibilities of the university for those who follow.

This important work is the mission—the "why"—at the root of *Writing Communities*. And it will be such work that will be the focus of you and your classmates' time together.

Steve Parks

Writing
Communities

A Text with Readings

PART ONE

Reading
& Writing
Communities

Reading Strategies and Intellectual Communities

Writing Prompt: "Strange Angels"

Perhaps all of us have met a stranger on the bus, on the train, or in line at the market who left us with more than we expected. He may have eased his way past our inhibitions, our guard up, and actually managed to adorn our ears with gems of wisdom. Maybe you came across a stranger who became family in a matter of minutes, someone who changed the tide of your morning, your afternoon. You smiled once that day. Maybe you caught her name, maybe you didn't. Remember. Then write a story of an encounter with a strange angel.

Response: "Mom Frasier" by Yolanda Wisher

From *Open City: A Journal of Community Arts and Culture*

New City Community Press/
Peter Hanley/Yolanda Wisher

Out of the house and up the sidewalk to the corner of 43rd and Chestnut Streets, we argued. The steeple of the ancient church across the street seemed to scold us for our pettiness but we kept on. On our way to 30th Street Station to catch the R5 to North Wales to see my mother, we hoped to catch a bus or cab at the corner. I was carrying an out of tune child's guitar, a gift for my sister. Already late, about to miss our train, and pissed at one another, we stood in our frowns on either side of the bus stop sign with our thumbs out. The world was moving in slow motion. Out of the hot air, out of the heat waves of the summer, out of nowhere, an old woman with a face decorated with pockmarks and black heads made her way with a cane across the street to us. As if she knew us, she started commenting on the downfall of young girls in clothes tighter than their friendships. She told us about the man she loved.

"You know how me and my husband made it through? We sang to each other. It make everything easy."

I kept looking for a bus, waiting for her to ask for change or hand us a religious pamphlet. I didn't know she would have us singing to each other on a hot day in July, late for our train with a huge rift between us. She reached for us, put our hands together as folks walked by on their way to and from the supermarket, the Rite-Aid on the next block. Her hands were swollen and rough, soft on the insides like dough. "Go 'head," she instructed. He sang an El DeBarge song to me, our hands gently rocking.

> Someone just like me
> Running into someone just like you
> An accidental touch
> Turning into a gentle kiss or two

I hesitated to have my voice all out in the open—I was embarrassed for myself, my lack of playing skills, my trembling alto. She said, "Honey, play that instrument in your hand and sing to this man. Look in his eyes." With her hand cradling my elbow, I sang the only song I could think of to the man I loved. Have you ever sung to your beloved? That day was a first for me. The words seemed to fly out of my mouth like confetti from a window and blow through the corridor to Chestnut Street.

> No words to say
> No words to convey
> These feelings I have for you
> Deep in my heart
> Safe from the guard
> Of intellect and reason

"See?" We smiled at each other, easily. The day was a fresh lily and this woman's face was a sun. Her pockmarks glittered. I pictured her man rinsed in her rough songs, his head thrown back, catching the jewelry of her voice around his neck.

"Where y'all going?" she asked. I told her we were going to 30th Street and she hailed a cab for us in less than 3 minutes. Told the driver where we were headed and held open the door as we got in. I asked her what her name was; I wanted to write a poem 'bout her. She said, "Mom Frasier. I've lived here for years. This is my neighborhood." She closed the cab door. Turned and walked away with the help of a cane. We made our train with one minute to spare. The woman had powers, the woman was love, and I didn't expect to see her again.

■   ■   ■

We have all encountered a "Mom Frasier." It might not have been at a bus stop on a hot day in July. Your moment might have occurred in a supermarket, on a practice field, or at a religious service. We have all had such a moment, though, a time when a stranger, an everyday person who might never cross our path again, offers wisdom to us. "Strange Angels" is a testament to the belief that everyday people — community intellectuals — can teach us important lessons.

You will be asked to share a similar faith in the intellectual insights of the people whose path you cross each day when you leave your classroom and your campus. Indeed, such faith is an essential premise of the work we will undertake together.

Of course, you might find this request somewhat odd, since you probably came to college to learn from experts. Indeed, access to expertise is the fundamental calling card of the university. Before we start our common journey, then, we will cover some reasons for this request to accept such a broad definition of the intellectual and why I am asking you to listen to intellectuals such as Mom Frasier.

What Is an Intellectual?

If asked to define an intellectual, most people would probably point to individuals such as professors, doctors, lawyers, religious leaders, or politicians. Because individuals in such positions have a larger institution — such as a college, hospital, church, or government — validating their expert knowledge in a particular area, most people would agree with this list. Then there is the case of individuals such as Mom Frasier. Her expertise is grounded in her own life experiences and knowledge gained on the streets of her community: "I've lived here for years. This is my neighborhood."

Antonio Gramsci, a political theorist, had a succinct way of describing the relationship between intelligence gained in the classroom and intelligence gained in the streets: "Everyone is an intellectual, but not everyone has the position of an intellectual." In other words, every person has an informed worldview—a sense of justice and values based on individual and collective experience—but not everyone has traditional institutions validating his or her expertise. Indeed, the vast majority of people are in the position of Mom Frasier: an ordinary person who is proud of her neighborhood and trying to work for its improvement. They are the people you meet on the street who might offer immediate advice—such as how to get to a local business—but also possess deeper knowledge of a community based on long-term experience and different educational experiences. Gramsci believes they also have lessons to teach us.

Gramsci even provided a set of terms to distinguish between such intellectuals: *organic* and *traditional*. Although there has been significant debate about the intricacies of these terms, the following might be useful definitions for our work together:

An **organic intellectual** is an individual who bases his or her worldview on the experiences and insights of those sharing a similar lifestyle or economic position.

A **traditional intellectual** is an individual who bases his or her worldview on the experiences and insights of mainstream religious, educational, and political institutions.

In an ideal world, Mom Frasier would find her "organic" interests in alignment with the "traditional intellectuals." They would all be pulling in the same direction. For Gramsci, though, that is not always the case.

Too often, the traditionally educated intellectual doesn't support the goals of the community-based organic intellectual. Whereas organic intellectuals like Mom Frasier generally work to bring people into a collective effort to change society for the benefit of everyday people, like those in their community, Gramsci argues that traditional intellectuals tend to support society staying the same. So for Gramsci, the question became, How do organic intellectuals (Mom Frasier) convince traditional intellectuals (lawyers, doctors, etc.) to take up working people's concerns, abandon their traditional roles, and become part of a larger effort to alter society accordingly?

To make this idea concrete, imagine a moment that might bring these different intellectuals together into a common conversation, such as a plan by a local university to build a new medical center in Mom Frasier's community. Who are the intellectuals that can provide the best information needed to make an informed decision? A lawyer could certainly talk about the legal framework needed to purchase land, hire employees, and so on. A doctor could talk about the improved health care. Perhaps architects could be on hand to discuss the actual building of the medical center. Initially, these varied knowledge bases might seem to be the most important. They certainly aren't unimportant.

Recognizing the insights of organic intellectuals, however, would mean that Mom Frasier should also be intimately involved. She would be uniquely situated to talk about the values and actual needs of the community, her neighborhood. She would be best positioned to understand the concerns of local residents about putting the building in a particular neighborhood block. She might be able to offer advice on how not only the health-care needs but also the economic needs of the community might be met by the project. For Mom Frasier, it becomes a question of how to shift an "intellectual" debate primarily focused on a university's interests in a medical center toward supporting the community's self-defined goals.

Yet even if she were invited to a meeting, how could Mom Frasier gain enough authority to actually impact public decisions, such as where the medical center might be built? Unlike doctors, lawyers, and architects, who have college degrees,

Mom Frasier might have insights based on the experiences and concerns of her neighbors, on the rich intersection of daily life with larger cultural and economic patterns. Her local knowledge would be valid in part because it represents the community's values. When individuals such as Mom Frasier speak, it is out of a conscious attempt to identify common values and theories about how the world works from their own neighborhood experiences—how, that is, numerous individual and collective forces have created and maintained the neighborhood they call home and how change can occur.

But to gain the type of leverage that can actually impact the power of lawyers, doctors, and architects to turn ideas into concrete actions, these local insights need to be recognized by those outside the immediate community. Mom Frasier's insights—like those of other organic community-based intellectuals—need to gain traction not just through the power of her thoughts but also from the power of having community support. Mom Frasier also needs to understand how to connect the power represented by her community with the arguments of traditional intellectuals to shift the terms of the debate to her advantage. Ultimately, it becomes a question of whose knowledge and whose insights are going to be valued by those around the table.

Thus, the question "Who is an intellectual?" is really just asking what type of knowledge will be valued (traditional or organic) and how such knowledge gains power to influence community and civic decisions. During your time in class, you will be studying how organic and traditional intellectuals gain power and how they produce knowledge designed to create change. Most important, you will be learning how the act of uniting these different ways of making knowledge can represent the most powerful form of intellectual work. The best conversations and the best answers are always based on the widest set of intellectuals being involved and with the broadest set of traditional and organic intellectuals at the table.

CHECKPOINT   Changing Communities

Think about a time when your home community faced a major change. Some examples might be trying to preserve a historic site or monument, protesting or supporting a new business, or resisting or negotiating plans for a new structure. Consider these questions:

- Why was this change important to your community, and how so?
- Who was involved in making the decisions?
- Were the voices of both organic and traditional intellectuals heard in the process?
- What kinds of strategies did the organic intellectuals in the community use to organize and rally support? Were those strategies successful? Why or why not?

Becoming an Intellectual

At this point, you might be thinking, "All this seems very far afield from a college writing class." Thinking about traditional and organic intellectuals might seem distant from your immediate goals of learning to read and produce academic writing, succeeding at your chosen major, and moving on to the life you hope college will enable. If you pause for just a moment, though, you can see how thinking about intellectuals poses deeper questions, questions that will potentially characterize almost every word you write during your time in college.

For instance, imagine that you are taking a philosophy class. As you learn the values that inform academic writing in philosophy, you will need to consider various questions. Are you writing to support the traditional values of the field of philosophy, or are you proposing a different set of values, perhaps ones that represent your home community? To what extent might your writing also be an attempt to bring together seemingly oppositional ideas into new collaborations, new forms of knowledge, and new forms of action? How might your writing bring, say, Mom Frasier, Aristotle, and community politics into the same paper? What is the writerly voice you want to create for the work you do after college? For the communities with whom you want to be in conversation? What do you hope to achieve as an individual? As part of a collective?

Or course, at this moment you might have more immediate concerns, such as juggling personal, college, and work commitments. Thinking beyond the current moment might seem a luxury. Still, throughout your time in college, you will be writing. That is, course after course and year after year, you will be crafting a writing voice that will ultimately exist outside of the classroom. Once you graduate, you will no longer be writing just for your class, but for real purposes. You will need to make real decisions about *with whom* and *for whom* you wish to write, about whether you see your writing as advocating for a *certain community* or working to bring *multiple communities* together, and about whether you want to support the *status quo* or seek *change*. When this moment arises, you'll want to be taken seriously on this important work. You will want the reading and writing skills that will support your efforts.

The fundamental belief of this book is that it is better to begin this work from your opening moment in college. This book will argue that you already need to listen and write not just to traditional intellectuals or to professors, but to organic intellectuals and communities as well. Ultimately, it is the ability to read and write in the intersections of such different kinds of knowledge that will allow you to develop a powerful and productive voice. Indeed, to delay developing such a voice, to limit your reading and writing to just a classroom exercise, is to allow yourself to learn a limited and reduced sense of the power of language. And that seems a profoundly anti-intellectual vision to adopt as a model for your college career.

How to Read Like an Intellectual

Now is the time, then, for you to begin to make the decisions about how you want to draw together different visions of intellectual work, different visions of what an intellectual community might entail, for your specific goals. To this end, your initial task will be to develop appropriate reading strategies. As highlighted above, people deploy different reading strategies depending on the type of community they hope to address or create. In the imagined community meeting about the health center, for instance, Mom Frasier was cast as reading the moment differently than the architect or lawyer. Each drew off different strategies, different knowledge bases to understand what needed to be done. Although it's a bit too simplistic, we might imagine this moment as one when traditional and organic reading strategies were deployed to study a particular problem. And, as discussed above, it is the work of combining these insights that will most likely produce the best results.

So as you start this course, it might be useful to learn some reading strategies that can produce these combined insights and to highlight the tools these strategies provide. For our purposes, it is useful to think of reading strategies as fitting into two categories: traditional and organic.

Traditional Reading Strategies

Classrooms are one of the primary engines for producing traditional intellectuals. There are numerous reading strategies that can be used to succeed in traditional intellectual work.

Asking Why the Reading Was Assigned

Before beginning any assigned reading, it is useful to look at the course syllabus to remember the goals of the class. Ask yourself these questions:

- What are the central questions the course is trying to discuss? Understanding the central issue of a course will help you understand the type of conversations the instructor hopes to create in the classroom.
- Who is the audience for the selection? Reading a book in a philosophy course is profoundly different from reading the same book for a business course.
- Where is the reading placed in the course? Readings early in the course might pose a series of general questions, and later readings might offer a series of specific answers to those questions.

If you are not clear about why a reading is assigned, you should ask your teacher to explain its purpose in the course. Don't feel awkward about such questions. It's your instructor's job to address such concerns.

Reading for Purpose

Assigned readings are usually full of data, facts, and information. It is easy to get bogged down in the details. For this reason, you might find it useful to read the essay quickly one time through just to get the main gist of its argument:

- What are the key questions the essay tries to address?
- Why are these questions important to the author?
- How does the author argue that the questions should be important to the reader?
- What type of answers does the author provide?

Reading for Evidence

When you identify the specific set of questions or topics that interest the author, you will also need to identify what particular evidence or support the author uses to support his or her argument. In your second reading of the selection, then, you should consider:

- What type of evidence does the author cite?
- How does the evidence help address the questions the author raises?
- What type of conclusions does the evidence allow the author to draw on?

Reading for Audience

As you assess the support an author provided, you will probably notice that the evidence is drawn from other authors, articles, and books. Consider how the author is addressing a specific audience of readers:

- Do the cited articles repeat key terms in their titles?
- What time period do the cited articles cover?
- Does the article appear to address an emergent or ongoing issue in this area of research?
- In what type of publications or publication formats do the cited articles appear?

Note-Taking Strategies

Although the above suggestions may suggest a particular order to these strategies, you will ultimately decide which order works best for you. What will remain constant, though, is that it is impossible to remember everything you have read or to hold all the points in your head at the same time. For this reason, engaged readers develop multiple strategies to help them understand a particular piece of writing.

Annotating

As you read, you should **annotate**—actively underline, write notes in the margin, and pose questions to the text. For instance, you might consistently underline all the times a key term is used. You could also write in the margins what you believe each paragraph is contributing to the overall argument. You might highlight passages that, despite your best attempts, make no sense and that you hope the class can discuss at your next meeting. Using these strategies makes you an active reader, and being an active reader will not only help you remember what you have read but also serve as the first step toward eventually drafting a response.

Sample Student Annotations

Below is a passage from Antonio Gramsci's writing "On Intellectuals" (which you can read more of on page 49) showing sample annotations and notes from a student.

However, every "essential" social group which emerges into history out of the preceding economic structure, and as an expression of a development of this structure, has found (at least in all of history up to the present) categories of intellectuals already in existence and which seemed indeed to represent an historical continuity uninterrupted even by the most complicated and radical changes in political and social forms.

> What's meant by "essential"?

> What kind of intellectuals? Ask reading group about this passage—copy into journal.

The most typical of these categories of intellectuals is that of the ecclesiastics who for a long time (for a whole phase of history, which is partly characterised by this very monopoly) held a monopoly of a number of important services: religious ideology, that is the philosophy and science of the age, together with schools, education, morality, justice, charity, good works, etc. The category of ecclesiastics can be considered the category of intellectuals organically bound to the landed aristocracy. It had equal status juridically with the aristocracy, with which it shared the exercise of feudal ownership of land, and the use of state privileges connected with property. *But the monopoly held by the ecclesiastics in the superstructural field was not exercised without a struggle or without limitations, and hence there took place the birth, in various forms (to be gone into and studied concretely), of other categories, favoured and enabled to expand by the growing strength of the central power of the monarch, right up to absolutism.* Thus we find

> Organic or traditional?

> Look up this word.

> What does "superstructural" mean?

> Is "organically bound" the same as an "organic intellectual"? Ask reading group?

> Gramsci uses history as evidence to support his claim.

This passage reminds me of Gloria Anzaldúa's essay.

the formation of the *noblesse de robe,* with its own privileges, a stratum of administrators, etc., scholars and scientists, theorists, non-ecclesiastical philosophers, etc.

Notes:
- Gramsci wrote this piece to understand what organic intellectuals had to do to change society.
- Who is the audience? Maybe other political theorists, activists?
- This section seems to talk about how "intellectuals" are created to help those in power. True?
- How does this "history" help explain the difference between organic and traditional intellectuals? It seems like a political analysis. Are intellectuals "political"? Ask group when we meet next.

Keeping a Reading Journal

An additional common reading strategy is to keep a reading journal in which you write down what you believe to be important quotes, interpretations, or connections within and among assigned readings. Such notes can be helpful when you begin to write essays because the journal already contains your initial thoughts. You could also do this work online or on a blog, which has the advantage of allowing others to respond to it, creating a community within your class that is committed to helping one another better understand the assigned readings.

Forming a Reading Group

A collective strategy for tackling the readings in class is to form a reading group—a group of classmates with whom you can meet to talk about how you read a text, choose particular sections of the essay for group focus, and draw on

The Star-Ledger/Robert Sciarrino/The Image Works

collective insights to form or refine your own opinions. If your schedule allows, a reading group can be a key support in your reading of assigned class texts.

Organic Reading Strategies

Of course, traditional intellectuals are not the only ones to use these kinds of strategies to gain understanding. People in every walk of life use some of these strategies daily, although they take slightly different forms in different contexts. Labeling the above strategies as "traditional" was simply to highlight how, in this course, they are all designed to aid you in understanding a particular academic writer's project within a particular academic community. As you move toward a major or career, though, you will find that there is great value in being able to learn, analyze, and work within many different communities. Learning the additional strategies given below—strategies based more in everyday communities—will also be useful.

Listening to Everyday Speech

Within any particular community, people might use certain sayings, refer to certain figures, or draw together different languages. Whether it is a single term or a whole way of speaking, these everyday speech acts represent a theory about the community and its ethical values. Speaking "Spanglish," for instance, might indicate a desire for the community to represent its complex identity to the larger culture. Similarly, a focus on Catholic imagery might represent an attempt to maintain a religious focus as an important community value.

Understanding the values of everyday speech, then, can give you a sense of the theoretical underpinnings of a community. To that end, you might ask yourself:

- How does the way families and neighbors speak represent a way of seeing the world?
- What are the ways individuals in the neighborhood learn to value this way of speaking?
- What happens when new community members bring in different terms or language patterns?
- Why might community members continually choose to speak this way?
- What values about the community does this way of speaking represent?

Recognizing Community Theories

As you explore the ways in which a community's way of speaking represents a theory of community, you will soon discover that many of these same people also have a theory on how the world works (and can be changed) based on their life experiences. As you listen to your neighbors, you might ask yourself:

- Are there common ways of talking about how the community, the state, the country, or the world works?

- How do these common insights represent a theory of social change?
- What is the role of the community in fostering positive change?
- Is that change just local, or does the community want to make changes in a larger context?
- Does change seem possible?

Recognizing Community Insights

It would be a mistake to imagine any community as being unified in its speech patterns or theory of social change. There will always be some variation. Indeed, this variation itself allows the community to adapt and change to new situations. Still, if you listen long enough, you will hear a series of community stories being repeated, such as when a particular business closed or when an accident occurred on a certain street corner. These stories represent a collective experience and, to some extent, represent a sense of communal history from which any future actions will be based. You might ask yourself:

- What stories are invoked to represent the history of the community?
- How do the stories provide a sense of what it means to live in the community?
- What do these stories try to show about the community's collective experience?
- In a world where endless stories probably exist about life in this neighborhood, why would the community want to repeat these stories?

Recognizing Community Solutions

Oft-repeated community stories or sayings often act as fables. They are invoked at a time of crisis or sudden change to provide a map for what should be done, giving insights on how to avoid mistakes or how to repeat successful strategies. As you think about the ways in which your community "solves problems," ask yourself:

- What type of solution tends to succeed?
- How do these solutions represent community values?
- Who typically benefits or loses out from such solutions?
- What is the process by which solutions are reached?

Making Connections

As with any reading process, how you begin is probably less important than the process of returning again and again to the text being studied, whether it is a printed essay, Web page, or local community. In the case of attempting to read like an organic intellectual, it will mean residing in the community, staying present, and interacting daily with those around you. Many of the "texts" you read will be conversations, so it is important to find ways to record what you hear, develop a way to understand the connections. Here are some common strategies useful in such work.

Double-Entry Journal

Keep a small notebook with you. Throughout the day, take notes on the left-hand side of the notebook. Write down common phrases, repeated stories, and recurring opinions you hear about the community. At the end of each day, write down on the adjacent right-hand page what common insights you can draw about how to read the community. This process will allow you to see where your common insights emerge from on a daily basis.

Audio Blog

Another strategy is to simply record your insights on your phone or computer. One interesting result of this method is that you will begin to hear how your voice, your insights, move between "everyday talk" and "academic talk" as you discuss what you hear on the streets in your neighborhood.

Community Archives

Communities produce a stunning amount of writing: local newspapers, pamphlets, flyers, and posters among other **artifacts** (a term for any material product that is produced by a community). Although each of these pieces of writing is "temporary," each provides an insight into how the community wants to represent itself to its fellow residents and to the larger public. You might begin to collect these varied community publications, analyzing any common terms, themes, or strategies you see among them. Such analysis will provide you with a sense of how communication occurs and how values are transmitted in your community.

Regardless of which methods you might choose, each one should serve as a reminder that "reading" a neighborhood — understanding its daily interactions as a text that can be studied and analyzed — is a constant process of observation and insight. In this way, it is not all that different in approach from working with classroom-based materials.

Sample Student Annotations

Below are annotations a student made when she was asked to analyze a piece of writing by Susan Hamilton, a resident of a neighborhood in Syracuse, New York, whose work appeared in a book called *Home: Journeys into the Westside*. The student's annotations were more organic than traditional in nature, as she was reading for an understanding about the neighborhood and its common stories. In doing so, she made notes for herself as well as notes to bring up later with her reading group.

Why the Near Westside Is Home

Susan Hamilton

My initial encounter with the neighborhood was accidental—I
got lost on streets that veer off on a diagonal and that took me to
an unexpected destination. In the same way, I didn't really plan
to live here. I owned a home on the Southwest side, and though
I was dissatisfied with its lack of porches, its small yard, and the
size of the mortgage payment, I was not actively looking to move.
Then an acquaintance who knows I like old houses urged me to
tour one that was coming up for sale on Holland Street. The previous owner had died in her 90s, leaving this house something like
a museum. Most of its Victorian splendor was intact, right down
to the intricately wrought metal pulls on the pantry drawers, and I

Repeats many stories told about crime/drugs in the neighborhood—also makes claim that it is her neighborhood, she "had a role to play."

was immediately hooked. The area didn't frighten me; it reminded
me of Deep Rondo, the inner-city, racially mixed neighborhood
in St. Paul where I lived as a young child. I had been working as
a community organizer on the Near Westside, so I already knew
some of my new neighbors. But I wasn't blind to the problems,
such as the drug house across the street and decades of neglect
by local government. The lot next door, where a house had been
set afire to cover up a burglary, had been vacant for more than a
decade and used as an informal dump. When I bought my house,
I began cleaning out the lot's trash and trying to mow the thicket
of weeds, some taller than my head, with a push mower. When
drug dealers would congregate at the curb, I walked around them,
picking up the food wrappers and subtly giving the message that I
too had a role to play and a claim to that space.

Storm stories are also repeated a lot.

A little over two years later, early in the morning of Labor Day
1998, a freak storm blasted Syracuse. I was awakened by the shriek
of a box fan being blown out of the window by 115 mph winds. I
closed windows and lay back down on the bed, which moved as the
whole house swayed. Lightning flashed green outside, like strobe
lights, and thunder punctuated the sound of falling trees. When I
got dressed and went downstairs, I could not see out the windows
because they were all streaked with rain. I opened the back door
and could see only leaves where my car was parked. My dog Che,
terrorized by the storm, cowered at my feet. Before I could decide
whether to take refuge in the basement, the worst of the storm
passed. The electricity went out—and would not be restored for a

week. Peering out the front door, I could vaguely see the shapes of big trees on the ground, power lines snared in their branches. <u>Then I heard voices from the darkness. A group of young men from the surrounding houses</u> appeared, holding cans of beer and flashlights. They asked if I was OK, and I told them I was afraid that my car had been crushed. Disregarding the danger of fallen electrical wires, a couple of them scrambled over branches to reach the backyard and returned to report that the car was unscathed under a mound of small twigs. Then the guys moved on to the next house, calling out to the tenants to see if they needed help.

As I came back inside to comfort my dog, <u>I realized that for the first time I really felt at home in this neighborhood, where people do look out for each other and pull together during crises.</u> During the next week of post-storm recovery, people shared food from their freezers, told where ice could be purchased, helped one another cut up trees that littered yards, and cheered together when the Hydro Ontario trucks sent from Canada finally restored power to our streets. Though still neglected by local government, we could take care of each other.

> Uses "crime" context to make it seem scary. This story wants to trick the reader, playing off stereotypes generated about the neighborhood. Ask group if they see similar strategy when talking to outsiders.
>
> It is also a common story—it is the caring community, not the drugs, that marks the community; feeling at home is being part of this caring community.

Notes:
- Possible research question: How does the community talk to outsiders about neighborhood? How does that represent the community's sense of how change can occur? How does this way of speaking alter the image of the community?
- This story is told in very direct language, with a lot of details about household fixtures, fridges, how houses looked, Victorian, who comes to help, Hydro Ontario. How is knowing such details evidence of knowing the neighborhood? How is this way of speaking showing the person "belongs"?

Note what is not included amid all these notes and comments: *There are no final conclusions.* Instead, the comments are used to understand how the text represents a deep knowledge of the neighborhood, how it attempts to reach out to nonneighbors, and how it attempts to make a public argument about how the neighborhood should be understood by the public. In doing so, the piece also seems to make an argument about how change occurs. Of course, to draw any firm conclusions about how this piece reflects the neighborhood as a whole, much more reading and documentation would have to take place. And as noted above, only after such documentation can the power of writing as a tool, with its ability to provide a format to link ideas together, be used to begin to talk about the community as a whole. (More about this type of intellectual work will be discussed in Chapter 2.)

By now it should be clear that reading as an intellectual is actually a three-part process: (1) working within the methods of any academic article to understand its possibilities and limitations, (2) articulating community-generated insights and values, and (3) discovering how each might work together on a specific issue or project. That is, at any moment, you are both learning new methods of analysis and placing them in dialogue with the insights you have gained from real life. This type of reading practice prepares you not only for success in college, but for success in using your education to collaboratively create (and work with) communities that represent your values and aspirations. That is the true work of intellectuals.

RUNDOWN Strategies for Reading

Traditional Reading Strategies
- Think about why the reading was assigned and ask questions of the text.
- Read for purpose.
- Read for evidence.
- Read for audience.

Take notes; annotate hard copies with a pen or pencil, focusing on important ideas and terms.

Keep a reading journal with reactions and thoughts.

Form a reading group with other members of the class.

Organic Reading Strategies
- Listen closely to everyday speech and think about what it implies.
- Learn to recognize how a community's ideas and theories come out in everyday speech.
- Learn how to acknowledge community insights into issues.
- Listen to a community's solutions for issues.

Keep a double-entry journal.

Keep an audio blog with your own thoughts and insights.

Access community archives.

Discussion Questions & Activities

1. Before the next class, write a response to the "Strange Angels" prompt that began this chapter. Share your response with your classmates.

2. Consider the writing you typically encounter during a single day. What percentage would you consider written by traditional intellectuals? What percentage would you consider written by organic intellectuals? How do you draw the distinction? Bring some samples of both to share and discuss with your classmates.

3. Assume for the moment that Gramsci is correct: "Everyone is an intellectual." How does your college foster or limit the interaction of students with the broadest range of intellectuals on and off campus? What is your relationship to the service employees, librarians, secretaries, business owners, wait staff, and others who surround your life as a student? What might that say about how the college is educating you?

4. Make a list of organic intellectuals in your community. Use the strategies outlined in this chapter to trace their worldview, the sense of values that shape their daily actions. What insights do these intellectuals bring to your life? To community issues? To your work as a student?

5. Choose one course in which you have already been assigned a particular essay to read. Bring that essay to class. Form small groups and talk about the margin notes each of you wrote while reading the essay. What do these notes say about how you read an essay? What strategies do you bring to the difficult work of reading academic writing? How might the traditional intellectual readings strategies discussed above expand your reading practices?

6. Choose an assigned essay from another course. Read it in terms of how your community, your neighbors, might approach it. Make marginal notes, underline key passages, and circle key terms. Bring that essay to class. Discuss how reading from this context provided a different lens through which to understand the essay. How might this reading strategy provide you with some insight into your own understanding of the value and goals of academic writing? How might these community-based reading strategies offer a critique or endorsement of the purposes and goals of academic writing?

2

Academic and Community Discourse

Writing Prompt: "Lessons Learned"

Describe a moment when you learned something in a classroom.

Response: Excerpt from "I'm Trying to Find a Midpoint between Two Cultures" by Mayra Castillo Rangel

From *Espejos y Ventanas/Mirrors and Windows: Oral Histories of Mexican Farmworkers and Their Families*. The following selection was originally published in both English and Spanish.

New City Community Press/ Jaeyun Jung

We arrived here on July 14th, I think, during the summer of 1993 right after I graduated from 6th grade, primary school there. When I entered school here I entered an all-English school, although I had some bilingual teachers and classes. Before I started I remember my dad bought my brother and me a blackboard, chalk, an eraser and lent us his English books to start preparing for school. He said I had to learn all I could alone and at times he would help with what he knew, which I now realize wasn't a lot—but even though it was not much, that and the encouragement helped. He showed me an alphabet, the numbers, and some basics. He also took us to a Puerto Rican friend of his at the mushroom plant where he worked so she could help us too. She read books for us and my first English book I read was by Dr. Seuss. I think it was something like *One Fish, Two Fish, Red Fish, Blue Fish*. . . .

In August I entered the Kennett Middle School in the 7th grade. Most of my classes were ESL [English as a Second Language] but I also had some regular courses. I had English, Science, Math, and Social Studies. I stayed at the Kennett District until the break at the December holidays because we moved from Toughkenamon to Avondale to West Grove school district. In January I entered a new school. By then I understood a lot of English but I still didn't speak it yet, so I still took ESL classes for another two or three years. Most of my middle-school classes were in English but I had a lot of help from my ESL teachers and, little by little, I ended up with only regular classes. By the time I entered high school I wasn't accepted into ESL as often anymore because I needed to complete my regular classes in order to graduate from high school.

Although it may seem like I progressed a lot from the time I first arrived, learned some basics, entered school and eventually graduated, I think entering school was very difficult. I was very afraid. I don't know why, but I was very afraid. My first day of school I took a bus with one of my neighbors because he was already bilingual. He helped me get on the bus and then took me to the main office. Sister Jane had previously registered me at the school but I had to present myself at the main office to get my schedule and be advised on how classes were going to work. There was another new girl in the main office with me. I learned that her name was Juanita when the principal, Mr. Carr, asked her—I was too nervous to speak at all, even to her. I was so happy when I learned that Mr. Carr spoke some Spanish. That comforted me, but I still couldn't help but cry in front of him and Juanita. I was very very nervous and afraid and couldn't help it. Juanita was very strong; I could tell she was nervous too, but she didn't cry or anything. Looking at her and the principal made me feel grief and shame and more fear and then I cried even more. Eventually I stopped and went on with my day. I don't remember anything else from that first day, I only remember that I cried again the night before my first day in the Avon Grove School. I was upset because I had already made friends at my previous school and was somewhat comfortable with my classes and professors and now I had to start all over again. My mom tried to comfort me by telling me that I had to go to the new school. She said it was necessary and that I couldn't stay home. I continued on, I went to my new school, made new friends and made it there, after all. I wanted to learn. I thought I wasn't very intelligent, but I wanted to learn, even by myself, and little by little, I was becoming more and more independent.

■   ■   ■

Mayra Castillo Rangel tells a compelling story of her movement through classrooms, of continually being asked to learn English to be able to achieve her high school degree. She is clearly successful in these efforts, eventually graduating from high school and then from college as well. One powerful element of her story is her honesty about the difficulty of learning a new language while continually being asked to enter new classrooms with new teachers at new schools. At each moment, it seems, her words and writing were being observed, assessed, and, ultimately, altered. It was a deeply stressful experience.

At no point, however, does Rangel criticize or characterize her teachers as being uncaring. Instead, she presents them as individuals in a system designed to help her learn "standard English." She recognizes that this requirement was a conscious decision by many different parts of the school district she was attending (as well as her family) about what every student in that system should know prior to graduation. It was not a whim of a teacher or the particular policy of the school, but rather a collective decision across multiple school districts.

If you look at your own college and across similar colleges and universities, you too will likely find evidence of such collective decisions. One of them is that students must learn academic discourse. The common opinion is that academic discourse is a necessary skill for success in college, but what exactly is it? How can students benefit from such a requirement? How can Chapter 1's discussion of community-based intellectuals shed light on its use? And what are some concrete strategies we might use when writing academic discourse?

What Is Academic Discourse?

Academic discourse is perhaps best understood as an umbrella term for the many different types of writing that exist and have power within the university to share knowledge. (In fact, the name *academic discourse* grows from the fact the university is also known as "the academy.") For instance, if you were to look at the writing done by your professors (which you can usually do by looking them up on their department's Web page), you might notice that each has a different research specialty. They study different topics (cell structure, literary texts, mathematical probabilities), use different types of evidence (geological data, theoretical models, archaeological evidence), use different types of reference systems (Modern Language Association, American Psychological Association, Chicago Manual of Style), and publish in different types of academic journals (English, anthropology, engineering), often in different formats (print, digital, video). Moreover, if you were to look at this writing, you would also notice that the ways of arguing are equally varied. Some authors will invoke personal experience and their home dialect; others will argue through the use of symbols, charts, and equations; and still others produce work that blends video, online, and print technologies to make their point. Sometimes professors will use all these methods at once. This mixing of technologies, this multimodal writing, is becoming increasingly popular among university researchers. In fact, it is this openness to many alternative ways of producing knowledge that should be one of the most exciting aspects of a college or university.

At its best, academic discourse is an incredibly inventive way of writing, and its inventive nature is not just its form. Academic discourse is also inventive in how it emerges from specific research communities, exploring a specific question, all the while actively searching out other research communities to support its work. Take the example of Gloria Anzaldúa, a famous a scholar of Chicana cultural theory, feminist theory, and queer theory (see page 387). Anzaldúa wrote about what it meant to her to live in the United States with Mexican heritage, to live within and across many personal, cultural, and political borders. Consider the following passages regarding snakes from Anzaldua's essay "How to Tame a Wild Tongue," in *Borderlands/La Frontera: The New Mestiza*:

> Snakes, *viboras*: since the day I've sought and shunned them.
> Always when they cross my path, fear and elation flood my body.
> *Coatlalopeuh* is descended from, or is an aspect of, earlier Mesoamerican fertility and Earth Goddesses. The earliest is *Coatlicue*, or "Serpent Skirt." She had a human skull or serpent for a head, a necklace of human hearts, a skirt of twisted serpents and taloned feet.
> After the Conquest, the Spaniards and their Church continued to split *Tonantsi/Guadalupe*. They desexed *Gualalupe*, taking *Coatlalopeuh*, the serpent sexuality out of her. (Gloria Anzaldúa, "How to Tame a Wild Tongue," *Borderlands/La Frontera: The New Mestiza*, 48–49)

Her writing blends Spanish and English, personal and historical experiences, and moves from formal to informal language. Both the form and the content are inventive. Using a wide range of sources, Anzaldúa creatively addresses important issues about identity, colonialism, and even religion with the goal of finding a new pathway to exist as a person and as a scholar. Perhaps because of this very fact, her work is widely taught in college classrooms, studied by professors, and written about in academic journals. She is understood as writing "academic discourse."

Anzaldúa's work points out another feature of academic discourse: It is also an inventive act of reading. If you look at the above passages, it quickly becomes clear that Anzaldúa read widely from both from her academic and her home communities for relevant insights on personal and political "borderlands" prior to writing her book. In fact, if you were to look at the endnotes for this particular essay, you would see how many diverse authors she studied to produce her work. Here's a small sample:

1. Ray Gwyn Smith, *Moorland Is Cold Country*, unpublished book.
2. Irena Kelpfisz, "*Di rayze aheym*/The Journey Home," in *The Tribe of Dina: A Jewish Women's Anthology*, Melanie Kaye/Kantrowitz and Irean Kelpfisz, eds. (Montpelier, VT: Sinister Wisdom Books, 1986), 49.

3. R. C. Ortega, *Dialectologia Del Barrio*, trans. Hortencia S. Alwan (Los Angeles, CA: R. C. Ortega Publisher & Bookseller, 1977), 1932.

4. Eduardo Hernandez-Chavez, Andrew D. Cohen, and Anthony F. Beltramo, *El Lenguaje de los Cicanos: Regional and Social Characteristics of Language Used by Mexican Americans* (Arlington, VA: Center for Applied Linguistics, 1975), 39.

5. Hernandez-Chavez, Cohen, and Beltramo, xvii.

6. Irena Klepfisz, "Secular Jewish Identity: Yidishkayt in America," in *The Tribe of Dina,* Kaye/Kantrowitz and Klepfisz, eds., 43.

7. Melanie Kaye/Kantrowitz, "Sign," in *We Speak in Code: Poems and Other Writings* (Pittsburgh, PA: Motheroot Publications, Inc., 1980), 85.

8. Rodolfo Gonzales, *I Am Joaquin/Yo Soy Joaquin* (New York, NY: Bantam Books, 1972). It was first published in 1967.

9. Gershen Kaufman, *Shame: The Power of Caring* (Cambridge, MA: Schenkman Books, Inc., 1980), 68.

10. John R. Chávez, *The Lost Land: The Chicano Images of the Southwest* (Albuquerque, NM: University of New Mexico Press, 1984), 88–90.

11. "Hispanic" is derived from *Hispanis* (*España*, a name given to the Iberian Peninsula in ancient times when it was part of the Roman Empire) and is a term designated by the U.S. government to make it easier to handle us on paper.

12. The Treaty of Guadalupe Hidalgo created Mexican-Americans in 1848.

13. Anglos, in order to alleviate their guilt for dispossessing the Chicano, stressed the Spanish part of us and perpetrated the myth of the Spanish Southwest. We have accepted the fiction that we are Hispanic, that is, Spanish, in order to accommodate ourselves to the dominant culture and its abhorrence of Indians. Chávez, 88–91.

The variety of different authors and subject matters listed and the varying type of knowledge represented is quite amazing. Anzaldúa's work demonstrates an attempt to draw together authors who may not necessarily see themselves in conversation and have them speak with one another. That is the function of academic discourse: It can create new communities and new ways of producing knowledge that move the conversation in interesting and important directions.

At its core, academic discourse is a form of writing in which an author explores how a particular research community has defined an important theoretical or public problem, with the author then using that community's insights to frame a response that moves the conversation forward. In the process, the author might expand the texts that are considered important when answering that question (see Anzaldúa's list above) as well as the forms of writing in which that response occurs (think multimodal texts that often blend words, images, and sounds). For instance, you might begin researching how academics have discussed ESL courses, be led to discussions of the politics of bilingual education,

> **CHECKPOINT**   Inventing Discourse
>
> Choose a piece of your own writing from either this course or from a previous high school or other college class. Consider these questions:
>
> - Would you consider your writing to be "inventive"?
> - How were you taught to think about the goals of academic discourse in the class for which you wrote this piece? Do you think you met those goals?
> - Moving forward, do you think you would like to try new kinds of discourse, to invent new ways of presenting your own writing?

connect that topic to concepts of social change from your own community, and end up writing a multimodal paper that embeds all these subjects in a discussion of Mexican-American cultural heritage. This type of inventive and connective reading, learning, and responding to particular research communities is, in the best sense, academic discourse.

Research Communities

A central point to understand about academic discourse is that it is a *community-based* activity. A research community can be understood as a group of individuals engaged in answering a common set of questions who typically also use common methods and strategies when looking for answers. Research communities are wide-ranging: they can be anything from the members of a particular academic department to a group of people on an e-mail list for news about Lady Gaga. Even though each community produces new insights for its members, it is useful to consider how *academic* research communities differ from *everyday* research communities.

Academic Research Communities

In academic research communities, the writing produced has been reviewed and assessed before being published. Unlike the writing produced in informal discourse communities (such as blogs or e-mail lists), academic discourse is a system that produces, evaluates, and validates the writing its contributors produce, deciding which articles or books successfully provide new answers to the questions being posed by the community and its members.

When you encounter an article in an academic journal or read a book published by a university press, for instance, the writing has already been reviewed several times by other academics, who often will ask for clarifications and revisions before considering it seriously for publication. Often, even when the author has made these changes, more revisions are requested. The work is published only when reviewers believe that the author of the article has shown a sufficient understanding of the journal's community of readers—their interests, knowledge base, ways of speaking, important books—and has demonstrated how his or her work moves the community's conversation forward.

Admittedly, this process might seem a bit circular in that academic writing is written for an academic audience and approved by academics, except for one element: Academic writing is also the site of struggle. Each generation, a new set of scholars pushes against previous ways of understanding and attempts to discuss new topics and use new technologies. In this way, every academic article is actually just a brief resting point in an extended conversation; new authors will always come along to expand or question the direction in which a given article wants to take the conversation. As the insights of more people point it in different directions, this ongoing dialogue endlessly shifts the contours of the community.

To a great extent, choosing a major means you have decided to join that particular academic research community and become a part of the conversation. As a member of that community, you will work collaboratively to define a problem facing the community, to use multiple methods to approach a solution, and to question if another method might not prove more useful. Your research community will be indebted to those who came before and will draw on existing scholarship while trying to open up new possibilities for answers and actions. An academic community's writers therefore draw on the existing language and terms of their given field, using them to discover the new truths that meet current challenges. As debate progresses, the community's terminology might become increasingly specialized, but if this development produces new insights from which the community can benefit, the community will accept it.

Academic research communities are a rich site of inventive writing *because* they are rich spaces of conversation and debate, of analysis and argument, over almost every facet of existence. In fact, one reason students are asked to participate in academic discourse communities is that these communities model what an *engaged* community looks like when it is investigating an important issue.

CHECKPOINT Identifying Discourse Communities

Choose a piece of academic writing that was assigned as a reading in a different class. Think about how it builds an argument, how it presents evidence, and how it examines certain terms. Now do the same work with a piece of nonacademic writing, such as an op-ed or a blog entry about a current event.

- What differences do you see between these two pieces? Who is the audience for each piece? What do these different ways of writing tell us about how knowledge is produced in each of these discourse communities?

Everyday Communities

As stated above, research communities are wide-ranging. One reason Chapter 1 emphasized the importance of organic intellectuals was to highlight that everyday communities also deserve to be understood as sites where important research strategies can be learned and essential knowledge can be produced. Any examination of a neighborhood would demonstrate coalitions of individuals engaged in intense conversations concerning how larger cultural and economic forces affect local issues. Moreover, these conversations are based on an inventive reading strategy, an attempt to draw different types of texts together. Consider how Mayra Castillo Rangel cites the different writing instruments and texts circulating in her community: blackboard, chalk, erasers, English-speaking friends, children's books, bilingual school staff, ESL classes, and textbooks. This array of writing and reading tools, of which there were probably more, were Rangel's bibliography page. They were the research community that she both invented and stepped into to produce the writing above.

As with academic communities, the pressure applied by these challenging conversations in everyday communities—based on an array of community issues and texts—could create ways of speaking that are specific to their context, potentially making it difficult for an outsider to immediately understand the conversation. As with academic research communities, however, these conversations can supply us with useful insights and methods. Ideally, these communities would work together, using their combined insights to find solutions to the pressing issues of the day.

There is really no specific reason that academic discourse must stay in the academy, nor is there any valid reason that community discourse can't productively travel toward the university. If "everyone is an intellectual," collaboration across contexts should be the hallmark of intellectual work. As noted above, a central premise of our work together is that the best writing, the best research, emerges when intellectuals located across a range of institutional and public locations join together to discuss an issue of concern. It is out of this bringing together of different communities that new solutions and possibilities are created. It is part of the power of a writer such as Gloria Anzaldúa, and it is why this chapter covers both forms of research.

Indeed, to imagine otherwise is to put false and damaging limitations on which resources any community can bring to the conversation. One motivation to learn the general investigative values of academic discourse might be to more easily pick up on the writing strategies of your particular major. The larger purpose, however, is to understand how research communities operate. By bridging the work of multiple research communities, you will be able to draw the conversations between any two communities into a dialogue, into common purpose. Just as you should be developing your writerly voice and

Paula Solloway/Alamy Stock Photo

reading strategies for roles beyond the university, you also should be developing your investigative and research skills for purposes beyond the university.

Joining the Community

Learning to write in the academy is not unlike learning to write or speak within
any new community. You need to learn the rules of conversation as well as what
counts as evidence. As noted in Chapter 1, one of the best strategies when reading academic discourse is to try to determine the communal values of the piece
you are reading. What do these authors consider to be important questions?
What are the important terms they use to explore these questions? What type
of evidence do they imagine as compelling, and what type of evidence do they
imagine as irrelevant? As noted above, you might also spend time looking at the
bibliography pages of the piece you are reading, skimming the titles of the works
listed to see if certain terms are repeated, perhaps in slightly modified ways. This
process will give you a sense of the larger conversation in which any particular
piece of writing appears.

   If you find that you are intrigued by the questions asked within this community and you choose to join, your role will be to push on these definitions, based
on your own values, and explore how their primary questions must change to
respond to your challenges. For instance, you might find architectural discussions
about sustainable buildings interesting, but wonder how such buildings might

work in your neighborhood or religious community. You might then explore how the community could address this concern, bringing your insight to bear on the issue. Such moments are not necessarily adversarial. As an incoming member of the community, your mission is not to dismiss the community's values or concepts. Rather, you should understand the community's writings as trying to value the work of others, extending or amending those voices. You are simply trying to continue that effort by bringing your insights to the conversation.

Your right to join and expand the conversation is an important point: Students often see academic writing as unrelated to their own interests and experiences. The language of the articles sometimes confirms this sense of distance. Although on one level it might be true that not every essay will speak to your values, you might also imagine that this distance—that failure to connect—is evidence that the conversation needs to consider additional experiences and additional pieces of evidence. For example, for many years, linguists understood African American speech patterns as having been based on eighteenth-century English. Scholars such as Melville Herskovits began to study the actual language patterns of African American speakers off the coast of North Carolina. Using his research, Herskovits demonstrated that the language patterns of the residents bore traces of a larger African heritage. Soon, words, phrases, and sentences spoken by African Americans began to be understood as representing this heritage. Today, there is a general acceptance of these connections, although as with all academic discussions, there is still a debate over the extent of such a heritage in everyday speech.

© Mike Greenlar/The Image Works

You should imagine that your experience, your communal values, can also act as an important lens to understanding the goals of any particular piece of academic writing. Of course, to fully engage with the essay, you will need to read closely and understand the conversation out of which the piece emerges as well as the multiple ways it answers important questions particular to its conversation. It is also best not to assume that you know more than those who have been involved in the conversation for years. After all, you want to be a generous participant. Throughout your reading of any text, however, your personal and communal experience can be an important tool. To some extent, you should picture yourself as an organic intellectual, drawing and affirming the worldview of your community, investigating the purposes and values of traditional intellectuals, and looking for ways to build alliances. Imagine that you are trying to hold both types of knowledge in your mind, determining what it means for where you now stand in your own beliefs.

Here it might be useful to return to Mayra Castillo Rangel. Her essay that began this chapter eventually discusses what it means to be from Mexico but live in the United States, an experience of being in one community but having the linguistic and cultural heritages of both communities present in her mind. She is consistently moving between her traditional and organic knowledge, as she addresses issues of family, marriage, and education. She explains, "I'm simply trying to find a midpoint between both cultures since I do still live in both, even though I live in only one country." This midpoint, as you might expect, requires a sense of inventiveness. It requires exploring multiple ways of speaking and writing—of respecting and valuing her home language and community, and working to bring it into dialogue with other ways of speaking. In some ways, Rangel's metaphor of a **midpoint** is an apt description of what it should mean to actively engage with multiple research communities. On one level, all writers strive to be a Rangel or an Anzaldúa.

CHECKPOINT   Bringing Voices Together

Revisit some recent conversations you had through an online community such as Facebook or Twitter. Choose several exchanges and explore how you conversed with the others who took part. Consider these questions:

- What was the discussion about? How did you speak? What did you use as evidence in staking your position?
- How did these online conversations differ from how you talk to your family? How did they differ from how you talk in your classrooms?
- Can you picture a way that these different conversations might be brought together in a single discourse community? If so, how?

Of course, you may not share Rangel's experiences. You may not wish to echo the strategies of Anzaldúa. You may have lived in one community your whole life and always spoken the same language. Anzaldúa's story has one final "lesson" to impart, though. As a student, you are most likely juggling your existing knowledge of home and school while also being asked to develop a new way of speaking and writing. Rather than assume that you must choose one community to which to belong, instead you might create an intellectual midpoint where the academic and the communal (traditional and organic) are in constant dialogue, constantly calling forth new questions, new ways of writing, and new types of solutions. If you remember the necessarily inventive nature of academic discourse, you will understand such work as central not only to your identity as a student but also to your life beyond college.

Writing Like an Intellectual

By now, it should be clear that *intellectual* is a multifaceted term that implies both communal and academic knowledge and incorporates both organic and traditional insights. What might not be clear, however, is that the writing produced by intellectuals is supported by a common set of principles and strategies that are used in their work. These principles guide them, enabling and directing the specific product they hope to produce. At the outset of our work, it is important to take a moment and embed these principles and strategies within an overarching vision of intellectual writing. This step is particularly important because your work during this term will potentially include not only academic papers but also newspaper editorials, community press books, and digital publications. To achieve your writing goals, we need a definition of the writing process that is as expansive as our definition of intellectuals.

Establishing a Research Focus

The first stage of any research project—academic or community-based—is to establish a **research focus**. It is different from developing a topic sentence or even, to some extent, a theme. A research focus represents the broad set of issues or problems that interest you. Rather than rushing in to find an answer, you should step back and try to consider all the different writers and voices that have a pointed concern or interest in the topic being considered. For instance, if you are exploring the topic of women's rights, you might want to start finding your focus by first making a list of potential topics, such as workplace discrimination, sexual harassment, and the suffragist movement. You might also want to make a list of important people to consult, such as women's studies scholars, community activists, political leaders, and opinion columnists. Your opening move is to create the largest possible constellation of intellectuals to help you understand the full scope of the conversation. In doing so, you put the inventive nature of academic reading to work to develop a rich community of people from whom you can learn and to whom you can respond in your essay.

- Develop a list of key terms for your research area; conduct a search through your library database and Internet search engines.
- Use the results of this search to create a list that contains a wide variety of sources, such as single-author essays, print academic journals, online publication sites, advocacy organizations, and online discussion groups.
- Explore how these different authors define important questions, discuss similar terms, develop evidence, and stake a position on the topic.
- Write a short statement detailing what you take to be the primary focus and goals of individuals or communities doing research in this area; also state how this community will allow you to address your particular concern(s) about this topic.

Organizing Research Materials

As you continue your research, you will have to manage a lot of information. Books, Web sites, essays, and interviews, among other materials, will accumulate on your desk or computer desktop. (Remember the range of materials Anzaldúa had to manage for her project; see pp. 23–24.) It is a good idea to have a system in place that will allow you to quickly access the appropriate material when needed and, even better, access the specific parts of that material.

- Keep a notebook or Word document where you dedicate a page to each resource you have found, listing its full bibliographic information, most relevant key terms for your project, and specific quotes (with page numbers).
- Create a blog where you keep a running commentary on what you are reading, assessing the key points of a text, noting additional areas of possible research, and discussing some possible connections among texts.
- Create a folder on your computer labeled "Current Research" where all digital texts are stored. Have two subfolders for "Read" and "Unread" to help you keep track of what work still needs to be done.

Understanding Your Research Community

As you work your way through these materials, you will soon discover that the writers tend to focus on certain types of questions and use certain types of evidence based on the particular community, or audience, with whom they are discussing the topic. Rather than quickly choosing a side in response to a particular piece, see if you can begin to draw connections between different authors by taking their singular arguments and creating a new understanding of the issue. Remember that your goal is not to accept or reject a particular author; rather, it is to build a research community based on your readings that enables you do discuss *your* topic in a way that meshes with your values, your instincts. (These texts are, in effect, the bibliography for your paper.) It is from this constellation of voices and writings that your particular research project will emerge. You might begin by taking the following steps:

- Choose three pieces of writing that share a common focus on a central term but define that term differently.

- Create a chart that details each piece of writing's method, form of evidence, and conclusion.

- Write a short statement detailing how each method will enable you to answer your particular concern(s) about this topic.

- Create a list of the information you will need to find about your topic so that you can effectively use these methods in your paper to offer your definition of the central term used in all the pieces you are analyzing.

Participating in the Research Community

You might be tempted to quickly take a side as you engage with your research community. It is more productive, though, to imagine yourself joining a conversation that you find important rather than just arguing for an already established point. Consider how you might talk through an important issue with friends or family. Would you ever reject someone's point outright? Or would you try to understand that person's opinion, add your own, and see if a new possibility might emerge? When writing academic discourse, you want to see how you can move the discussion forward and determine what possibilities for progress you can find in the arguments being proposed. Will you disagree with some of the arguments? Sure you will. Still, you must approach these authors with respect and see what other ideas and arguments can be developed from their viewpoints. Here again, you might begin by taking the following steps:

- Determine the current stance of the broad research community toward your concern(s) about this issue.

- Write a short statement on how your stance on this topic will further the discussion on this issue, by both endorsing and critiquing current work being produced.

- Create an outline indicating, among other elements, sources to be used to establish the state of the current research, the value of your particular intervention in this research, researchers to be used to support your particular stance, and evidence to be used to prove the value of your stance.

The Writing Process

Once you have completed the initial stages of your research, you will need to begin formulating your thoughts in writing. This moment is when your voice begins to enter the conversation. Admittedly, such moments can be simultaneously exciting ("Finally a chance to speak my piece!") and overwhelming ("Where to begin?"). A useful guide at such moments, an initial way to begin to organize your efforts, is to follow the steps of the writing process: prewriting, drafting, revising, and editing.

Prewriting

Typically, **prewriting** is framed as a brainstorming exercise in which you write continuously for a period of time, putting down on paper every idea or thought you have about the topic at hand. It might be better, however, to imagine that you are brainstorming within a particular research community, developing or addressing issues within that community. So far, you have written several short statements about your writing goals. This step is an opportunity to expand those statements and begin to create an extended text to use as the basis for your essay. With that in mind, spend 15 to 20 minutes answering the following questions:

- What are the key terms or key questions within that community that interest you?
- How do you want to approach them?
- What questions might you want to research? (You might also consider what questions the research community does not address.)
- What questions do your personal or communal experiences raise about the topic?
- How do those personal or communal experiences influence how you understand the work of the research community?
- What might it mean to include these insights as well?

Once you have spent time responding to these questions, read what you have written. Do you see a question or specific topic emerging on which you want to focus your paper? Spend some additional time writing a paragraph that further clarifies your particular interest in the work of this research community.

Drafting

Here is the moment when our discussion of organic and traditional intellectuals—and the idea that the best research draws these types of knowledge together—comes into play. The tension between a research community's focus and your personal experiences of an issue that you addressed in prewriting is an example of the need for academic discourse to remain endlessly inventive and open to change. As you draft your essay, the work is to bring these multiple forms of insight into the same paper.

Perhaps one of the best ways to start drafting is to imagine an example, a real moment, that captures what you are trying to write about. For instance, if you are generally concerned about the lower wages that women typically receive compared to men, you might begin by writing about an actual example where this situation occurred. You can use this example to draw out your broader points on this issue: "This story of Mary not receiving the same wages as her male counterparts, because she was married, points to how traditional gender roles are used to justify economic discrimination." You might even begin each paragraph with a moment in the story and then detail the larger issue it encapsulates. As you move forward with the essay and revise it (see below), the structure might change. As one way to begin, you might find that beginning with a case study is very useful.

It should be stated that drafting is not an easy task, nor should it be. After all, you will be using your writing to produce new and important insights. It might be helpful to look at some of the writing featured in this book to get a sense of how other writers have approached this task. You might look at the essays by Gloria Anzaldúa (see p. 387) and Carmen Kynard (see p. 127) for examples of how they draw everyday experience and academic terminology into their writing. You might look at the work of Gerald Graff (see p. 114) or Christopher Wilkey (see p. 146) to understand how to include personal testimony into more traditional research-based writing. In any event, you should keep in mind that the richest conversations are those that blend the insights of many and develop unique ways of addressing (through writing or speech) important community problems. It is this goal that should frame your initial draft of any piece of writing.

Revising

Revision is sometimes cast as editing, or checking your paper for obvious logical errors or grammatical mistakes. Although that check is clearly an important step to take, revision is more deeply connected to revising the content of your paper, not just the grammar and syntax. Revision should focus on making sure that your paper moves a conversation forward and brings together the multiple academic and community insights that have led to your specific set of conclusions. As a way to begin revising, you might consider these questions:

- Who is the audience for this argument?
- Why is the argument in my paper important to them?
- Will the facts used be persuasive to this audience?

You might also have your peers (school or community-based) read your draft to see if it makes sense to them. Do they understand how the argument is developed, the rationale for the sources used, and the necessity of the conclusions drawn? If they are confused or less than convinced, you should talk with them about how the writing might be improved. Be open to the possibility that you may need to change your mind in the essay. In this sense, revision means developing writing that is brought into dialogue with its intended communities and that is understood *by them* as a persuasive and important piece of work. To make that happen, you might have to move paragraphs, expand or delete certain points, or conduct more research. Revision, then, is really the act of producing the next draft of your paper. As mentioned earlier, academic writers produce multiple drafts of their work before it moves to any public audience.

Final Editing

At some point, you will decide that a draft of an essay represents the strongest version of your insights and that now is the time a public audience (whether your class or your community) should be invited to respond to your work as a completed argument. It is only at this moment that you should focus on issues of grammar and formatting. Even these general "editing" categories will need to be understood within the genre in which you are writing. Social scientists document research differently than English literature scholars, and articles are formatted differently than brochures or annual reports. Keep these issues in mind as you do your final editing and speak to your instructor about what kind of reference and documentation guidelines you should follow.

Note on publication: As noted many times throughout this chapter, intellectuals participate in conversations; they work to produce new knowledge that is important to their community. For this reason, you should consider how your writing might eventually become part of a discourse community, whether in your college or as part of the local community. If you have written a traditional academic research paper, you might explore journals that publish undergraduate writing; if you have produced an opinion piece, you might consider a campus or community publication; if you composed a brochure, you might consider where to place it so that members of your community will encounter it. That is, if you have taken seriously the work of participating and producing knowledge on a topic on which you have a sincere interest, you should consider how it might reach its intended audience. (For a more in-depth discussion about publication, see Chapter 7.)

Sample Intellectual Strategies

The following essay was written by Vera Beaton, a member of a community writing group who was exploring the connection between work, community, and organic intellectuals. (This excerpt comes from *Pro(se)letariets;* more excerpts appear in Chapter 3.) The author would not be typically understood as a student; rather, she had an advanced academic degree and was trying to blend her academic and community knowledge to understand a particular moment in her job. The essay represents one model of how such work might be done.

Different parts of this author's discussion explore different types of insights, which are annotated through the excerpt.

The Tree of Thanks

Vera Beaton

My daughter came home for the Canadian Thanksgiving holiday, and we had some very interesting family times together. Specifically, we talked about family and times, in short bursts and in extended sessions. I have no clue about what prompted this, but part of it came from my reflections about a little boy who is currently in treatment at my place of work.

    I don't usually discuss people at the hospital with family or friends—it usually seems like a violation of one kind or another. But this little boy had kind of hit me where I live, and I wanted to share this with someone that I knew would consider this from a loving perspective, rather than discount the story as more eccentric blithering from the strange mind of Minerva Jones.

    The little boy in question is a child who ended up in a group home following a time of chaos in his family. His parents were getting divorced, and he was caught in the crossfire of their battle. He became angry, and began to act out. His misbehavior took the form of writing long stories with violent themes. When he went to the group home, this activity did not stop. In fact, after some time in the group home, he started writing stories about the group home.

    He was sent to the psychiatric hospital after a staff member found a seven-page story about his plan to kill his enemies at the group home by turning on the gas stove and letting the residence fill with gas. At the end of the story that he wrote, "everyone perished in the resulting explosion."

    People are taking this sort of early warning very seriously these days. When this boy arrived on our doorstep, the lessons from the Columbine High School shooting came to the fore. Staff speculated about this boy's "sociopathy." Was he signaling some horrendous intention?

    The Demon Seed. The boy seemed like a regular kid, but unusually intelligent. He is extraordinarily creative. He developed a daily newspaper on the ward, and he started a lottery by putting a winning symbol on a piece of paper in pencil, then coloring over it with a crayon. He'd pass these out to the other kids, and they would scratch off the crayon, revealing a winner. There were no

Annotations (right margin):

Family (home) relationships

The writer's academic (medical) community; relationships

The boy's home community

The writer's academic (medical) community; the boy's home community

The boy's home community

prizes involved. Kids liked the idea of being winners, and he'd post the results on his bedroom door, with the daily winner acknowledged. He made a *Jeopardy*-type game. When I saw this, I asked for "Animals, $300."

The question: What animal has eyes bigger than its brain? Answer: See below.

Relationships (the writer's and the boy's)

I started to tell my daughter about this kid because he had done a funny and interesting thing. The recreational therapist had made a construction paper tree for the unit, entitled *The Tree of Thanks*. The therapeutic task assigned to the children was to cut leaves from various colored paper, and then write something they were thankful for on each leaf. I saw the finished product when I came to work in the evening.

Relationships; home communities

These kids were thankful for so many things—their moms, pets, grandparents, toys. One kid was even thankful for me, which was nice. But buried in the leaves of this Tree of Thanks was a kid who was thankful for "[his] evilness." It was written in jagged purple crayon on a peaceful green background.

I had to laugh. "What a little beauty!" I thought.

I knew this had to be the work of my creative/sociopathic boy. So many people were telling him that he was having bad thoughts. In fact earlier in the week, during a treatment meeting, one of the social workers had gone on about his attempt to blow up his group home after I recommended that we test this boy's IQ. I had to remind the social worker that the boy had not tried to kill anyone; he had only written about it. He did not fight with his peers physically, but he did occasionally have disputes. For the most part, he adapted to his environment, and dealt with his episodic anger through written expression. For example, he

Relationships; the boy's home community (and his place in it)

became angry at a certain staff member when she wouldn't allow him to use the phone to call his mother. He wrote on the floor of his room "Mrs. S. is a mean bitch."

This seemed like a natural response to powerlessness, in my way of thinking.

He was congenial with his peers and had moments of generosity and compassion with them.

I told my daughter about this boy, in the same general terms as I have here—no names, no identifying details. No loss of confidentiality, no betrayal. But I wanted to tell someone how glad

I was, after all the trials of this young boy's life—the breakup of his family, and the involuntary commitments—how he was still able to retain a sense of himself and the integrity to be thankful for the "evilness" that allowed him to explore and display his anger without causing harm to anyone else.

I'm hoping one day we'll all catch up to this kid.

(Answer to the *Jeopardy* question: OSTRICH. My first instinctive response was people, but then I remembered that, generally, our brains are bigger than our eyes. This may not be a good thing.)

More Tree of Thanks Stuff

So after I discussed the young boy with my daughter, my strange and tangential mind moved onto another young boy who grew up with heavy burdens: my mother's grandfather.

Ambrose "Amby" O'Connell had responsibility from an early age. His father had kept going on after going out for a "quart of milk." In the way of that time, Amby was lucky to have been given his father's job in the coal mine. He was nine years old. No fourth-grade primer for this boy—his path was to help feed a family.

The writer's home community and family relationships

Such is life.

He went on to be a well-respected man, a dragger man, the man who dragged others out of the mine following a cave-in or a fire. He also became the fire chief of his local area, a man who led other small-town saviors into the very heart of all that intended to destroy everyone: ruin, despair, death. Along these same lines, he was an early union organizer. Somebody forgot to tell him he "owed his soul to the company store," and he didn't believe it when they tried to influence him after the fact. Union supporters were having unfortunate accidents, and there was outright brutality in the streets of New Waterford, Dominion Beach, and Glace Bay, courtesy of the companies (and the Canadian government). Mr. O'Connell started a credit union in his house so that the miners would have a place to come for funds. Some place not owned by the Dominion Coal Company.

"A man's a man for a' that . . ."

I told my daughter that her great-great-grandfather was one of the reasons that sociologists love to hang around Nova Scotia. And then I moved onto another strange and wonderful story . . .

Academic
(MUMS)
community;
discussion
continues
for several
paragraphs

Another Strange and Wonderful Story. MUMS is the acronym the women gave their union as they emerged from the battered women's shelter, empowered to take on all manner of injustice and brutality.

MUMS stands for Mothers United for Metro Shelter.

This was 1984. *Brave New World* was available, if only we had the map, and the wisdom to use it.

MUMS had a great start by six women who had joined together to protest the prejudicial and falsely inflated Halifax rental housing market. They held up traffic on the Alexander A. MacDonald Bridge one day, and handed out fliers describing the pitiful state of housing for poor women and children in Halifax. They described how they were dubbed the welfare bums, but how $700 out of the $900 they were "given" each month to support a family, really went to line the pockets of landlords. How hard it was to feed and clothe children on $200 a month. (Have you ever noticed the "nickel-and-diming" that goes on? It'll be the death of us.)

MUMS were radical in that they suggested (aside from the fact that the bulk of the fund they were given was going to the fattest people in town) the true state of affairs implied they were, in essence, paid employees of the government, bringing up the next generation of wage slaves in the absence of that brutal "milk cow" they used to call their husbands. They were a union of mothers, employed by the government, enduring the full stigma of the handout. No benefits except the health and happiness of their children, the sort you can fashion on the most meager of wages—a very hard job.

They called for a public demonstration of their powerlessness, and they gave a date for their intended act of civil disobedience. They planned to march on City Hall, hand the mayor an eviction notice, give him a bogus check for $900, and tell him to find new accommodations for his activities.

On the designated date, they set out from a site halfway down Gottigen Street, a place heavily damaged by munitions explosions in the various world wars. It was a place where the corpses of the *Titanic* washed up, along with their sad, water-logged possessions. These six women walked along the waterfront to City Hall, so purposeful, proud, and adamant.

On the way, they gathered others—folks watching from the sidelines, but invigorated by their passion. When they passed the docks next to the bridge separating Halifax from Dartmouth, the entirety of the union of dock workers joined them.

The MUMS members' home community

A half dozen women and several hundred men. The women served their eviction notice, and the mayor, noting so many potential voters in his presence, made the necessary promises.

A rent-controlled apartment complex with a daycare.

The mayor never made good on this.

But I told my daughter about this story to tell her about the people we come from, the places we've been. The dreams lost, the promise shown and denied. The ability of people to rise above the squalor. The hope of brotherhood and sisterhood.

The writer's relationships and home community

I can't tell the story about those dock workers joining the *Mother's Union* without crying, and I did some serious boohooing when I told my daughter about them. Me, a silly middle-aged woman, crying while she sat on her living room floor in the middle of America, so far away from the fray.

And I cry now. But it's for the same reasons that I told my daughter as she patted my head and kissed me while I cried on the *Tree of Thanks* day.

"Sometimes, people are so good, and they have so much dignity, that they just break your heart."

I only wish I could've laughed.

A Man's a Man for All That
Robert Burns, 1795

A poem by Robert Burns ties together themes from the writer's discussion: community, relationships, the struggle for justice

Is there for honesty poverty
That hangs his head, an' a' that;
The coward slave—we pass him by,
We dare be poor for a' that!
For a' that, an' a' that,
Our toils obscure an' a' that,
The rank is but the guinea's stamp,
The man's the gowd for a' that.
What though on homely fare we dine,
Wear hoddin grey, an' a' that?

Give fools their silks, and knaves their wine,
A man's a man for a' that.
For a' that, an' a' that,
Their tinsel show, an' a' that,
The honest man, tho' e'er sae poor,
Is king o' men for a' that.

Ye see yon birkie ca'd a lord,
Wha struts, an' stares, an' a' that;
Tho' hundreds worship at his word,
He's but a coof for a' that.
For a' that, an' a' that,
His ribband, star, an' a' that,
The man o' independent mind
He looks an' laughs at a' that.

A prince can mak a belted knight,
A marquise, duke, an' a' that;
But an honest man's aboon his might,
Gude faith, he maunna fa' that!
For a' that, an' a' that,
Their dignities an' a' that,
The pith o' sense, an' pride o' worth,
Are higher rank than a' that.
Then let us pray that come it may,
(As come it will for a' that,)
That Sense and Worth, o'er a' the earth,
Shall bear the gree, an' a' that.
For a' that, an' a' that,
It's coming yet for a' that,
That man to man, the world o'er,
Shall brothers be for a' that.

Of course, your own academic writing will sound different from that of Vera Beaton or Gloria Anzaldúa. You should nonetheless keep in mind the voices of Beaton, Anzaldúa, and Rangel (who opened this chapter) as examples of what it means to maintain a midpoint between traditional and organic knowledge, between the academy and their communities. During your time in college, you will constantly be asked to find your own midpoint between different cultures and communities. Ideally, writing can serve as a space for you to begin to find your voice, your midpoint, as you navigate your way through college.

Bridging Academic Communities

Thus far, we have spent considerable time developing an intellectual framework that can encompass both traditional and organic intellectuals, arguing that the most productive discussions—and the most innovative solutions to communal issues—emerge from such a sustained dialogue. Along the way, we have looked at different writers to see how they use their writing to cross over or blend different communities. Implicitly, we have been creating a template that will take such writing outward toward partnership work that links the academy and the community. For that to be possible, we will need to develop the pragmatic skills that can enable such discussions to occur. In Chapters 5 through 7, we move toward this work.

Now, however, it is important to delve deeper into the different ways writers have blended the academic and the communal, the scholarly and the personal, to argue for the goals of "higher education" and the "writing classroom," the very locations in which you are encountering this book. In other words, before moving toward partnership with a community, it is important to have a strong understanding of your own location. For that reason, you will read how writers have discussed the goals of "higher education" in Chapter 3, exploring the work of Antonio Gramsci, David Bartholomae, and Andrew Delbanco as well as writing by working-class students and writers in the United States and the United Kingdom. You will also see how policy organizations have attempted to formulate the goals of colleges and universities. In effect, you will get a sense of the current issues facing colleges and universities.

In Chapter 4, you will have the opportunity to read about the "writing classroom" to see how professors are reshaping its goals for the current moment. Here you will read the work of Gerald Graff, Carmen Kynard, and Christopher Wilkey, who attempt to model a dialogue between the "classroom," the "students," and the "community." In doing so, they invite you to offer your own opinion, to join the conversation, on how the modern university should imagine the goals of one of its most-taught courses—freshman writing. After having done this work and explored this research, you will be in a position to understand what it might mean to blend the university and its classrooms with the goals of the surrounding communities. You will be ready to consider the value of bringing traditional and organic intellectuals together for common purpose.

RUNDOWN   Strategies for Research and Writing

Creating a Research Focus

- Establish a research area.
- Understand the goals of its research community.
- Develop a reading list of relevant research.
- Determine your stance regarding the relevant research.

  Create a list of authors across academic, popular, and community contexts who speak to the issue you are exploring.

  Create a note, folder, or blog to help organize your response to the research.

  Develop a list of key terms as well as how different authors define them.

  Write a short statement about how you define key terms and where you believe the research conversation can be productively developed.

Producing Research

- Respond to the current questions within the research community.
- Establish how your response will move the conversation forward.
- Bring together research to develop your response.
- Demonstrate the value of your response to academic and community researchers.

  Spend 20 minutes writing a short essay on what you understand to be the key issues of your research area. Use this essay as your first draft.

  Share your completed draft with your peers in your class and community for feedback, revising it to address their concerns.

  Edit for grammar only with the final draft.

  Consider a public venue in which to publish your work.

Discussion Questions & Activities

1. Before the next class, write a response to the "Lessons Learned" writing prompt that began this chapter. Share your response with your classmates.

2. Choose a piece of "academic writing" assigned to you in a different class. Describe its features—how it argues, presents evidence, and examines

certain terms. Do the same work with a piece of "nonacademic writing." What differences do you see between these two pieces? What do these different ways of writing tell us about how knowledge is produced in each of these writing communities?

3. Reread this chapter. As a class, identify places where you believe the writer is doing the work of a traditional intellectual. Now point to moments where the writer is doing the work of an organic intellectual. How would you describe the differences? Based on your analysis, how does this writer define the purpose of academic discourse? Do you agree? Remember that your goal isn't to take a position on the actual argument being produced by the writer. Rather, your role is to have a discussion about the goals of academic writing.

4. As discussed above, a writer exists within a research community (whether the community consists of neighbors, academic scholars, or both). Choose one essay discussed in this chapter. As a class, attempt to define the research community of the author. From whom is the author drawing information? To whom is the author addressing the essay? To what end is the author making an intervention in the conversation? Then, having done this work, discuss what other research communities might be brought into this conversation to expand, amend, or critique that author's approach to the subject. That is, what was the overarching framework that seemed to inform how the author created a research project? Remember that your role here is not to stake out your own position. Rather, it is to imagine what research the author excluded from the essay and, in doing so, enable a larger discussion of what values might have informed the development of that author's research community.

3

Writing Education: Moving from Home to College Communities

The readings in this chapter will help you to better understand and explore the many goals of higher education. As a jumping-off point for this work, here's a short essay describing a unique piece of writing and its importance to a particular community.

"Ban Fascism"

I t is written in huge four-foot letters. It can be seen clearly streets away. It is a white paint daubing on a high brick wall which shouts BAN FASCISM.

It has been there ever since I can remember and that's almost twenty years.

Its paint is now beginning to fade. I remember seeing it when I had no conception of the word's meaning, and I remember not asking my parents in case it was something rude.

It is unfortunate that I ever did grow up to know what it meant, that it should still be a word still relevant in the modern world.

Maybe it was scrawled up there by two young Jews with a brush and a bucket of paint at the time of the Mosely street riots. I can almost see them in the dark night slapping on the paint carefully but quickly and all the time keeping a watchful eye on the empty streets.

Having finished their night's labour I imagine them running off into the dark not daring to look at the slogan until the following morning when along with a hundred others they could tut and gasp at the cheek of the graffiti artist's work.

"Who could have done such a thing," they would say mockingly and sharing a grin.

There's a funny thing about that sign. If you stand very close to the wall it's just lines and circles. It tells you nothing. Yet just by standing back a few yards its message is clear.

Sometimes one must be free of oppression to understand that he has been oppressed.

But what of them now? What of the brave hotheads who felt they could not live that night through without advertising their emotions. Are they still as heated and eager to alight the world or have the drops of time extinguished the flame. Maybe they are tired and apathetic, maybe they are dead. No matter if they are either. For a little while at least they have left a tribute to the people they were and the politics of compulsion.

The work of those graffiti artists is as deep and honourable as anything hanging in the National Gallery. Maybe more so. It doesn't belong in a museum though but where it is, in the street. Its audience is you and me. It is a plea and a warning.

Pray the fading white paint need never be renewed.

—**Roger Mills, Basement Writers, England**
From *Federation Magazine*, 30th Anniversary Special

It might seem odd to begin a chapter focused on helping you understand what it means to write for college with a story about graffiti and even odder to use an essay about writing placed high up on a brick wall as the introduction to a chapter focused on the goals of "higher education." As noted in Chapters 1 and 2, however, higher education is changing. Students are increasingly being asked to consider how their education can be a bridge to local community concerns and directly link students' education to community needs. So although only a few of us might imagine graffiti activism as part of our future, higher education is increasingly asking us to consider how we might take our writing public, how we might link it to larger causes.

For this reason, the goals of higher education and the way it works in practice might be different from what you expect. As you begin your work in college, it is important that you consider the context in which your education is occurring and look at the dynamics of the community in which you are being asked to participate. It is equally important to consider the larger social context in which education itself occurs and the ways in which the country frames the goals of higher education in relation to our communities and our economy. We need to consider why some individuals who are seen as educated are given power whereas others are placed on the wrong side of privilege. And we need to assess how our education is asking us to stand along this divide.

As these questions emerge, we will have to return to our earlier discussion of the role of the university in combating such divides. Although almost everyone might agree that a university education should prepare you for the real world, it is not clear that there would be equal consensus on the role of the university in altering that real world—tilting it toward a particular sense of community values and social justice. Nor is it clear that students themselves should be called on to take part in a university's push toward a greater role in public affairs. At this very moment (and to some extent with this book), however, you will be asked to take on such work, to become part of a classroom, college, and institutional vision of the "public good" and endorse what is an emerging community consensus on the role of higher education. As you move through college, you will also need to decide where you stand on such goals.

Of course, all these questions might seem distant to you. As you begin your college career, your immediate goals might be to succeed in particular classes and be accepted into a particular program. It is important to remember, however, that these classes and programs exist within colleges, which exist within communities, which exist within national conversations. We are part of these discussions whether or not we chose to be. So to consciously participate in those discussions, to understand what it means to be (and succeed as) a college student, to learn how we want to navigate this difficult terrain, we might also find it useful to take the advice of Roger Mills: "If you stand very close to the wall it's just lines and circles. It tells you nothing. Yet just by standing back a few yards its message is clear." Perhaps we need to stand a few yards back from our education for a moment to see the broader message higher education is trying to send.

You will not be alone in this exploration of the goals of higher education. In addition to the support of your teacher and classmates, this chapter will share with you the insights of writers and activists who have also attempted to think through how our culture determines the goals of education, the role of higher education in implementing those goals, and the type of public stance students should learn in the process. As you read their writing, you will see how they establish a research area, read widely the work of others in that area, and attempt to move the conversation forward. You will see how they try to address not only other academic writers but students and neighbors as well. That is, they understand their work as moving across many different communities. Through engaging with their ideas, not only will you get a sense of the "big picture" in which your education occurs and develop some new reading and writing strategies to use in your own work, but you will also be able to join an ongoing conversation about the goals of higher education today.

References and notes for the readings can be found in the appendix on page 427.

ANTONIO GRAMSCI

On Intellectuals

Universal History Archive/
Getty Images

Antonio Gramsci was an Italian Marxist imprisoned by Benito Mussolini's Fascist government. Much of Gramsci's work can be understood as an attempt to understand how a political movement like Fascism could gain such power. In particular, he explored the role of intellectuals in legitimizing certain political ideologies. He was concerned, that is, with how an idea becomes a fact, which then allows it to be an unquestioned basis for how a society operates. It is this unquestioned belief in certain facts that Gramsci defined as "hegemony." He understood his work as questioning the hegemonic status of Fascism in an effort to open up alternative ways of organizing society. For his beliefs, as noted above, Mussolini imprisoned him. Hegemony, it seems, had more than intellectuals on its side.

In the following excerpt taken from *The Prison Notebooks* (1926), Gramsci attempts to work out his ideas, exploring what it means to be an intellectual and what role intellectuals have (and should take) in fostering a more just society.

■　■　■

Are intellectuals an autonomous and independent social group, or does every social group have its own particular specialized category of intellectuals? The problem is a complex one, because of the variety of forms assumed to date by the real historical process of formation of the different categories of intellectuals.

The most important of these forms are two:

1. Every social group, coming into existence on the original terrain of an essential function in the world of economic production, creates together with itself, organically, one or more strata[1] of intellectuals which give it homogeneity and an awareness of its own function not only in the economic

but also in the social and political fields. The capitalist entrepreneur creates alongside himself the industrial technician, the specialist in political economy, the organizers of a new culture, of a new legal system, etc. It should be noted that the entrepreneur himself represents a higher level of social elaboration, already characterized by a certain directive [*dirigente*] and technical (i.e., intellectual) capacity: he must have a certain technical capacity, not only in the limited sphere of his activity and initiative but in other spheres as well, at least in those which are closest to economic production. He must be an organizer of masses of men; he must be an organizer of the "confidence" of investors in his business, of the customers for his product, etc.

If not all entrepreneurs, at least an *élite* amongst them must have the capacity to be an organizer of society in general, including all its complex organism of services, right up to the state organism, because of the need to create the conditions most favorable to the expansion of their own class; or at the least they must possess the capacity to choose the deputies (specialized employees) to whom to entrust this activity of organizing the general system of relationships external to the business itself. It can be observed that the "organic" intellectuals which every new class creates alongside itself and elaborates in the course of its development, are for the most part "specializations" of partial aspects of the primitive activity of the new social type which the new class has brought into prominence.

5   Even feudal lords were possessors of a particular technical capacity, military capacity, and it is precisely from the moment at which the aristocracy loses its monopoly of technicomilitary capacity that the crisis of feudalism begins. But the formation of intellectuals in the feudal world and in the preceding classical world is a question to be examined separately: this formation and elaboration follows ways and means which must be studied concretely. Thus it is to be noted that the mass of the peasantry, although it performs an essential function in the world of production, does not elaborate its own "organic" intellectuals, nor does it "assimilate" any stratum of "traditional" intellectuals, although it is from the peasantry that other social groups draw many of their intellectuals and a high proportion of traditional intellectuals are of peasant origin.

2. However, every "essential" social group which emerges into history out of the preceding economic structure, and as an expression of a development of this structure, has found (at least in all of history up to the present) categories of intellectuals already in existence and which seemed indeed to represent an historical continuity uninterrupted even by the most complicated and radical changes in political and social forms.

The most typical of these categories of intellectuals is that of the ecclesiastics, who for a long time (for a whole phase of history, which is partly characterized by this very monopoly) held a monopoly of a number of important services: religious ideology, that is the philosophy and science of the age, together with schools, education, morality, justice, charity, good works, etc. The category of ecclesiastics can be considered the category of intellectuals organically bound to the landed aristocracy. It had equal status juridically with the aristocracy, with which it shared the exercise of feudal ownership of land, and the use of state privileges connected with property. But the monopoly held by the ecclesiastics in the superstructural field was not exercised without a struggle or without limitations, and hence there took place the birth, in various forms (to be gone into and studied concretely), of other categories, favored and enabled to expand by the growing strength of the central power of the monarch, right up to absolutism. Thus we find the formation of the *noblesse de robe,* with its own privileges, a stratum of administrators, etc., scholars and scientists, theorists, nonecclesiastical philosophers, etc.

Since these various categories of traditional intellectuals experience through an "esprit de corps" their uninterrupted historical continuity and their special qualification, they thus put themselves forward as autonomous and independent of the dominant social group. This self-assessment is not without consequences in the ideological and political field, consequences of wide-ranging import. The whole of idealist philosophy can easily be connected with this position assumed by the social complex of intellectuals and can be defined as the expression of that social Utopia by which the intellectuals think of themselves as "independent," autonomous, endowed with a character of their own, etc.

One should note however that if the Pope and the leading hierarchy of the Church consider themselves more linked to Christ and to the apostles than they are to senators Agnelli and Benni,[2] the same does not hold for Gentile and Croce, for example: Croce in particular feels himself closely linked to Aristotle and Plato, but he does not conceal, on the other hand, his links with senators Agnelli and Benni, and it is precisely here that one can discern the most significant character of Croce's philosophy.

What are the "maximum" limits of acceptance of the term "intellectual"? Can one find a unitary criterion to characterize equally all the diverse and disparate activities of intellectuals and to distinguish these at the same time and in an essential way from the activities of other social groupings? The most widespread error of method seems to me that of having looked for this criterion of distinction in the intrinsic nature of intellectual activities, rather than in the ensemble of the system of relations in which these activities (and therefore the intellectual groups who personify them) have their place within the general complex of social relations. Indeed the worker or proletarian, for example, is not specifically characterized by his manual or instrumental work, but by performing this work in specific conditions and in specific social relations (apart from the consideration that purely physical labor does not exist and that even Taylor's phrase of "trained gorilla" is a metaphor to indicate a limit in a certain direction: in any physical work, even the

10

most degraded and mechanical, there exists a minimum of technical qualification, that is, a minimum of creative intellectual activity). And we have already observed that the entrepreneur, by virtue of his very function, must have to some degree a certain number of qualifications of an intellectual nature although his part in society is determined not by these, but by the general social relations which specifically characterize the position of the entrepreneur within industry.

All men are intellectuals, one could therefore say: but not all men have in society the function of intellectuals.[3]

When one distinguishes between intellectuals and nonintellectuals, one is referring in reality only to the immediate social function of the professional category of the intellectuals, that is, one has in mind the direction in which their specific professional activity is weighted, whether toward intellectual elaboration or toward muscular-nervous effort. This means that, although one can speak of intellectuals, one cannot speak of nonintellectuals, because nonintellectuals do not exist. But even the relationship between efforts of intellectual-cerebral elaboration and muscular-nervous effort is not always the same, so that there are varying degrees of specific intellectual activity. There is no human activity from which every form of intellectual participation can be excluded: *Homo faber* cannot be separated from *Homo sapiens*. Each man, finally, outside his professional activity, carries on some form of intellectual activity, that is, he is a "philosopher," an artist, a man of taste, he participates in a particular conception of the world, has a conscious line of moral conduct, and therefore contributes to sustain a conception of the world or to modify it, that is, to bring into being new modes of thought.

The problem of creating a new stratum of intellectuals consists therefore in the critical elaboration of the intellectual activity that exists in everyone at a certain degree of development, modifying its relationship with the muscular-nervous effort toward a new equilibrium, and ensuring that the muscular-nervous effort itself, in so far as it is an element of a general practical activity, which is perpetually innovating the physical and social world, becomes the foundation of a new and integral conception of the world. The traditional and vulgarized type of the intellectual is given by the man of letters, the philosopher, the artist. Therefore journalists, who claim to be men of letters, philosophers, artists, also regard themselves as the "true" intellectuals. In the modern world, technical education, closely bound to industrial labor even at the most primitive and unqualified level, must form the basis of the new type of intellectual.

On this basis the weekly *Ordine Nuovo* worked to develop certain forms of new intellectualism and to determine its new concepts, and this was not the least of the reasons for its success, since such a conception corresponded to latent aspirations and conformed to the development of the real forms of life. The mode of being of the new intellectual can no longer consist in eloquence, which is an exterior and momentary mover of feelings and passions, but in active participation in practical life, as constructor, organizer, "permanent persuader" and not just a simple orator (but superior at the same time to the abstract mathematical spirit); from technique-as-work one proceeds to technique-as-science and to the humanistic conception of history, without which one remains "specialized" and does not become "directive" (specialized and political).

Thus there are historically formed specialized categories for the exercise of the intellectual function. They are formed in connection with all social groups, but especially in connection with the more important, and they undergo more extensive and complex elaboration in connection with the dominant social group. One of the most important characteristics of any group that is developing toward dominance is its struggle to assimilate and to conquer "ideologically" the traditional intellectuals, but this assimilation and conquest is made quicker and more efficacious the more the group in question succeeds in simultaneously elaborating its own organic intellectuals.

The enormous development of activity and organization of education in the broad sense in the societies that emerged from the medieval world is an index of the importance assumed in the modern world by intellectual functions and categories. Parallel with the attempt to deepen and to broaden the "intellectuality" of each individual, there has also been an attempt to multiply and narrow the various specializations. This can be seen from educational institutions at all levels, up to and including the organisms that exist to promote so-called high culture in all fields of science and technology.

School is the instrument through which intellectuals of various levels are elaborated. The complexity of the intellectual function in different states can be measured objectively by the number and gradation of specialized schools: the more extensive the "area" covered by education and the more numerous the "vertical" "levels" of schooling, the more complex is the cultural world, the civilization, of a particular state. A point of comparison can be found in the sphere of industrial technology: the industrialization of a country can be measured by how well equipped it is in the production of machines with which to produce machines, and in the manufacture of ever more accurate instruments for making both machines and further instruments for making machines, etc. The country which is best equipped in the construction of instruments for experimental scientific laboratories and in the construction of instruments with which to test the first instruments, can be regarded as the most complex in the technical-industrial field, with the highest level of civilization, etc. The same applies to the preparation of intellectuals and to the schools dedicated to this preparation; schools and institutes of high culture can be assimilated to each other. In this field also, quantity cannot be separated from quality. To the most refined technical-cultural specialization there cannot but correspond the maximum possible diffusion of primary education and the maximum care taken to expand the middle grades numerically as much as possible. Naturally this need to provide the widest base

15

possible for the selection and elaboration of the top intellectual qualifications—i.e., to give a democratic structure to high culture and top-level technology—is not without its disadvantages: it creates the possibility of vast crises of unemployment for the middle intellectual strata, and in all modern societies this actually takes place.

It is worth noting that the elaboration of intellectual strata in concrete reality does not take place on the terrain of abstract democracy but in accordance with very concrete traditional historical processes. Strata have grown up which traditionally "produce" intellectuals and these strata coincide with those which have specialized in "saving," i.e., the petty and middle landed bourgeoisie and certain strata of the petty and middle urban bourgeoisie. The varying distribution of different types of school (classical and professional) over the "economic" territory and the varying aspirations of different categories within these strata determine, or give form to, the production of various branches of intellectual specialization.

Reading

1. How does Gramsci define *intellectual*?

2. How does Gramsci believe intellectuals are created?

3. How does he define the responsibilities of the organic intellectual? The traditional intellectual?

4. How does he define the responsibility of working-class organic intellectuals?

Inquiring

1. Rather than just looking to colleges or universities, Gramsci wants his readers to consider how economic systems produce the need for particular types of intellectuals, individuals who can explain why a particular economy is necessary as well as make sure that economy runs smoothly. Assume that Gramsci is correct. How does his viewpoint challenge more typical visions of intellectuals and academic work? How does it recast typical visions of the purpose of a university? Then, having done this work, step back and consider whether you actually find his argument persuasive.

2. Gramsci argues there are two types of intellectuals—organic and traditional. Why do you think he might have chosen these terms? What type of intellectual work does each of these terms describe? What do you think he was trying to indicate about the relationship of each type of intellectual to the larger public? At this point in your life, do you see yourself as a traditional intellectual or an organic intellectual? Why?

3. Gramsci writes: "All men are intellectuals, one could therefore say: but not all men have in society the function of intellectuals" (para. 11). What does he mean by this statement? How does this statement challenge the idea of who

is considered an intellectual in a society? Develop a list of individuals who you think prove this statement to be true, and then discuss the value (or lack of value) for using Gramsci's viewpoint to understand the term *intellectuals*.

Composing

1. One way to imagine this current moment in your life is to see it perched on a threshold—as poised between lessons you have already learned from your home community and lessons you will learn in college. Gramsci might frame this moment as a deciding point between becoming an organic intellectual or a traditional intellectual. In a short essay, describe how each of these terms provides a particular type of road map for how people should lead their lives. Then imagine how each of these terms might shape your own life after college. Conclude your essay with a discussion of whether "organic" or "traditional" intellectual goals (or some possible combination) best reflect what you hope to accomplish in the future.

2. In paragraph 3, Gramsci describes how every social group creates its own "strata of intellectuals." Look at this passage closely. Write an essay that attempts to explain the claims Gramsci makes about the process by which intellectuals are created. To do so, you might start by defining key terms, examining how he develops these terms in light of his larger argument, and considering the context out of which he was writing. (Do a little research online if you would like more background information.) Then, having done this work, reflect on modern economic forces, such as social media. Consider how Facebook and Apple have created new ways for individuals to interact and, in doing so, have created very profitable companies. How might Gramsci study these forces to understand how they are also creating particular types of intellectuals with particular types of social and political functions?

3. Gramsci argues for there being "organic intellectuals." He does not, however, provide many examples of such individuals. Write a short essay that discusses someone from your home community who might fit this definition. How does this individual give your community an "awareness of its own function not only in the economic but also in the social and political fields" (para. 3)? What makes this person an organic intellectual in your community? What work does this person do as an intellectual? Why (or why not) might your home community also consider this person an organic intellectual? Finally, what might you have learned from this individual that will be useful for you in college? Possibly even in this class?

Connecting

Gramsci claims that education is an element in keeping the economy going, a claim that conflicts with the claim set forth in the *Wingspread Declaration* (p. 93) that students and universities should never be seen strictly in economic terms. Write an essay in which you discuss the basis for each argument and detail your position on this seeming conflict.

DAVID BARTHOLOMAE

Inventing the University

Courtesy David Bartholomae,
photo: Jing Yun

David Bartholomae is a professor of English at the University of Pittsburgh. His work emerges out of a concern for how working-class students can succeed in the university. In particular, Bartholomae argues that from the moment students enter college, they need to be placed in the position of academics when being asked to write essays; students must write as historians, biologists, and literature scholars if they are to fully understand the rules of the community in which they are trying to succeed. He is not, however, arguing that students should leave behind their home community's values and ways of understanding the world. Rather, he challenges students to undertake this difficult balancing act of "inventing a university" in which they blend the work of the historian with the historical insights of their community.

In the following excerpt from his book *Writing on the Margins* (2005), Bartholomae describes what he understands as the work of the university, the work of the student, and the difficult balance that must be struck if both are to succeed in their unique missions.

■ ■ ■

> Education may well be, as of right, the instrument whereby every individual, in a society like our own, can gain access to any kind of discourse. But we well know that in its distribution, in what it permits and in what it prevents, it follows the well-trodden battle-lines of social conflict. Every educational system is a political means of maintaining or of modifying the appropriation of discourse, with the knowledge and the powers it carries with it.
>
> —Foucault, *The Discourse on Language*

. . . the text is the form of the social relationships made visible, palpable, material.

—Bernstein, *Codes, Modalities and the Process of Cultural Reproduction: A Model*

E very time a student sits down to write for us, he has to invent the university for the occasion—invent the university, that is, or a branch of it, like history or anthropology or economics or English. The student has to learn to speak our language, to speak as we do, to try on the peculiar ways of knowing, selecting, evaluating, reporting, concluding, and arguing that define the discourse of our community. Or perhaps I should say the *various* discourses of our community, since it is in the nature of a liberal arts education that a student, after the first year or two, must learn to try on a variety of voices and interpretive schemes—to write, for example, as a literary critic one day and as an experimental psychologist the next; to work within fields where the rules governing the presentation of examples or the development of an argument are both distinct and, even to a professional, mysterious.

The student has to appropriate (or be appropriated by) a specialized discourse, and he has to do this as though he were easily and comfortably one with his audience, as though he were a member of the academy or an historian or an anthropologist or an economist; he has to invent the university by assembling and mimicking its language while finding some compromise between idiosyncracy, a personal history, on the one hand, and the requirements of convention, the history of a discipline, on the other. He must learn to speak our language. Or he must dare to speak it or to carry off the bluff, since speaking and writing will most certainly be required long before the skill is "learned." And this, understandably, causes problems.

Let me look quickly at an example. Here is an essay written by a college freshman.

> In the past time I thought that an incident was creative was when I had to make a clay model of the earth, but not of the classical or your everyday model of the earth which consists of the two cores, the mantle and the crust. I thought of these things in a dimension of which it would be unique, but easy to comprehend. Of course, your materials to work with were basic and limited at the same time, but thought help to put this limit into a right attitude or frame of mind to work with the clay.
>
> In the beginning of the clay model, I had to research and learn the different dimensions of the earth (in magnitude, quantity, state of matter, etc.). After this, I learned how to put this into the clay and come up with something different than any other person in my class at the time. In my opinion, color coordination

and shape was the key to my creativity of the clay model of
the earth.

Creativity is the venture of the mind at work with the mechanics
relay to the limbs from the cranium, which stores and triggers this
action. It can be a burst of energy released at a precise time a thought
is being transmitted. This can cause a frenzy of the human body, but
it depends on the characteristics of the individual and how they can
relay the message clearly enough through mechanics of the body
to us as an observer. Then we must determine if it is creative or a
learned process varied by the individuals thought process. Creativity
is indeed a tool which has to exist, or our world will not succeed into
the future and progress like it should.

I am continually impressed by the patience and goodwill of our students.
This student was writing a placement essay during freshman orientation. (The
problem set to him was: "Describe a time when you did something you felt to be
creative. Then, on the basis of the incident you have described, go on to draw
some general conclusions about 'creativity.'") He knew that university faculty
would be reading and evaluating his essay, and so he wrote for them.

5   In some ways it is a remarkable performance. He is trying on the discourse
even though he doesn't have the knowledge that would make the discourse more
than a routine, a set of conventional rituals and gestures. And he is doing this,
I think, even though he *knows* he doesn't have the knowledge that would make
the discourse more than a routine. He defines himself as a researcher working
systematically, and not as a kid in a high school class: "I thought of these things
in a dimension of . . ."; "I had to research and learn the different dimensions of
the earth (in magnitude, quantity, state of matter, etc.)." He moves quickly into a
specialized language (his approximation of our jargon) and draws both a general,
textbook-like conclusion — "Creativity is the venture of the mind at work . . ." —
and a resounding peroration — "Creativity is indeed a tool which has to exist, or
our world will not succeed into the future and progress like it should." The writer
has even picked up the rhythm of our prose with that last "indeed" and with the
qualifications and the parenthetical expressions of the opening paragraphs. And
through it all he speaks with an impressive air of authority.

There is an elaborate but, I will argue, a necessary and enabling fiction at
work here as the student dramatizes his experience in a "setting" — the setting
required by the discourse — where he can speak to us as a companion, a fellow
researcher. As I read the essay, there is only one moment when the fiction is
broken, when we are addressed differently. The student says, "Of course, your
materials to work with were basic and limited at the same time, but thought help
to put this limit into a right attitude or frame of mind to work with the clay."
At this point, I think, we become students and he the teacher giving us a lesson

(as in, "You take your pencil in your right hand and put your paper in front of you"). This is, however, one of the most characteristic slips of basic writers. (I use the term "basic writers" to refer to university students traditionally placed in remedial composition courses.) It is very hard for them to take on the role—the voice, the persona—of an authority whose authority is rooted in scholarship, analysis, or research. They slip, then, into a more immediately available and realizable voice of authority, the voice of a teacher giving a lesson or the voice of a parent lecturing at the dinner table. They offer advice or homilies rather than "academic" conclusions. There is a similar break in the final paragraph, where the conclusion that pushes for a definition ("Creativity is the venture of the mind at work with the mechanics relay to the limbs from the cranium") is replaced by a conclusion that speaks in the voice of an elder ("Creativity is indeed a tool which has to exist, or our world will not succeed into the future and progress like it should").

It is not uncommon, then, to find such breaks in the concluding sections of essays written by basic writers. Here is the concluding section of an essay written by a student about his work as a mechanic. He had been asked to generalize about work after reviewing an on-the-job experience or incident that "stuck in his mind" as somehow significant.

> How could two repairmen miss a leak? Lack of pride? No incen-
> tive? Lazy? I don't know.

At this point the writer is in a perfect position to speculate, to move from the problem to an analysis of the problem. Here is how the paragraph continues, however (and notice the change in pronoun reference).

> From this point on, I take *my* time, do it right, and don't let cus-
> tomers get under *your* skin. If they have a complaint, tell them
> to call your boss and he'll be more than glad to handle it. Most
> important, worry about yourself, and keep a clear eye on every-
> one, for there's always someone trying to take advantage of you,
> anytime and anyplace. (Emphasis added)

We get neither a technical discussion nor an "academic" discussion but a Lesson on Life. This is the language he uses to address the general question, "How could two repairmen miss a leak?" The other brand of conclusion, the more academic one, would have required him to speak of his experience in our terms; it would, that is, have required a special vocabulary, a special system of presentation, and an interpretive scheme (or a set of commonplaces) he could have used to identify and talk about the mystery of human error. The writer certainly had access to the range of acceptable commonplaces for such an explanation: "lack of pride," "no incentive," "lazy." Each commonplace would dictate its own set of phrases, examples, and conclusions; and we, his teachers, would know how to write out each argument, just as we know how to write out more specialized arguments of our own. A "commonplace," then, is a culturally or institutionally authorized concept or statement that carries with it its own necessary elaboration. We all use commonplaces to orient ourselves in the world; they provide points of reference and a set of "prearticulated" explanations that are readily available to organize and interpret experience. The phrase "lack of pride" carries with it its own account of the repairman's error, just as at another point in time a reference to "original sin" would have provided an explanation, or just as in certain university classrooms a reference to "alienation" would enable writers to continue and complete the discussion. While there is a way in which these terms are interchangeable, they are not all permissible: A student in a composition class would most likely be turned away from a discussion of original sin. Commonplaces are the "controlling ideas" of our composition textbooks, textbooks that not only insist on a set form for expository writing but a set view of public life.

When the writer says, "I don't know," then, he is not saying that he has nothing to say. He is saying that he is not in a position to carry on this discussion. And so we are addressed as apprentices rather than as teachers or scholars. In order to speak as a person of status or privilege, the writer can either speak to us in our terms—in the privileged language of university discourse—or, in default (or in defiance) of that, he can speak to us as though we were children, offering us the wisdom of experience.

I think it is possible to say that the language of the "Clay Model" paper has come *through* the writer and not from the writer. The writer has located himself (more precisely, he has located the self that is represented by the "I" on the page) in a context that is finally beyond him, not his own and not available to his immediate procedures for inventing and arranging text. I would not, that is, call this essay an example of "writer-based" prose. I would not say that it is egocentric or that it represents the "interior monologue or a writer thinking and talking to himself."[1] It is, rather, the record of a writer who has lost himself in the discourse of his readers. There is a context beyond the intended reader that is not the world but a way of talking about the world, a way of talking that determines the use of examples, the possible conclusions, acceptable commonplaces, and key words for an essay on the construction of a clay model of the earth. This writer has entered the discourse without successfully approximating it.

10   Linda Flower has argued that the difficulty inexperienced writers have with writing can be understood as a difficulty in negotiating the transition between "writer-based" and "reader-based" prose. Expert writers, in other words, can better imagine how a reader will respond to a text and can transform or restructure what they have to say around a goal shared with a reader. Teaching students to revise for readers, then, will better prepare them to write initially with a reader in mind. The success of this pedagogy depends on the degree to which a writer can imagine and conform to a reader's goals. The difficulty of this act of imagination and the burden of such conformity are so much at the heart of the problem that

a teacher must pause and take stock before offering revision as a solution. A student like the one who wrote the "Clay Model" paper is not so much trapped in a private language as he is shut out from one of the privileged languages of public life, a language he is aware of but cannot control. . . .

Linda Flower and John Hayes, in an often quoted article,[2] reported on a study of a protocol of an expert writer (an English teacher) writing about his job for readers of *Seventeen* magazine. The key moment for this writer, who seems to have been having trouble getting started, came when he decided that teenage girls read *Seventeen;* that some teenage girls like English because it is tidy ("some of them will have wrong reasons in that English is good because it's tidy—can be a neat tidy little girl"); that some don't like it because it is "prim" and that, "By God, I can change that notion for them." Flower and Hayes's conclusion is that this effort of "exploration and consolidation" gave the writer "a new, relatively complex, rhetorically sophisticated working goal, one which encompasses plans for a topic, a persona, and the audience."[3]

Flower and Hayes give us a picture of a writer solving a problem, and the problem as they present it is a cognitive one. It is rooted in the way the writer's knowledge is represented in the writer's mind. The problem resides there, not in the nature of knowledge or in the nature of discourse but in a mental state prior to writing. It is possible, however, to see the problem as (perhaps simultaneously) a problem in the way subjects are located in a field of discourse.

Flower and Hayes divide up the composing process into three distinct activities: "planning or goal-setting," "translating," and "reviewing." The last of these, reviewing (which is further divided into two subprocesses, "evaluating" and "revising"), is particularly powerful, for as a writer continually reviews his goals, plans, and the text he is producing, and as he continually generates new goals, plans, and text, he is engaging in a process of learning and discovery. Let me quote Flower and Hayes's conclusion at length.

> If one studies the process by which a writer uses a goal to generate ideas, then consolidates those ideas and uses them to revise or regenerate new, more complex goals, one can see this learning process in action. Furthermore, one sees why the process of revising and clarifying goals has such a broad effect, since it is through setting these new goals that the fruits of discovery come back to inform the continuing process of writing. In this instance, some of our most complex and imaginative acts can depend on the elegant simplicity of a few powerful thinking processes. We feel that a cognitive process explanation of discovery, toward which this theory is only a start, will have another special strength. By placing emphasis on the inventive power of the writer, who is able to explore ideas, to develop, act on, test, and regenerate his or her own goals, we are

putting an important part of creativity where it belongs—in the
hands of the working, thinking writer. (p. 386)

While this conclusion is inspiring, the references to invention and creativity
seem to refer to something other than an act of writing—if writing is, finally,
words on a page. Flower and Hayes locate the act of writing solely within the
mind of the writer. The act of writing, here, has a personal, cognitive history
but not a history as a text, as a text that is made possible by prior texts. When
located in the perspective afforded by prior texts, writing is seen to exist separate
from the writer and his intentions; it is seen in the context of other articles in
Seventeen, of all articles written for or about women, of all articles written about
English teaching, and so on. Reading research has made it possible to say that
these prior texts, or a reader's experience with these prior texts, have bearing
on how the text is read. Intentions, then, are part of the history of the language
itself. I am arguing that these prior texts determine not only how a text like the
Seventeen article will be read but also how it will be written. Flower and Hayes
show us what happens in the writer's mind but not what happens to the writer
as his motives are located within our language, a language with its own requirements and agendas, a language that limits what we might say and that makes us
write and sound, finally, also like someone else. . . .

15   It is one thing to see the *Seventeen* writer making and revising his plans for
a topic, a persona, and an audience; it is another thing to talk about discovery,
invention, and creativity. Whatever plans the writer had must finally have been
located in language and, it is possible to argue, in a language that is persistently
conventional and formulaic. We do not, after all, get to see the *Seventeen* article.
We see only the elaborate mental procedures that accompanied the writing of the
essay. We see a writer's plans for a persona; we don't see that persona in action.
If writing is a process, it is also a product; and it is the product, and not the plan
for writing, that locates a writer on the page, that locates him in a text and a style
and the codes or conventions that make both of them readable. . .

It is possible to see the writer of the *Seventeen* article solving his problem of
where to begin by appropriating an available discourse. Perhaps what enabled
that writer to write was the moment he located himself as a writer in a familiar
field of stereotypes: Readers of *Seventeen* are teenage girls; teenage girls think of
English (and English teachers) as "tidy" and "prim," and, "By God, I can change
that notion for them." The moment of eureka was not simply a moment of breaking through a cognitive jumble in that individual writer's mind but a moment of
breaking into a familiar and established territory—one with insiders and outsiders; one with set phrases, examples, and conclusions.

I'm not offering a criticism of the morals or manners of the teacher who wrote
the *Seventeen* article. I think that all writers, in order to write, must imagine for
themselves the privilege of being "insiders"—that is, the privilege both of being

inside an established and powerful discourse and of being granted a special right to speak. But I think that right to speak is seldom conferred on us—on any of us, teachers or students—by virtue of the fact that we have invented or discovered an original idea. Leading students to believe that they are responsible for something new or original, unless they understand what those words mean with regard to writing, is a dangerous and counterproductive practice. We do have the right to expect students to be active and engaged, but that is a matter of continually and stylistically working against the inevitable presence of conventional language; it is not a matter of inventing a language that is new.

When a student is writing for a teacher, writing becomes more problematic than it was for the *Seventeen* writer (who was writing a version of the "Describe baseball to an Eskimo" exercise). The student, in effect, has to assume privilege without having any. And since students assume privilege by locating themselves within the discourse of a particular community—within a set of specifically acceptable gestures and commonplaces—learning, at least as it is defined in the liberal arts curriculum, becomes more a matter of imitation or parody than a matter of invention and discovery. . . .

Let me draw on an example from my own teaching. I don't expect my students to *be* literary critics when they write about *Bleak House*. If a literary critic is a person who wins publication in a professional journal (or if he or she is one who could), the students aren't critics. I do, however, expect my students to be, themselves, invented as literary critics by approximating the language of a literary critic writing about *Bleak House*. My students, then, don't invent the language of literary criticism (they don't, that is, act on their own) but they are, themselves, invented by it. Their papers don't begin with a moment of insight, a "by God" moment that is outside of language. They begin with a moment of appropriation, a moment when they can offer up a sentence that is not theirs as though it were their own. (I can remember when, as a graduate student, I would begin papers by sitting down to write literally in the voice—with the syntax and the key words—of the strongest teacher I had met.)

What I am saying about my students' essays is that they are approximate, not that they are wrong or invalid. They are evidence of a discourse that lies between what I might call the students' primary discourse (what the students might write about *Bleak House* were they not in my class or in any class, and were they not imagining that they were in my class or in any class—if you can imagine any student doing any such thing) and standard, official literary criticism (which is imaginable but impossible to find). The students' essays are evidence of a discourse that lies between these two hypothetical poles. The writing is limited as much by a student's ability to imagine "what might be said" as it is by cognitive control strategies. The act of writing takes the student away from where he is and what he knows and allows him to imagine something else. The approximate discourse, therefore, is evidence of a change, a change

20

that, because we are teachers, we call "development." What our beginning students need to learn is to extend themselves, by successive approximations, into the commonplaces, set phrases, rituals and gestures, habits of mind, tricks of persuasion, obligatory conclusions and necessary connections that determine the "what might be said" and constitute knowledge within the various branches of our academic community. . . .

The purpose of the remainder of this [essay] will be to examine some of the most striking and characteristic of these problems as they are presented in the expository essays of first-year college students. I will be concerned, then, with university discourse in its most generalized form—as it is represented by introductory courses—and not with the special conventions required by advanced work in the various disciplines. And I will be concerned with the difficult, and often violent, accommodations that occur when students locate themselves in a discourse that is not "naturally" or immediately theirs.

I have reviewed 500 essays written, as the "Clay Model" essay was, in response to a question used during one of our placement exams at the University of Pittsburgh: "Describe a time when you did something you felt to be creative. Then, on the basis of the incident you have described, go on to draw some general conclusions about 'creativity.'" Some of the essays were written by basic writers (or, more properly, those essays led readers to identify the writers as basic writers); some were written by students who "passed" (who were granted immediate access to the community of writers at the university). As I read these essays, I was looking to determine the stylistic resources that enabled writers to locate themselves within an "academic" discourse. My bias as a reader should be clear by now. I was not looking to see how a writer might represent the skills demanded by a neutral language (a language whose key features were paragraphs, topic sentences, transitions, and the like—features of a clear and orderly mind). I was looking to see what happened when a writer entered into a language to locate himself (a textual self) and his subject; and I was looking to see how, once entered, that language made or unmade the writer. . . .

In general, as I reviewed the essays for this study, I found that the more successful writers set themselves in their essays against what they defined as some more naive way of talking about their subject—against "those who think that . . ."—or against earlier, more naive versions of themselves—"once I thought that. . . ." By trading in one set of commonplaces at the expense of another, they could win themselves status as members of what is taken to be some more privileged group. The ability to imagine privilege enabled writing. Here is one particularly successful essay. Notice the specialized vocabulary, but notice also the way in which the text continually refers to its own language and to the language of others.

> Throughout my life, I have been interested and intrigued by music.
> My mother has often told me of the times, before I went to school,
> when I would "conduct" the orchestra on her records. I continued

to listen to music and eventually started to play the guitar and the clarinet. Finally, at about the age of twelve, I started to sit down and to try to write songs. Even though my instrumental skills were far from my own high standards, I would spend much of my spare time during the day with a guitar around my neck, trying to produce a piece of music.

Each of these sessions, as I remember them, had a rather set format. I would sit in my bedroom, strumming different combinations of the five or six chords I could play, until I heard a series of which sounded particularly good to me. After this, I set the music to a suitable rhythm (usually dependent on my mood at the time), and ran through the tune until I could play it fairly easily. Only after this section was complete did I go on to writing lyrics, which generally followed along the lines of the current popular songs on the radio.

At the time of the writing, I felt that my songs were, in themselves, an original creation of my own; that is, I, alone, made them. However, I now see that, in this sense of the word, I was not creative. The songs themselves seem to be an oversimplified form of the music I listened to at the time.

In a more fitting sense, however, I *was* being creative. Since I did not purposely copy my favorite songs, I was, effectively, originating my songs from my own "process of creativity." To achieve my goal, I needed what a composer would call "inspiration" for my piece. In this case the inspiration was the current hit on the radio. Perhaps, with my present point of view, I feel that I used too much "inspiration" in my songs, but, at that time, I did not.

Creativity, therefore, is a process which, in my case, involved a certain series of "small creations" if you like. As well, it is something, the appreciation of which varies with one's point of view, that point of view being set by the person's experience, tastes, and his own personal view of creativity. The less experienced tend to allow for less originality, while the more experienced demand real originality to classify something a "creation." Either way, a term as abstract as this is perfectly correct, and open to interpretation.

This writer is consistently and dramatically conscious of herself forming something to say out of what has been said *and* out of what she has been saying in the act of writing this paper. "Creativity" begins in this paper as "original creation." What she thought was "creativity," however, she now says was imitation; and, as she says, "in this sense of the word" she was not "creative." In another sense, however, she says that she *was* creative, since she didn't purposefully copy the songs but used them as "inspiration."

While the elaborate stylistic display—the pauses, qualifications, and the use of quotation marks—is in part a performance for our benefit, at a more obvious level we as readers are directly addressed in the first sentence of the last paragraph: "Creativity, therefore, is a process which, in my case, involved a certain series of 'small creations' if you like." We are addressed here as adults who can share her perspective on what she has said and who can be expected to understand her terms. If she gets into trouble after this sentence, and I think she does, it is because she doesn't have the courage to generalize from her assertion. Since she has rhetorically separated herself from her younger "self," and since she argues that she has gotten smarter, she assumes that there is some developmental sequence at work here and that, in the world of adults (which must be more complete than the world of children) there must be something like "real creativity." If her world is imperfect (if she can only talk about creation by putting the word in quotation marks), it must be because she is young. When she looks beyond herself to us, she cannot see our work as an extension of her project. She cannot assume that we too will be concerned with the problem of creativity and originality. At least she is not willing to challenge us on those grounds, to generalize her argument, and to argue that even for adults creations are really only "small creations." The sense of privilege that has allowed her to expose her own language cannot be extended to expose ours.

25   The writing in this piece—that is, the work of the writer within the essay— goes on in spite of, or against, the language that keeps pressing to give another name to her experience as a songwriter and to bring the discussion to closure. . . . Its style is difficult, highly qualified. It relies on quotation marks and parody to set off the language and attitudes that belong to the discourse (or the discourses) that it would reject, that it would not take as its own proper location. . . .

These are educated and literate individuals, to be sure, but they are individuals still outside the peculiar boundaries of the academic community. In the papers I've examined in this chapter, the writers have shown an increasing awareness of the codes (or the competing codes) that operate within a discourse. To speak with authority they have to speak not only in another's voice but through another's code; and they not only have to do this, they have to speak in the voice and through the codes of those of us with power and wisdom; and they not only have to do this, they have to do it before they know what they are doing, before they have a project to participate in, and before, at least in terms of our disciplines, they have anything to say. Our students may be able to enter into a conventional discourse and speak, not as themselves, but through the voice of the community; the university, however, is the place where "common" wisdom is only of negative values—it is something to work against. The movement toward a more specialized discourse begins (or, perhaps, best begins) both when a student can define a position of privilege, a position that sets him against a "common" discourse, and when he or she can work self-consciously, critically, against not only the "common" code but his or her own.[3]

It may very well be that some students will need to learn to crudely mimic the "distinctive register" of academic discourse before they are prepared to actually and legitimately do the work of the discourse, and before they are sophisticated enough with the refinements of tone and gesture to do it with grace or elegance. To say this, however, is to say that our students must be our students. Their initial progress will be marked by their abilities to take on the role of privilege, by their abilities to establish authority. From this point of view, the student who wrote about constructing the clay model of the earth is better prepared for his education than the student who wrote about playing football in white shoes,[4] even though the "White Shoes" paper is relatively error-free and the "Clay Model" paper is not. It will be hard to pry loose the writer of the "White Shoes" paper from the tidy, pat discourse that allows him to dispose of the question of creativity in such a quick and efficient manner. He will have to be convinced that it is better to write sentences he might not so easily control, and he will have to be convinced that it is better to write muddier and more confusing prose (in order that it may sound like ours), and this will be harder than convincing the "Clay Model" writer to continue what he has already begun.

Reading

1. How does Bartholomae define his audience for this essay?

2. How should students define the audience for their writing?

3. How does Bartholomae understand the term *writer-based prose* (para. 9)?

4. How does he understand the term *reader-based prose* (para. 10)?

Inquiring

1. Bartholomae begins by stating that students "invent" the university every time they sit down to write an essay. This act of invention seems to apply to Bartholomae's essay as well. How would you describe his "invention" of the university in this essay? What type of work does he see the university as performing? What are its goals? As someone who has been thinking about what it means to study at a university, do you find his definition compelling? Why or why not? How might you want to revise his understanding based on your own goals?

2. One way to talk about writing in the academy is to focus on the specific requirements of individual disciplines, such as anthropology, business, theater, and so on. Bartholomae, however, attempts to define the common characteristics that are part of *all* academic writing. He points to the essay about music and creativity (para. 23) as a good example. What does he see in the paper that makes it academic? What does he value in the voice created by this author? What does

he think could be improved? As you think about your other college classes, do you believe this type of authorial voice would be acceptable? Why or why not?

3. Bartholomae makes the claim that student writers are "made or unmade" by language (para. 22). In other words, writers who know how to use language have distinctive writing, whereas writers whose style is general and indistinctive tends to feel divorced from any particular writer's actual beliefs. Reread the passage where Bartholomae makes this point (paras. 22–23). Then, using one of your papers written for this class, work with several of your classmates to see whether your papers could be seen as "made" by language rather than by you. How might you revise those sections? Based on this experience, what do you see as the difference between your being "made by language" and actually writing an essay?

Composing

1. Bartholomae writes that students should not be expected to produce a new or original argument without first understanding "what those words mean with regard to writing, [expecting this from students] is a dangerous and counterproductive practice" (para. 17). Write an essay in which you discuss how Bartholomae reaches that conclusion. What implications does this conclusion have for how you approach your work as a writer? Do you believe his conclusion makes it easier or harder for you to write in college? Why?

2. In the middle of his argument, Bartholomae steps away from discussing specific student papers to reflect on the work of Linda Flower. He does so to strengthen his point about the difficulties students face when beginning to write in the academy. These difficulties, it seems to Bartholomae, are more than developing a "writerly" voice, as Flower argues. Write an essay in which you frame the difference between Bartholomae's and Flower's understandings of what student writers need to learn to succeed at college. Be sure to account for the different research data they use to support their claims. Then, having done this work, use your own experience as a student writer to assess whether Bartholomae or Flower better expresses the difficulties of learning to write in the university.

3. In discussing the development of the student writer, Bartholomae makes it clear that students' writing is never invalid, only that it is indicative of "a discourse that lies between what I might call the student's primary discourse . . . and standard, official literary criticism. . . . The approximate discourse, therefore, is evidence of a change, a change that, because we are teachers, we call 'development' " (para. 20). Note that Bartholomae puts "development" in quotation marks. Write an essay in which you discuss how you understand Bartholomae's use of quotation marks in this passage. What was he trying to indicate about the value of a student's "primary discourse"? What does

Bartholomae see as the ultimate role of a student's primary discourse in writing within an academic community?

Connecting

Bartholomae argues that when students sit down to write, they are inventing the university. Andrew Delbanco, however, demonstrates some of the historical forces that have shaped the university's development (p. 70). Write an essay in which you discuss how this history shapes a student's ability (both positively and negatively) to invent the university in his or her writing.

ANDREW DELBANCO

Who Went? Who Goes? Who Pays?

Kristin Murphy/Getty Images

Andrew Delbanco is a professor of American studies at Columbia University. Although the original framework for his research was American literature, his recent work has concerned the American university. Delbanco argues that the economic forces confronting the university and the larger society have lessened the ability of students to use college as a means to test ideas and grow as individuals; in other words, utility has replaced inquiry. Along with this cultural shift, he argues, has been an equal diminishment in the commitment to supporting diverse student populations (in terms of race, ethnicity, and class) at the vast majority of universities—excepting only elite and community colleges from this charge. In response, Delbanco attempts to argue for a new type of university, one that upholds its historic commitments but recognizes the new economic context in which such commitments exist.

In the following excerpt from his book *College: What It Was, Is, and Should Be* (2012), Delbanco discusses the economic forces that are affecting the modern university and its students while offering a vision of education that is about both inquiry and utility.

■ ■ ■

The modern university was an entirely new entity—in part an educational institution focused on graduate and professional training, but in larger part a research enterprise driven by science. Where, in this house of many mansions, was the college? Did it—does it—still exist as a place of guided self-discovery for young people in search of themselves?

One way of coming at this question was suggested around a century ago by Max Weber, who, not long before Sinclair Lewis invented "Winnemac," proposed a distinction between two "polar opposites of types of education." The types he had in mind correspond closely to the terms "college" and "university" as I have been using them. The first, associated with religion, is "to aid the novice to acquire a 'new soul' . . . and hence, to be reborn." The second, associated with the bureaucratic structures of modern life, is to impart the kind of "specialized expert training" required for "administrative purposes—in the organization of public authorities, business offices, workshops, scientific or industrial laboratories," as well as "disciplined armies."[1] Many other serviceable terms could be substituted for Weber's—knowledge versus skill; inspiration versus discipline; insight versus information; learning for its own sake versus learning for the sake of utility—but whatever terms we prefer, a good educational institution strives for both. "The two types do not stand opposed," as Weber put it, "with no connections or transitions between them." They coexist—or at least they should—in a dynamic relation.

Beginning with the rise of the research university and continuing ever since, American higher education has struggled to maintain this dialectic. For good or ill, the oldest and richest institutions have been looked to as models, so it mattered for more than Harvard when the president who succeeded Eliot, Abbott Lawrence Lowell, decided that the college was being overwhelmed by the centrifugal force of the university, and that something had to be done about it.

In the early 1920s, with the help of a $13 million gift (at least $150 million in today's dollars) from the Harkness family, Lowell oversaw the creation of undergraduate "houses," each with resident faculty, dining hall, common rooms, and library. Yale initially declined a gift from the same source for the same purpose, but soon reversed itself and built a comparable cluster of what, with more explicit deference to the Oxbridge originals, it called "colleges." More than a decade earlier, at Princeton, Woodrow Wilson, president from 1901 to 1910, had attempted something similar, but he failed in part because Princeton students had long organized themselves into "eating clubs" that provided, according to tradition-minded alumni, sufficient social coherence. In fact, by sorting students according to class and caste, the clubs reflected what one enterprising reporter for the *Harvard Crimson*, after a field trip to Princeton, called its "frank institutionalization of arbitrary and unreflective prejudices."[2] . . .

But opening up college to previously excluded groups has always been a process of ebb and flow, and academic leaders have been divided within, as well as among, themselves about how far or fast to go. When it came to admitting undergraduates, Nicholas Murray Butler, president of Columbia for virtually the whole first half of the twentieth century, favored a Jewish quota; but he also pressured the old boys of the English Department to grant tenure to a brilliant young Columbia College graduate, Lionel Trilling, whom they had written off as a Marxist, a Freudian, and, most damningly, a Jew.[3]

At Harvard, mindful of the "Jewish invasion" that ruined Columbia in the eyes of its blue-blood alumni, Lowell, too, clamped down on admitting Jewish students, suspecting they were long on brains but short on "character." He also favored excluding Harvard's few black students from its freshmen residence

5

halls, and, in his role as public figure, supported restrictive immigration laws. Yet Lowell's motive in creating the house system was to close the divide between wealthy and needy students. He was appalled to see rich boys segregating themselves in "gold coast" apartments while those with less money were relegated to rooming houses where they paid the rent by working a (usually) menial campus job. "Snobbish separation . . . on lines of wealth," he felt, threatened "to destroy the chief value of the College as a place for the training of character."[4] . . .

We tend to look back at this exclusionary history with a combination of incredulity and indignation, and to praise the present at the expense of the past. There are good grounds to do so. Admissions procedures originally devised as ways to screen out Jews—personal essays, letters of recommendation, interviews—are touted today as ways to identify qualities that may not be captured by grades or tests. Formerly excluded groups such as blacks or Hispanics, once virtually barred from many institutions, are now beneficiaries of "race-conscious" admissions policies. College, we say, used to be about preserving uniformity, but today it is about achieving diversity.

How we got from one to the other is a stirring story. It has many chapters, of which the democratizing of elite institutions is only one—and, as a matter of scale, a minor one. At the turn of the century, when Stover was prepping for Yale, fewer than a quarter-million Americans, or around 2 percent of the population between eighteen and twenty-four, attended college. By the end of World War II, that figure had risen to over two million. In 1975, it stood at nearly ten million, or one-third of young adults. Today, including those students whom we call "nontraditional," the number has almost doubled. . . .

The most important force in democratizing American higher education was the explosive postwar growth of what had once been known as junior colleges—two-year institutions whose origins were in the "normal schools" that had been founded in the nineteenth century and flourished early in the twentieth, and whose primary focus had been on training schoolteachers. For some students, these institutions served as conduits to a nearby or affiliated university where graduates of a two-year college could go on to earn the bachelor's degree. By the 1950s, the junior colleges were evolving into a national system of what are now known as community colleges, which today number more than twelve hundred, with an enrollment exceeding six million—roughly a third of all undergraduates in the United States. In California, under Kerr's master plan, community colleges were designed as entry points into a system of higher education that provided students with the opportunity, if they did well in their first two years, to advance to one of the four-year state colleges or even to a research university.

10   Meanwhile, private and selective public institutions made increasing use of standardized tests for the purpose of identifying talented students outside their usual "feeder" schools. Also in the 1950s, the Ivies established the principle of "need-based" financial aid. This was an effort to replace the scattershot philanthropy of the past, by which scholarships had been awarded on somebody's

hunch about who deserved what, with a rational system of discount pricing based on careful evaluation of what a family could afford. It was a push for distributive justice — or, some might say, a dose of socialism ("each according to his need") — in a world otherwise run according to the rules of the market. . . .

Progress in the public universities was even more remarkable, both in expanding opportunity for low-income and first-generation college students, and in supporting first-class teaching and research across all fields. Over the first half of the twentieth century, Brooklyn College and the City College of New York established themselves among the most intellectually vibrant institutions in the world. At midcentury, the University of California at Berkeley challenged and in some respects exceeded [Harvard, Yale, and Princeton] in both accessibility and quality, while the flagship branches of other state universities such as Ohio, Michigan, Wisconsin, Indiana, Illinois, and, more recently, Texas, North Carolina, Oregon, Washington, and Florida, rose into the ranks of the world's leading institutions. And in many cases, these huge institutions have sought to provide a true residential experience for undergraduate students. The America that Alexis de Tocqueville had described in the early nineteenth century as a nation where "primary education is within the reach of everyone" but "higher education is within the reach of virtually no one" seemed to be turning itself upside down.[5]

The foregoing story is usually told as a triumphant one. But there are a number of things wrong with it. For one thing, it fits too neatly the progressive narrative we like to tell about ourselves. Need-blind admissions, for instance, is an admirable ideal, but it can be little more than a feel-good slogan if a college concentrates its recruiting in places like Scarsdale or Riyadh, where it won't encounter candidates with much need. As one college president told me when I first tried to understand these policies, "If you really want to practice need-blind admissions, cover up the zip codes when the applications come in." Campus interviews may seem to be about, as the phrase goes, getting to know the whole person, but since they are often conducted by alumni volunteers or student interns with little input into the ultimate decision, they tend to be, as the Stanford sociologist Mitchell Stevens calls them in a book entitled *Creating a Class*, "heavily symbolic" — designed "as much to affirm the college's commitment to personalized evaluation as to learn more about applicants."[6]

Less likely to be resolved anytime soon are the pervasive problems that low-income students face not only in gaining admission to elite colleges but in getting to and through college at all. One leading authority, Donald Heller of Pennsylvania State University, asserts that "college-going rates of the highest-socioeconomic-status students with the lowest achievement levels are the same as the poorest students with the highest achievement levels."[7] This sobering statement doesn't tell us much about the advantages or obstacles (adequate or inadequate financial resources; stable or broken families; strong or weak schools) that help or hurt a student's chances of getting to college; and it is striking that children growing up in economically deprived circumstances who attend good high schools do much better than those in poor schools—although they still lag significantly behind their wealthier peers.[8] But however one slices the data, it is clear that the progressive story of expanding opportunity has slowed or stalled, and there is reason to doubt that the United States can truly be described today as a nation of equal opportunity where talent and effort trump poverty and prejudice.

One reason for the slowdown can be traced to the late 1970s, when California's Proposition 13 (1978) initiated a series of populist tax revolts that became chronic tax resistance, and eventually led, state by state, to "massive disinvestment" in higher education.[9] The University of Virginia, for example, founded by Thomas Jefferson for the public welfare, has recently been described as "a public university in name only" since it now receives a mere 8 percent of its funding from the state of Virginia, down from nearly 30 percent a quarter century ago.[10] At the University of Wisconsin, in a state with a long progressive tradition, only about 19 percent comes from public funds—also down from around 30 percent just a decade ago. To make up for the decline in public money, tuition rates at public universities have been climbing even faster than at private institutions—a trend likely to accelerate, while state universities are also recruiting increasing numbers of out-of-state students, who pay higher tuition than in-state residents. To make matters worse over the past couple of decades, financial aid to individual students administered by the states has been allocated more and more on the basis of so-called merit rather than need. (Between 1999 and 2009, merit aid grew by more than 150 percent, while need-based aid rose by less than 100 percent.)[11] This means that scholarships have been going increasingly to high-achieving students who come disproportionately from high-income families, leaving deserving students from low-income families without the means to pay for college.

15   The same shift of support from more needy to less needy students has been evident at the federal level. In 1976, the maximum federal Pell grant for a low-income student covered nearly 90 percent of the average cost of attending a four-year public institution, and almost 40 percent at a private university. By 2004, Pell grants covered under 25 percent of the cost at a public college, and less than 10 percent at a private institution. And while funding of grants for low-income students has failed to keep up with the rising cost of college, there has been robust growth in the amount of unsubsidized federal loans that go mainly to students from middle-income families.[12] Before the election of 2010, President Obama and the Democratic Congress were trying to reverse this trend by enhancing Pell grants and turning them into an entitlement whose value would keep pace with inflation. But with tax revenues falling and tuitions continuing to rise, and now with the government in a deficit-cutting mood, such initiatives seem likely to be rolled back—although at this writing (August 2011), the Pell grant program has been spared in the first deficit-reduction deal.

As for private institutions, at least since the rise of need-based aid in the middle years of the last century, the prevailing financial model has been a "Robin

Hood" system whereby relatively affluent students pay a larger share of college costs than needier students—something some parents find objectionable. "Why should I pay full freight when Johnny's roommate is getting a free ride?" is a question familiar to financial aid officers. It is usually asked in ignorance of the fact that even families paying full "sticker price" (now over $50,000 at the most expensive colleges) are meeting far less than the full cost of their child's education—calculated as a proportional fraction of faculty and staff salaries, dining, library, health, and athletic services, as well as overhead costs such as keeping the lights on, the heat flowing, and the buildings in good repair. In other words, all students, rich and poor, in America's private colleges—except at those run for profit—are subsidized to one extent or another. What this means for the college is that it must make up the difference between operating costs and tuition revenue with other sources of income such as endowment return, government grants, and private donations.

Since the crash of 2008, this has become much harder to do. Endowments, government support, and the amount of giving have all fallen or are rising more slowly, while pressure on financial aid budgets has sharply increased. This is not a pretty symmetry, and it puts financial aid offices under heavy strain to keep up with demand. Even those parents who have not lost their jobs have probably seen their retirement assets dwindle and the value of their homes drop, leaving them ineligible for home equity or other loans that were once among their options for financing their children's education. . . .

Ticking off such inequities is easy to do, and creates opportunities for righteously condemning individual and institutional behavior. Yet all these practices raise difficult ethical questions—of just the sort, in fact, that should be part of a college education. How many of us with the means to help would look our own son or daughter in the eye and say, "I will put you at a disadvantage by refusing to spend our family's money helping you prep for the test"? And while it's natural to feel resentment when other people's children enjoy advantages denied to our own, for centuries very few people objected to what amounted to affirmative action for whites. Most of the beneficiaries took their preferential standing for granted, while most of the excluded were remarkably gracious about their exclusion. Today, however, a lot of people object to affirmative action for minorities, which as Anthony Kronman puts it, entails "a contest of right against right—a conflict between the defensible claim of minority applicants to a form of special treatment and the equally defensible claim of non-minority applicants to be judged by their individual qualifications alone." Nor is affirmative action for alumni children (though it is rarely called by that name) a simple matter of right or wrong. Not many colleges can afford to alienate loyal alumni, on whose benefactions they depend for educating all students—including low-income students—by turning away their (qualified) children in larger numbers than they already do.[13]

The more one delves into the intricacies of selective college admissions, the more such questions force themselves into view. Is it legitimate to offer lower aid to students who seem likely to accept an offer of admission (alumni children, for example, or candidates who have proven their zeal by traveling a long way to campus for an interview), and thereby conserve the budget for students who might need to be "incentivized" to enroll? Should a wealthy institution offer grants instead of loans to all students whom it deems eligible for any amount of financial aid, so they won't be deterred by debt from pursuing relatively low-paying careers in, say, teaching or public service? Or, given the market value of its prestigious degree, should such an institution reserve grants for the more needy students and stick with loans for the less needy, who probably won't have much trouble paying back whatever they have borrowed? Is it a fair use of resources to provide extraordinary aid to families making as much as $200,000 per year (as Harvard and Yale announced they would do before the crash of 2008) in view of the ensuing pressure on less wealthy colleges to follow suit, thereby leaving themselves unable to offer adequate support to needier students? One former Harvard dean, Theda Skocpol, put this dilemma in the form of a stinging question: Why should America's leading universities make "the annual cost for families up to the 95th income percentile less than half the cost of purchasing a new luxury car"?[14] . . .

20   None of these questions—and there are many more—has an ethically simple answer. What's beyond dispute is that the practices they bring into view are heavily weighted in favor of students from families with means. Before the economic debacle of 2008, a national discussion seemed to be getting under way about ways to respond to this inequity, which was clearly growing. Between the mid-1970s and mid-1990s, in a sample of eleven prestigious colleges, the percentage of students from families in the bottom quartile of national family income remained roughly steady—around 10 percent. During the same period the percentage of students from the top quartile rose sharply, from a little more than one-third to fully half. And if the sample is broadened to include the top 150 colleges as designated by the *Chronicle of Higher Education*, the percentage of students from the bottom quartile drops to around 3 percent.

There are many reasons for dismay at this situation, one of which was stated by former Princeton president William Bowen, who wrote in 2005 that "the sense of democratic legitimacy is undermined if people believe that the rich are admitted to selective colleges and universities regardless of merit while able and deserving candidates from more modest backgrounds are turned away."[15] As a step toward restoring some sense of legitimacy, Bowen proposed that academically promising students from low-income families get "a thumb on the scale"—an advantage comparable to what alumni children, athletes, and minority candidates already get. If they have lower test scores or fewer AP classes of the sort that high schools in the inner city or in rural areas rarely offer, these deficiencies should be considered in the context of limited opportunities, and evidence of success in overcoming obstacles should also be taken into account. Proposals of this sort were responses to the fact that at most private selective colleges, the already-small enrollment of low-income students was getting smaller even before the financial crash, when endowments were soaring. But they have been put into practice at only a very few elite institutions, notably Harvard and also Amherst, which, during the presidency of Anthony Marx (2003–2011), recruited aggressively in low-income communities and took an increasing number of Pell-eligible students as transfers from community colleges—without apparent negative effect on the academic strength of its student body.[16]

If we step back from these particulars, what kind of general picture emerges? The stark truth is that America's colleges—with such notable exceptions as community colleges, historically black colleges, distinctive institutions such as Berea College in Kentucky (which charges no tuition and requires campus work from its students, all of whom are first in their families to attend college), along with a very few elite institutions with large endowments—have lately been reinforcing more than ameliorating the disparity of wealth and opportunity in American society. One writer goes so far as to call our leading colleges "propaganda machines that might as well have been designed to ensure that the class structure of American society remains unchallenged."[17]

Even if admissions policies were to change fundamentally at selective colleges, there will never be room for more than a fraction of the students worthy of going to them. Some of these colleges are expanding, but mostly with an eye toward admitting more students from abroad, who are often the children of the globetrotting business and political elite. Moreover, too many worthy students in today's America are unable to continue their education beyond high school at all—and of those who do, too many find themselves in colleges that are underfunded and overcrowded. "Over the last forty years," as one community college president writes, "enrollment in community colleges has expanded at a rate four times greater than in four-year public and private universities, yet they are able to expend only one third as much per full-time student as their better-financed private and public counterparts." This means that the very students who most urgently need mentoring and support—first-generation college students, often minorities—are the ones who find reduced hours in the library and laboratory, cutbacks in advising, remedial tutoring, and child care, and who are likely to be taught by underpaid, overworked part-time faculty trying to cobble together a living by teaching at two or three campuses at the same time. It is hardly surprising that evidence of substantial learning is scant and that rates of graduation among many college students are low—especially in public institutions.

And yet there seems to be much less indignation about the present than about the past, in part, perhaps, because as our society divides more and more between those with "advantages" (our euphemism for money) and those without, the two camps know less and less about each other. It's hard to know whom or what to hold accountable. Should we blame political or academic readers, or maybe taxpayers—that convenient abstraction that includes ourselves? If we sat in the legislature, are we sure we'd cast the right vote when forced to allocate scarce funds between, say, Medicaid and higher education? The hard fact is that in the absence of fundamental change in our tax structure and political priorities, the days of "both . . . and" are over, and the days of "either . . . or" have arrived.

Reading

1. How does Delbanco define "the university"?

2. How does Delbanco define the "democratizing of elite institutions" (para. 8) in the university?

3. How does he question whether a university education in the United States is really an "equal opportunity" for everyone?

4. How does he question whether education can be made affordable and equal to everyone?

Inquiring

1. Delbanco seems unsure of how to assess the commitment of elite colleges to sponsoring diverse student populations. Although he acknowledges that elite colleges have overcome their traditional exclusion of certain populations— such as African Americans and Jews—he seems less sure about the overall diversity of campuses today. What forces does Delbanco believe originally opened up colleges to greater diversity? What forces are currently working to exclude certain students today? Does Delbanco provide an answer to how to continue to diversify the student population? What type of solution might you propose?

2. Near the end of his essay, Delbanco argues that many community colleges are unable to provide the support required for nontraditional students—first-generation students, students from traditionally excluded backgrounds—that are vital to their success. Delbanco then contrasts these disadvantages with the wealth often associated with elite schools, which have large endowments to finance such support. Consider how your own school supports nontraditional students, a term that will mean something slightly different on each campus. How might Delbanco assess the efforts on your campus to support such students? How might your campus leadership respond?

3. One of the primary issues facing college students is cost—the rising cost of tuition, books, and housing. Delbanco discusses the shifting role of the government and universities to address this issue. What does he believe to be the primary reason college costs are rising? What does he believe has been the historic role of the government? Does he have faith that colleges can take on such a role in at the current moment?

Composing

1. Delbanco writes that, with a few exceptions, American colleges "have lately been reinforcing more than ameliorating the disparity of wealth and opportunity in American society. One writer goes so far as to call our leading colleges 'propaganda machines that might as well have been designed to ensure that the class structure of American society remains unchallenged'" (para. 22). Write an essay in which you examine the evidence Delbanco uses to support these rather large claims. Do you find that evidence compelling? How might you complicate or expand his conclusions about colleges supporting the current economic class structure based on your own experience, your own research, or both?

2. In an ideal university, according to Delbanco, students would gain an understanding of "learning for its own sake versus learning for the sake of utility." He then adds a "good educational institution strives for both" (para. 2). Write an essay in which you support or challenge Delbanco's claim. As a college student, do you believe a college education should include both learning for its own sake and for utility? Given that many students are paying for their own education, do you believe they should have to take "core curriculum" courses, such as those in English, linguistics, math, or Romance languages? Or should they be allowed to just take courses related to their careers? Based on your own experience, do you believe Delbanco's vision of education meets the needs of students today?

3. Throughout his essay, Delbanco repeatedly argues that colleges need to be open to all students and that campus populations should approximate the diversity of the city, state, or country in which they exist. Colleges might also be seen as primarily educational institutions, however, dedicated to working with students who meet their strict admission requirements. Write an essay in which you trace the development of Delbanco's argument about the need for diversity on college campuses. How do you respond to his argument? Do you believe universities have an ethical commitment to diverse student populations? If so, what policies might support such a goal? Would such policies be ethical in themselves? Why or why not?

Connecting

Delbanco argues that the university's commitment to a diverse student population is often in conflict with how resources are allocated, that is, how the university receives and spends its money. The authors in *Pro(se)letariets* (p. 80) offer an educational manifesto to support working-class students, the very students Delbanco believes are most often hurt by a lack of dedicated resources. Taking Delbanco's argument into consideration, write an educational manifesto for students attending U.S. universities.

VARIOUS AUTHORS

Selections from *Pro(se)letariets*: The Writing of the Trans-Atlantic Worker Writer Federation

New City Community Press/
Elizabeth Parks

Pro(se)letariets is the result of a university–community partnership between the Writing Program at Syracuse University (SU) and the Federation of Worker Writers and Community Publishers (FWWCP). FWWCP members and SU students collaboratively wrote on the theme of education for one year, with a particular focus on what it meant to be a working-class student. At the end of the project, the SU students and FWWCP members met in London to develop an "education manifesto," a document that was then used to create college courses and FWWCP projects. Ultimately, the writing from the project, named the Trans-Atlantic Worker Writer Federation, was published in book form, circulating in both the United States and the United Kingdom.

In the following excerpts, writers from the project discuss their educational background as well as present their manifesto.

■　■　■

DEANA CATER

The First Day of Third Grade (USA)

When I was younger, say around six or seven, I was a little fireball. I learned all of my lessons, but I learned them better than any of the other second graders. I was brilliant, passionate, confident and not afraid to speak out. I could wow all of my teachers and peers and without even noticing or trying. We had these little journals we were supposed to write in every day. Every morning before we began our lessons, we would take 15 minutes or so to write in them. They'd be simple prompts like "What do you want to be when you grow up?" or "What did you do this weekend?", and because I learned my lessons so well, I didn't need to think about it. I'd get all fired up about the prompt and put pen to paper and begin scribbling. It was like the lessons were innate. I was born to write and to write well. I was never sure exactly how I was writing that made my teachers smile and point and brag to other teachers about what a brilliant little fireball I was; in fact, I didn't think I was doing anything out of the ordinary, but whatever I was doing, I kept it because it worked.

Soon after completing the second grade, my parents decided to send me to another school. They told me that I would be going to a school in a better area, a more influential part of town far away from the rinkydink part of town I knew. They told me that there were more opportunities where I was going. Better education, more money, and the people were the movers and shakers of the city. They were confident that I would fit right in. They knew their little fireball would just assimilate right into that culture. Everyone was so excited about the move. All of my family knew it was the best thing for me, and my teachers and peers cheered me on and supported the decision. They all thought that I could fare well in this new part of town. "Not too many of us over here get a chance to go over that way," my 60-year-old neighbor told me "and worse yet, not all of us do so well when we get over there, but you're a little fireball, you'll do fine."

Soon after the move was my first day of third grade. I wake up, excited to experience the great opportunity that everyone was telling me about. I wash extra good so I'm extra squeaky clean. I think I washed my face three times. I put on my best outfit. Have mom fix my hair just right in braided pigtails. My dad bought me a new Hello Kitty bookbag with a matching lunchbox. Oh yes hunny, I thought I was looking sharp, draped down and done up. I kiss my parents goodbye and they wished me well as I boarded the city school bus.

I watched the trees whip by the bus window. Even the trees are more beautiful in this new place. The grass is greener. The houses are bigger, better, brighter. There are cool looking cars riding alongside the bus. There were kids around my age sitting in the back seat of these cars, I suppose getting dropped off to school. Some of the cars' names are easier to pronounce than others. "Hummer," I whisper to myself before looking at another vehicle behind it. "Fer . . . feaer . . . feaer . . . , no, looks like a short 'a', ferar . . . ferari," I whisper wondering to myself.

Finally, I arrived at my new school. I walk through the heavy, glass double doors. Then I stand, looking. These people, these new people don't look like me. I walk around a little bit. No one looks like me. They wear their hair differently. They walk differently. Even dress differently. I begin to think that maybe I don't look as sharp as I thought. I've seen some of these people before. I've seen them pass through my old town from time to time. I've seen them on television, too, advertising their boat dealerships and restaurants. I've seen people that look like them

5

on billboards. These look like the type of people that run for mayor or governor or justice chair or whatever else.

I walk up to a student to ask if she would show me around. We begin to converse, but I can hardly understand from the way she was speaking. She was speaking the same language, no doubt, but it was as if she was speaking a different dialect. I had to listen carefully to catch snippets of her phrases to piece together what she was saying to me. I was thinking to myself that maybe she's new to the country, but she introduces me to a lot of her friends and teachers and they were speaking in the same manner. So perhaps I do not speak correctly. Perhaps I need to try to speak like them I wonder to myself.

"Would my parents understand me?" I ask myself.

She continues to show me around the school and introduces me to another student who is in my class. The student looks puzzled. She speaks the same as all the rest of the people in the school, so it was hard to understand again, but I believe she asked me if I was dirty. "Dirty?" I asked, "why do you think I'm dirty?"

"When my little brother plays outside on our jungle gym, sometimes he gets brown dirt spots on him. You look like you have them all over. Did you wash this morning? Did you fall on your way to school?"

10   I try to explain to her that I'm not dirty, but she has a hard time understanding. I guess she's never seen anyone like me before. I begin to wonder where she must live that she has never had a friend of darker skin.

Finally, it's time for class. We all pile into our little desks. The teacher begins to write a series of sentences on the board as a student volunteer passes out spiral bound notebooks. I begin to get excited because I recognize this activity. It's journal time. The teacher explains we will write a series of quick writes of about two paragraphs each. We will stop after each prompt and select volunteers to share theirs before we begin the next one. We'll complete three prompts.

The first prompt was "What did you do this summer?" This is easy enough I think to myself. I let the words fall onto the paper. I begin to write about the trips to the park with my parents, going to the swimming pool, and visiting my grandparents. I write about how my grandparents make the best barbecue ribs and how I prefer my dad to make Koolaid because he puts more sugar in it than Mom does. I scribble, erase, and scribble until I am confident that I have the best two paragraphs possible.

The teacher asks for volunteers to share their writing. Immediately, my hand shoots up, but as luck would have it, she calls on someone else. A boy stands and begins to read. He tells us of his summer trip to Mazatlan, Mexico. Another student gets called on next and tells us of her sailing trip with her family in their boat along the east coast. Another student spent a few weeks at her family's beach house. My story doesn't sound so great anymore. Their experiences are all so different than mine. Would they even relate to my experiences? Would they care since theirs seem so much more worthwhile? The way they write even sounds different. Their word choice and the way they put things together doesn't quite sound like my style. "I bet they don't even drink Koolaid," I say to myself.

The time comes for the last prompt. "Who is your role model?" I decide to write about my grandmother, and her struggles raising nine brothers and sisters while her parents left to find work in another state. It was taking me a while to get started this time. Nothing was sounding right. Everyone else seems to not be having a problem. Am I the only one struggling? Everyone else seems to be comfortable and doing well. The ideas weren't coming as quickly, in fact, writing was becoming a chore. I wasn't sure if I should try to write like them again, or just go back to how I write. The problem is, I never had to think about it before. I'm not sure what to do, but I finally pound out something.

This time when the teacher asks for volunteers my hand stays down. Volunteer   15
after volunteer stands up to read and I listen, wondering what it was about their writing that sounds different, asking myself if it's possible for me to write like they write, or if I should continue to not think about it and let it just come, like I've been doing.

Soon, school ends. I wave goodbye to many of the friends I made that day as their parents come one by one to pick them up. I board the city bus to go home. My parents ask me about my first day of school and I tell them with a smile that I had a great day and that I made a lot of friends.

Morning comes. It's the second day of third grade. I try to fake sick so that I wouldn't have to go, but my parents are too smart for that. I get out of bed. I go to my closet. Nothing looks right. I scramble about trying to put together a better outfit than before. I then wash extra, extra squeaky clean this time. I think I washed my face five times. There's no way anyone can say I'm dirty now. I board the bus to school after kissing my parents goodbye. I look at the trees whip by thinking about what kind of prompts the teacher will assign today, asking myself if it will be as difficult today as it was yesterday and if I have what it takes to make it in this new school.

JO BARNES

Scholarship Boy (UK)

He knocked at the door.
"Come in sit down.
Now what newspapers do your parents read?"
"The Pictorial and the Daily Herald, sir."
"Who is your favourite comedian, boy?"
"Max Miller, sir!!"
"Tell us one of his jokes."
"I can't remember one, but I can tell you one of Frankie Howard's."
"What does your father do?"
"He's a docker, sir."   10
Each word a nail hammered his fate.
Their words, his words.
Not grammar school material, they said.

ALONNA BERRY

Failure to Assimilate (USA)

I remember my first encounter with Syracuse University. It was on a college visit, I had been invited to compete in a Maxwell Scholarship program that my high school grades had earned me a spot in. My parents were so excited, I have to admit—I was too. I thought after being rejected from Yale and Dartmouth, being accepted in the top ten percent of the incoming class of Syracuse University wasn't bad—and if I got another scholarship it wouldn't have been that bad of a deal. Well anyway—back to the story. When I first walked up the stairs to Maxwell School of Citizenship—I thought, this is the place for me to be. As we all filed into the auditorium I began to think this may be a little harder than I thought. I wasn't surprised to see that I was maybe one of five African-American students there out of an auditorium of maybe 200 or so. This is what I was used to. Throughout my entire high school career if I wasn't the token "black kid," I was definitely always the token "black girl." So to say the least I felt right at home . . . Or at least I thought.

Even though I was used to my surroundings, I wasn't used to the atmosphere. Everyone looked at me differently. They even seemed surprised when I spoke— I couldn't understand. Suddenly it all seemed so foreign to me. I began to look around and nothing that I saw was familiar anymore. I began to feel so out of place, and then I felt my body begin to tremble. It was my turn to speak in front of the group for the competition. The topic was Immigration. Most of the people before me who had spoken simply said build a wall—we don't need any more foreigners in this country. They seemed so insensitive to me. Didn't they understand that immigration is what founded this country, and that most of the immigrants that cross the Mexico-America border don't tarnish our country—they are helping to rebuild it. I did not come from an immigrant family, but some my closest friends did and their parents have worked hard to build a home, and gain citizenship. I couldn't imagine what it could be like to live a life that close-minded.

Well that was just the beginning of my experience at Syracuse University. I later learned that there are many class, race, and social microcosms there. When I was 17, I started taking classes at Syracuse, in a SummerStart program. After visiting for my shocking scholarship competition I was surprised to see the vast difference in the students attending SummerStart. I was not the "token black girl or person"—in fact I was surrounded by more African American students than I had ever been in my life. Almost every person in the SummerStart program was a person of color. I had to admit I was excited, and astonished. I had never been in a learning or living situation like this before. When I walked into Watson Hall, and found my way up to the 2nd floor, room 204 (my key envelope said), I was the first one to arrive—so I began unpacking and decorating with my parents. This was going to be my new home for the next 6 weeks . . .

When we were almost finished unpacking I heard the door open, it was my new roommate. She came in with a man helping her who was not much older than us. After he moved her things in, they said goodbye and he left. I was surprised at how quickly he had left, but I didn't want to get in her way as she began to unpack her belongings. My parents and I decided that we should make our Wal-Mart run now to allow her to unpack. Before we left, I introduced myself, and asked her if she wanted us to pick her up anything from Wal-Mart. Surprisingly she responded, "I've never been to a Wal-Mart before, I don't really know what they have there." I didn't know what to say, where I am from, in the country-suburban community of Delaware, Wal-Mart was the pinnacle of every-one's being. I couldn't comprehend. In order to combat my confusion my mother said, "Well if you want to come along you're more than welcome." She agreed, and by this time our Chevy Suburban was now full with two other new students as we made our way to Wal-Mart. As we were driving I discovered a few things.

None of my "new friends" had ever been to Wal-Mart before, they were all   5
from New York City, and their names were Shaquana (my roommate), Myranne, and David. David was Colombian, Myranne was Puerto Rican, and Shaquana was black like me. As we continued to drive I began to realize what a different environment college life was going to be. To me, Syracuse seemed like a big city; to them it seemed like the country.

I couldn't imagine a country with an interstate, freeways, and highways. I was dumbfounded. I live on Woodlytown Road, across the street from a corn field in Magnolia, Delaware. This all seemed so foreign to me—not just the interstates, free-ways, and streetlights, but the people too—the people were the most foreign of all.

As we made our way into Wal-Mart the absolute look of amazement on their faces astonished me (but my parents didn't seem so surprised). When everyone was finished shopping, we were on our way back to Watson Hall.

When my dad pulled up the hill in our Big Blue Suburban, and pulled in front of the door of Watson to let us all out I knew what had just happened. I had just been labeled: "the uppity, rich black girl from Delaware or Maryland or something like that." The scary feeling began to come back, and even though like during the scholarship completion I was amongst my peers . . . this time I didn't stand out because of my skin, I stood out because of who I was. I talked different, I walked different, I dressed different—I was different.

Sometimes it's not just about race, it is about class too. As SummerStart came to an end, and I was chosen to give the speech at the ending ceremony—I talked about my experiences in SummerStart. I spoke about what I learned, and what we had to look forward to in a few weeks in August. The speech was hopeful and reflective—just like a good commencement speech should be. But I have to admit, as I stood on the stage, and looked at my audience I knew that an audience of my peers would never look so colorful again. As my hands began to tremble, and my body to shake, I wasn't nervous, I was fearful. Fearful of what I had seen in the scholarship competition, fearful of what I encountered in the

Suburban my first day of SummerStart, I was fearful . . . because what I had done
and would continue to do is fail to assimilate.

STEVE OAKLEY

No Right to Write (UK)

I an't got no right to write
Cos evrythin I do is shite
I cant make my words fit
    into a neat rhyme
And novels just take too bloody long
I tried once you knowst
Wrote me life story, took nearly a week
An I typed it out all nice n neat
An posted it to London to a big book
10   Company but it must ave got lost
So a year later
I was visiting my sister there
I took a copy to the building
    on the address
An spoke to a bloke at the front desk,
he were a right ponce
He says to me I need an appointment
That I had to leave,
And calls over this handy looking
20   security guard
Name on the badge says Steve
He looks pretty hard
So I make my way to the door
An ah says to him
"What they treating people like
that for?" He inna bad sort after all
An he says to me,
"I guard the building mate,
but they guard British culture 'rate"
30   I didna ave a fuckin clue
What'd just happened
And that was ma writin days done
I gave up there n then
I an't got time for smarmy gits
I went back home n called it quits—
    put telly on
But ah can wax lyrical

An I no all the big words
I use em to confuse em
Dine at the Birds—that's ma local   40

KAY EKEVALL

Education (UK)

At school, I knew history:
Kings and Emperors
Battles and heroes
There was something called
The White Man's burden
We seemed to do well under it,
But the black man didn't.

I didn't know about
Miners and dockers:
Their work and their battles,   10
I did hear about Peterloo
But those Chartists were bloodthirsty rebels,
They had to be put down!

My education began when I met
The hunger marchers from Aberdeen and Dundee
On their way to London.

DAVID KENT

Priceless (USA)

In 1982, while in high school looking forward to graduation, my world as I knew it crashed and burned. I was told by educators I could not graduate based on my competencies, which were under state education requirements for graduation at the time. "You will have to stay back another year to make them up."

Well, at the time the United States President was Ronald Reagan, who signed a bill that basically said you must be enrolled in college curriculum by the age eighteen in order to keep receiving social security disability benefits on my mother's behalf. Mom was disabled physically by then. We could not afford to lose her SSD benefits or we would lose everything. I could not allow this to happen. So, without any college prep classes and no high school diploma, I had to enroll in a college curriculum at Onondaga Community College (OCC). I wanted to enroll in an electronics technology program at OCC. The program had been filled for two years and there was a waiting list, but based on my entrance exam I was put at the bottom. Yes—a very low exam score. Again, I said to myself, "Damn, where do I go from here? Enroll in another curriculum or what?"

So I swallowed my anger and my stress, and went to go talk to my advisor. She suggested that I consider a humanities program for now, until an opening in my choice program occurred. After a bout of self-doubt, I said I'm going to do it. Boy, was I stupid. The study of the human mind, I didn't even make matriculation (the grade point average). The best I received was a 1.9 (of a 4.0 scale). I had 10% participation in this class!

By May 1982, I was out, and wondering how I was going to pay back a $1,700 school loan. Higher education services knew. At a 1982 education and vocation seminar, I met with Karl and May Knowlton. They operated the industrial work division at Olsten Temporary Services. While under a lot of stress, I approached and asked what types of temporary employment they offered.

5   "We have industrial labor position right now," they said. So I figured with my background as a laborer I had a good chance of getting a pretty good job with Olsten Temporary Services. For once, I was right.

They had a position opening for an industrial laborer at Bristol Myers Squibb Company, a very large international pharmaceutical business. They offered me a temp assignment for about one year on the third shift, which gave me time to plan ahead and start an active full time employment search and access those employment and training programs available for dislocated workers, which I was at the time. Even knowing I would not receive a great employment opportunity, I still pounded the pavement, read the classified ads daily in the Syracuse Herald-Journal, and bussed the distance to the suburban Syracuse area or where a classified might take me. Still, I never gave up the search; being an optimist permits me to do that. Perseverance was my partner.

I stayed with Olsten Temporary Services until June 1985 in different areas of industrial employment. Yes, I did return to Bristol Labs to various positions. All I knew is that I was receiving a weekly paycheck that helped my family's economic hardship. I was very thankful for this opportunity.

Let's remember the important issues in my life are about being from a working class family and, yes, my relationship was much different than those who are privileged to have two working parents and are able to have the finances to afford a good education. I do not have a chance to return to school in the future. What matters to me is to make sure that my mother is able to pay our monthly responsibilities without falling under. Through this sacrifice in my life, it was all worth it and if I had to, I would do it all again. The lessons I learned as a youngster and in working helped to bring money into the home to make sure there was food on the table and a roof over our head. To sacrifice this and to persevere — there is a light at the end of the tunnel. Just walk forward to the next step and soon enough you'll be there. Don't give up. If you fall, get up and keep walking. Strive to survive. Look at me. I made it. I did not stop. I kept my chin up and my feet in front of me.

I have my own responsibilities now. I am happily married and gainfully employed, handling life's financial responsibilities a day at a time and ready at a moment's notice to handle my family's financial occurrences as they happen—which has not happened for quite some time. Most importantly, a true statement that stands with me twenty four hours a day: family comes first.

I can only see a good ending to come to add to this collection of my life. As a young man who has struggled through education, earned an hourly wage at an early age, who had an alter ego who loved to dance and drink and have fun, I have matured into a hardworking, responsible man, with a voice for change, a workforce leader with recognition as a voice for organized workforces.

"In order to be the 'man', you have to beat the man." As an SEIU 1199 delegate and political organizer and activist, I have proven my character time and time again. My voice was heard in Albany, N.Y., in the largest rally in the history of labor organizing; it was myself along with 37,000 of my brothers and sisters from SEIU 1199 on April 1, 2001—a day I will never forget. Being forced into the labor force at an early age made me responsible, struggling through education made me a survivor, and dancing and moonlighting gave me a personality. Building a family made me a man. Being a member of SEIU 1199 gave me a voice and made me a leader. Working for a living and earning a wage made me an adult. It led me to having all this today, a job, a loving family, a workforce leader, waking up every day. This is for me, simply put, PRICELESS.

DANIELLE QUIGLEY

Server (USA)

Perhaps you have seen her
Rushed and flustered
Belittled and beaten down
Forcing smiles
With strained politeness
Biting her tongue?

Perhaps you mock her
"Ignorant profession"
A server tending to your needs
Her trite existence
With meager means—
A lifestyle unlike your own

Perhaps you pity her
"Oh look she's pregnant!"
"And so young!"
Quick, ring check—
"at least she's married . . ."
Poor baby

20
Or perhaps you are her—
Struggling, hardworking
A college student with honors
A writer with potential
A happily married woman
An excited mother-to-be

Perhaps if you saw me
As more than a server
Grant me the credit I merit
Dispose of your pity or mockery —
Recognize the resemblance?
30
Could I be you?

PAT DALLIMORE

Mum's Writing (UK)

Sit down be quiet read a book
Don't you dare to speak or look
Shush Mum's writing
She's left the dishes in the sink
All she does is sit and think
Shush Mum's writing
Nothing for dinner not for tea
And all she ever says to me is
Shush Mum's writing
10
But what's all this Mum's wrote a book
Why not buy one have a look
No need to shush now we can shout
And tell all our friends about
MUM'S WRITING

The Trans-Atlantic Worker Writer Federation Manifesto

1. Education should teach a global humanity (not the humanities) based on an alternative sense of history and where cooperative values and restorative justice are primary.

2. Education should take place in a safe environment free from traditional social/economic biases with self-respect for each other as individuals as well as members of different classes, heritages, and sexualities.

3. All educators must move from subconsciously teaching students to be Westernized versions of "them" to teaching the essential equality among all individuals and cultures.

4. The conceptual equality taught to students must also be manifested in equal funding and equal access to well-maintained school facilities.

5. To base an educational system on any other values accepts a fundamental inequity in society and acceptance that now all human potential will be fulfilled.

Reading

1. How do you understand the term *proletariat*? (If you are unfamiliar with this term, look it up.)

2. How does *pro(se)letariet* alter or expand the meaning of *proletariat*?

3. How does the *Pro(se)latariet* manifesto define the goals of education?

4. How does the manifesto say the "conceptual equality" taught to students needs to be demonstrated?

Inquiring

1. The writers in *Pro(se)letariets* attempt to define being working class through highlighting particular details of their lives. What types of details do they use? Do these details have any common traits? How do they cumulatively define *working class*? Finally, if you were asked to define *working-class experience*, would you use such details? What details might you add? How might those details change the *Pro(se)letariets* writers' definition of this term?

2. Many of the essays and poems featured in *Pro(se)letariets* discuss the ways in which the writer's home life conflicted with the expectations of school. These conflicts involved a lack of time, untraditional ways of speaking, and difficult economic circumstances. Have you encountered similar obstacles? Would you place these experiences under the umbrella term *working-class experience*? How might such a term help explain your experience? How might it distort your experience?

3. Although each writer in *Pro(se)letariets* identifies as working class, not all writers limit their experience to this term. Some also discuss how race and gender affected their educational experience. Choose one essay or poem. Use it as a way to begin discussing the relationship between race, gender, and class. Does it make sense to choose one of these terms as the most important? What difficulties might writers face when speaking about themselves in terms of class, race, and gender simultaneously?

Composing

1. The writers in *Pro(se)letariets* write personal stories because they believe such stories can capture as much complexity as academic writing while also being more accessible to readers. In doing so, the authors hope to show to their

audience the personal effect of race, class, gender, and opportunity on their education. They hope to stir individuals to collective action. Write an essay or poem in which you use your personal experience to discuss how class, race, and gender affected your own education. Demonstrate how these different forces might have interacted with one another or have opened or closed opportunities for you. When you are done, read the essay aloud. Do you think an individual might be called to action based on your essay? If not, revise the essay until you believe it would create such action.

2. *Pro(se)letariets* is based on a belief in working-class experience. Moreover, the book argues that this term can be used to represent the experience of working-class students not only in the United States but in the United Kingdom as well. Write an essay in which you define what *Pro(se)letariets* means by the term *working class*. How does this term relate to other such terms such as *race* and *gender*? Discuss whether you believe in such a "transatlantic" definition of class. How might you amend, revise, or reject this category when discussing your own experience as a student?

3. *Pro(se)letariets* concludes with "The Trans-Atlantic Worker Writer Manifesto" (p. 90), a statement that was collaboratively written by students attending Syracuse University and by members of the Federation of Worker Writer and Community Publishers (FWWCP). The FWWCP was a network of working-class writing and publication groups in the United Kingdom that had been corresponding with the U.S. students over the course of an academic term. The goal of the manifesto was to represent the groups' collective vision of a just and equitable education. Write an essay in which you respond to this manifesto. At the end of your essay, write your own manifesto in which you state your beliefs about not only what it means to be educated but what society must do to ensure students have an opportunity for such an education.

Connecting

Pro(se)letariets provides many examples of how working-class students experience classrooms, from grade school to college. David Bartholomae (p. 56) might be read as imagining his classroom as a space where such experiences could be put in conversation with academic writers. Write an essay in which you discuss whether *Pro(se)letariets* would see Bartholomae's classroom as supportive of working-class voices and writing. Is such support important to you as a beginning college writer?

HARRY BOYTE AND ELIZABETH HOLLANDER

Wingspread Declaration on Renewing the Civic Mission of the American Research University

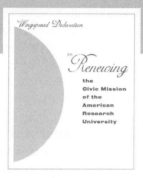

The *Wingspread Declaration on Renewing the Civic Mission of the American Research University* is the result of a set of conferences involving university presidents, provosts, and faculty and was composed by Harry Boyte and Elizabeth Hollander on behalf of the conference participants. These conferences emerged as a response to criticism that the modern university was failing to live up to its historic mission of creating civically engaged citizens and being an active participant in its local community. Instead, the argument went, the university had become a bastion for theory unrelated to practice, of scholarship disconnected from public need. The *Wingspread Declaration* was not just a statement of commitment to such work but also a road map to accomplishing such work.

In the following excerpt, the authors discuss the need for a civically engaged university. They also examine what such work might look like in practice.

■ ■   ■

Those document is the result of collaboration by participants at a Wingspread conference involving university presidents, provosts, deans, and faculty members with extensive experience in higher education as well as representatives of professional associations, private foundations, and civic organizations. The purpose of the conference was to formulate strategies for renewing the civic mission of the research university, both by preparing students for responsible citizenship in a diverse democracy, and also by engaging faculty members to develop and utilize knowledge for the improvement of society.

The Wingspread conference was held December 11–13, 1998. At the end of the conference, participants formed working groups and committed themselves to action strategies for renewing the civic mission. They reconvened for a second conference on July 19–21, 1999.

The conference was coordinated by the University of Michigan Center for Community Service and Learning, with sponsorship by the Association of American Universities, American Association for Higher Education, American Council on Education, Association of American Colleges and Universities, Campus Compact, New England Resource Center for Higher Education, University of Pennsylvania Center for University Partnerships, and the Johnson Foundation, with support from the W. K. Kellogg Foundation.

Wingspread is an international educational conference center designed by Frank Lloyd Wright and maintained by the Johnson Foundation in Racine, Wisconsin.

5   Civic engagement is essential to a democratic society, but far too many Americans have withdrawn from participation in public affairs. Higher education can contribute to civic engagement, but most research universities do not perceive themselves as part of the problem or of its solution. Whereas universities were once centrally concerned with "education for democracy" and "knowledge for society," today's institutions have often drifted away from their civic mission.

At the same time, however, there are new stirrings of democracy in American higher education. From one campus to another, there is increasing interest in efforts to better prepare people for active citizenship in a diverse democracy, to develop knowledge for the improvement of communities and society, and to think about and act upon the public dimensions of our educational work.

What are some strategies for renewing the civic mission of the American research university? This question was the focus of a conference of higher education leaders at Wingspread that produced the following declaration about the renewal process. We are indebted to Barry Checkoway of the University of Michigan, Elizabeth Hollander of Campus Compact, and Stanley Ikenberry of the American Council on Education for preparing an initial draft, and to Harry Boyte of the University of Minnesota and Elizabeth Hollander for their leadership roles in preparing the final statement.

> . . . most of the American institutions of higher education are filled
> with the democratic spirit. Teachers and students alike are pro-
> foundly moved by the desire to serve the democratic community.
> —Charles Eliot, President, Harvard, 1908

Across the country a historic debate is underway over the future of America's great public and research universities. From many sources, including state legislatures, governing boards, public constituencies, and the mass media, research institutions are challenged to justify what they do and how they do it. The beliefs and practices that universities have espoused, affecting research, teaching, and outreach, are under review, spurred by calls for accountability, efficiency, and utility as well as by questions about the theories of knowledge embedded in prevailing reward and evaluation systems. The controversies of this debate also reflect trends and questions in higher education as a whole.

At their broadest and most engaged, research institutions of higher education in America have been, in Charles Eliot's words, "filled with the democratic spirit." Such spirit took many different forms. Columbia University, according to Seth Low, breathed the air of the city of New York, its working class population, its problems, and its opportunities. At the University of Chicago, America's pragmatic philosophy and world-renowned sociology department emerged, in part, from vital partnerships between the Hull House settlement and scholars. At land grant institutions, the cooperative extension system of county agents saw itself as "building rural democracy" and helping to develop communities' capacities for cooperative action. As late as 1947, the President's Commission on Higher Education titled its report, *Education for Democracy.*

In the postwar years, American research universities have seen an explosion in numbers of students, in fields of study, and in international prestige. Questions of diversity and justice, issues of who universities choose to admit and serve are central to the democratic spirit. On these grounds our schools have made clear advances. Today, research universities are more richly varied in the cultures, economic backgrounds, and outlooks of our students. Our curricula are more inclusive of diverse cultures, traditions, and ways of knowing. Fields of research and scholarship have proliferated, and path-breaking advances have been made in areas scarcely imagined a generation or two ago. Research universities today evidence renewed engagements with communities. Many have joined the service-learning movement that involves students in real world problems and issues.

10

Though incomplete, such changes nonetheless represent substantial progress toward a more inclusive and a more just system of higher education. Yet despite such gains, few leaders in research universities today would make Eliot's claim that their fundamental mission is to serve democracy or that they are filled with the democratic spirit.

Today, higher education mirrors the democratic discontents of the larger society. Nowhere is this truer than in our great research universities. T. S. Eliot's haunting question in his 1937 poem *The Rock*—"where is the wisdom we have lost in knowledge, where is the knowledge we have lost in information?"—has become a question for our age.

Research institutions are subject to the same forces in the society that focus on "efficiency of means" and neglect continuing discussion about civic purposes and public meanings of our individual and collective work. Ends are regarded as fixed. Even when debated they are separated from the larger tasks of democracy.

Such dynamics take the form of proposals to make colleges more responsive to the demands of students redefined as customers. Allocations of resources are pushed toward their most remunerative uses with a slighting of other institutional values. A powerful new trend is the "virtual university." Public service today often has a commercial cast. All of these developments can have value as parts of a larger whole. But they cannot be taken for the whole. Students are far more than "customers"; they need to be understood as co-creators of their learning. Universities are far more than data banks for distance learning; they are places where students, faculty, and staff interact in multi-dimensional ways and, at best, learn and develop together. And communities are far more than sites of economic growth; they are places where a variety of public and private values need articulation, recognition, and cultivation.

15   As agents of the democracy, colleges and universities will consciously prepare a next generation of involved citizens reflecting the full and immensely varied cultural and economic mix of America, by creating innumerable opportunities for them to be in college and to do the work of citizenship. This means conceiving of institutions of higher learning as vital, living cultures, not simply an aggregation of discrete units in competition with each other. The public dimensions of our common cultures require intense and self-conscious attention. Opportunities for students, faculty, staff, administrators to use their many talents for the greater good must once again pervade every aspect of our work.

Yet today, many students feel that college is out of their grasp and those who are in college often feel disengaged and powerless. They find few opportunities for civic participation. Every department, every discipline, every unit of our research universities experiences pressures to draw back from connection to the whole. Cultures of research-oriented schools have become increasingly competitive, individualist, and characterized by the "star system." Faculty identities are drawn away from the local civic community and toward national and international disciplinary and sub-disciplinary reference groups. Moreover, faculties are socialized throughout their graduate school preparation to think in highly individualized and privatized terms about their work in ways that make it difficult to believe in the possibilities for effective cooperative action for change.

Despite these trends and pressures, many faculty devote themselves to the pressing tasks of our commonwealth and seek out colleagues, inside and outside their disciplines, to work with in their efforts. We need a far ranging examination of our purposes and practices so that such work is honored, celebrated, and built upon.

Against this background, we issue this Wingspread Declaration based on the conviction that now is the time to boldly claim the authority and ability to focus our energy on the civic purposes of higher education. Those of us in higher education can change its directions and commitments. We can mobilize support for change from outside constituencies by making alliances with those constituencies. We can shape our cultures, renew our civic missions, and guide our destinies.

The challenges facing higher education go beyond the need to add more service-learning experiences or to reward faculty for community-oriented research. As important as these objectives are, the more fundamental task is to renew our great mission as the agents of democracy. This task points to deep strategic challenges: How to tap and free the powers and talents of all elements of our schools—our faculty, our students, our staff, our administrators—for public engagement? How to break down the artificial and arbitrary "silo cultures" that now stifle creativity, connection, and community? How to renew throughout our institutional life and cultures a robust sense that our work contributes to the commonwealth of our communities, our nation, and the world?

How might this vision of public engagement be made manifest? It will take   20
many different forms in different universities. Here we suggest some ways that an engaged university will embody its mission.

1. Students

What will it mean for our student bodies to be filled once again with the democratic spirit?

A. A core element in the mission of the research university is to prepare students for engaged citizenship through multiple opportunities to do the work of citizenship. Such work involves real projects of impact and relevance, through which students learn the skills, develop the habits and identities, and acquire the knowledge to contribute to the general welfare.

B. The university curricula and courses challenge students' imaginations, draw on student experiences and interests, and cultivate students' talents and public identities. This means sustained attention to how our curricula help to develop civic competencies and civic habits. These include the arts of public argument, civic imagination, the ability to critically evaluate arguments and information, the capacities and curiosity to listen constantly, interest in and knowledge of public affairs, capacities for intergroup dialogue, and the ability to work with others different from themselves on common projects and problem solving in ways that deepen appreciation of others' talents.

C. Campus co-curricular activities on and off campus offer multiple opportunities for students to get engaged in community projects that enhance the civic welfare and common good, to register to vote, and to participate actively in political campaigns and other change-oriented activities. Further, such activities create space for constant reflection about how such experiences might shape their future careers and life work.

D. Students help build and sustain genuinely public cultures full of conversation, argument, and discussion about the meaning of their learning, their work, and their institutions as a whole. Students encounter and learn from others different from themselves in experience, culture, racial background, ideologies, and views.

E. Students have multiple opportunities to help create knowledge and do scholarship relevant to and grounded in the public problems of society, while learning rigorous methodologies and the demanding crafts of fine scholarship.

2. Faculty (including teaching staff)

What will it mean for the faculty to be filled with the democratic spirit?

A. Faculty help create, participate in, and take responsibility for a vibrant public culture at their institutions. Such a public culture values their moral and civic imaginations and their judgments, insights, and passions, while it recognizes and rewards their publicly engaged scholarship, lively teaching, and their contributions through public work.

B. Faculty members have opportunities and rewards for socially engaged scholarship through genuine civic partnerships, based on respect and recognition of different ways of knowing and different kinds of contributions, in which expertise is "on tap, not on top."

C. Faculty teaching includes community-based learning and undergraduate action research that develops substantive knowledge, cultivates practical skills, and strengthens social responsibility and public identity for citizenship in a diverse democratic society.

D. Faculties' professional service is conceived of and valued as public work in which disciplinary and professional knowledge and expertise contributes to the welfare of society, and also can occasion the public work of many other citizens.

E. Faculty members are encouraged and prepared when they desire to pursue "public scholarship," relating their work to the pressing problems of society, providing consultations and expertise, and creating opportunities to work with community and civic partners in co-creating things of public value.

F. Faculty members engage in diverse cross-disciplinary work projects that improve the university and create things of lasting value and significance.

G. Faculty are encouraged to mentor students, providing out-of-classroom opportunities to build communities of learning on and off campus. These opportunities have the potential to expose students to the public work of faculty whose own moral imaginations and public talents are vitally engaged in relevant scholarship and work of social significance.

3. Staff

What will it mean for staff to be filled with the democratic spirit?

A. Staff, in association with institutions, make visible their multiple (and now largely invisible) experiences, talents, and contributions to student learning and to the community–building process at institutions of higher education. Further, their rich contributions to the broader intellectual enterprise of our institutions become more visible and recognized.

B. Staff build upon and receive recognition for the often extensive ties that many have with the local community, seeing such community knowledge and connection as a resource for community-university partnerships, for student learning, for engaged scholarship, and for the broad intellectual life of the institution.

C. Staff gain a voice in governance, receive fair salaries and benefits, and are encouraged to participate in ongoing intellectual conversation and public life. The staff assist in the creation of multiple opportunities for staff development and continuing education.

D. Faculty and others come to recognize that educating students for democracy is an institution-wide enterprise in which staff play key roles in providing opportunities for public work, dialogue with others far different from oneself, and democratic practice on campus. Staff are encouraged to work with faculty to examine and change the campus culture to support engagement.

4. Administrators

What will it mean for administrative leaders to be filled with the democratic spirit?

A. It will mean that the president and other leaders give consistent and sustained voice to the broad public purposes of our institutions. This will involve articulating the philosophical and intellectual meaning of research universities as agents of democracy, helping to highlight the specific and unique quality and character of their particular institutions, and making visible the public work and contributions of faculty, staff, and students.

B. Administrators take leadership in creating institutions that evolve to reflect changing demographics and to engage the diverse cultures of our places and our world. This leadership includes promoting hiring policies to achieve broad representation and social diversity among faculty members and administrative staff, not simply out of moral imperative but out of full recognition that a diversity of backgrounds, cultures, and views is essential to a vital public culture within our institutions.

C. Administrators create and improve infrastructures that sustain creativity, flexibility, and public contribution in many forms, and develop mechanisms for a continuing process of collective self-examination and reflection on organizational learning.

D. Administrators support and create multiple opportunities to develop the public leadership skills and capacities of diverse members of the institution.

5. The institution

What will it mean for our institutions, comprised of faculty, students, staff, and administrators and guided by the deliberations of trustees, to be filled with the democratic spirit as whole institutions?

A. This will mean that our institutions develop admissions policies and financial arrangements that are shaped by the imperative to create diverse "publics" within our institutions. This imperative understands economic, ethnic, racial, religious, and ideological diversity to be a crucial ingredient in learning cultures for the world that is emerging.

B. Trustees, like administrators, think of themselves as public philosophers as well as stewards and promoters of institutional resources, seeking to articulate and to advance the public and democratic purposes of higher education.

C. Stakeholders in our universities define institutional work as a whole in ways that highlight civic mission broadly, that tie work to large public questions and issues, and that unearth distinctive civic histories, cultures, and contributions. In this context, part of the challenge is for leaders, at all levels, to develop a variety of infrastructures of support, including multidimensional understandings of "scholarship" in promotion and tenure procedures for faculty work that serves its civic mission. Such support includes creating high standards, demanding expectations, and rigorous methods of evaluation of engaged scholarship, teaching, and public work.

D. The university creates and sustains long-term partnerships with communities, with K-12 schools in an integrated system of democratic education and education for democracy, and with a range of civic bodies. These will be framed in ways that reflect the university's commitments to and self-interests in community building and civic vitality, that integrate community experience into the learning of students and the professional service opportunities for staff, and that fully reflect the public dimensions of scholarly work.

E. The university promotes public understanding of its work as an essential part of its mission, recognizing an institutional responsibility for publicly useable knowledge, developing formal structures to sustain such uses.

F. The university similarly creates structures that generate a more porous and interactive flow of knowledge between university and communities. These aim at making the university's knowledge more accessible to communities, and constantly informing university scholarship with the experiences, knowledge, and public issues that arise from the life of communities. Such structures might include public forums co-created with community partners that enliven public cultures and conversations in locales; infrastructures of support for public scholarship based on a partnership model between university and community and civic groups; and efforts to disseminate exciting scholarship and findings.

Research universities and leaders from all levels of our institutions need to rise to the occasion of our challenge as a democracy on the edge of a new millennium. We need to help catalyze and lead a national campaign or movement that reinvigorates the public purposes and civic mission of our great research universities and higher education broadly. We need to renew for the next century the idea that our institutions of higher education are, in a vital sense, both agents and architects of a flourishing democracy, bridges between individuals' work and the larger world.

In this spirit and to these ends, we call upon all associations, professions, disciplines, faculty bodies, employee associations, and student organizations related to research universities and higher education to consider these questions, to debate, revise, and expand these propositions, and to join with us in renewing the civic mission of American higher education. Our challenge in a time of change is to transform knowledge into wisdom and to make democracy come alive, for ourselves and for those who follow after us.

Reading

1. How does the *Wingspread Declaration* define the need for universities to be civically and democratically engaged with local communities?

2. How does each group identified in the *Wingspread Declaration* demonstrate its "democratic spirit" (para. 5)?

3. How does the *Wingspread Declaration* define the benefits for students to attend such universities?

4. How does it define the obstacles to a civically engaged university?

Inquiring

1. The *Wingspread Declaration* consistently speaks about democracy, civic values, and public purpose. These powerful terms carry a lot of emotional appeal. They are also terms with meanings that are hard to capture, however. As you read the *Wingspread Declaration*, what do you believe the authors specifically mean

by the university supporting democracy? Do they mean civic engagement? What does this work look like in practice to them? Do you believe such work should be an important element in a student's education? Why or why not?

2. The authors of the *Wingspread Declaration* are clearly concerned that the traditional public role of the university has been lost. What do they believe led to the university abandoning its public role? What has to change for the university to once again take up this work? Do you believe such work is the mission of the university?

3. The *Wingspread Declaration* provides guidelines for how universities should create "structures that generate a more porous and interactive flow of knowledge between university and communities. These aim at making the university's knowledge more accessible to communities, and constantly informing university scholarship with the experiences, knowledge, and public issues that arise from the life of communities" (para. 20). Spend several days exploring your own university. Walk around campus and look at what types of events are offered. Search the university Web site for academic programs or offices that seem dedicated to such work. Then, as a class, discuss the value of such an "interactive flow of knowledge between universities and communities." Do you see it improving your own education? Can you see evidence that it is improving the communities around your campus?

Composing

1. The *Wingspread Declaration* provides many examples of the work the authors hope students undertake as part of their education. For instance, they imagine having students "help build and sustain genuinely public cultures full of conversation, argument, and discussion about the meaning of their learning, their work, and their institutions as a whole" (para. 20). They also imagine that students will "encounter and learn from others different from themselves in experience, culture, racial background, ideologies and views" (para. 20). As described, there is little doubt such experiences might indeed be beneficial to the students and the community members, but these examples are also quite idealistic, devoid of the complications such experiences often entail. Choose an example from the *Wingspread Declaration* that you believe matches an experience you have had. Contrast the ideal description with reality by writing an essay that compares your own learning experience with the description. How were the two similar? In what notable ways were they different?

2. The authors of the *Wingspread Declaration* seemed concerned that "students" have become "customers." Although that is seemingly just a change in terms, the authors see it as representing a more fundamental shift in how the university conducts its business. The authors describe how business forces working in society have negatively impacted research institutions, ultimately

casting public service, universities, and students in a commercial light (paras. 8–12). Do you believe the concerns expressed in the *Wingspread Declaration* were justified, especially considering that it was written in 1999? Has the university become just like a business, its students customers, their goals cast only in economic terms? To answer this question, use your own university as a research site. Explore its Web site, admission documents, and other official materials. How do they describe the goals of an education? How might the authors of *Wingspread Declaration* respond? Do you find such a response persuasive?

3. The *Wingspread Declaration* was written in 1999, before many aspects of Web 2.0 had come into being. Facebook, for instance, was launched in 2004, YouTube in 2005, and Twitter in 2006. This work, then, only imagines democracy and civic engagement in terms of traditional practices such as public forums. Write an essay in which you discuss how the advent of social media might have altered the very workings of democracy. If that is the case, what does it mean to be civically engaged as a student, faculty, and university now? In essence, write an essay that attempts to frame the university as a publicly engaged actor in the era of social media. In writing this essay, you might find it useful to use a structure similar to the *Wingspread Declaration*, with a general statement about the work of the university followed by a set of proposed actions by students, faculty, and administration.

Connecting

The *Wingspread Declaration* imagines a bold future for the university. It is a future in which faculty, students, and neighbors work collaboratively to support local communities. The work of Andrew Delbanco (p. 70), however, points to some of the historical forces that might work against such lofty goals and on where and how money might be spent at the university. Write an essay in which you discuss whether "community partnership" work should be a primary goal of "higher education" in the current economic climate.

Projects for Chapter 3

The following are group and class projects. You should talk to your instructor about which projects you will be completing in your course.

PROJECT 1 Evidence of Intellectuals

Gramsci argues that "all men are intellectuals, one could therefore say: but not all men have in society the function of intellectuals" (p. 52). One way to read this statement is that all forms of knowledge are equal—that everyone's insight deserves to be respected. It states an important moral value. It is unclear, however, how this value might help us decide between differing opinions. It does not provide us a road map for how to assess the different evidence that individuals might use to support their beliefs, and when you write for the university, the type of evidence you use to support an argument is vital.

As a class, divide into five equal groups. Assign each group a reading from this chapter. Have the group list the types of evidence used by each author, developing categories to define what type of evidence it represents (statistics, personal experience, historical evidence, etc.). Once this list is done, each group should share their work (both categories and evidence) with the class. Have one student write each group's list on the classroom's dry-erase board or blackboard, or somewhere else the rest of the class can see it.

Now consider the types of essays you have been asked to write so far in your education. Does one type of evidence seem better suited to the typical essay you have been asked to write for your classes than others? If so, what conclusions might you draw about what is valued as knowledge, as intellectual, in your educational experience? Can you draw conclusions about what type of knowledge is least valued? Finally, what type of writer have you had to become to gain the position of a successful intellectual in college?

PROJECT 2 Writing across the Curriculum (and Beyond)

Writing as college faculty, Bartholomae (p. 56) and Delbanco (p. 70) speak about the common values that should inform a university education. Bartholomae speaks about a common intellectual stance that students will have to take toward writing to enter the "university" successfully. Delbanco argues that a common stance for universities should be to embrace diversity in student populations. In their writings excerpted in this chapter, neither author details what such commitments look like in terms of actual classes. Neither makes clear how these commitments translate into what students study, what they are asked to write, and how they are assessed. A university might be invented through their writings, but it is unclear the type of work it is meant to produce in practice—in detail—through actual courses.

As a class, bring in the syllabi of all your current classes. Break into small groups of three to four students. Spend some time analyzing the syllabi in terms of the following questions:

1. What type or types of knowledge do these syllabi value? Do you see common definitions of what students should know? Of what students should be able to do?

2. What type or types of writing do these syllabi value? Do they share common assumptions about what it means to write in the university?

3. What type or types of student bodies do these syllabi imagine? Do you see a commitment to diversity in the works assigned?

4. Can you develop a common sense of the mission of the university based on these syllabi?

Once all groups have done this work, one member of each group should share the group's answers. Now decide what type of "university" these courses develop. Does it mesh with Bartholomae's and Delbanco's visions? Does it meet your own goals for a university education?

PROJECT 3 What Was (and Is) Your College

Many of the readings in this section have argued that universities should take on a public role. For Delbanco (p. 70), this public commitment is expressed as a commitment to a diverse population and an affordable college system. For the *Wingspread Declaration* (p. 93), it is expressed in terms of professors working with communities and students linking their education to the neighborhoods around the university. Every college, however, will take up this public commitment in a different way, based on its own history and on its own traditions.

Before the next class, research how your own college understands its public commitments. You might begin by doing a search on the college's Web site, typing in key words from the *Wingspread Declaration*, such as "service-learning movement," "community partnership," and "democratic values." You might research the cost of your college versus the average income of the community surrounding the college. Finally, you might talk to individual students or professors to see how they understand the mission of the university.

Discuss your findings at your next class meeting. How might you describe your college's public commitments? What values does your college express? What programs does its support? Does it meet the goals of the *Wingspread Declaration*? Do you believe that the *Wingspread Declaration* should even be part of the goals of a college?

PROJECT 4 Performing Community

A central emphasis in *Pro(se)letariets* (p. 80) is the belief that individuals and communities have their own organic understanding of how the world works, often expressed in their unique ways of talking and writing. In this sense, *Pro(se) letariets* might be seen as an example of "organic intellectuals" organizing to support their own vision of education, yet it also demonstrates that when these values and understandings are placed within a grade school or college classroom, conflict emerges. As demonstrated in the excerpted writings, the student does not always win.

It is difficult, however, to gain an awareness of how a community understands itself—how its way of interacting on an individual basis—represents a particular set of values, a particular belief about the goals of education. This difficulty makes it even harder to assess whether the university is attempting to work with (not against) a community's vision.

Later in the semester, you will develop skills in interviewing individuals to gain this understanding. For the moment, however, you can use public forms of writing to begin this work. You can also use these public forms to understand how the goals of the university support (or fail to support) the goals of the community. Over the next week, begin to collect the writing that circulates in the community in which your college exists. Don't just grab the local newspaper: pick up flyers, church bulletins, and zines; collect writings from local Internet forums, Twitter posts, YouTube channels, and community Facebook pages; explore local government, nonprofit organizations, and community group Web sites for community strategic plans or development efforts. Bring these materials to class.

Using what you have found, what conclusions can you draw about how the community understands itself? What values bring these different pieces of writing together into a singular vision? While recognizing that much more research would need to be done, what can you tentatively say about how your college supports (or fails to support) the goals of the community?

PROJECT 5 The Students' Right to Their Own Language

Much of the discussion in this chapter has been broad, theoretical, and perhaps a bit idealistic. In the abstract, few might disagree that organic and traditional intellectuals should be valued equally, with each seen as bringing unique and important insights to the conversation at hand. Nor might there be much debate about arguments claiming academic discourse can be an inventive form of writing; numerous examples of similar arguments could no doubt be brought forth to support such a claim.

In the day-to-day reality of students and teachers situated in specific college writing programs, however, it might be difficult to encapsulate how this concept might work in practice. What does a belief in organic intellectuals mean for students who enter the class with their communal ways of speaking? How might teachers be affected by a program's pressure to enable students to become traditional intellectuals? How might this tension play out in the actual writing done by students for class?

One way to begin discussing these questions is to consider the Students' Right to Their Own Language resolution, approved by the Conference on College Composition and Communication (CCCC), a professional organization of college writing instructors. Since 1974, when it was first adopted, the CCCC has endorsed and reaffirmed a resolution that states the following:

> We affirm the students' right to their own patterns and varieties of language—the dialects of their nurture or whatever dialects in which they find their own identity and style. Language scholars long ago denied that the myth of a standard American dialect has any validity. The claim that any one dialect is unacceptable amounts to an attempt of one social group to exert its dominance over another. Such a claim leads to false advice for speakers and writers, and immoral advice for humans. A nation proud of its diverse heritage and its cultural and racial variety will preserve its heritage of dialects. We affirm strongly that teachers must have the experiences and training that will enable them to respect diversity and uphold the right of students to their own language.

You can read the entire statement on the Web site of the National Council of Teachers of English (www.ncte.org).

This resolution is interesting in that it argues that students should not be stopped from using the "dialects of their nurture or whatever dialects in which they find their own identity and style." In effect, the CCCC equates a student's language with his or her home community's values. In this sense, the resolution represents an attempt to authorize the organic knowledge of the student in the classroom by limiting teacher authority to enforce a "standard American dialect." Although the resolution does not stop the student who wants to learn the "standard," it is clearly an important recognition of nonacademic ways of knowing, writing, and speaking in a writing classroom.

As someone who has been reflecting on the possible importance of "organic" and "traditional" knowledge in learning how to write, both for college and beyond, how do you respond to this resolution? Do you believe students have a right to their own language? Do you agree with what it might mean for the goals of a college writing class? That is, which set of goals do you believe represent your own interests in taking a college writing course?

One way to begin to answer these questions is to consider your experience so far in this course. Where do you see this book positioning itself in relationship to the students' right as defined by the CCCC? Go through the chapters you have read and annotate these moments. (For a refresher on annotating strategies, see p. 11.) How might your class frame a resolution about the role of organic and traditional intellectual knowledge in your writing classroom? How might you, as a collective, balance the competing values and demands inherent in a college writing course? How might you frame its work in relationship to the surrounding community? That is, how might you revise the Students' Right to Their Own Language resolution to reflect your class's emerging sense of the purpose and goals for taking a course in college writing?

PROJECT 6 The Forgotten Bottom Remembered

Throughout this text, two consistent values have been expressed:

1. Community members must be understood as intellectuals and as having the authority to determine how their neighborhood is represented.

2. Communities have their own sense of good writing and how writing should be used to represent their communities.

Interpreting these values and turning these values into actual practices can be difficult, however. In fact, deciding who has the authority to choose how a community is "represented" is a central moment of tension in almost any project that brings community and university members together.

This tension is well represented in a story about the Forgotten Bottom community in Grays Ferry, a Philadelphia neighborhood. A class at a nearby university worked with Forgotten Bottom residents to create a book, based on resident interviews, that would show the tolerance, friendship, and genuine affection that was the hallmark of this multicultural neighborhood. The book was also intended to distance the community from a nearby neighborhood's history of hate crimes. Because many of the Forgotten Bottom residents were older, the book was also intended to be an indirect history of the neighborhood and the city. As part of the project, many residents shared photographs from their childhoods, sharing memories in their interviews based on these images. For many, it was an opportunity to reflect on a meaningful and joyful life.

When the book was finally published, however, many Forgotten Bottom residents were concerned about the cover. There was a sense that the cover did not accurately reflect the neighborhood's history or self-image. There was anger that the university partner did not share the cover image or the final versions of the published interviews before publishing the book. Indeed, community residents demanded that, at the very least, a new cover be created. (There was also some concern about how the resident interviews were represented in the book.)

Here are both covers:

Original Cover

New City Community Press/
Jaeyun Jung

Revised Cover

New City Community Press/
Jaeyun Jung

As a class, discuss what you see as the "message" of each cover. Why would members of the Forgotten Bottom community be concerned about the original cover? How might the revised cover appear to address those concerns? Indeed, how does the Forgotten Bottom story illustrate the potential problems of such publicly engaged work? How does it illustrate the need for clear guidelines about how decisions will be made among community and university partners? Does the *Wingspread Declaration* provide guidance on the proper role of the university? Would Bartholomae (p. 56) or Delbanco (p. 70) see such efforts as even being the work of the "university"?

After discussing these questions, break into small groups of three to five. Develop guidelines that would detail the different responsibilities of the university and community intellectuals with a goal of creating guidelines that would stop such a situation from occurring again. How might these guidelines value the insights of the community? Of university scholars? Of students? What might it mean in practice to value both traditional knowledge and organic knowledge?

Writing Classrooms: Discovering Writing within Classroom Communities

The readings in this chapter are designed to help you think about the many ways in which writing can work in a classroom. As a jumping-off point, here's a poem about one student's classroom experience — and how that experience felt at odds with her life elsewhere.

Untitled

You sit still
Stiff
Rigid as the walls that climb behind you
Walls plastered with portraits
Men of science, math and literature
They told you the men were important
They told you to learn their names
They told you to commit their words to heart
And to take their thoughts as truth
But for now
In this moment
Your only thoughts are your bones
And of their struggle to hold you upright
They are heavy lead pipes
At odds with the smooth contours of your wooden desk

You notice how the others sit with ease
How they raise their hands as if they were feathers
But your hands are too heavy to lift
A woman stands
Paces
Her mouth moves in rhythm less motion
And the drone she spins makes you think of the factory
Where machines buzz and whir in mindless constancy
You realize the factory is your place
Where your time and your body are your gifts
Gifts that you are forced to give
And which are never returned
The clock ticks
Steady
You follow the second hand with your eyes
A bell rings out and the crowd surges
Up and out and away
Only you remain as the walls crumble into plaster puddles
Replace themselves with colder, grayer walls
Walls without portraits
Walls that house the whir and buzz of machines
There are no men of science here

—Natalie Pascarella, Junior, Writing Major
From *Pro(se)letariets: The Writing of the Trans-Atlantic Worker
Writer Federation*

■   ■   ■

As both Mayra Castillo Rangel's and Natalie Pascarella's writings demonstrate (see pp. 20 and 111, respectively), you enter a classroom with a wealth of knowledge, some gained in textbooks and some gained through daily life. Then, through conversations with your teachers and classmates, you slowly learn new knowledge and new skills that you hope will enable you to fulfill personal as well as communal goals. In this way, the classroom, at its best, acts as an incubator for you to grow into the person you hope to be in the future.

The classroom is also a space where you are asked to make important decisions about who counts as an intellectual. From whom you can learn? With whom you can imagine a different way to see the world? Sometimes your teachers determine who counts by announcing the importance of particular authors; at other times, a class research project allows you to discover new and important voices.

Throughout this process, you are engaged in the work of learning *who* is an intellectual, but you are also being asked to *become* an intellectual. You are asked to read and write in a certain way, with a certain conception of depth, rigor, and understanding. You are also told to write for a particular audience and enact specific strategies to gain their interest. These definitions or strategies, though, may or may not intersect with your own sense of intellectual work based on your own experiences with intellectuals in your community. In this chapter, you will focus on this more immediate level of decision making and the ways in which classrooms engage you in the continual task of deciding and enacting what it means to read and write like an intellectual. That is, rather than assume that the academic community is correct in its definition, in this chapter you will consider the following questions. What does it mean to do intellectual work? What does such work look like? To whom is it addressed? To what goal is it pointed? What larger purpose might it serve?

As you undertake this work, you will also be provided the opportunity to test your definition in a variety of contexts—the classroom, the campus, and the community—because what you ultimately decide counts as intellectual work will necessarily place you in relationship to a specific audience, with specific expectations. This chapter, then, will also allow you to act on your decision and test the usefulness of its possibilities.

As before, you will not be alone in these efforts. In addition to the support of your teacher and classmates, this chapter contains the insights of writers and community activists who have also attempted to think through how work in the academy frames, supports, or hinders certain types of intellectual projects. In the work of Gerald Graff, Carmen Kynard, and Christopher Wilkey, you will find models of writers who attempt to think through the experience of students in writing classrooms. In doing so, they attempt to develop a more open and inviting atmosphere for the knowledge students bring with them from families and communities into the classroom. These authors see writing as an opportunity to explore issues, imagining that opening up such a dialogue is the hallmark of intellectual work. Through engaging with their ideas, you will be able to join an ongoing conversation about the purpose of classrooms and further develop your own goals for undertaking intellectual work.

Too often, you are asked to sit in classrooms and listen to professors lecture about the value of an education, an experience where lists of important intellectuals are often handed to students to be studied and admired. Yet you have your own views on what schooling should consist of and how it should be structured. You have your own set of community intellectuals through which to judge their academic counterparts. What is needed is a space that will allow you to draw together the communal and the academic to develop your own vision.

References and notes for the readings can be found in the appendix on page 427.

GERALD GRAFF

The Problem Problem and Other Oddities of Academic Discourse

Courtesy of Gerald Graff

Gerald Graff is a professor of English and education at the University of Illinois at Chicago (UIC). During his career, Graff has become a public figure on the goals of a liberal arts education, once appearing on the *Oprah Winfrey Show* to discuss the importance of the humanities. Early in his career, Graff focused on the importance of literature as a space for rational discussion of public issues. Later, he helped found Teachers for a Democratic Culture in an attempt to create space for other academics to take on an active role in public debates over education. More recently, he has turned his attention to the classroom. Here his primary concern is to argue that although teachers might understand the necessity of a particular type of academic work—studying literature, for instance—their students may not. Rather than mask over such misunderstandings, he argues that this implicit conflict should be the focus of classroom discussion.

In the following excerpt from his book *Clueless in Academe: How Schooling Obscures the Life of the Mind* (2003), Graff attempts to represent the experience of students when given the requirement to "read deeply" into a piece of writing.

■ ■ ■

As teachers we often proceed as if the rationale of our most basic academic practices is understood and shared by our students, even when we get plenty of signs that it is not. We take for granted, for example, that reflecting in a self-conscious way about experience—"intellectualizing"—is something our students naturally see the point of and want to learn to do better. If they don't, after all, why are they in school? At the same time, we cannot help noticing that many students are skeptical about the value of such intellectualizing. When students do poorly, the reasons often have less to do with their lack of ability than with their reluctance to become the introspective type of people who relish and excel at such tasks.

Aversion to the apparent pretentiousness of intellectual ways of communicating is often central to this reluctance. In *The Unschooled Mind* Howard Gardner observes that the problems students have in comprehending texts are often magnified by their "insensitivity . . . to the vocabulary of argument—'contend,' 'hypothesize,' 'refute,' 'contradict'. . . ."[1] Gardner is right about the connection between poor reading comprehension and students' lack of a "vocabulary of argument." The problem, however, often lies not in the students' "insensitivity" to this vocabulary but their disinclination to acquire it. In some high schools and colleges, students would risk ostracism if they use expressions like "hypothesize" or "I contend." As the saying goes, nobody likes a smart-ass.

Hillel Crandus, a teacher of eleventh-grade English, asked his class to write short papers (which Crandus shared with me) expressing how they felt about analysis, especially the kind of close interpretative reading of texts that's the staple of literature courses. One student, call her Karen, wrote, "Personally, I don't like analyzing everything that happens to me. Some of it would be a big waste of time. I sometimes find myself analyzing dreams that I've had, but it's usually pretty pointless. To me a lot of things happen for a very obvious reason that does not need a lot of discussion or insight." Another stated flatly that "the only thing that overanalyzing leads to is boredom."

In my experience, the distaste Karen feels for "analyzing everything that happens" to you, and the belief that some things "happen for a very obvious reason" and therefore need no further inquiry, don't necessarily disappear once students move on to college, though by then students have become more guarded about betraying such views in the presence of their teachers. As a University of Chicago undergraduate put it, "'Academic' type people take life too seriously and don't let themselves read for enjoyment. There's more to life than intellect . . . you can read for fun." A UIC freshman told his composition instructor that "I don't want to dig deeper into the meaning of something. What I say is what I mean." Whenever I survey students on the question, many admit they have a problem with academia's tendency to turn everything it touches into grist for the analytic mill, almost as if teachers were deliberately trying to spoil everybody's fun.

In this chapter, I look at some standard academic practices that often seem second nature to teachers and A-students but come across to many students as bizarre, counterintuitive, or downright nonsensical. These perceptions of the absurd nature of intellectual practices underlie the familiar stereotypes of the educated: eggheads, nerds, sissies, snobs, braniacs, know-it-alls, brown-nosers, control freaks, ideologues, and manipulative propagandists. These characterizations may be rooted in misperceptions of the life of the mind, but ones that are unlikely to be dispelled unless teachers flush them out and address them.

5

The Problem Problem

Nothing better exemplifies the apparently counterintuitive nature of intellectual practices than their preoccupation with what often appear to be bogus "problems." Academic assignments ask students not only to become aggressive know-it-alls, but to cultivate problems to an extent that seems perverse or bizarre. I call this syndrome the "problem problem."

One reason why students often resist the academic fixation with problems is suggested by Wayne Booth, Gregory Colomb, and Joseph Williams in their valuable primer on academic writing, *The Craft of Research*. Booth, Colomb, and Williams discuss the difficulties inexperienced students have with the conventions used to set up the problems that form the starting point of most expository essays.[2] Yet the difficulties students have in constructing the kind of problem that launches an essay stem not only from their unfamiliarity with the conventions of problem-posing, but from deeper uncertainties about the "problematizing" role itself.

Booth, Colomb, and Williams do not mention these uncertainties, but they provide a clue to them when they distinguish between problems that are recognized to be such and those that are not.[3] Problems of the first kind, such as earning a living, finding a mate, curing heart diseases, preventing air pollution, or eliminating poverty and homelessness come to us with an apparently *pre-given* quality. These problems are already so widely acknowledged that writers can take them up without having to make an argument for seeing them as problems, though there are situations in which they might have to (for example, talking about poverty with an audience of social Darwinists). Many of the problems with which academics deal, however, lack this pre-given quality, as when they concern the meanings of words, abstract concepts, and texts, or the actions of people long dead. In such cases, where we can't assume that others will see the problem we are taking up *as* a problem, we have to work to sell them on its reality and importance. Academics not only cultivate problems that are unrecognized as such, they like to *invent* problems that most people are unaware of, or look for new ways to describe already recognized problems.

In this penchant for problematizing, academic research scholars resemble avant-garde artists who "defamiliarize" previously familiar subjects, using alienation effects to make what seems obvious and unproblematic look strange. But despite the lip service given to Socrates' maxim that the unexamined life is not worth living, searching out new problems can seem profoundly counterintuitive: are there not already enough problems in the world without our straining to invent new ones? From a certain commonsense point of view, academia's cultivation of problems looks manufactured, perverse, and silly, and academic problem-posers resemble the dotty scientists on the island of Laputa in Jonathan Swift's *Gulliver's Travels*, who grapple earnestly, for instance, with the problem of turning excrement back into its original food. . . .

The academic faith in the singular virtue of finding problems in subjects— 10
love, in Gornick's case—generally thought to be unproblematic seems especially
bizarre and forced when the problems have to do with the meanings of texts. The
idea that, below their apparent surface, texts harbor deep meanings that cry out
for interpretation, analysis, and debate is one of those assumptions that seems so
normal once we are socialized into academia that we forget how counterintuitive
it can be. In fact, this assumption has probably never been comprehensible, much
less convincing, to much of the general population or even to some academics.
(A certain college Dean is said to have wondered aloud why entire departments
are needed to study the books he has no trouble reading on the train to work
every day.) An exception might seem to be scriptural texts, whose meanings have
been picked apart and debated for so many centuries that the practice does not
seem odd—except to sects that see even scriptural interpretation and theological
debate as coming between the believer and God.

In their written responses, many of Crandus's eleventh-graders confess that
most classroom analysis of texts and interpretations seems tedious and pointless, an infinite regress that goes nowhere. As one student, Elaina, put it, "A
student will make a comment that, maybe to me, seems straightforward, yet
we still seem to dig deeper into just what that comment meant." Karen, the
student whose reservations toward "analyzing everything that happens to me"
I quoted above, wrote as follows about a class discussion of Richard Wright's
autobiography, *Black Boy*:

> [I]t seems to me that we analyzed things that didn't seem to have
> much to analyze. For instance, the fire episode in the beginning of
> the book. In my opinion, Richard started the fire out of curiosity
> and boredom. The discussion we had in class got into things like
> it symbolizes his imagination or internal impulses, or even how he
> feels about his racial impression. I'm not saying that these aren't
> good ideas, but I think it's making something out of nothing. . . .
>
> Another reason I do not like [to] analyze, though this might
> sound arrogant, is because it is not important to me. I don't care
> what the fire in *Black Boy* symbolizes. It doesn't really make [any]
> difference to me. To some people, it does make a difference, and
> that's fine with me. But I don't really see how this helps me out in
> my life, the past, the present, or the future. It could end up help-
> ing me a lot, you never really know. I know it will help me out in
> college English classes.

Karen suspects that the symbolism attributed to works like *Black Boy* is simply not *there* in the text—in any case, she can't see it. Just as for her "a lot of
things happen for a very obvious reason that does not need a lot of discussion

or insight," what a text means is apparent on the surface and therefore needs no analysis. But even if deeper meanings are indeed present in the text, Karen adds, she doesn't care, though she acknowledges that such things do matter to some people and might some day to her, if only to help her get through college English courses. . . .

The problem is exacerbated by uncertainties about *intention*—a concept that has itself been endlessly debated by aestheticians and philosophers of language. Jay, another of Crandus's eleventh-graders, finds classroom analysis of textual intentions "not interesting": "Like when we are asked to think about the way an author would respond to our responses, how are we supposed to know? As far as I know most of us are not close personal friends with any of the authors we have read so far. So why would we know what the author would think?"

Laura writes that, when asked why something happens the way it does in a text, "I would have trouble analyzing why it happened because I wasn't there, I have never personally talked to the author. . . ." A tenth- grader at another school expressed a view similar to Jay's and Laura's in a symposium on Shakespeare's *The Tempest*, when I asked her if she thought Shakespeare shared the preference she had expressed for Caliban over Prospero: "I wouldn't know," she replied. "I never met the man." As these students see it, either a text's intention is obvious on the face of it or it isn't. If it isn't, we can phone the author and ask what his or her intention was, but if the author is dead or otherwise unavailable, there is nothing much to be done. So again, where's the problem?

If what authors intend does not seem a genuine problem, then making a problem of *unintended* psychological or social meanings in texts seems all the more patently a waste of time. A college teacher reports the following exchange between a freshman student on Mark Twain's *Adventures of Huckleberry Finn*. The teacher, hoping to get her class to see the ambivalent treatment of racial injustice in the novel, called attention to the apparent discrepancy between the novel's satire on slavery and racism and the many passages in which the slave Jim is made a comic butt of Huck and Tom Sawyer's pranks. One student, however, offered an explanation of the discrepancy that seemed more plausible to him than the presence of cultural contradictions.

> Teacher: So what do you all make of the apparent contradiction here?
> Student: Hey, maybe Mark Twain was having a bad day. Or maybe he just didn't care.
> Teacher: How's that?
> Student: I mean, maybe he was just lazy, or he had to make a deadline?

The teacher retorted that even if we assume that Twain was lazy, indifferent, or in a hurry, that would not explain why these qualities expressed themselves in such a racially coded way. She realized, however, that her response was not convincing the student nor many of his classmates. They resisted entertaining the kind of richly symptomatic reading that she, as a good intellectual, was angling for, one in which textual anomalies betray deeper, more interesting problems.

The instructor reflected that she had not prepared the class for looking at contradictions in texts, or even mentioned the topic. She also reflected that it had only been in graduate school that she had discovered that texts might be all the more interesting and valuable for the contradictions they contained. In both her high school and college she had been taught that great works of art are unified, and she had learned to write papers that discovered the principle of unity in the works' themes, language, or symbolism. If there were contradictions in a work, it presumably was second-rate. In her future classes, she resolved to introduce the issue of textual contradictions and discuss it with students rather than expect them to watch for such contradictions or to know what to say about them. . . .

There is a difference, in other words, between legitimate critical skepticism toward over-the-top symbolic readings that fail to justify themselves with reasons and evidence, and the anti-intellectual dismissal of any reading that challenges the received understanding of a text or event. That said, however, it is important that teachers not dismiss students' skepticism of the academic obsession with the problem of hidden meanings. Unless those doubts are respected and fairly aired and discussed, students will feel they have no choice but to play along with an interpretative game whose validity they do not accept.

When this happens, students repress their anxiety and alienation and some end up resorting to Cliffs Notes — or increasingly nowadays to the Internet. In his recent book, *The Crafty Reader*, Robert Scholes quotes a sampling of recent Internet postings by desperate students who have been asked to produce accounts of what something in a text means:

1. Subject: Huck Finn symbolism of river.
   I am writing a paper on the symbolism of the Mississippi River in Huck Finn. How is the river a symbolic mother to Huck? I need examples from the book too. Please help fast.

2. Subject: Oedipus Rex — Irony
   I need help finding Irony in Oedipus Rex. There's supposedly a lot in there but I've been assigned Scene II and there's only so much.

3. Subject: symbolism: gardens
   what do gardens symbolize? are there any sexual innuendos? anything one could dig up on the symbolism of gardens would be of great help. Thanks.[4]

What is striking here is that the writers of these posts see interpretation as an occult process rather than one that might be mastered by learning disciplined reading. As they see it, rivers and gardens in themselves have some fixed but secret meaning that you either get or don't get; if you're one of those who doesn't, you can only get on the Web and try to find one of those who do.

Some, of course, would argue that this kind of student desperation only shows what a serious mistake it has been to put the interpretation of hidden meaning at the center of the academic humanities, thereby turning texts into crossword puzzles and trivializing reading. To me, however, these student postings demonstrate not the folly of asking students to search for deep meanings in texts, but the failure to give students the help they need to conduct that search well, with a sense of how and why it can be useful. As Scholes comments, "These students are crying for help."[5] Students who run to the Web to find out what gardens and rivers symbolize have no other recourse when their teachers treat such questions as self-evident. The practice of searching out and inventing "problems," whether posed by texts or other objects of study, needs to be discussed with students, with an open invitation to air their doubts about the practice and its value.

Negativism and Oppositionality

For many students, academia's fixation on seemingly superfluous problems seems linked with another off-putting trait, its relentless negativism and oppositionality. In *Errors and Expectations*, her classic book on the problems of basic-writing students, Mina P. Shaughnessy touches on this trait in describing the problems novice writers have when they are "expected to make 'new' or arguable statements and then develop a case for them."[6] To make "a case" for yourself, to make statements that are "arguable," you must be oppositional and defensive, if not cantankerous. Furthermore, the value academia places on making "arguable" statements can seem not only needlessly embattled, but flatly illogical. Why would any sane person go out of his or her way to say things that are "arguable"? Just as common sense suggests that it is foolish to invent problems that did not previously exist, it also suggests that the point of writing and speaking is to make statements that *nobody* is likely to dispute, so that provoking disagreement is a sign that the writer has failed. A sound essay, according to this way of thinking, consists of uncontroversially true statements. In fact, this way of thinking once dominated the academic disciplines, where knowledge was seen not as a conversation or debate but an accumulation of positivist truths, a sort of pyramid of discrete facts built up brick by isolated brick.

20   As often, however, common sense has things wrong, which explains why we do not find many essays with titles like "Human Beings Have Elbows," "Breathing Is Possible," and "Washington Is the Nation's Capital," though all these propositions are perfectly true. As Booth, Colomb, and Williams point out, "Readers think a claim significant to the degree that it is contestable,"[7] or, in Shaughnessy's term, "arguable." Precisely because nobody disputes them, uncontroversially true statements are by definition inarguable and therefore not worth making, at least not as an essay's main thesis. The reason why official prose sounds

notoriously banal is that it goes out of its way to be uncontroversial. A college of education mission statement I have seen declares, "We are committed to preparing individuals to become outstanding teachers, who understand and teach students in thoughtful, caring, and intelligent ways." The College here takes a courageous stand against those who would prepare teachers to be thoughtless, uncaring, and unintelligent.

Paradoxically, claims that are arguable and solicit disagreement are a sign of an argument's viability, not its failure. A completely uncontroversial proposition does not even qualify as an "argument"—we would never say, "The man argued that Washington, D.C., is the nation's capital." Unless this paradox is explicitly addressed, however, many students will labor under the misapprehension that the goal of an essay is to string together a series of uncontroversially true statements. A student who turns in such an essay will—and should—draw an instructor's comment of "So?" or "Who disputes it?"

On the other hand, imagine such a student, chastened by such comments, trying to do as he or she is told. Instead of making an uncontroversial and therefore negligible claim, our student goes to the other extreme and offers a claim that is outrageously controversial. Now the instructor's response shifts from "Who disputes it?" to "Surely not," or "What's your evidence for that?" Clearly, formulating a tenable point is a tightrope act in which students have to court controversy, but only as much as they can anticipate and deal with. Here is why finding a makable "point," as Shaughnessy points out, can be harder than it looks.

Expert players of the game of public discourse know that the easiest way to set yourself up to make a tenable point is to contest a point somebody else has made or, even better, has taken for granted. Such experts have acquired an inventory of formulaic templates for this kind of contestation. In *Lives on the Boundary* Mike Rose cites fellow compositionist David Bartholomae's suggestion that "when stuck, student writers should try the following 'machine': 'While most readers of ____ have said ____, a close and careful reading shows that ____.'"[8] According to a walker's guide to the city of Chicago, freshmen at the University of Chicago are given the following advice: "If someone asserts it, deny it; if someone denies it, assert it."

Rose observes that this reflexive negativity "perfectly expresses the ethos of the university," though "university professors have for so long been socialized into this critical stance, that they don't realize how unsettling it can be to students who don't share their unusual background."[9] Rose is right, but it also needs to be added that some professors find this contentious ethos as "unsettling" as students do and perhaps for that reason fail to call students' attention to it. As students go from teacher to teacher and from subject to subject, they often receive confusingly mixed signals about the value of controversy: Mr. B the physicist regards it as a distraction from the uncontroversial truths of science, whereas for Ms. J the chemist the clash and warfare of competing hypotheses is at the center of science; Mr. R the embattled moralist philosopher and Ms. C the feminist political scientist love to stir up debate and they reward contentious students, but Ms. A the feminist art historian regards debate as an unfortunate expression of macho agonism.

25   To the confusion created by these mixed messages add the fact that what counts as a wildly controversial statement in one course or discipline may be seen as uncontroversial or old hat in another. As a consequence, students are often left unsure whether controversy is to be courted or avoided, and since their teachers' different views on the question are screened from one another in courses that do not communicate, the question is rarely posed in an overt way. No wonder, then, that many students end up opting for docility. Whereas high-achieving students intuit the conventional templates of contestation and contravention ("While most think X, I argue Y . . .") from their reading, others won't acquire them unless such templates are explicitly supplied. When this doesn't happen, students are forced to play the academic game with one hand tied behind their backs.

Persuasion as Aggression

When the academic penchant for problematizing and negativity goes unexplained, the intellectual energy expended on academic tasks tends naturally to look like mere aggression rather than reasonable behavior. There is thus a connection between the impenetrability of intellectual practices and the tendency to associate intellectualism with bullying and other unattractive personal qualities, especially those that involve persuasion. To argue persuasively, you have to have an axe to grind, to want others to do something they are not already doing, if only to think differently about something than they do. Such an attitude will seem at best presumptuous, and at worst arrogant and coercive. . . .

For many students, the very word "argument" (like "criticism") conjures up an image not of spirited conversational give and take, but of acrimonious warfare in which competitors revile each other and make enemies yet rarely change each other's minds. Disputes end up producing winners and losers or a stalemate that frustrates all parties; either way they are useless except for stirring up bad blood.

This tendency to equate persuasion with aggression is especially rife among students who grow up in liberal pluralist surroundings, where "Live and let live" is a ruling maxim and "whatever" the popular mantra. As students often put it, "You have your opinions, I have mine, so what's the point of either of us trying to persuade each other? Everybody's an individual, so nobody has the right to tell anybody else what to do or think." There seems little value in becoming the type of person solicited by academic writing assignments—in other words, those who seem guided by the arrogant premise that everyone should think the way you do or that you have the right to generalize about or speak for others.

On the other hand, students from more traditional backgrounds often share their liberal classmates' dim view of persuasion. To Christian fundamentalists, the surrounding secularized society may seem too far gone to be open to persuasion, just as the culture of persuasion and argument seems in league with a Godless secular humanism that views moral issues as endlessly subject to debate. Whether from secular or religious backgrounds, then, American students are often trained to regard persuasion as a waste of time at best and asking for trouble at worst.

This student attitude toward persuasion is tied up with a deeper refusal to become the sort of *public* self that schooling assumes we all naturally want to be. Often when I am struggling unsuccessfully to help students master sentence structure or paragraphing, I realize that what I'm up against is not the students' inability to perform these operations, but their aversion to the role of public spokesperson that formal writing presupposes. It's as if such students can't imagine any rewards for being a public actor or even imagine themselves in such a role.

This lack of interest in entering the public sphere may in turn reflect a loss of confidence in the possibility that the arguments we make in public will have an effect on the world. Today's students' lack of faith in the power of persuasion reflects the waning of the ideal of civic participation that led educators for centuries to place rhetorical and argumentative training at the center of the school and college curriculum. Underlying the centrality of this training was a classical conception of public citizenship that has come to seem unreal as the small town has given way to urban massification and as the ideal of the citizen has been displaced by that of the consumer. If even successful adults find it hard to imagine themselves influencing public policy through their rhetorical and argumentative skills, students figure to find it all the harder to visualize themselves in such public roles.

The standard theme assignment that asks students to take a stand on public issues like homelessness, poverty or abortion rests on the increasingly hollow pretense that what we think and say about such issues can actually make a difference. Given the notoriously widespread cynicism about the chances that our opinions (or votes) will influence public policy, it is hardly surprising if students are fatalistic too. These doubts about the payoff of persuasion underlie much of the student relativism that has been so widely deplored for half a century now. When students say that value judgments are merely matters of subjective opinion, what looks like philosophical relativism may actually be an inability to imagine a world in which one's arguments might have consequences.

The emergence of the Internet, the electronic town meeting, and talk-back radio hold out some promise that this cynical fatalism can be reversed. We may also be witnessing a revival of student idealism and activism, qualities that may not have completely disappeared. The same student who claims at one moment that all beliefs are subjective can often be found a moment later arguing passionately for a cause. Adolescent cynicism and fatalism often mask uncertainty, as

30

if students were challenging their elders to talk them out of it. Again, these are important issues to be raised in class. . . .

In this [essay] I have inventoried some of the main features of academic discourse that seem odd or counterintuitive when left unexplained. I have suggested that the best way to deal with these apparent oddities is not to duck them, but to build classroom discussions and writing assignments around the questions they pose and to let students debate these questions. What is the point of looking for hidden meanings in everything you read? Why must expository writers have a "point" all the time? How do you know if the meanings a reader ascribes to a text are really there or not, and how can you debate the issue? Do works of entertainment have hidden meanings as the acknowledged classics do? Why summarize and restate other people's views even when those people are present? Does academia reward or punish students who are aggressively argumentative? Is it in fact arrogant to try to persuade other people that you are right? Is debate about ideas a form of warfare or a way of getting beyond warfare? Do you want to intellectualize, and why or why not? All these challenging questions are central to education, yet they have been allowed to fall through the cracks between courses and disciplines.

35   Whatever side students come down on over these questions—and students will divide on them as much as most of us do—opening these questions for discussion has the educationally desirable effect of positioning students as anthropologists, intellectual analysts, of their own academic lives. Even if some students end up rejecting academic roles, they at least may discover that their rejection will be more powerfully expressed if they draw on the resources of academic discourse to formulate it. This tactic may not eliminate student anti-intellectualism, but it can give it a more intellectual cast, and for teachers this is more than half the battle.

Reading

1. How does Graff define the "problem problem"?

2. How does he argue that "claims that are arguable and solicit disagreement" (para. 21) are more likely to hold up than claims that don't?

3. How do students come to believe that "persuasion" means "aggression" when crafting an argument?

4. How should professors alter their teaching to address student responses to the "problem problem"?

Inquiring

1. Graff suggests that many students are turned off of education because of how academic work is framed, such as academics' tendency to cultivate "problems" or locate contradictions in texts that seem fairly straightforward. According to Graff, these habits create social resistance among students,

who often turn against their schoolwork in response. What are some of the other characteristics Graff attributes to academic culture, and what do you think of his claims about their effect on students? Has he—an academic himself—found a problem that appears rather insignificant, or has he discovered something crucial about students' relationships with academic work? As you read this piece, based on your experience, do you find his description of students and student culture persuasive? Which of his contentions do you find especially pertinent or misguided? Why?

2. For Graff, the academic world is a profoundly different *culture* from that which students (and other educated adults) encounter in their daily lives. He claims the academy is too theoretical and students, it seems, work better with pragmatic issues. However, you may have your own theories about what it means to study an issue, theories based on your family and communal experiences that lead you to question Graff's claims. Perhaps the academy fails to recognize these community-based theories as important. How might exploring the way your home culture defines and explores "important problems" provide a different sense of intellectual argument for the classroom to consider? How might it change what it means to "read deeply"?

3. At the end of his essay, Graff suggests that teachers should address students' concerns directly and "build classroom discussions and writing assignments around the questions they pose and . . . let students debate these questions. What is the point of looking for hidden meanings in everything you read? Why must expository writers have a 'point' all the time? How do you know if the meanings a reader ascribes to a text are really there or not, and how can you debate the issue? . . . All these challenging questions are central to education, yet they have been allowed to fall through the cracks between courses and disciplines" (para. 34). What do you think of Graff's proposed solution? Will direct confrontation—through class discussion and writing assignments—with the questions he raises help address the gap between students and the academic culture they encounter in college? Will it open up a space for alternative forms of analysis in the classroom? Why or why not?

Composing

1. Graff's essay appears as a chapter in his book *Clueless in Academe: How Schooling Obscures the Life of the Mind* (2003). Graff's intended audience is fellow professors and teachers who confront student resistance to academic analysis and argumentation in their classes. As a student, you come to Graff's work from a different perspective. You may or may not share the reactions Graff describes to academic culture. Write a short essay in which you discuss Graff's investigation of student responses to academia. Present your own interpretation of the relationship between students and the analysis in which they are asked to participate in school. To be more precise, it might be useful

to refer to specific courses, texts, or assignments that illustrate the forms of academic work that you do or don't find valuable. Where do you stand in relation to Graff's reading of the problems students encounter in their college courses? What other insights can you offer as a student that add to, challenge, or complicate his views as a professor?

2. In making his argument, Graff relies primarily on the statements of a single eleventh-grade English class taught by Hillel Crandus, who asked his students to write short papers on what they thought of performing academic analysis. Expand on Graff's research by conducting your own survey of student responses to what Graff calls "intellectualizing" or "reflecting in a self-conscious way about experience" (para. 1). What do your friends, classmates, or home community members have to say about the academic habit of thoroughly analyzing whatever subject arises? After you've explored this issue with a variety of other students, write an essay in which you discuss how they understood the ways in which academic analysis—of life, culture, or texts—can be a practice that is valuable (or not so valuable) to develop. How would you position yourself in relation to your fellow students and the students you interviewed or those quoted in Graff's essay? Which of their views do you share or oppose, and why? In what ways does the academy or students (or both) need to change to address the problems you see in the strategies and goals of academic argument?

3. In discussing students' equation of academic persuasion with aggression, Graff argues that students are experiencing an "aversion to the role of public spokesperson that formal writing presupposes. It's as if such students can't imagine any rewards for being a public actor or even imagine themselves in such a role" (para. 30). Write an essay in which you discuss the type of "public actor" Graff believes academic writing is trying to produce. Why might students resist that role? What type of writing (and argumentation) do you believe would be most effective for someone who wants to take on the role of being a public actor, a public intellectual? What is public persuasion like, or what should it be like? Finally, is it true that students "can't imagine any rewards" for taking on the "role of a public spokesperson" (para. 30)? Can you?

Connecting

Graff argues that a primary reason for students' disengagement in academic writing is a lack of interest in how topics are discussed. Academic problems generated by close reading, for instance, simply do not seem relevant to many students' lives. By contrast, Carmen Kynard (p. 127) points to issues of racism when discussing students' alienation from the academy. Write an essay in which you imagine how Graff's argument about the "problem problem" would be altered if he imagined his students as other than "white."

CARMEN KYNARD

From Candy Girls to Sista-Cypher: Narrating Black Females' Color-Consciousness and Counterstories in *and* out *of School*

Courtesy of Carmen Kynard

Carmen Kynard is an associate professor at John Jay College of Criminal Justice. Her work examines the relationship between race, literacy, and urban education. In the essay featured here, Kynard is primarily concerned with how new technologies enable African American women in college to maintain a sense of communal identity, particularly when confronted with course work and departments that seem not to recognize their literacy skills. For Kynard, it is the inability (or unwillingness) of mainstream education (public and college level) to understand the skills such students bring into the classroom that results in the creation of a hostile and unproductive learning environment. Notably, Kynard has not only worked to expand the literacies allowed in her own classroom but also worked systemically to broaden the curriculum in public and college-level classrooms. Among her efforts are teaching in the Coalition of Essential Schools (Bronx, New York), a Community Learning Center Project in Harlem, and developing curricula for the African Diaspora Research Institute and Caribbean Cultural Center in New York.

In the following essay, originally published in the *Harvard Educational Review*, Kynard connects her childhood experience as part of an academically focused friends club, the Candy Girls, with the struggles of African American women in college.

■ ■ ■

I think it was the penny loafers that started it all. Though we did not know each other, both LaNita and I had spray-painted our penny loafers for the first day of school; hers were a sparkly, iridescent fuchsia and mine were a glossy, bright baby-blue. We even had shirts and shiny ties to match, always paired with crisply creased blue jeans. It was the early 1980s, so we were funky fresh in that gear right there, couldn't nobody tell us nuthin. We garnered one another's full respect through our identical responses to boys who tried to take the dollar bills out of our loafers (we wasn't about no pennies even when dollars were hard to come by): we kicked 'em. It was only natural that from then on we became best friends, initially spending most of our time talking about one thing: the R&B boy band of the time, New Edition. After attending a New Edition concert (with red, spray-painted loafers), we decided that we were the Candy Girls who New Edition sang about. (LaNita's intention, though she denies it now, was to marry Bobby Brown, and I was the one with the good sense to choose Ralph T despite LaNita's insistence that he sang like a girl.)

As Candy Girls, we decided to wear only red and white in Bobby's and Ralph's honor. We soon became five Candy Girls, one for each boy of the band and all with C-letter nicknames. We eventually discarded New Edition altogether when we grew to more than five members and incorporated two more friends who liked one another and not boys. We talked on the phone for hours, since all of our mothers were single and worked long days and long nights. We made up cheers, dance steps, and raps. We orchestrated classroom pick-ups, timed-out suck-teeth for our own calling and responding, prearranged lunchtime seating and discussions, syncopated our steps when walking as a group, and exchanged intricate chain letters during period switches—all while wearing, of course, matching gear, even if it meant we had to tie red shoestrings around our heads like bandanas because we couldn't afford much else. In the context of our integrated Ohio junior high school, where white-on-black fights and black-on-black fights were the way to work out the issues the adults would not address, your crew, your Candy Girls, was all you had. You couldn't walk the halls alone or go to the bathroom alone, and you certainly couldn't count on a teacher to care.

In our first year, we competed to get 100 percent on assignments. Each of us had come from black teachers' classrooms; we had either been funneled into black teachers' classrooms in newly integrated white schools or been in black teachers' classrooms in all-black elementary schools. After our time with those teachers, we walked into junior high school fully armored with a sense of worth and intelligence and a notion that we would someday be sumbody. We were also what you might call, siditty. We had many good times torturing our peers for their bad grades and even took it so far as to visit their homes when we knew they'd be on punishment, all in the hopes of receiving candies and dollars from their parents, and, especially, catching a glimpse of a peer getting bopped upside the head after we showed off our good report cards.

We didn't like our schoolwork, but we did make a sacred dare: whoever didn't get A's in our first year of junior high would have to roll up on the social studies teacher and tell him that his breath be stankin (which was very true). Almost all of us had his class but during different periods. He would make us come up to his desk for individual conferences to a chorus of groans and feigned faintings from black students who relished such classroom shenanigans (or at least I did). LaNita and I had the class during the same period, and we both rounded out the semester getting A's. As a matter of principle, and as founders of the Candy Girls, our thirteen-year-old selves needed to take a stand for what was right. And so I was elected to tell the dude that his breath stank. I was sent immediately to the office, and LaNita, in solidarity, threw some mints at him on her way out the door when the bell rang. (Candy Girls always carried red-and-white mints.)

I remember going to the guidance office to see Mrs. N, the only African American guidance counselor, who all black kids had to go see when there was a problem—and there was always a "problem" with us. I explained to Mrs. N that the man had dragon-fire breath and needed to be told about it cuz maybe he just didn't know, though anybody next to him sho nuff did. I also distinctly remember explaining to Mrs. N, "That man breath be hummin," and even started humming to let her hear the kind of bass his halitosis had. I assumed that was legitimate for her, because she simply sent me to my next class with a "girl, git yo butt to class." She didn't reprimand me or even tell me to apologize. (Today, I am convinced that her smirk was an attempt to not laugh.)

I don't ever remember the Candy Girls getting into any real trouble in that school; after all, we did do well academically. But there were never any praises or Scooby Snacks thrown our way either. We were never selected for the special trips, events, or honors. On a good day, we were ignored, like the problem that would eventually go away, and on a bad day, we were accused of violent tendencies, hyperaggression, self-segregation/self-ghettoization, and gang affiliation. And we were always marked because our dress, speech, volume, hair, and directness didn't match schooling's most sacred R: the *right-white* bourgeois etiquette. Mrs. N saw a whole lot of us and our "problems."

It was not simply that school did not match the cultural and social capital of our families, communities, and peer stylings; it was that school actively disempowered what we brought to the table and left us materially under-rewarded in comparison to our white peers.[1] It is certainly true that the rich tradition of linguistic and educational research on African American language and culture was not as available when I was in junior high school and thus resulted in wholly negative experiences with cross-racial communication. However, this fact doesn't change the racism that targeted working-class black children, like the Candy Girls, under state-sanctioned integration experiments, as representative of a "particular challenge": "usually poorer, sometimes ill fed,

5

[working-class black children] tended to be more unruly than middle class white children . . . noisy, ill-disciplined children who could not keep still, had short attention spans, and defied [white teachers] at the drop of a hat."[2] The thing is, all folk ever really needed to do was listen and they could have known that we thought our social studies teacher was pretty cool; he just needed to get hisself some real strong breath mints before he wanted to go and do all that touchy-feely, come-sit-close-to-me-and-let's-pretend-ain't-no-hierarchy foolishness. We didn't explicitly articulate our disbelief and distrust of the social studies teacher's claims of a democratic classroom in this school where he and white students were hyper-privileged, but we certainly had an embodied reaction to his hypocrisy, to his coloring within the lines.

I am not interested in showing (i.e., proving) the humanity and sophistication of the Candy Girls. It is time for a different kind of project and rhetoric. Alongside realizing the Candy Girls as a kind of community of practice, a discourse community, and as masters of out-of-school literacies, I want to think about the Candy Girls as enacting and embodying discursive spaces that teach working-class/working poor people alternate gendered and racialized roles in white institutions. I am interested in a paradigm that locates these roles and discourses as the contemporary reinvention of "hush harbors," African American sites of resistance that functioned as "hidey" spaces for multiple literacies that were officially banned via institutional and state structures that prohibited African American humanity during slavery.[3] I am insisting on these literacies as an African American site of memory that inherently represents a critique of and action against hegemonic languages, discourses, and identities as well as an alternative, black cultural aesthetic that organizes hidey spaces.

At its heart, this article is a *narrative ethnography of sistahood* where the Candy Girls serve as a kind of guiding symbol and centripetal force for examining the intersections of race, class, and gender in education. I am particularly interested in how such black women's ciphers[4] represent practices, epistemology, and histories of hush harbors. The Candy Girls mark my own politics of location in white educational settings where physical occupation of the institution was always wedded to an ideological hush harbor. I intend to highlight my own conscious role and identity as a Candy Girl as a kind of foreshadowing of the relationships and experiences of black female college students with whom I have been politically and psychically linked. Overall, I want to excavate a cultural ecology[5] of literacies with a sequence of multiple narratives that explore how digital technologies offer hush harbors for black female college students' social and literacy practices — my contemporary and digitized Candy Girls. I offer a series of online conversations among young females of African descent as the discourses and social language of black women who work toward color consciousness in higher education and away from its institutional racism.

Joining the Cyber Sista-Cipher: A Digital Transplant's Narrative

When I got to my new university, Champion State University (CSU)[6]—a large 10
urban institution in the Northeast that boasts the most diverse student campus
of all PhD-granting institutions—I found many young black women who either
were unwilling to speak in their classrooms or, when they did, used very cryptic
and prescripted undertones. In the early days at CSU, I had three young women
of African descent in my class who did not talk for the first few weeks. In the
second week, one of them asked if she could meet me after class for a grammar
lesson, since I was the English teacher type. I said *sure*, hoping to talk to her
about more things. We did in fact talk about a paper she was working on, but the
conversation turned when she asked, *How you get this far and stay so comfortable
with yourself?*[7] Today, I remember that question most and the thoughts in my
head: *Why wouldn't I be comfortable? What . . . we ain't s'posed to be here? Who been
tellin' her that and how and why?*

I remember wanting and needing to hear what was happening at this college, and so the student and I talked for hours that Friday and many Fridays
thereafter. Before I knew it, there were other young black women I was meeting
who were not in my classes. I was soon looped into an online world, something
akin to a listserv, a hush harbor with plotting, scheming, and planning that no
one else in the institution seemed to imagine was happening. This hush harbor
worked in the way that Nunley argues: "camouflaged locations, hidden sites,
and enclosed places" that become "emancipatory cells . . . [to] untie [members']
tongues, speak the unspoken, and sing their own songs to their own selves in
their own communities."[8] The notion of "hidden" here is also complex, since
these literal and metaphorical meetings and gathering points are unauthorized
by the white gaze and its hegemonic centers but "hidden in plain sight" at these
very centers.[9]

In addition to thinking of hush harbors as spaces, Nunley reminds us that this
"distinctive relationship to spatiality" is both "material and discursive" and rests
on an "audience, African American nomoi (social conventions and beliefs that
constitute a world view or knowledge), and epistemology."[10] These are not only
physical gatherings of black folk but a process and institution for the embodied
presence of African American nomos, "rhetoric, phronesis (practice wisdom and
intelligence), tropes, and commonplaces."[11] Thus, hush harbors enact African
American rhetoric, as opposed to merely providing utopian safe havens or survival strategies, and have done the historical and current work of maintaining,
rescripting, and retheorizing African American challenges to white hegemony.
At a university such as CSU, the hush harbor can do the important work of
disrupting the social reproduction of bourgeois whiteness that the majority of
classrooms and college faculty maintain.

By the middle of my first semester at CSU, I began communicating with a
group of thirteen young women of African descent (with families who reflected

the breadth of the African diaspora) who maintained an informal, e-mail distribution list using their own private e-mail accounts rather than their school accounts. The e-mail discussions took place during the school months and lasted for almost three years, comprising hundreds of e-mails. All of these women were nineteen- to twenty-three-year-old, first-generation college students; they all worked a minimum of thirty hours per week and finished their college studies in five to six years. When I met them, they were all in their third to final year at CSU, and so I got to know many young women of African descent on that campus in ways that I would never have gotten to know them in the classroom.

School-like practices certainly governed the work and writing of these young women in the cyber cipher,[12] and so my use of an in-school and out-of-school dichotomy of literacy will serve a specific function. The hush harbor in the context of CSU certainly mirrors what we know from educational research about out-of-school literacies.[13] As Schultz and Hull[14] remind us, research on out-of-school contexts via ethnographies of communication, Vygotskian perspectives, and New Literacies Studies has had a significant impact on redefining the terrain of literacy. Where literacy once was something connected solely to school, reading, and writing, academic discussions of literacy today are specifically connected to discourses, identities, practices, and ideologies, making the work that hush harbors do logical. In college settings, however, we do not often talk about out-of-school literacies. Students are seemingly transplants who have left their homes and neighborhoods and sometimes countries of origin to live in dormitory environments. And even when college students are commuters, they travel from such a wide range of places and neighborhoods and often spend most of their time at their jobs rather than on the college campus. Research on literacies in college settings, in-school and out-of-school, is sometimes similarly confined. When the American Institute for Research and the National Endowment for the Arts[15] set out to pursue the first full-scale attempts at researching college students' literacies, they reduced literacy acquisition to a set of skills and behaviors; they totally ignored contexts and practices and settled on quantifying how few novels college kids read today, as if that could capture the complexity of literacies in a student's life or today's world. Wilber[16] further contends that there is still a gap in research on college students' digital technologies and identities, since the existing research is often limited to a focus on professors' instructional changes, effective pedagogy, or learning outcomes rather than on students' everyday practices.[17] Thus, research on new digital technologies in college settings is just more "business as usual" in the sense that the purpose is to make "the business of teaching or delivering content . . . simply more technologized."[18] The women in this study are, therefore, multiply silenced and erased in research due to the reductive nature of how literacies in college settings are imagined, the lack of attention paid to out-of-school literacies, and the ideological ignoring of the transformative possibilities of the hush harbors that are always present.

The notion of a hush harbor rather than the in-school and out-of-school dialectic allows for a kind of political location that does the work of challenging the racialized policing of language and being in schools. Many of these women's conversations are about school, school assignments, school discussions, school writing, and racist or Western assumptions underlying the tasks they have been given in school. The setting of the college classroom and the discursive and intellectual experiences out of classroom are spaces that are completely siphoned off from one another. As an institution that circulates its own specific modes of learning, CSU, like all schools, determines the ways in which white discourses get allowed and centered. Hush harbors work against this.

Step into the Arena: A Hush Harbor's Narrative

The institutional names I had used for these students were all different now in the cyber cipher and became missinSOULmusic, oh_so_fabulous, leaning2-wardgrace, PrplPhiyah, yup_thedarkertheberry, and many reconfigurations of Ill Nana, for example. In this way, the Internet allowed for renaming/nicknaming (just like the first order of business for the Candy Girls) according to the meanings by which the sistas of the cipher elected to be identified. As Banks[19] has shown in positing a black digital ethos on BlackPlanet.com, users' names and messages — the spellings, tonal semantics, and phonologies that get deployed — do transformative work. Thus, even the names used for e-mails demonstrate how African American technology users rewrite cyber-space as a black space and cultural construct and, thereby, redefine their access to it.

At first, I was a bit hesitant to be looped into this online community, because, frankly, I thought, I am just too old to be all up in these young women's biz'ness. My first response to their request that I join their e-mail conversations was a thank-you and a question:

> I love that yall are communicating and connecting like this—makes me feel like, whew, thank the lawd that somebody at this place is tryna work toward some consciousness, and I am grateful and honored that yall loopin me in, but, now are yall sure about this . . . remember: I'm old.

There were many responses back to me. A brief sampling sounds something like this:

> U aint old my sista.
> Gyrl, u betta stop trippin.
> You betta stop that type of talk b4 I need to put my foot up ur behind, ya hear?

15

After these e-mail loops, I knew I was in like Flynn, really part of this sista-cipher, because you only threaten a sista like that. And so it was on!

The e-mail where I officially entered the cipher involved a forwarded message about a forum to teach black women to eat and exercise better. These kinds of forwards in the cipher were always related to Web texts or events involving black women and were always accompanied by commentary. The forwarded message about the black women's health program was cast as a polemic of why and how it was assumed that black women *don't* know how to eat right.

> You know what, Americans think Black women don't know how to eat right . . . Now, I'm not one to talk since I eat from the truck, but . . . eating healthy requires money and access to the right distribution venues . . . are these workshops gon teach us how to organize for this in our communities or just lecture us, yet again, on everything we be too dumb to do right? [ellipses are the student's]

The solution, if the claim against black women was true, called for a change in access and equity as it regards food, wealth, and grocery store distribution and not a change in individual behavior. The charge in these turns of the sista-cipher was to analyze social ills from a black female-centered perspective that in turn necessitates a different set of social solutions. Ethos and participation in this example do not rest on literal healthy eating, marked by the sista's own narrative insertion, "Now, I'm not one to talk," but on the ability and desire to recognize and counter the negative assumptions about black women.

20   Functioning similarly as the forwarded messages were e-mails that described personal, racist encounters as an invitation for all in the group to think through structural racism as it pertained to black women. Here is a typical invitation to interrogate interactions between upper-middle-class white women and working-class black women in the context of black caretaking of white middle-class children.

> was walking with my sister and mother through the park this weekend. only white women and their children were there, as we passed, these women went and grabbed their baby carriages and purses as if we wanted to rob them and kidnap their white babies, walk through that same park any monday to friday and you will see only people like us takin care of them same white babies, and yet today they scared, what that about?

The charge in these turns of the sista-cipher was to take up the seemingly everyday, run-of-the-mill racist encounters and trouble their normativeness. This work might be the most distinct from what happens at the institution where we met because the goal of these exchanges was not to perform individualized, feel-good sessions but to take on the communal task of warding off the possibility of (more) internalized racism. There is a kind of marking of these personal events as regular occurrences, but there is also the call *"what that about?"* to look into these settings and deconstruct every single instance for wholeness and sanity. This deconstruction of the outside world would happen right alongside the deconstruction of interactions and assignments that occurred at the college. . . .

SMH or *it bees dat way sometime:* A Cyborg's Generational Narrative

The cipher often fully explored and enacted black language's "generational continuity [that] provides a common thread across the span of time, even as each new group stamps its own linguistic imprint on the Game."[20] It was those moments when *SMH* and/or *it bees dat way sometime* appeared in a message that showed a kind of generational weaving.

SMH (*shakin' ma head*) was how you responded to another sista in the cipher when you didn't have the time to really write more but had to say sumthin, when you didn't quite have the words, or when words just wouldn't do. And when the response was to a description of an encounter where another non-conscious sista got dissed and didn't know it or refused to engage other black women on campus or made a point of distancing herself from black culture/language/aesthetics or publicly and adamantly articulated the position of color-blindness, there was only one in the digital cipher that could tackle the job: *it bees dat way sometime.* This is an acknowledgment of racist oppression as still an ever-present reality, an acknowledgment that lets you know you are not just imagining things. The expression is not acquiescence to racism but recognition of its history and presence. Sometimes, when the possibility for doing what Bob Marley called for—"emancipat[ing] [our] selves from mental slavery"—just seemed way far away, the message might just say, "*SMH . . . it bees dat way sometime . . . SMH . . . SMH.*" SMH and "it bees dat way sometime" worked in multiple ways: (1) as call-and-response, a shared and embodied language practice in communities of African descent, and (2) as hybridized forms that might be thought to do what Bhabha[21] describes as disrupting authority with both mimicry and mockery.

If you know research on black language, you immediately think of Smitherman's *Talkin and Testifyin* (1977) and her now-infamous chapter 2 named after this very same Nina Simone song. Issues such as signifying, semantic inversions, and the blues notes in Simone's "It bees dat way sometime" made Smitherman move away from coinages like "dialect" and "Black English" to calling this system of speaking/thought a "language." She argues:

> Here the language aspect is the use of the verb *be* to indicate a recurring event or habitual condition, rather than a one-time-only occurrence. But the total expression—"it bees dat way sometime"—also reflects black [language] style, for the statement

suggests a point of view, a way of looking at life, and a method of adapting to life's realities. To live by the philosophy of "it bees dat way sometime" is to come to grips with the changes that life bees putting us through, and to accept the changes and bad times as a constant, ever-present reality.[22]

25   This was an expression that I knew well but thought of as old skool, so when I heard the women talking this stuff, I just had to ask the cipher:

> ME: it bees that way sometime? if i didn't know it befo, i know fo sho now that yall some old souls! what yall know about it bees-ing dat way sometime?
> SISTA #1: every bonafide sistah know em some Nina Simone, Miss Carmen.
> ME: my bad, my bad . . . since i see i done become Miss Carmen now
> SISTA #2: sistas, don't be listening to Nina alone, because if you down, that sista will really mess witcha head on some things. yeah, we oldheads, C, tragic that so many young people don't know Nina

"It bees dat way sometime" represents a shared language, history, culture, and set of political interests that formulated the new local community of the sista-cipher, a local community within an institutional setting. The combination of the women's expression, alongside language in computer-mediated communication, like SMH, all within the context of the institution where we met, marked black womanhood in this cipher as a kind of black cyber transmutation. In one sense we were all physically estranged from places that we had called home or community, but the cipher was consciously used to do the work of stretching our institutional discourses and identities back to the figurative places we called home. Though the cipher was really only an informal type of e-mail listserv, as users we understood how these technologies affected our lives and the information we shared and learned from it.[23]

Harraway's[24] notion of cyborg agency makes a critical nod toward us sistas in the cipher as embodied beings in information-rich technological worlds, black literate-historical communities, and inequitable state institutions.[25] Harraway's theory is a reminder that we can define feminist identity and sista kinship in ways that are not overly idealized and romantic but, instead, realized through deliberate negotiations, polyvocal play with language, transgression of existing boundaries, and a conscious stance where machines and technologies are dynamically connected to the consciousness of its users. Harraway's cyborg—in the sense of postmodern identities, knowledges, and political ties that are formed through computer-mediated communication and environments—engage a kind of work, agency, and productive action when we challenge the possibilities of our circumstances with "conscious coalition," "affinity," and "political kinship."[26] Thus, the kind of "play of writing" from sistas in the cipher is starkly different from the kind of writing sanctioned by schooling.[27] Digital writing in this cipher connects alienated subjects, challenges the binaries of orality and print, and blurs the boundaries between nonstandard and standardized language/meaning.

"The Window Dressing of White Supremacy": An Institutional Narrative

These students have all graduated, and I have moved on to a different university. We still keep in touch — yes, via e-mail — but we do not use the cipher the way that we did when we were at CSU together. On the one hand, the intellectual work, writing, and literacies of this sista-cipher are worth celebrating. This was a daily subversion and resistance of the dominant discourses that decided what counted as valued language, experience, and knowledge. On the other hand, we cannot ignore the fact that the sistas spent their undergraduate years in classrooms where they said very little and edited out the most charged, political content from their assignments. In the least, the story of the cyber sista-cipher compels us to ask some uncomfortable *what-if* questions. *What if* success in higher education for working-class black women is not about the stuff we researchers/educators usually write about — understanding disciplinary paradigms, mastering academic codes and literacies, managing work and school, etc.? *What if* school success is really — most of the time or even some of the time — about eradicating pan-African/black conscious identity and language or, at least, having to hide it and develop it somewhere else (which is still eradication)? The women in the cipher were at the top of the academic food chain — dean's lists, graduate fellowships, and high grades. But *what if* the successes of these women were contingent on the fact that they mastered a kind of public performance of racelessness?[28] Where, when, and how does this paradigm get imposed and what does it mean for literacies and institutions? If we take up the idea that there is "no single locus of great Refusal, no soul of revolt, source of all rebellions" but instead a "multiplicity of points of resistance,"[29] then the sista-cipher is part of that multiplicity. But is that enough?

At CSU, most of the students I met at the beginning of the program in the introductory classes, the classes that were the most racially and linguistically diverse, did not make it to the end of the program. When I went into a department meeting and described what I saw happening in my classes and named it as a problem, I was told that I needed "to remember Martin Luther King's dream and work with everyone." No single other professor said a word in support, though some shared their agreement in hallway whispers. I include this memory because I want to trouble the notion of silence and challenge prevalent inklings toward distant, objective, neutral, detached researcher stances and collegial relationships—a kind of silence that can do real violence to communities of color. Calling the women in this study "silent" will not pave the path for radical reinventions; what if, instead, we called and thought about our research and researcher-activism as silent?

30   In this department where we never talked about race or the active displacement of students of color, every single professor did research, published articles, collected data, and spent grant dollars in poor communities of color. And yet, whenever I didn't talk in a department meeting, I was the only one who was considered silent. The silence that gets enabled by detached research and departmental involvement is inherently violent and smacks of a kind of renewed Tuskegee experiment: from 1932 to 1972, the U.S. Public Health Service experimented on 399 black men in the late stages of syphilis, men who were never told what disease they were suffering from or its seriousness, but data were collected from their autopsies after they were deliberately left to die from tumors, heart disease, paralysis, blindness, and insanity.[30] My allegation of and comparison to the Tuskegee experiment may seem extreme, and perhaps you could argue that this is my own rhetorical ride or die. Yet, it hardly seems like such a far stretch to question whether educational researchers really intend to alleviate inequity and human suffering when we exhibit no outrage or voice while daily observing the denigration and disappearance of the communities we "study." There was no institutional halt on white faculty chasing and receiving very real, material credentials while working in black communities, all the while ignoring the vanishing of black students at their own school. It seems worth saying here that the Tuskegee experiment was seen as legitimate and necessary research for forty years. It was an insider at the site who finally blew the whistle. In this case, the informant had to forgo (some of) the material effects of whiteness in order to question the discarding of black bodies in the name of compiling research and knowledge. While some of the twentieth century's *specific* racisms may have been addressed, we now face the problem of the "new racialized ethnic hierarchies, discourses, and processes of domination and subordination in the context of economic globalization and neoliberal public policies."[31]

That these black female students in the cipher felt ignored or marginalized at the same time that their bodies were highly marked and supervisible was no figment of imagination on their parts. In my time in the department during the duration of the cipher, no student of African descent was ever awarded one of the departmental graduation prizes. Every year a young white woman won an award (and/or coveted department job), though they only constituted 7–10 percent of any entering freshman class. Black women's work and insights were never the conversation among faculty around the watercooler or photocopier or in departmental meetings—except for one black woman whose dress, speech, and demeanor were called "too street." As Barajas and Ronnkvist[32] argue, colleges and K–12 schools whose demographics have large percentages of students of color (and even a few critical, conscious administrators of color) still function as white spaces, which is an important reminder for those fooled into thinking that a "different" demographic of college students means a different kind of education. We know very well in K–12 research that even in multiracial, "integrated" schools, it has been the middle-class white kids who end up in the accelerated classes.[33] There were no accelerated classes that siphoned off the black women of this study, but their everyday invisibility as strong readers, writers, and thinkers who were also race-conscious served the same function of "within-school segregation."[34] Instead of the white-black divide that mapped itself on to an honors/regular divide of the twentieth century, new racialized divides mark the twenty-first century: color-conscious/colorblind, street/bourgeois, diva/AbercrombieandFitch, multilingual-multidialectal/standardized speaker.

These years of being schooled for and as a "mainstreamed-everyone-else"[35] functioned as what Shor (personal communication, November 1999) calls the "window dressing for white supremacy," a kind of tokenization where (some) people of color get to be in the front row, on the marketing pamphlets, or in the picture windows. This window dressing, however, only serves to camouflage a daily, omnipresent whiteness and its materialist effects[36] in every decision- and selection-making body and institutional rewards system. . . .

Ya Betta Recognize: Looking B(l)ack as Researcher-Narrator, Candy-Girl, and Ciphered Sista

I opened with a story about the Candy Girls, a story of myself with a group of young women in junior high school who stuck together and stayed up, and so I will close here with them. In our second year in junior high, somehow, some way, we all set our sights on what we thought were "competitive" high schools: a conglomerate of Catholic high schools, where we could receive merit- and need-based scholarships in exchange for cleaning the school after school, and a conglomerate of vocational high schools (none of which exist today) that promised middle-class stability after graduation. We all went to separate high schools and naively thought our Candy Love would keep us tight and get spread across the city. It didn't quite work out that way. Each of us rounded out our high school years as what we promised one another we'd never become: ABGG—another black girl gone. Drug addiction, alcoholism, incarceration, prostitution, domestic abuse, or illegal trades had each one of us in its grip in some way. The promise of a job and livable wage offered by the vocational schools did not pan out during Ronald Reagan's counterreformation and left those graduates skill-less and jobless in a postindustrialized midwestern city with little to no economic opportunities. The promise of educational advances governed by meritocracy rang hollow for us Candy-Girls-turned-domestic-servants at private schools. We learned very quickly — and experientially — that rich white kids' parents went away for long weekends and left homes to teenagers who could drink and do drugs with absolute impunity, a stark contrast to the hyperpoliced, just-say-no warfare that was happening daily in *our* neighborhoods. And there was no more Mrs. N for any of us. Today, I would say that we Candy Girls were each hell-bent on what West calls "asserting" our "somebodiness" in a context where our bodies had no public worth.[37] However, we were not explicitly and consciously interrogating the racism that was schooling us and our bodies, the work that I would argue the cyber sista-cipher did daily as digital bodies.

The conversations that I had with the sistas in the cipher were not ones I had with any other faculty on my campus. Those e-mail chains gave me a lifeline as an academic as much as it did for the young women within a space that was as toxic for me as it was for them. Since the days of this cipher, I find myself always transferring the racialized and racist interactions of white faculty with me into images of how they must be similarly engaging young black women and people of color in their classes.

35   On the days when I wonder if the sista-cipher sold out, if we just cowed down too much instead of rioting at the gates, and if we accepted the madness so that we could "gracely walk through that door that was once closed," I remember the hard work that hush harbors do. And I wonder: if the Candy Girls had stayed together, if we would have stayed in the cipher and spoke back, in hush harbor mode, to our institutions, what would and could have happened? I know that navigating racist structural inequalities cannot be simplified, but I also live an *embodied* understanding and continued experience (as opposed to just representing an intellectual, political, or historical investigation) of the work that hush harbors do in countering the state-sanctioned oppressive institutions that we inhabit. Everyday folk, "stealin and meetin," as was the expression during slavery, continue to educate one another within and from their own syncopated discourses in the face of insurmountable odds.[38] The extracurricular practices of the sistas in the cipher did not and will not provide us, as black women and black communities, the "property" rights of whiteness.[39] It is unlikely that issues like equitable pay in comparison to white men and women or even equal access to job hiring and promotion will be granted, making it a seeming contradiction for these groups to so actively pursue literacy and rhetoric in hush harbors. These hidey spaces contradict and challenge a white, capitalistic tendency to purpose literacy solely in monetary/power terms and have been doing this work for America since slavery.[40]

To understand why these women would so actively engage in going back and rereading the books and articles that they had been assigned in their classes, for instance, a practice that will not make them richer, A-grade-granted, or even noticeable to white institutions, we must conceive of their philosophies of literacies within the political and ideological space of what hush harbors do. The counterstories that these women and black communities have historically told us about the purposes of literacy map out a set of practices that are diametrically opposed to how institutions enact literacy.

My own participation in multiple sista-ciphers/hush harbors also conditions the political arguments that I am making here. I never actually thought about writing about these conversations until the sistas asked me to tell our story for education scholarship. I was a sista in the cipher at the time, not an ethnographer. The process of going back and looking at the previous discourses and experiences of the cipher might be best described as an *unhushing narrative methodology* rather than an ethnography, since I was always an active agent in the cipher's sense making, decision making, and survival making. Only 10 percent of the conversations that happened in the sista cyber cipher have been relayed here. Every unhushing has been preplanned and executed with multiple approvals and ongoing readings from each sista: the naming of ourselves and our personal experiences with racism; the rhetorical battles and agreements we engaged in in regards to images of black women in the mainstream and in the classroom; and our counterattacks on the criminalization of our language and, therefore, knowledge.

I, as the faculty professor and educational researcher, am now the intentional storyteller of an intentional community's narrative where my own counterstory as a black woman in schools has been purposefully made visible.[41] Just as the cipher worked against the isolationism of sistas' lives, this methodology works against the isolating of researcher and participant.[42] Thus, the overarching purpose of this unhushing narrative methodology is to (re)value a black radical female subjectivity. Borrowing from the ideological force of critical feminists like Young,[43] we want these counterstories of multiple black female lived experiences to achieve more than the Western academic genre of squirreling away empirical cases. Instead, these counterstories represent sketches of black female experiences that hold "conceptual alternatives" and "alternate ideals."[44] The public-ing of our private conversations attempts to capture our experiences as black women in ways that move beyond victimization or celebration and, instead, portray our hush harbor as a site for new political lenses into, and therefore struggles against, schooling's processes of ethnic cleansing.

What might it have looked like for those outside of this hush harbor to intervene in the institution that warranted these harbors' functioning? As we see it, the most radical challenge would be, in the worldview lingo of hip hop, to *recognize*. In urban youth language, "recognize" is about publicly acknowledging what is going on and who the central perpetrators are. It can be a directive expression in the sense that this act of acknowledgment has dire consequences if not performed, from light punitive action to getting straight-up called out on the rug like it ain't even funny. It is worth saying again: no one in the department where I met the sistas in the cyber cipher noticed their displacement or talent; nobody recognized. It didn't have to be that way, and it can't be that way if we intend to really dismantle the race, gender, and class hierarchies of educational institutions.

40   Just as literacies have their own lifespans — overlapping and competing with existing and dominant models, growing and working through periods of transition, and one day fading away[45] — the cyber sista-cipher also had its lifespan. We do not talk like we used to, but it is also not coincidence that we have each joined new ciphers in the new institutions that we inhabit, new hush harbors. I'd like to think that we are doing what LaNita, myself, and all of the Candy Girls did not know to continue after we left one another but *recognized* when we first met: sing that song . . . *Candy Girl, you are my world . . . Candy girl / All I want to say / when you're with me / you brighten up my day.*[46]

Reading

1. How does Kynard understand the Candy Girls not getting "any praises or Scooby Snacks" (para. 6)?

2. How does she argue education is often "window dressing for white supremacy" (para. 32)?

3. How does she define the purpose of a "hush harbor" (para. 8)?

4. How does Kynard believe the university should address "white supremacy" in the classroom and in academic departments?

Inquiring

1. Kynard claims that some students — in this case, working-class African American females — suppress their thoughts, experiences, and ideas in the classroom because they won't fit in with what Kynard calls "schooling's most sacred R: the *right*-white bourgeois etiquette" (para. 6). This etiquette includes supposedly proper ways of speaking and writing along with things like fashion and social customs. Even at the highly diverse public university where Kynard taught, she encountered students whose African American language was criticized for not being appropriately "academic." As you discuss Kynard's essay, examine her claims about language restrictions in the classroom. What does she mean by the "*right*-white bourgeois etiquette"? Can you point to examples from your own experience in school? Based on your experience, does this etiquette alter how teachers and students respond to African American language or the language of other ethnic groups? (You might focus on your own campus.)

Do you agree with Kynard that schooling is largely about "the social reproduction of bourgeois whiteness" (para. 12)? If not, how would you talk about the relationship between race and education?

2. Toward the end of her essay, Kynard discusses the need for educators to recognize the ways in which certain students (and individuals and groups more generally) get marginalized because of their difference from the mainstream (para. 39). She argues that such recognition is a form of action, the first step toward addressing inequality. If teachers, students, and individuals were to "publicly acknowledg[e] what is going on and who the central perpetrators are," what might such acts of recognition look like? What might be said or done? By whom? Where and when? To answer these questions, select—and then describe—one moment when the dismantling of "race, gender, and class hierarchies" Kynard calls for might begin either inside or outside the classroom. How might Kynard's insights help you understand the work that needs to be done?

3. Kynard draws some dramatic parallels between schooling and other social ills. She claims, for instance, that the silence in her department over matters of race "smacks of a kind of renewed Tuskegee experiment," a secret government study from 1932 to 1972 in which hundreds of black men with syphilis were left to die for the sake of collecting data from their cadavers. Later, she refers to "schooling's process of ethnic cleansing" (para. 39), and her central metaphor—the hush harbor—comes from the era of slavery. What risks as a writer does Kynard take with such comparisons, and what is their effect? For what reasons might Kynard think these analogies are worth the risk of stating them? How might they help (or hinder) the effect she hopes to have on her readers?

Composing

1. Kynard's essay begins with her recollection of her membership in the "Candy Girls," a small group of African American females who bonded with one another in middle school. This group made good grades in their classes, but they were ignored when it came to academic awards or events, and they were sometimes accused of "violent tendencies, hyperaggression, self-segregation/self-ghettoization, and gang affiliation" (para. 6). Kynard writes that this experience foreshadowed what she would encounter years later as a teacher, when she partook in a "hush harbor" created online by a group of female African American college students who often felt silenced by the dominant social and cultural expectations at their university. Kynard's claim that schooling alienates the innate intelligence and culture of certain students can be understood as referring to more than just African American girls/women. Write a short essay in which you explore some version of a

hush harbor in which you've participated either in college or during your earlier schooling. The idea is not merely to choose any group or club to which you've belonged but to examine a group whose language and conduct were "actively disempowered" by the school you attended (or currently attend). In what ways was this group implicitly or explicitly silenced in the classroom? How did its hush harbor compare to the "cyber sista-cipher" Kynard describes? Be sure to analyze specific examples of the language, behavior, and judgment of this group as you flesh out your portrait. What purposes did your hush harbor serve, and in what ways do you think it succeeded or failed in its endeavor?

2. Kynard at times employs African American language in both her article and her cybertalk with her students, yet this essay was published in an elite academic journal, the *Harvard Educational Review*. In other words, for all the talk in college classrooms about the "appropriate" language for academic writing, Kynard managed to go public in an academic setting without entirely relinquishing a form of discourse generally discouraged (and penalized) in school. Write an essay in which you examine Kynard's use of language. Locate examples of supposedly academic and nonacademic discourses in her article and discuss how and why Kynard brings them together. What do you think of the way she speaks with her students in the hush harbor? Should teachers model forms of discourse that are presumed not to be acceptable by the academic world? Why or why not? What does Kynard's use of language in this article suggest about the possibilities for academic writing?

3. Kynard poses the "what-if" questions of whether "school success is really — most of the time or even some of the time — about eradicating pan-African/ black conscious identity and language" and whether the successes of the women in the cipher "were contingent on the fact that they mastered a kind of public performance of racelessness" (para. 28). By asking "what if," Kynard urges us to contemplate the possibility that success in school depends on conforming to a language and code of conduct that eradicates race. Write an essay in which you explore the questions Kynard raises here. *What if* those who don't already belong to the dominant racial group have to put their forms of expression and behavior on hold to succeed in school? Does this pressure to conform to an existing academic code only affect African American girls? Are there other forms of exclusion? Reflect on the questions Kynard asks and attempt to address them. In what ways are students expected to perform "*right*-white bourgeois etiquette" (para. 6) in school? What are the effects of this requirement? In what way should (or shouldn't) schooling be changed to allow for alternative language patterns and behavior?

Connecting

Kynard discusses how "hush harbors" are important to students who feel discriminated against at their universities. Such spaces provide them with communal support. Wilkey (p. 146) seems to argue that another viable option is to teach students overtly oppositional rhetoric to protest such conditions. Write an essay in which you discuss the relative merits of both positions for students facing discrimination in their classrooms and academic programs.

CHRISTOPHER WILKEY

Engaging Community Literacy through the Rhetorical Work of a Social Movement

Courtesy of Christopher Wilkey,
photo: Donelle Dresse

Christopher Wilkey is an associate professor at Northern Kentucky University. His work concerns the relationship between literacy, advocacy, and writing classrooms. He is also deeply involved in Cincinnati's Over-the-Rhine community, helping support the revitalization of that neighborhood. In the following essay, Wilkey describes how these commitments come together in his writing class. Over the course of the semester, students study literacy, learn about the community, and ultimately engage in an oppositional activist rhetoric in support of organizing efforts. In the process, Wilkey argues, students learn what it means to be an active citizen struggling for social justice.

In the following excerpt, originally published in *Reflections: A Journal of Writing, Service Learning, and Community Literacy,* Wilkey frames the goals for his work for both students and the community.

■ ■ ■

I see the community literacy project as a seed to start recording our history, our efforts, and our perspectives. History leaves us out. If the truth of our experience is never told, then much is lost. Knowledge is power. It's not everything, but it's a piece of how we get left out. If the history of Over-the-Rhine only gets written by the dominant forces, then there is a lot of blank pages. We have always said in our effort, a step out of oppression is expression.
—Bonnie Neumeier, Over-the-Rhine People's Movement activist

Neumeier's words above reflect the power of literacy when courageous individuals on the margins of society decide to "speak truth to power." For Neumeier and others like her, literacy has the potential to call attention to social injustices by enabling people to realize that "a step out of oppression" is indeed expression. And, these peoples' stories of oppression and exclusion are not without their opposites—liberation and inclusion. The very act of giving expression to lived experiences of hardship and struggle is an act of justice and redemption, one that helps assure that a people's history no longer goes unheard.

In the best of circumstances, speaking truth to power presents fundamental themes of tragedy and struggle aligned with genuine hope and possibility for the present and future. As antidotes to social injustice, hope and possibility are quite distinct from merely "wishing" or "dreaming." As Paula Mathieu points out, "To take on hope is to take on risk and responsibility while maintaining a dogged optimism."[1] In the context of a social movement, retaining what might be called a "critical hope" requires mobilizing actions that inspire and motivate while simultaneously calling out instances of social oppression and/or disenfranchisement. Literacy works to connect these actions associated with critical hope—actions expressing both a critique of the status quo and a progressive vision of the future—when communicating that the need for social change is necessary. It is at these moments, when speaking truth to power becomes much more than simply protesting on behalf of "truth" against those in power, that the work of a social movement becomes the work of literacy pedagogy.

The challenge for community literacy practitioners is to align our work with social movements and to use literacy and rhetoric to advance distinct causes. Community literacy practitioners can initiate pedagogical practices embodying critical hope which dramatize the interplay between critique and progressive social action, between social protest and a discourse of possibility. Locating the most opportune times to build strong working relations with social activists is not a straightforward task; the platforms for literacy associated with such a community are bound to differ in significant ways from the comfort many of us, along with our students, identify with the university classroom. Building productive alliances with social activists and the communities they represent is necessary to develop a pedagogical framework that utilizes a diverse set of literacy practices and to bring people together across radically different social standings and cultural backgrounds. Speaking truth to power requires exposing social injustices and directly calling out those who are responsible and holding them accountable. When considered side-by-side, these dual objectives—using literacy to bring people together to build community across difference while directly calling out others to expose their complicity with social injustices— may seem at odds. How, for instance, are we to reconcile the virtues of respect and reconciliation—the hallmarks of community-building—with a strident, confrontational rhetoric designed to target particular audiences deemed complicit in maintaining an unjust status quo?

This essay argues that community literacy projects can appropriately utilize the progressive rhetoric of community-building across difference, together with the provocative rhetoric often associated with speaking truth to power, when initiated within the context of a social movement committed to social justice. Drawing from rhetorical analyses and community literacy work in support of a local grassroots movement in the Cincinnati neighborhood of Over-the-Rhine, I show how social protest and community building—and by extension radical critique and direct social action—can function together as pedagogical activities that use public discourse to challenge dominant perceptions of inner-city life. In the community activism described throughout this essay, the seemingly contradictory poles of what Edward P. J. Corbett has identified as "the rhetoric of the open hand" and "the rhetoric of the closed fist" are combined through the pedagogical work of a particular social movement, signaling the power of rhetoric and literacy to advance critical hope. Ultimately, I argue that classroom practices employing the oppositional rhetoric of speaking truth to power have key advantages over the conciliatory rhetoric usually associated with work in community literacy when it comes to engaging our students in social justice work. . . .

Community Activism in Action: Rhetoric and the Over-the-Rhine People's Movement

5   Cincinnati's Over-the-Rhine neighborhood is not unlike many inner-city communities across the nation where attempts at community development clash with the reality of economic disenfranchisement and social oppression. According to the *Over-the-Rhine Community Housing* website, "In 1950 approximately 30,000 people resided in Over-the-Rhine, with whites constituting 99% of that population. Recent data show a population of about 7,600 residents, 80% black. Of the current residents, the median household income for four is less than $13,000. Of Over-the-Rhine's 7,500 habitable units, 3,000 are below housing code standards. About 300 buildings stand vacant." Over-the-Rhine continues to suffer from many of the typical problems associated with low-income urban environments, "including population decline, homelessness, increased segregation, building abandonment, high rates of unemployment and underemployment, and little access to political power."[2]

The professional class has long sought to rehabilitate this urban space, adhering to the belief that developing the area merely requires the free-market and entrepreneurial spirit to take center stage. This movement toward economic rejuvenation is very much underway. As described in an airing of National Public Radio's Weekend Edition Sunday, "The first time you come and drive through Over-the-Rhine, you'll focus on the street corner drug sellers. The second time, you'll notice the Italianate architecture, the bright colors. And then you'll see the coffee shop that sells used books, the art galleries, music clubs."[3]

The neighborhood is currently being gentrified. The threat of further displacement continues, and the future viability of a long-term local grassroots movement to secure the livelihood of low-income residents and workers remains under siege. Over the past forty years, the Over-the-Rhine People's Movement, "a network of organizations based in social service, community education, the arts, welfare rights, and affordable housing development,"[4] has consistently addressed issues of racial equity and social justice as well as provided needed services for residents. The success of People's Movement activists over the years is most evident in their historical efforts to stave off economic development plans done at the expense of low-income people.

My ongoing work in Over-the-Rhine follows my deep conviction that recent corporate efforts to transform the neighborhood make it essential that the work of the community organizations affiliated with the People's Movement be supported to enhance equitable redevelopment. The rich history of community activism affiliated with the People's Movement through the years signals the power of literacy to effect change in the community. Even though the powerful have tended to downplay their point of view, these activists understand how their own voices are central to the movement toward community self-determination.

A People's Account of Over-the-Rhine: Then and Now

The history of the Over-the-Rhine People's Movement dates back to the late 1960s and early 1970s when neighborhood activists took it upon themselves to organize and advocate for direct services for an ever-increasing homeless and poverty-stricken population residing in the neighborhood. Very much a product of a time when radical social movements across the globe were flourishing, the People's Movement utilized a rhetoric that framed the conditions of poverty engulfing the neighborhood as local manifestations of broader, global structural injustices. And for these activists, remedying social injustices at the local level was largely a matter of linking their work to social movements challenging the status quo more broadly. Specifically, arguments revolving around issues such as affordable housing, homelessness, welfare rights, and education in the neighborhood, employed direct appeals to struggles associated with movements advancing anti-imperialist, feminist, anti-war, and pro-labor agendas. A major forum for disseminating People's Movement rhetoric in Over-the-Rhine during the 1970s and the 1980s was *Voices: The Over-the-Rhine Community Newspaper*, a neighborhood publication raising awareness of political and civic matters facing residents and workers. A predominant goal for People's Movement activists and *Voices* writers during these early days was to directly connect the hardships of poor residents and workers in Over-the-Rhine to the plight of oppressed groups everywhere. For instance, at times, movement activists and *Voices* writers equated the social forces creating the poverty conditions in Over-the-Rhine with the imperialist practices spawning the forced removal of American Indians onto reservations:

> We recognize that Indian people are not alone in the fight to force the rewriting of history. Other "nations" of oppressed people are struggling to expose the truth of how they have been exploited by the American system—Black people, Appalachians, the Vietnamese. And we here in Over-the-Rhine, in our struggle for good living conditions, face some of the same oppressive problems American Indians face—and face the same small rich class of people who rule this land. Our struggles are the same. . . . If we understand the true history of genocide of Indian people, we can better understand the many exploitations of the present American system."[5]

Putting aside the problem of validity in associating gentrification to Indian genocide, the target of protest for these activists was the American system itself and the interests it served. It is clear who they regarded as responsible for its maintenance and legitimization: "In America, where power is held in the hands of a small rich class of people, the present-day news and history is written to support the money interests of that small group; not all the masses of people."[6] The workers and residents of Over-the-Rhine are portrayed as casting their lot with the masses of disenfranchised and exploited people, in opposition to the small group of people holding a disproportionate share of wealth, status, and power in American society.

10   The direct association of Over-the-Rhine with the historical struggles of disenfranchised and exploited people everywhere would find fuller expression in later accounts of the gentrifying process taking place in the neighborhood. In addressing the continuing gentrifying practices leading to the inevitable displacement of low-income people in the neighborhood over the last forty years, it has not become uncommon to characterize an individual working to "revitalize" Over-the-Rhine as the "modern 'urban pioneer'" who seeks to "wipe out native populations under the new manifest destiny—the promise of a bohemian culture, a vibrant business life, and bustling streets filled with walking consumers."[7] . . .

In terms of speaking truth to power, what is most striking about Dutton's account of gentrification as essentially an imperialist project is the boldness—the utter lack of timidity—in its charge that there are those who remain directly complicit in the perpetuation of social injustices done at the expense of society's most vulnerable members. In this account of gentrification, the misery felt by Over-the-Rhine workers and residents calls attention to the suffering experienced by excluded and dispossessed peoples everywhere. "Displacing the poor and arranging their disappearance," Dutton writes, "is the game plan."[8] For Dutton and other People's Movement activists, calling out those in power for their deliberate efforts to legitimate fundamentally unjust actions is largely a matter of defending the oppressed from the assaults of the oppressor. Protecting the interests of the poor and the dispossessed is what motivates their outrage directed toward those they deem culpable.

The potential value that social protest holds for activist work in inner-city communities like Over-the-Rhine is something that I try and teach my students. Introducing students to the People's Movement history of social protest encourages them to explore the grittier side of community activism and take sides on issues of public concern. The fallout of the neighborhood Uprising of 2001, which brought national attention to the city of Cincinnati during a four-day period in April of that year, is a prime example of the kind of issues facing Over-the-Rhine residents and workers over the last decade. It all began in the aftermath of the police shooting of Timothy Thomas, a 19-year-old black man. Officer Steven Rouch shot Thomas in the back during an on-foot pursuit — several police officers were chasing Thomas because of old traffic violations.[9] The incident ignited a storm of protest from the city's black community in general, and Over-the-Rhine residents and workers in particular. Subsequent rioting that followed the shooting drew local and national media attention. A *Cincinnati Enquirer* article sub-heading read: "Violence tears open the city, and it takes a curfew to bring calm. Bodies, property and the city's reputation are damaged in the worst urban unrest here in 30 years . . ."[10] Buried in news reports from media outlets across the city and nation focusing on the violence were acknowledgements that peaceful protests were organized over the four-day period of civil unrest. Protests expressed the deep-seated anger and frustration with, among other things, the fact that fifteen African-Americans had been shot to death by city police officers during the preceding six years.[11] While looting and property destruction took place in a number of Cincinnati neighborhoods, Over-the-Rhine activists organized peaceful protests that sought to explain why many of the "rioters" felt under-siege by the city establishment. "If you're fine when things are normal, then you want things to stay normal," said protest organizer Rev. Damon Lynch III. "If you're not, then normal is an uncomfortable place to be."[12]

Through extended inquiries into the Uprising of 2001 and the peaceful protests, including the subsequent civil unrest and its aftermath (which has both renewed efforts to improve race relations in the city and emboldened efforts to gentrify Over-the-Rhine), students in my Writing for Social Change class are encouraged to locate meanings that express something other than the uncritical view that "these people" were simply "immoral rioters" searching for an excuse to create mass havoc and chaos. Furthermore, students are asked to situate the violent acts of looting and property destruction in relation to the well-organized and peaceful demonstrations calling the city officials and police force into account for their ongoing discriminatory policies and practices against the poor and people of color. In doing so, students complicate ready-made assumptions regarding the nature of organized social protest and the value of using discourse to confront a culpable establishment head-on.

Rather than viewing proclamations of indignation—expressed through such slogans as "Stop Killing Us, or Else!" and "Don't Shoot!"[13]—as the mark of an "uncivil" or "unreasonable" response to an unfortunate situation, students come to question the all-too-easy identification of the direct challenge to authority such slogans clearly represent with any subsequent acts of violence that may eventually be wielded against that authority. Rather than viewing the confrontational rhetorics of social protest on display in the organized street demonstrations as *the cause* of much of the violence that was to ensue, students consider if the real culprit might actually be the unjust and oppressive living conditions forced on communities like Over-the-Rhine. Students inquire into the possibility that governmental policies that do little good for the poor, virulent racism, and a capitalist economic system increasingly assure that entire communities in our inner cities are left off the map. In this context, protest placards proclaiming "Cincinnati Cops: Stop Killing Black People!"[14] do more than lay blame at the feet of Cincinnati police officers; such discourse positions the police officers as agents of the State who have a responsibility to resist the oppressive and domineering charge to control, and make submissive, black bodies on the streets. Speaking truth to power, students learn, involves articulating a "truth" that those in power may not be comfortable hearing but that nonetheless prioritizes the necessity of expressing indignation directed at an unjust system that perpetuates the indignant conditions many are forced to live under. . . .

Speaking Truth to Power: Hands, Fists, and Social Protest

15   The approach to speaking truth to power described above suggests a distinct conception of political rhetoric. As an expression of political rhetoric, being competent in naming the oppressor and systems of oppression is not all that is required for People's Movement activists to effectively call into question unjust actions. Rather, what is needed is a rhetorical framework to critically interrogate the unjust activities enacted by those who wield power over the oppressed and to hold them accountable. At the same time, the oppressed must use discourse to challenge each other to "unchain themselves," and in so doing, build community for the purpose of coming together for self-determination.

In proclaiming who and what are actively working against the interests of the poor in Over-the-Rhine People's Movement, activists complete only one half of the equation necessary to speak truth to power. The other half entails convincing others that their critique, or protest, is worth engaging. However, the rhetoric deployed by the People's Movement must contend with a number of obstacles, the most obvious being the tendency to be labeled by audiences as "extremist" or "coercive." In this sense, the People's Movement shares much in common with the rhetorical legacy of American radicalism. According to James Darsey, American radicalism is best exemplified by "its concern with the political roots of a society, its fundamental laws, its foundational principles, its most sacred covenants."[15] Subsequently, its rhetoric might be characterized as "a steadfast refusal to adapt itself to the perspectives of its audience," and as a result, be perceived by the majority as "uncivil" or "extremist."[16] The backdrop for establishing what might come to be stigmatized as an incendiary rhetoric is the promotion of its opposite: a civil, conciliatory rhetoric. Nonetheless, the form and content of a "civil discourse" is wholly dependent on the rhetorical situation from which it derives. In the case of the People's Movement's employment of social protest, it is useful to examine the form of "civility" it is in response to.

In "Corbett's Hand: A Rhetorical Figure for Composition Studies,"[17] Richard Marback examines composition studies' continuing disavowal of confrontational rhetorics in favor of the humanist rhetorics associated with our professional discourses, which are portrayed as conciliatory, civil, and effectively reasoned. Turning to Edward P. J. Corbett's 1969 article, "The Rhetoric of the Closed Fist and the Rhetoric of the Open Hand," Marback traces composition's inability to effectively engage the public on issues of justice to the field's response to the turmoil of the late 1960s, when numerous protest movements centering on issues of race, class, and gender were ultimately positioned as "coercive" by the broader culture. Drawing from the classical rhetorical figure of "the open hand and the closed fist," composition studies constructed "the humanizing, liberating potential of the writing hand in opposition to the externally and physically enforced violence of the closed fist."[18] Corbett argued that composition studies needed to side with the "reasoned, sustained, conciliatory discussion of the issues" of the open hand, in contrast to the "non-rational, non-sequential, often nonverbal, frequently provocative means [of persuasion]" of the closed fist "prevalent in the late 1960's."[19] According to Marback, however, the uncivil attributes ascribed to social protest concealed the actual violent and coercive dynamics of certain rhetorics marked as "civil" or "progressive." It is this privileging of a civil discourse, in opposition to the "unseemly" confrontational discourse of social protest, that composition studies has inherited.

While the People's Movement clearly operates in a different context from composition studies, its positioning as a movement on the margins of the broader culture suggests that much of its work remains a response to dominant rhetorical modes and styles. In the case of composition studies in the late 1960s, the rhetoric on society's margins that presented the biggest challenge to the field's conception of itself as promoting the democratic ideal of the open hand was the closed-fist rhetoric associated with Black Power. Through the discourse of civility marked by the open hand stood its opposite—the Black Power fist, made emblematic of the exact kind of discourse that was understood to be an anathema to a democratic polity. "From the perspective of liberal democracy," Marback writes, "the image of the conciliatory open hand gives expression to the most significant opportunities for discursive mediations of civic life, while the closed-fisted refusal to engage in a discussion in these terms signals all that is opposed to democratic values and civic participation."[20] On the other hand, "In a society where racial identity correlates with power and privilege, the Black Power fist gives expression not only to belligerence, but to the feelings of anger and frustration with systemic indifference to discrimination and segregation."[21]

In the same way that the anger at the white establishment and the moral indignation expressed through the clenching of fists stood as a justified response to racial oppression and discrimination, the People's Movement's targeting of Over-the-Rhine "urban pioneers" as "colonial rulers"[22] signals an appropriate response to the real-world violence of gentrification. As an Over-the-Rhine developer recently put it in describing his great fortune to expand and develop his area of operations to revitalize the neighborhood, "We're having a lot of success. This area is like a low-hanging fruit."[23] The People's Movement use of social protest is a response to precisely this kind of "open-hand" rhetoric, which in actuality operates as a coercive, imperialist project disguised in the cloak of "civility" and "conciliation."

20   As Marback demonstrates, the rhetoric of civility embedded in the image of the open hand has provided composition studies with an idealized version of writing to intervene in public affairs to challenge social injustices, and contribute to social change. Insofar as the "open hand" pits the expression of a privileged group in opposition to an "unreasonable" and "coercive" closed-fist rhetoric, teachers can imagine students getting training in a privileged discourse that will give them access to public audiences. However, when communicating effectively means using a discourse to "move out of the realm of the disenfranchised into the realm of privilege,"[24] then it is difficult to imagine how that same discourse might address the concerns of a socially disenfranchised group, other than to say that one is providing critical insights from a position of privilege entirely divorced from the discursive exchanges and material conditions giving rise to the social injustices in the first place. The capacity of teachers and students, then, to use public discourse in ways that matter is severely contained because the mere expression of critical insights purporting to challenge the system is understood as equal to actually *changing* the system.

Unlike this idealized image of an open hand, for those speaking truth to power it is precisely the discursive exchanges and material conditions determining the everyday lives and concerns of the socially disenfranchised that mark the terms of engagement with systems of privilege and oppression. Rather than using rhetoric to fashion a critical-distancing from issues as a way to direct social change from above, speaking truth to power confronts power head-on to *critically engage directly with issues*, and in so doing, upends the figure of the open hand raised up and the closed fist clenching. Turned downward, the open hand is now envisioned as moving down grasping, engulfing, and smothering everything within its reach; while the closed fist rises up from the ground, and asserts itself, disrupting attempts made by the open hand to hold it down. In this sense, the closed-fist rhetoric of the People's Movement finds ways to disrupt the established symbolic order so as to call attention to a new social order, one that re-thinks everyday perceptions of inner-city life.

It is exactly at this point of discursive disruption where we can theorize that the operation of the hand and fist ultimately becomes paradoxical: the disruptive movement of the closed fist pushing upward becomes enmeshed in the open hand, but rather than smothering the closed fist, the open hand now works to embrace it. Combining fist with hand, the new figure links the power of critical assertion with the receptiveness of listening—the capacity of the fist to assert itself becomes an act of self-determination which is nevertheless dependent on the good will of the embracing hand to give full recognition to the capacity of oppressed peoples to express their own self-worth and dignity on their own terms. . . .

Implications for Community Literacy Pedagogy

Speaking truth to power has significant pedagogical implications for the prospects of initiating community literacy projects in tandem with the work of a social movement. Before describing my community literacy work in alliance with the Over-the-Rhine People's Movement, it is helpful to clarify the role of community literacy pedagogy as a form of action sustained by the work of a social movement that supports the kind of rhetorical dynamics outlined in the previous section. When it comes to creating a pedagogical framework, my account of speaking truth to power suggests that simply mobilizing critical resistance on the part of students as a solution to the problem of community disempowerment disengages the work of community literacy projects away from local communities. Simply having students provide academic critiques as a literate strategy for countering social injustices in a local inner-city neighborhood like Over-the-Rhine has consequences not unlike what may happen in a writing classroom on a university campus if the discourse used remains largely disengaged from the real-life rhetorical situations of the everyday lives of people residing in that community. While emphasizing that the solution to social injustices is actualized in students' use of literacy to *identify*—and perhaps theoretically challenge—the work of hegemony, all too often community literacy pedagogy fails to consider ways in which literacy might be used as an *activity* for combating social injustices keeping the status quo in place.

This opposition between critical insight and structural change marks the gulf between engagement and rhetorical action in community literacy projects that simply ask students to write critically about the social injustices they observe in the community. For community literacy projects to work toward structural solutions to systemic problems, they need to take into account the necessity of using writing as a tool for collectively critically engaging those problems. For community literacy projects to fulfill their promise of social change, proposing solutions is not enough. Implying that when individuals simply identify the work of hegemony this automatically satisfies the conditions for acting more justly in the world draws attention away from structural solutions. The stark divide between critical insight and social action inherited from the broader discipline of composition studies helps explain why community literacy practitioners interested in social change often find it so difficult to provide an institutional framework for effectively challenging the status quo in the local communities in which they work. Whenever community literacy pedagogy solicits individual students to articulate critical insights at the expense of genuine social reform in partnership with local grassroots movements for change, the possibility of instituting actions that work for social justice is greatly compromised.

25 Positioning community literacy pedagogy within the context of a movement for social change requires finding ways for literacy education to provide opportunities for learning what is at stake in activist work. This pedagogy brings students and teachers into dialogue with community members and activists to critically engage issues and to disrupt established hierarchies across systems of privilege and oppression. In the process, community building across difference is initiated by providing material space for critical assertions that challenge structural injustices. In this sense, speaking truth to power operates as a literacy practice that provides opportunities for enacting critical hope by grounding writing in the material conditions giving rise to the most pressing issues facing a community while bearing witness to the possibility of enacting genuine transformation in the service of social justice. Going beyond merely identifying and critiquing social injustices, inviting students to work with community members and activists to use writing critically to speak truth to power can be a genuine act of civic engagement.

Community Literacy Work with the Over-the-Rhine People's Movement

My involvement with community literacy work in Over-the-Rhine began when I first made contact with a few People's Movement activists and heard them express a strong desire to document and publicize the long history of community activism in Over-the-Rhine. I had already engaged in a number of social justice related activities in the neighborhood during the previous four years and was viewed as a credible partner because I had earned, as a People's Movement activist once told me, the required "community credits." Furthermore, I had already internalized much of the vocabulary and ideological dispositions of the People's Movement. This ability to "talk the talk" of the movement gave us a shared language for discussing issues that mattered and provided me with an entry point for learning more deeply about the people, including their struggles, hopes, and fears.

I eventually established a working relationship with Thomas A. Dutton at the Miami University Center for Community Engagement in Over-the-Rhine. I teach my Writing for Social Change course at the Center. Students in this class meet regularly at the Center and interact with Over-the-Rhine community residents and activists as a way of examining how an actual social movement and everyday people use rhetoric and writing to work for social change. Significantly, the university where I teach—largely a commuter campus with many first-generation college students—is in the suburbs across the river from Cincinnati. My students are very familiar with "how Over-the-Rhine, within the cultural imagination of the entire Cincinnati region, has become so symbolic of all the negative images and things that are supposedly wrong with the city: crime, blight, dirtiness, general poverty, etc. . . ."[25] Most of my students come from suburban environments and many claim "to know" Over-the-Rhine, although their familiarity with the neighborhood often comes "from watching the crime reports on the 11 o'clock news." It is not a stretch to say that many students are often "afraid to visit the neighborhood."[26]

As an example of community literacy emphasizing public writing, this Writing for Social Change course culminates in an "Over-the-Rhine Campaign Project" in partnership with People's Movement activists. Over the course of the semester, students are introduced to ongoing activist campaigns in Over-the-Rhine to assist low-income individuals and the homeless. Students have numerous face-to-face interactions with community activists and take on many critical investigations into media and community texts dealing with Over-the-Rhine. Students also have substantial opportunities to participate in the formation of actual campaign projects through interactions with these community activists. The components of a given campaign can take many forms, including: designing and producing a "street newsletter" or "'zine," creating a Display Board based on oral history interviews of Over-the-Rhine residents and workers, and working with Over-the-Rhine residents and workers on their writing. The basic requirement is that the project be done in consultation with our community partners.

As part of their Over-the-Rhine Campaign Project, a recent class of students designed and produced a 'zine entitled *The People's Friend*, in recognition of their support of the Over-the-Rhine People's Movement. One of the students, Dana Divine, had the opportunity to read a poem that he wrote which was published in this 'zine at an Open Mic gathering at InkTank, the previously mentioned community writing center in Over-the-Rhine. Writers and poets from the Men's Recovery Program at the Drop Inn Center homeless shelter direct this event.

I facilitate a weekly writing group at the Drop Inn Center with these men, who use writing as a tool for recovery from drug and alcohol abuse. Central to my pedagogical approach in facilitating this writing group is to make connections with the broader social issues in Over-the-Rhine as a way of strengthening their work through the recovery progress.

30   The poem Divine wrote for the 'zine and Open Mic is entitled "Gentrification— a.k.a. Get the Fuck Out!" During one of my meetings with the Drop Inn Center writing group, I passed out my students' 'zine to the men. I asked them to write in response to the pieces in 'zine. One of the men, "The Mad Poet," wrote a poem in direct response to Dana's poem. The Mad Poet's poem, entitled "Serfication—a.k.a. I am One With the Land," completes a textual interaction that demonstrates the capacity that speaking truth to power has in using social protest to build community across difference. Below, I present both poems in their entirety:

Gentrification—a.k.a. Get the Fuck Out!
by Dana Divine

Out with the tired, old, poor,
we want something easy on the eyes.
How about a nice café,
Maybe some upscale clothing shops.
The people need better living conditions,
I'm for some new condos (market rate of course!)
Why don't these people get their shit together,
Pull themselves up from their bootstraps?
Turn that frown upside down,
make those lemons into lemonade.
Try getting a goddamn job,
make a contribution to society.

This community is growing, expanding,
we're trying to rebuild and reinvent.
We don't want to kick people to the curb,
maybe they can just scoot out of the way.
Let's not allow anyone to slow us down,
change must be painless and quick.

This world is forever changing,
Only the strongest can keep up,
it's a Darwinian thing,
the survival of the richest.
There is no progress without casualties,
it's the American way by God!

***

Serfication—a.k.a. I am One With the Land
by The Mad Poet

I am tired, old, and poor,
I line up twice in soup kitchens for more.
Can you see that I am down but not out,
Why must I get the fuck out?

I am one with the land,
You must seriously reconsider your plan.
Please grant me more time to pay,
I am currently learning the right way.

By simply taking it day by day,
I know what they say.
I am society's so-called ill,
Lost my job, can't pay the bills.

No matter what the sun always shines,
Today I opposed a sip of wine.
Instead I drank cold lemonade,
Things not perfect, but soon I'll have it made.
My pain is sometimes un-bearing,
Upscale society is so uncaring.
A smile gets me through the pain,
I do this even in the rain.

The community is growing and expanding,
I am taking vocational classes through understanding.
The poor cannot compete with the riches,
Does Darwin's theory mean I must sleep in ditches?

Is your community redevelopment approved by God,
Or should I march and scream a Christian Jihad?
Unnecessary causalities is so unkind,
What happened to no man left behind?

Can you see that I am down but not out,
Why must I get the fuck out?
I am one with the land,
You must seriously reconsider your plan.

Speaking in the voice of the Over-the-Rhine market-rate developer, Divine uses sarcasm to highlight the dangers unfettered market-rate development holds for low-income individuals in communities like Over-the-Rhine. A culmination of what he learned through his critical inquiries into the rhetoric surrounding the historical and contemporary struggles in Over-the-Rhine, the poem reaches back against systems of privilege and oppression to make space for an alternative perspective to be heard. In the process, the poem invites an encounter with difference as an opportunity to learn more about the lived experiences of the "other." The Mad Poet accepts Divine's invitation by speaking in his own voice and on his own terms, proclaiming boldly the true impact that gentrification has on the lives of the most vulnerable in society. Taken together, both poems illustrate how speaking truth to power calls direct attention to unjust political arrangements and holds the oppressor accountable—all the while providing the material conditions necessary for encouraging community ties across difference. . . .

I have attempted to show how an oppositional rhetoric might be utilized to directly engage social injustices, and in doing so, hold accountable those who are perpetuating an unjust status quo. Instead of asking, "How do we teach the rhetorical art of ongoing inquiry versus position taking (even when that position is inspired by a liberatory ideology)?"[27] I would have us ask, How do we work with students to show that position taking is essential and that the "art of ongoing inquiry" is not limited to the conciliatory acts of a "civic dialogue"? How do we teach that the oppositional rhetoric of speaking truth to power is an important dimension of many effective organized efforts to collectively inquire into social injustices and confront directly head-on those entities responsible for maintaining unjust political and economic arrangements? How, in other words, do we confront a conciliatory rhetoric that would have us believe that building a community of individuals to organize and express outrage directed at an establishment that clearly perpetuates social injustices is at best rather impotent and at worse reactionary, even violent? . . .

Community literacy projects such as the one I have outlined in this essay offer one way for students to learn the links between writing and social change through direct engagement with an actual social movement on the ground. Students in my Writing for Social Change course become first-hand witnesses to oppression, as they come to experience—both dramatically and vividly—ordinary people organizing efforts to fight social injustices. Through practices of both collective inquiry *and* collective position taking, students learn that sometimes placing demands for change on established audiences is the only alternative available for people who have been historically marginalized and disenfranchised.

As community literacy practitioners, aligning our work with social movements committed to progressive social change can introduce us, along with our students, to rhetorical strategies that have the potential of transforming community relations. At the same time, oppositional rhetorical strategies that speak truth to power have the potential of disrupting power relations in the context of community-building while also calling attention to the legitimacy of critical assertions and receptive listening in the more general, global debates involving issues of social justice. While creating an atmosphere of productive discursive engagement across racial, class, and gender lines may prove extremely challenging in public spheres where dominant voices effectively work to silence those on the margins, engaging grassroots social movement activities on the ground is more likely to provide substantive opportunities for discursive exchanges that challenge dominant conceptions of the lives of the socially disenfranchised and dispossessed. As an invitation to encounter people's organized efforts to challenge social injustices, engaging community literacy through the rhetorical work of a social movement holds the promise of encouraging us, along with our students, to experience writing and rhetoric as tools for genuine social change.

Reading

1. How does Wilkey define the purpose of the current "conciliatory rhetoric" taught to students engaged in community partnership work?

2. How does he define the purpose of teaching these same students "oppositional rhetoric" (para. 4)?

3. How does oppositional rhetoric lead to alternative forms of writing by residents and by students?

4. How does Wilkey argue that students need both conciliatory and oppositional rhetoric to be fully prepared for community work?

Inquiring

1. Wilkey makes a rather unusual claim in his essay. He seems to argue that if the college classroom is meant to prepare students to be active citizens in their community, that classroom needs to provide students with an opportunity to engage in writing that is strident, direct, and confrontational. He writes, "I argue that classroom practices employing the oppositional rhetoric of speaking truth to power have key advantages over the conciliatory rhetoric usually associated with work in community literacy when it comes to engaging our students in social justice work" (para. 4). That is not the way writing classrooms—or college classrooms, in general—typically operate. Researched and nuanced opinions tend to be the goal. And usually students *study* movements for social justice; they are not asked to *participate* in them. As a student in a writing course, how do you respond to Wilkey's belief in the social goals of the writing classroom? Do you share his belief in the power of oppositional rhetoric? Based on your experience, what type of writing do you believe would best prepare students to be socially engaged writers? How would you respond to being required to take part in a social movement campaign as part of a college course?

2. Wilkey describes his class as an example of "community literacy pedagogy" (para. 24). For Wilkey, this pedagogy means asking students to study theories of literacy and rhetoric, travel to the Over-the-Rhine neighborhood, meet local residents (such as Bonnie Neumeier), and engage in different community-based projects (such as the poetry reading). The strategy of having students

study a topic and then explore the "real-life" implication of that topic in a local community has become increasingly popular in some college courses. Many universities and colleges now have entire programs and institutes dedicated to supporting such community partnership and service-learning courses. Indeed, you might have already participated in such classrooms during high school or in a previous college class. It is unclear, however, whether students and community members find this pedagogical method as useful as their teachers and universities hope. Having read Wilkey's essay, what do you believe his students learned from being in the class? How would you describe the value of the community partnership aspect of the course? About the goals of community literacy pedagogy?

3. Wilkey's classroom is intimately connected to his larger commitment to the Over-the-Rhine neighborhood. By the end of his essay, he highlights students who have also endorsed this commitment, showcasing poetry written for a public reading. Reread the poem by student Dana Divine (p. 158). What do you believe the student writer means when writing "we"? What type of relationship is the writer claiming with the Over-the-Rhine community? Do you see him endorsing the social and political goals of the movement? Should the taking of such positions be the goal of a writing course? Of any college course? How do you understand the connections between writing, the classroom, and civic engagement?

Composing

1. Wilkey attempts to create a class that will provide students the writing strategies necessary to become active public citizens. Although he locates his students in a local struggle to which he is committed, his hope is that the strategies acquired through his classroom will be applicable to any social issue or cause. In effect, he attempts to think through what it might mean to create a classroom (or set of classrooms) that supports the work of the next generation of community leaders.

    You and your classmates are that next generation of leaders. Write an essay in which you discuss what specific economic, cultural, and international challenges your generation will face upon graduation. Using Wilkey's article as a model, imagine a writing classroom that would provide both the writing strategies and hands-on experience necessary to become an effective leader. Where might they go for their community writing experience? What actual type of writing would students engage in? A poem, a paper, a protest?

2. Community-based classes are becoming increasingly popular on college campuses. Wilkey provides the reader with one example of such a class, in this case a class linked to a larger social movement for community justice. There

are also many other ways students are asked to connect their education with a community. To understand what a community-based class means, more examples must be found, studied, and assessed.

Write an essay in which you discuss what the term *community-based class* means on your campus. To do this work, you might visit the campus community partnership or service-learning office (if there is one), collect campus brochures that highlight service-learning opportunities, or survey course offerings in various departments. After studying these materials, what can you say about how they represent the work of such courses? What values or goals do you see being expressed? How does Wilkey's understanding compare to the definition of such work on your campus? As a student who might have to take such courses, which do you believe offer the more important learning experience?

3. In 2011, Occupy Wall Street became a national movement, with activists staging protests in cities across the United States. The central slogan of this movement was "We are the 99 percent," a phrase used to indicate the movement's belief that 1 percent of the country possessed an unfair portion of the nation's wealth. Among those taking part in the protests were large numbers of college students or recent college graduates. Some of them no doubt were enrolled in a required writing course during their academic career, and many might have been involved in a class structured around a community-based project. Write a short essay in which you explore the language of a recent social movement, such as Black Lives Matter or Marriage Equality. How would you describe the methods those involved in that movement use to persuade the public to endorse their position? What types of language do political leaders use to respond to those demands? How might the movement be said to have succeeded or failed in shifting public debate over toward their understanding of the issue? Reflecting on Wilkey's belief in the usefulness of "speaking truth to power," how might this movement justify or critique the belief that writing classrooms should prepare students to engage in oppositional social justice? How do you understand the relationship between social justice movements and the goals of a college education?

Connecting

Wilkey claims his students learn valuable lessons about writing through their community partnerships. Such experiences, he claims, make the work of their academic classroom "real." In making this argument, Wilkey is coming to a much different solution to Graff's "problem problem" (p. 114). Write an essay in which you discuss how each author attempts to overcome students' lack of interest in academic work. Be sure to discuss which argument you find more persuasive and why.

Projects for Chapter 4

PROJECT 7 Crossing Boundaries

Graff (p. 114) and Wilkey (p. 146) tell stories of the classroom, stories in which students' thoughts and actions are represented in writing. With a rare exception, however, the students discussed do not control how they are portrayed; instead, their tales are told by others. The emergence of social media, though, has provided a seemingly endless array of places where students can tell their version of their own classroom experiences. Sites such as ratemyprofessor.com, wehatecollege .tumblr.com, and studentactivism.tumblr.com offer students a space in which to describe their experiences without engaging in the kinds of formal academic analysis that professors often expect from student writing.

For this assignment, research three Web sites where undergraduate students discuss their education. In examining the sites, pay attention to how students represent their experiences in school. What key terms and phrases appear on these sites? How do these terms and phrases express certain values about the writers and their view of education? How are comments assessed by those who read the Web site? In what ways does the writing on the Web site differ from the writing you have read this term? For instance, thinking back to Graff's essay, how might these Web sites be said to "read deeply"? Is there a sense that classrooms should, as Wilkey argues, prepare students for activist work as citizens?

Having done this analysis, join one of the conversational threads and express your opinion on the issue using one of your emerging theories on the goals of a university classroom or what makes a good writing classroom (perhaps developed previously in an assignment). Be sure to use the writing style that fits that site. Follow any comments and traffic about your post, responding and exploring how the site allows your theory to develop. Be prepared to discuss and present to your class the way in which this experience helped you understand the relationship between the kind of writing done in a college classroom and the kind done on a social media site. How do you understand the strengths and weaknesses of both forums for engaging in public dialogue about education?

PROJECT 8 Hush Harbors

The authors of the essays in this chapter have indicated (directly and indirectly) a variety of strategies students might use to initiate or participate in discussions about the goals of education on their campus. Kynard (p. 127) points to online forums such as "hush harbors"—a resource she finds both important and troubling—to build a collective student identity on what education may or may not mean on campus. Using a community-based pedagogy, Wilkey alludes to the power of public forums such as poetry readings as possible arenas for building a collective identity among different populations and effecting change. Notably, each of these authors is writing and offering suggestions from the position of the teacher, however sympathetically aligned with student interests.

Yet students themselves often strategize, create, and maintain a variety of publications designed to give them a voice on campus. Research the student-led publications on your campus, either in print or online. Explore the mission and goals of these publications, paying particular attention to how each frames itself as a voice for students. What do these publications see as the important issues that students confront? What do the publications see as their role in fostering debate on these issues? In what ways does each publication enable individual students to take part in a campus dialogue about education—or prevent them from doing so? Having answered these questions, choose one publication you think provides the best forum for your views on a specific educational issue facing students and write a piece to submit for consideration by the editors of that publication. Keep track of their response as well as any student responses if the piece is published.

Be prepared to discuss and present to class the way in which this experience helped you understand the relationship between the kind of writing done for college professors and that supported by a campus publication. What do you see as the strengths and weaknesses of both forms of writing for creating a public dialogue on campus about the goals of education?

PROJECT 9 A Community of Classrooms

A campus map is both informative and deceptive. It provides information for students, but it also has a limited vision of where a student can learn and what constitutes an educational space. It also fails to represent all the locations community members can go for their own educational needs. For this reason, such maps fail to represent a complete sense of the community and divide individuals into students and nonstudents.

For this project, you will revise your college's "campus map" into a community educational map—understanding the entire community as a campus offering educational opportunities. In doing so, you should think beyond limited visions of educational sites as being just classrooms; don't simply add in all the local public and private schools. Instead, consider the parks where individuals gather to talk politics, the churches where sermons sponsor public debate, and the sports arenas where discussion of football soon lead to politics. Take seriously that individuals can learn — can gain an education — in spaces that are not enclosed by classroom walls.

As you develop your map, create a key that allows you to record all the "locations" you think teaching or learning might occur. Think broadly here and try to indicate the many types of education that go on in a vibrant community. You might also create symbols for different types of learning. For instance, public schools might be marked with a triangle, health centers with a square, and athletic programs with an asterisk. The goal is to begin to map out how your classroom is part of a larger educational context.

Of course, you and many of your classmates might be new to the area. If so, your map might have a lot of empty space or unused key symbols. Here is where the collective wisdom of your classmates becomes vital. Once you have finished your map, share it with the entire class, creating one large map and key through which to understand the teaching and learning that occurs community-wide. Even with the whole class participating, however, you still might not have many organizations listed on the map. Before the next class, go online and find organizations in the city that match the different "keys" developed in class. (This research will also show whether your keys are useful terms to chart education in your community.) Bring this list to class along with a brief explanation of each organization. Work collaboratively as a class to add more detail and nuance to your map.

Once you have added in all your new data, discuss what this map tells you about education (and educational opportunity) in the community. What types of education are offered in the city? Does the type of education change based on which part of the city is being considered? How does the education offered in your college classroom relate to the larger educational efforts occurring in the city?

Note: Actual campus maps are copyrighted, and more often than not, university administrations are not open to allowing them to be revised. For that reason, you might take advantage of Google Maps, which can generate an image of a particular area, often as an aerial photo. The Map Builder function can then develop a set of pushpins that, when clicked, show any posted photos and text. Use this program to develop the map. Then consider how this map might circulate among students and community members, becoming a public document that details all the spaces in which one can acquire an education.

PROJECT 10 Community Voices

A consistent theme in this chapter has been the "public" nature of the writing classroom. As many have argued, it does not make sense to see a classroom or campus as separate from the neighborhoods that surround it. For instance, Wilkey attempted to locate his classroom projects in the history of a neighborhood, seeing the classroom as a space affected by and responding to a local history and culture. He took this argument even further by imagining how the classroom itself could be used to foster activism on behalf of neighborhood residents. Like Graff, he imagined the classroom as potentially preparing students for a "public role."

Yet few of these authors actively included the voice of city residents—local community intellectuals who might also have a sense of how the city could be re-formed or transformed. While the classroom was expanding in focus, the definition of *intellectual* seemed firmly rooted in the academy and the purview of professors who granted or failed to grant this status to community members. Very few of us, however, would be happy with such a definition. Indeed, many of us would be able to point to community members who represented much of what we might value about intellectual work, such as curiosity, thoughtfulness, or a commitment to issues larger than themselves. These individuals, however, have rarely gained access to college classrooms or academic departments—until now.

Taking seriously the idea that classrooms and universities should be responsive to the local environment, you are being tasked with creating a vision for a new academic department where students would go to learn about your community prior to doing any academic work on campus. The department must be staffed with community members (which for the moment will be defined as "nonacademics"). Write a department mission statement that explains what will be taught about your community. Also list at least six community members who would teach, and determine what they would teach. Give a brief biography of each individual, stating what each person will bring to the classroom and students in terms of knowledge. (A local community organizer, for instance, might bring a sense of the neighborhood's history.)

Be prepared to discuss and present to class how the knowledge contained in this new "department" could (or should) alter what students need to learn before becoming active in the community and before taking community-based courses. How does such a department also challenge what it means to be an intellectual? To be someone from whom others can learn?

PROJECT 11 A Community of Intellectuals

Every community has intellectuals, but as you read in Chapter 1, not every community intellectual is recognized as such. In many ways, universities and colleges are the best example of this statement. Too often, it seems, only the professors are seen as intellectuals. Everyone else who works on campus—perhaps serving food, cleaning classrooms, or tending to the grounds—is seen as merely supporting the professors' or students' work. Clearly, this view of "intellectuals" is very limited.

Working with your classmates, develop a list of "campus intellectuals." These individuals should possess wisdom not only about the campus but also about life and about what it means to be an active member of a community. Develop a set of questions that will allow them to share their wisdom and insights with students on campus about what it means to be someone who is actively engaged in this community, working for a better future.

Once completed, transcribe and edit the interviews into narrative form, with each interviewee signing off on the final version. Create a Web site that features an introductory essay written by the class and the interviews, and share the site's URL with campus publications.

(For strategies on how to conduct interviews, pp. 213–15. For information on publication permission letters, see pp. 240–41.)

PROJECT 12 Activist Scholars

Many of the readings in this chapter have focused on how students should acquire the skills necessary to take on the role of a public intellectual. For Graff (p. 114), this role seems pointed primarily toward rhetorical argument; for Kynard (p. 127), this role seems pointed to activism on campus; for Wilkey (p. 146), this role seems to require linking both campus and community activism. None of the authors, however, provide a full guide for these skills. In that sense, their essays are more contemplative than concrete.

For this project, you will develop such a concrete guide. As a class, put together a list of student organizations that could be described as "activist." In developing this list, you should not limit your self to organizations with overtly political titles; you should also consider organizations whose members understand their mission as changing the campus around cultural issues as well. Then develop a list of questions that will enable the organization members to speak about the skills they use in this public work, including what skills were learned in the classroom and what skills were learned outside the classroom. Assign each class member one organization to contact, interview, and document its work and insights.

Having collected this information, prepare a small photocopied chapbook entitled "The Campus Activists' Handbook," in which each page discusses one of the skills necessary to be a campus activist, providing an example from one of the interviewed activists of when this skill was used on campus. Once the chapbook is complete, share it with the student organizations, allowing them to reproduce it for their own use.

(For strategies on interviewing, see pp. 213–15. For information on publication permission, see pp. 240–41. For information on print publishing considerations, see pp. 244–46.)

PART TWO

Collaboration & Publishing

Community Partnerships

Writing Prompt: "Ode to an Intersection"

Write about an intersection that inhabits your heart.

Response: "Intersections" by Laura Lau

From *Open City: A Journal of Community Arts and Culture*

The intersection is the corner of the city that demands the most attention, where pedestrians gingerly cross the street at the sound of a siren; where the UPS truck sometimes parks beyond the end of the rounded curb and into the street, blocking everyone's view. It is the meeting place of people and cars, where they do the dance of I'm going first. The intersection is the crossroads of comings and goings. The intersection is a place of decisions and indecisions: "Should I cross here or there? Am I going or stopping?" It is the place of contemplation and motion. It is the place where you always wind up. It is the place where you must decide. The intersection defines the neighborhood. Sometimes it is the neighborhood; after all, this is where the action ends and sometimes begins.

Walking down the tree-lined sidewalk from the bus stop, I approach an intersection that I've lived with for four years, a place that sees a lot of excitement regardless of the season, regardless of the time of day. At least twice a week I enter the mom and pop general store to get a quart of milk or a bag of chips. It is the place with the hanging "Enjoy Coca-Cola" sign above the doorway, the place where I'll always get a "hello" and "see ya, babe." Phil and Mrs. Phil

New City Community Press/
Peter Hanley/Yolanda Wisher

have run the place for years. Phil opens the place early in the morning by sweeping the sidewalk. I'm not sure when Mrs. Phil relieves him; all I know is that I usually see her on my nightly visits, talking with her friend who likes to play the poker machine. Two summers ago, on a balmy weeknight, coming from the bus stop, I had to be buzzed into the store, a first. I found out later from Phil that Mrs. Phil had been robbed at gunpoint just hours before my arrival. I remember she was no longer the happy, smiley woman with the dyed red hair. She was a woman who looked her age, her dye job showing its roots, a storeowner who was afraid. Soon after the incident, Mrs. Phil's friend was always in the store with her. And the poker machine soon followed.

Across the street from Phil is the hoagie shop, the place with the signs on the front that proclaim the "Best Hoagies in Philly." Aside from this Italian-American specialty, they also sell beer, which I believe to be far more popular, evidenced by the paper bag holders who mill across the street at the long-abandoned house.

The hoagie shop is also a popular place with non-paper bag holders, out of town teenagers who want to get their fix of beer. Last summer, a bunch of teenagers in a black Jeep Cherokee walked in and walked out, shoplifting some beer. The owners, rumored to be part of organized crime, promptly rushed out with baseball bats and smashed the windows and lights of the car. The teenagers called the police. The police, teenagers and owners held a standoff for hours. The teenagers hoped to fault someone before going home to their parents. The police stood around looking bored and wished they had water ice on this hot humid night. I'm not sure what the end result was, but the police left around 2 a.m. I got this story from Phil.

Don't get me wrong, my intersection isn't all bad. This is the city and crime happens; it's inevitable. You've got to be careful and know what's happening around you. You have to be streetwise.

On the last corner is an empty store that is rented out to a construction company to hold building materials. It is the corner where I stand whenever my friends with cars come to pick me up and I get nasty looks from passersby for hangin out. At least I'm not holding a paper bag.

Whenever I stand on this corner, I see the fire engine whose home is blocks away roar past me. Pedestrians, some running across the street, others pausing, take a step back onto the curb, and cars move to the side. It is a flash of red and chrome rushing to stop a catastrophe at someone's house, a vehicle that must maneuver through the intersections all over the city.

Recently, on this very corner, a pregnant Mrs. Rodriguez waited with her sister for traffic to pass, and then her water broke. An eyewitness hailed an empty cab coming down the street and she was taken to Pennsylvania Hospital. She had a healthy nine-pound baby boy named Jesus. So named because he must have been looking out for her; after all, how many empty cabs come by when you need one? So Phil tells me.

Sometimes one's life becomes part of an intersection, adding to its history. One's life becomes synonymous with the very ordinary bisecting streets that cover this city. It is that very moment when you pause and realize your life will be changed forever, that you have left your mark, your story, on that corner. You are a part of this city, no matter how large or small it may be, you are not anonymous. It is the corners of this city that hold the stories of its people. What if there were no witnesses like Phil to tell these stories?

■   ■   ■

The work you have done in the first part of this book has been primarily campus-based, with your writing aimed primarily toward your teachers and fellow students. Now, however, you will begin the process of stepping outside the classroom to the streets and neighborhoods that exist around your college and university. You will begin to put your writing and labor into partnership with local individuals and communities who were here before your class began and who will be here long after.

Indeed, partnerships are about respecting intersections. They are about honoring the experiences of individuals who share a communal history and coming to understand your role in supporting their future. As you take your initial steps outside the classroom and into the flow of conversation and activity that mark any community, you should first give some consideration to the dynamics of university-community partnerships.

CHECKPOINT   Finding Your Place

Before you move on in this chapter, spend 10 to 15 minutes writing a response to the following questions:

- What do you think it means to be a student physically entering into someone else's space, literally into that person's home community?
- What do you anticipate will be the relationship between the "academic" knowledge you are learning in the classroom and the "community" knowledge you encounter in local neighborhoods?
- How do you envision your role, your place, in such a partnership?

Getting Started

The beginning of any partnership often has a lasting effect on its long-term success or failure. First impressions really do linger. For that reason, at the outset of any partnership, it is worth reflecting on a selection from the Tao:

Do you have the patience to wait
till the mud settles and the water is clear?
Can you remain unmoving
till the right action arises by itself?

The first step to becoming an active participant in partnership work, then, is to quietly wait before taking any significant action. Part of this advice is just common respect. You would not want strangers to enter your community and assume they can tell you how to fix your neighborhood. It would both belittle your neighbors' daily lives and assume an expertise that is unearned. So until you know enough about the community to be an informed participant, it is best just to listen, asking questions only for clarification.

Being quiet, however, should not be seen as being passive. Being an active listener, constantly taking in information, is actually a hallmark of an effective academic researcher. Indeed the work of attempting to fully understand a community—its strengths and areas of concern—will parallel many of the research strategies you will learn in college, such as defining an area of interest, developing data, and making informed decisions on how to proceed. So although you might initially find yourself a bit quiet in community gatherings, you should be an active researcher, taking notes and attempting to understand the new culture in which you are participating. (See Chapters 1 and 2 for a discussion of such research practices.)

Beyond developing academic research strengths, there's another reason to take a humble stance when beginning partnership work, one that has to do with respect. In some ways, this reason can be encapsulated through Laura Lau's story of the teenagers in the black Jeep Cherokee. As portrayed in her piece, the teenagers come into the community for the express purpose of stealing beer. Because they are outsiders, this act is a significant sign of disrespect. Her piece reads as though the teens had already assumed that it was a high-crime area and that such actions were expected. This vision of the neighborhood is clearly at odds with Lau's, who portrays her home as a rich intersection of lives and histories. Lau sees the teens' behavior as being based on a lack of knowledge and respect for her neighbors.

Communities often feel similar disrespect when partnering with colleges and universities. For local residents, the experience of university partnerships is typically one of college students entering their community, gathering data for a class project, and then leaving, never to be seen again. At such moments, the community's personal and communal experiences are transformed into little more than academic fodder for a student to earn a grade and receive a degree. Indeed, the insights gained from the student's research are often not even shared with the residents. This experience, which feels like an intrusion and a theft to many residents, can cause an undercurrent of tension within any university-community partnership.

So even when it is unspoken, even when your project may have put in place many of the safeguards against such an occurrence discussed below, residents may still be responding out of that history. They might still perceive you as someone more concerned with "getting a grade" than sincerely joining their community efforts. For this reason, humility and respect, a sense of quietly waiting, followed by informed conversation, and listening to the goals the community hopes to achieve are all signals that you wish to be a sincere partner. These signals demonstrate your commitment to working with (and not just taking from) the local intellectuals with whom you have just come into contact and with whom you hope to accomplish important work.

Tenants and activists seeking stronger rent laws in New York City march across the Brooklyn Bridge in 2015. Extreme, rapid gentrification has driven higher rents in many of the poorer neighborhoods in the city, particularly in Brooklyn. ©Andrew Lichtenstein / The Image Works

---

CHECKPOINT   Intruding

Think about a time when you felt like a space you consider personal — whether your community, your home, your dorm room, or even your computer — was being intruded upon. Why did it feel that way? How did you respond to the intrusion? What could the intruder have done differently to make the situation not feel so disrespectful?

Learning about the Community

One of the first things to consider, then, is what you will need to know about the community to be an effective and trustworthy participant. For instance, in the response to the above writing prompt, Lau is able to demonstrate a firm understanding of the "intersection" because she knows the key community players, has a sense of its history, and has been understood (by insiders and outsiders) to be a committed member of the neighborhood. It is easy to imagine Lau as being able to work effectively with neighbors on important issues, such as housing, because she would be able to demonstrate both respect for the neighborhood and, from that outlook, be trusted to understand its faults without generalizing about the residents. As she notes, "Don't get me wrong, my intersection isn't all bad." There are also, she argues, individuals like Mr. Phil.

One of the most difficult aspects of researching a community is to understand that the specific issue you are being asked to focus on, such as education, may not be indicative of the neighborhood as a whole. For instance, many college students who are asked to tutor at local middle schools and high schools assume that education is not important to the community and that its students don't try or that parents don't care; otherwise, they reason, outside tutors would not be needed. These college students, however, would not be in the school tutoring if there were not a committed community enabling their presence and if this community did not see education as an element of a larger effort to build its future. To understand the complexity of a community, you need to move beyond your specific experience, your specific involvement, to larger systemic questions about the economic, political, and legislative histories in which a neighborhood exists. You must constantly check your immediate experience against larger understandings of the neighborhood.

Researching the Neighborhood

Prior to entering a neighborhood, you should undertake research to help you understand the historic trends that have shaped the moment in which you are now participating. Initially, these questions might focus on the community as a whole:

- What is the cultural and economic makeup of neighborhood?
- What are the languages spoken in the community today? Fifty years ago? One hundred years ago?
- What is the percentage of home ownership versus rental units?
- What local businesses and nonprofit organizations exist in the neighborhood today? Which ones were there fifty years ago? One hundred years ago?

Indeed, the work of finding this information will demonstrate very powerfully the connection between your academic research and what it means to be an involved citizen. To discover this knowledge, you might use some of the academic research skills discussed in Chapter 1, skills that asked you to locate your interests within a set of ongoing scholarly conversations. For instance, you might research how historians of your region have framed the changes that have occurred over the past hundred years, or you might look at how economists have discussed the employment trends in that part of the country.

At the same time, however, such questions ask you to draw from a different pool of information: data that are produced by government or community organizations. To retrieve such data, you might go to the Web site of the U.S. Census Bureau (www.uscensus.gov), which provides various types of search engines — congressional districts, county businesses, and so forth — as well as apps that allow you to access this information on your smartphone. What is important to remember about such data is that even though the data might be presented as "facts" — say, in a numeric chart — the information presented is the result of many decisions about what type of data to collect, what particular terms mean, and how the data should be assessed. It is as much an interpretive framework as scholarly articles are. Indeed, as a class, you should not just accept such data, but use the data as a springboard for conversations about how the information frames community research.

At this moment, being an active listener within your community partnership becomes even more vital than before. When analyzing research and data, it is best not to think in terms of change as having happened for better or worse because such terms tend to simplify the dynamics of a community. For instance, it might be a fact that a neighborhood used to have more local businesses and higher employment, but residents might see the reduction of these attributes as not as important as an increase in parking spaces and greater diversity within the neighborhood. It is your responsibility to constantly balance data with the perceptions of the neighborhood residents; you must see the neighborhood as always actively redefining what is "better or worse" about living there and gauge your response appropriately.

CHECKPOINT   For Better or Worse

Think about a time in your home community when something happened that might have seemed objectively good or bad — such as a when a business closed or opened, or when an old building was torn down or a new one was built — but the reaction to the event was the opposite. Why was it seen in a positive or a negative light? What kinds of lasting effects did the event have on your neighborhood?

Engaging with Residents

As you have already learned, your research within a community should be more than simply book based. Indeed, if it were only book based, an argument could be made that you are privileging the opinions of traditional intellectuals over local organic intellectuals. Early in your study of a community, then, it is important to actively engage with residents to learn about their experiences of what has changed and what has stayed constant in their neighborhood as well as their sense of the values that have simultaneously endured and allowed progress. Here, prior to any "work" being done, your teacher and community partners might sponsor some initial small group meetings or listening circles where residents could share stories that capture important moments in the community and frame the specific issues of your project. As you listen to their stories, you might ask the residents:

- What does it mean in that story to be an active and productive member of the community?
- What does that story demonstrate about the values in the community?
- What does that story demonstrate about how the community manages change?
- What does the story portray about current challenges and future possibilities in the community?

You might also take the opportunity to share stories about your own neighborhood, linking a particular resident's story to something that happened in your neighborhood. When telling your story, you do not have to recast your experiences to fall in line with the experiences or expectations of the local residents; your goal is to simply express truths about your own home community and how it manages and enacts change. To alter your experiences to artificially bond with local residents would be disingenuous to both those to whom you are speaking and those whom you are representing.

Indeed, through such honest storytelling you might find that you share a common set of values with members in the community, values that cross the boundaries of student/resident. That should not be surprising: if you think about it, each individual involved in this project probably had multiple other places they could have chosen to go to instead of this particular meeting. Even if a student's participation were required for the class, there was still a set of decisions that led that student to enroll in a program or a college that had such requirements. In other words, *some* common set of beliefs led everyone in that room toward the same project, the same effort. This set of beliefs is also worth exploring as you begin your partnership because it is these latent but common values that will sustain the project and allow it to grow.

"Story of Self" Workshop

Beyond an informal meeting to share such stories, another important way to learn about the community and to build trust is to conduct what scholar Marshall Ganz calls a "Story of Self" workshop. Ganz is a professor at Harvard, perhaps one of the most "traditional" intellectual habitats one could imagine. He began his career, however, by working for civil rights campaigns, specifically the Student Nonviolent Coordinating Committee and the United Farm Workers of America. Watching how they organized their campaigns, he came to understand that what brought people out of their houses and into the streets was discovering a common set of values. Ganz went on to use this experience to develop an entire model for community organizing. (You can learn more about his work by visiting his Web site at marshallganz.com/http://leadingchangenetwork.org/.)

Marshall Ganz, second from the left, with United Farm Workers members in 1977. Cathy Murphy/Getty Images

For our purposes, we might find it useful to use his "Story of Self" workshop to begin a conversation among your classmates and community partners about the values that brought them together to undertake collaborative work. As you will see, it is a rather simple exercise in which the only requirement is that everyone be in the same room.

Divide those participating into equal groups of four, with equal numbers of students and residents in each group if possible. Tell them that they will be developing a 2-minute story about the values that informed their decision to join this project.

Choose a timekeeper. This person must ensure that everyone stays within time limits.

Ask each person to take 5 minutes to create a 2-minute response to the following question: Why are you here today?

Stress that the answer cannot be something like "Because I'm in the class" or "Because I work here." Rather, the reason given in the answer should point to the deeper set of values, the values that led to a whole set of decisions that ultimately resulted in this moment of sitting in this room.

Give each participant a chance to practice his or her response with someone in the group one time. Ideally, the groups would break into two resident/student pairings. Dedicate 2 minutes for one person in the pairing to tell his or her story, allowing 3 minutes for advice from the partner. Once the first story is complete, the other person should share his or her story for 2 minutes, with a 3-minute response from the partner.

Then have each person retell his or her story to their whole group, dedicating 2 minutes for a person to tell his or her story followed by 5 minutes for advice from the group members.

Finally, choose one person to present to the group, telling his or her story to the entire room.

After each selected person speaks, have one person write down on poster-sized paper the "key values" that the entire group heard expressed in the stories. They will be the values that structure your work together.

"Story of Self" Practice Work

TEAM BREAKOUT SESSION:

Goals

- Practice telling your "Story of Self" and get good, constructive feedback
- Learn to coach others so that they become better storytellers

Agenda

TOTAL TIME: 40 MIN.

1. Gather in your team. **Choose a timekeeper. Listen to your facilitator tell** (5 min.)
   his or her 2-minute "Story of Self" as an example.

2. Take some time as individuals to **silently develop your "Story of Self."** (5 min.)
   Use the worksheet that follows.

3. **Choose a partner. Practice telling your "Story of Self."** (10 min.)

   2 minutes each to tell your story:
   - Focus on the values you want to convey—what specific experiences shaped those values in your life?
   - Be specific and give lots of details.

   3 minutes each for feedback:
   - What values did the storyteller convey? How specifically?
   - What is the **Challenge, Choice, and Outcome** in each story? Write them in the boxes below.
   - Were there sections of the story that had especially good details or images (sights, sounds, smells, or emotions of the moment)? How did those details make you feel?

4. As a team, **go around the group** and tell your stories one by one. (20 min.)

   For each person:
   - 2 minutes to tell his or her story
   - 3 minutes to offer feedback from the group

NOTE: You have just 2 minutes to tell your story. Stick to this limit. Make sure your time-keeper cuts you off. This encourages focus and makes sure everyone has a chance.

Developing Your "Story of Self"

WORKSHEET

The "Story of Self" will answer the following question:

What brought you to this room today?

Before you decide what part of your story to tell, think about these questions:

1. What choices in my life have I made to get me to this point?

2. What values move me to take action and might also inspire others to similar action?

3. What stories can I tell from my own life about specific people or events that would *show* (rather than tell) how I learned about or acted on those values?

Family and Childhood	Life Choices	Organizing Experience
Parents/family	School	Introduction to civic work
Experiences growing up	Career	First experience of leadership
Your community	Partner/family	Connection to key books or people
Role models	Hobbies/interests/talents	Role models
School	Experiences finding passion	
	Experiences overcoming challenges	

A good public story is drawn from the series of choice points that have structured the "plot" of your life: the **challenges** you faced, **choices** you made, and **outcomes** you experienced.

Challenge: Why did you feel it was a challenge? What was so challenging about it? Why was it *your* challenge?

Choice: Why did you make the choice you did? Where did you get the courage—or not? Where did you get the hope—or not? How did it feel?

Outcome: How did the outcome feel? Why did it feel that way? What did it teach you? What do you want to teach us? How do you want us to feel?

Think about the challenge, choice, and outcome in your story. The outcome might be what you learned in addition to what happened. Try drawing pictures here instead of words. Powerful stories leave your listeners with images in their minds that shape their understanding of you and your calling.

Challenge	Choice	Outcome

Coaching Tips: "Story of Self"

WORKSHEET

The following questions will help you coach one another in your small groups as you practice telling your stories of self. Remember to balance positive feedback with constructively critical feedback.

"Story of Self" Coaching Questions

What worked: What images struck you? What did you like? What moved you? What did you connect with? How did the story make you feel? Were there sections of the story that had especially good details or images (e.g., sights, sounds, smells, or emotions of the moment)?

_____

_____

_____

_____

Challenge: What were the specific challenges the storyteller faced? How were those challenges made most vivid? What details would help make the challenges seem even more realistic?

_____

_____

_____

_____

Choice: Was there a clear choice or choices that were made in response to a challenge? How do those choices make you feel? (Hopeful? Angry? In solidarity?)

_____

_____

_____

_____

Outcome: What was the specific outcome that resulted from those choices? What does that outcome teach us?

_____

_____

_____

_____

Values: Could you identify what this person's values are and where those values come from? How specifically can you do so? Why is the person working to organize people in his or her neighborhood?

_____

_____

_____

_____

Questions: Where would you like to know more? How could this good story become a better story?

_____

_____

_____

_____

Record Feedback/Comments from Your Team Members Here:

Coaching Tips: Story of Self *(continued)*

Coaching Your Team's "Story of Self"

As you hear each other's stories, keeping track will help you provide feedback and remember details. Use the grid below to track your team members' stories in words or images.

Name	Values	Challenge	Choice	Outcome

Often as you listen to the stories, it will become clear that despite differences in background and location, a sense of commonality can be developed among those working on the project. This sense of commonality is the new space of opportunity that community/university partnerships can create. It is on the basis of these shared values that future work can be premised and endure. (For specific advice on how to structure such an event, see "Sponsoring Community Dialogue" on p. 216 in Chapter 6.)

Admittedly, these initial moments of sharing and partnership might seem awkward at first. You are, after all, talking to strangers as part of a project for your class. It is important to realize that many nonprofit and community organizations choose to take part in these kinds of partnerships because they want to help *you*. Although the work you help them complete will be valuable to them, most communities also want to be part of teaching you about civic uses for your academic studies and about what it means to connect traditional intellectual training with the needs of an actual neighborhood. They have an interest in your success. If you are humble in your interactions and sincere in the values that bring you all together, the community will provide you with all the necessary guidance and support. In fact, the more you respect community members by attempting to learn their history and understand their values, the more they will work toward ensuring that you learn from the experience. That is, awkwardness will fade as true partnership emerges.

Understanding Your Role in the Community Partnership

Your specific role in any partnership will depend on the goals of your class. That said, it is important to understand the entire scope in which partnership work occurs. The best model of community/university partnership work is one that is jointly developed, is sustained in its efforts, and provides for many different avenues for participation among a broad range of individuals. For instance, a partnership with a local school might support an after-school tutoring program, and that might be your initial involvement. Ideally, that tutoring program might also be part of an effort to support parents with homework struggles, to provide links between university and public school curricula, to offer students tuition aid to the university, or to lobby legislators for increased education funding. In such a situation, once you have finished tutoring students, you could then work at another area in the partnership, gaining a full experience of the structural elements necessary for an adequate education. Indeed, the importance of such fully articulated partnerships is that they engage with the entire culture in which education exists. That is, it is not only an after-school program that improves a student's education; it is the classroom teacher, curriculum, school supplies, funding, and so forth. Undergirding effective partnerships, then, is a commitment to joining two specific cultures and working toward creating a new space in which innovative types of work can occur. It is this middle space, this new possibility, that draws out the full possibility of different intellectual communities to address local concerns.

When involved in a community/university project, you need to imagine that your role not only encompasses the task at hand but also makes you part of the creation of a new cultural and activist space. For that reason, it is important not only to understand the specifics of your task but also to understand the larger set of local reasons that led to the partnership in the first place. Knowing these reasons will tell you why the partners have taken certain actions as well as indicate what future actions they might find necessary. If you do not undertake such research, you will be walking into an intersection with no sense of which way to turn or knowledge of what led to the creation of the intersection in the first place. Therefore, it is important not to equate the length and specificity of your involvement with the actual scope and intent of the partnership—usually you are stepping into an ongoing set of events of which your participation is one particular moment. The collective ethical commitment to the project as a whole transcends your specific involvement.

As you begin your work with the community, as you share your stories of self and listen to the stories that surround you, it is also productive to ask the following questions:

- What is the stated goal of my specific community project?
- Why did my community partners choose that goal?
- How does my project fit into other projects developed to reach this goal?
- How does my work support the partners' overall vision of the community's future?
- What is the relationship between the university and the community toward fulfilling these goals?

The answers to these questions will help you understand how your specific task, such as tutoring a student, carries importance beyond your involvement. They allow you to see the big picture that your work is enabling.

Discovering the answers to these questions, however, will require that you use all the academic and community research skills discussed previously (see Chapters 1 and 2). You might, for instance, need to read extended documents in which an organization's purpose and goals are overtly expressed. You might need to invite the community partners to your class to discuss their goals and overarching vision. As you do this work, you will also need to test these stated goals against your own research on the community (e.g., how do these plans intersect with your understanding of the community's historical development?). In other words, you will be asked to integrate quite a bit of information into a coherent understanding of the importance and work of the partnership.

Defining Your Role

Of course, although you should keep in mind this fully articulated version of your community/university project, all the partners recognize that your involvement will not go on forever and that your role will be limited, almost necessarily, by the length of time you have left in your education. You well might continue in the project beyond college (many students will find a home through such work), but more than likely your engagement will be for a specific period. For that reason, it is useful to remember what it means to bring such a complex understanding of partnership work into the expectations of specific tasks and to bring the world of the partnership into your specific role.

For the sake of clarity, it might be useful to define these relationships and your involvement with them. There are three types of involvement—limited, sustained, and transformative—which can be defined as follows.

Limited Involvement

One way a class can be structured is around a project in which students develop and present a particular written artifact to a community partner. Often the final product is a set of flyers, brochures, or Web sites. In this type of class, students spend the majority of their time studying a particular theory or set of skills that are then used to create the requested artifact. This work usually occurs in the final third of the course, making your work with the project **limited**. In such classes, it is easy to assume that the goal of the work is to demonstrate knowledge of the academic material. Although that is certainly true, it will still be important to demonstrate a keen sense of the community partners' needs. You will need to research the community, engage with its residents, and understand the values that undergird the project. The brevity of the time used in the class to complete the community project has no relationship to this research. Any successful product must mesh with the needs of its audience. Your community research ensures that your project will do that. In addition, you will probably need to develop a very strong relationship with the person who will be using the materials. To some extent, you are almost a hired hand. If your specific work occurs within a larger institutional commitment, however, the work produced will still be of long-term value, even though it might have taken only several weeks of your time.

Sustained Involvement

Another way a class might be structured is to support a semester-long partnership with a local community. This work might result in a chapbook publication, the development of a community event, or a digital/social media networking project. In this type of class, you will typically have the opportunity for multiple interactions with your resident partners. These interactions might include an initial group meeting, classroom visits by residents, class visits to the community, and individual or small group planning sessions based on the complexity of the project at hand. Such **sustained** engagement will allow you to develop the types of relationships from which you can *begin* to understand how to offer your own insights into the work at hand, whether they emerge from academic experience or from personal experience. Although you still need to be mindful of your limited experience, you will also be gaining the necessary experiences to hear how what is being done might mesh with elements of your academic/community expertise.

Transformative Involvement

Although your specific class project might conclude at the end of the semester, the work of any partnership exceeds the limitations of the academic calendar. Indeed, what makes a project **transformative** is its ability to exist beyond the confines of the academic school year. When such year-long commitments occur, you can be sure that there is support among the partners for the new cultural space to continue and expand. In such a situation, you might explore other avenues through which to stay involved, perhaps through enrolling in a different class that is working with the same community or taking on an independent or directed study (a situation in which you work directly with the faculty engaged in organizing the community partnership). Finally, you can always continue your work as a volunteer or paid staff member. Indeed, such roles speak to the transformation of academic and community knowledge into a singular force for creative change.

Volunteers with Jersey Cares working at Jefferson Elementary School in Plainfield, New Jersey. Volunteers painted murals in the school and helped clean and organize the library. The Star-Ledger/Ed Murray/The Image Works

Of course, your individual class might blend elements of all these models. And as the term progresses, you might suggest that the class incorporate elements of sustained or transformative strategies. Indeed, one of the most interesting elements of community partnership classes is how they need to change based on the specific cultural and economic contexts of the neighborhood in which a project is occurring. As someone active in the work, you should feel qualified to have such conversations with your instructor. Everyone in the class is taking the same collective journey, and to a great extent, reaching the imagined destination will take everyone's insights.

A final point about community partnership work is one that speaks directly to your role as a student. As the early chapters of this book emphasized, your time as a student is limited. When cast over the course of your entire life, the time you spend in a university classroom will be relatively short. So although you want to succeed in your classes and meet the goals of individual professors, it is incumbent on you to continually imagine a role for your education beyond the classroom. Community partnerships provide you with multiple avenues to explore how the specifics of a class, a major, or a degree might support a full and meaningful life after college. They allow you to witness and experience how traditional intellectual insights can be integrated, explored, and critiqued by the demands of daily life and the give-and-take inherent in any collective effort. If you open yourself up to such experiences, you will find that community partnership work—whether limited, sustained, or transformative—will help you see the full potential of the difficult work so often demanded in college.

To invoke Laura Lau, by taking on such work, we become part of a story larger than ourselves and more important than we might imagine:

> Sometimes one's life becomes part of an intersection, adding to its history. One's life becomes synonymous with the very ordinary bisecting streets that cover this city. It is that very moment when you pause and realize your life will be changed forever, that you have left your mark, your story, on that corner. You are a part of this city, no matter how large or small it may be, you are not anonymous. It is the corners of this city that hold the stories of its people. What if there were no witnesses like Phil to tell these stories?

RUNDOWN   Strategies for Community Partnerships

Preparing for Partnership Work

- Wait to act.
- Listen to community stories and histories.
- Research the community's economic, political, and demographic history.

  Spend time in the community before engaging in any partnership work.

  Ask community members how they understand the changes in their neighborhood and what they see as problems and solutions.

  Use resources such as published scholarship and the data from the U.S. Census Bureau to gain a big-picture understanding of the community, both its past and its present.

Engaging in Partnership Work

- Listen carefully.
- Understand the complete partnership structure.
- Understand your role in the partnership (limited, sustained, or transformative).

  Sponsor a "Story of Self" workshop with residents to create a sense of common values for the project.

  Invite community partners to come to class to learn about all aspects of the project, of which your role is one part.

  Have frequent discussions in class about the imagined and actual role being enacted by students and engage with community partners to ensure a common understanding of the work involved.

Discussion Questions & Activities

1. Before the next class, write a response to the "Intersections" writing prompt that began this chapter. Share your response with your classmates.

2. With your instructor, conduct a Ganz "Story of Self" workshop (p. 178) in your class, clarifying the values that bring each of you into this common space to engage in this collective work.

3. Develop a set of research questions that will enable you to understand the community in which you are about to work. (See Chapters 1 and 2 for advice on how to develop such questions.) Create small groups responsible for addressing those questions and present that information to your class.

4. Choose a specific online community, such as fan club's Facebook page or a nonprofit organization's Twitter account. Develop a set of research questions that will enable you to understand this community. Create small groups responsible for researching these questions, with each group presenting its information to the class. (Note: If you are also partnering with a geographic-based community, discuss how the different nature of each community altered your research.)

5. Analyze the elements of your class's proposed community partnership. Decide which role (limited, sustained, transformative) best describes the work your class will undertake. Discuss how your participation—your role—will advance or support the project. Do you believe it will be the most effective way to support the project? What other roles could you imagine the class undertaking?

6

Establishing Community Writing Groups

Writing Prompt: "The Writing Machine"

Form groups of no more than four people per group and give each group its own number. Using the passages below, each group should begin with the word "We" and count the individual words in the passage until it reaches its group number. Circle that word. Count forward for five more words and circle that word. Continue until the end of the third passage is reached. (For instance, Group 5 would begin by circling *Gifford* in Passage 1 and then would count five more words and circle *in*. The counting and circling every fifth word would continue until the end of Passage 3.) Using only these circled words and only in the form in which they appear in the passage, each group should then spend 25 minutes collectively writing a poem that answers the following question: What values inform your community publishing project? Share your group poem with the entire class.

Passage 1: We, the members of Gifford Street Community Press unite in the spirit of collective work and responsibility to coordinate a neighborhood Press where the multilingual and multicultural voices of the people will be heard and shared. We hope to be part of this community's kinship by sharing in personal and neighborhood struggles, triumphs, and producing collected works of creative expression. *The Press wants to support conversation and to build relationships, which will foster greater civic awareness of local issues and when necessary, support resident driven change in the neighborhood.* This Press hopes to produce

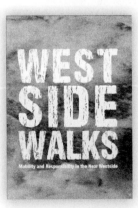

Gifford Street Community Press

and showcase artwork, writings, and other meaningful cultural pieces that represent authentic voices from the community. The Press will gather local compositions through writing workshops, Westside community events, and forums. Our mission is to contribute to the promotion of love, healing, and respect within the Westside, and validate the existence of peoples and cultures represented in the Westside Community. (Gifford Street Community Press Mission Statement)

Passage 2: All men are intellectuals, one could therefore say: but not all men have in society the function of intellectuals. (Antonio Gramsci, *On Intellectuals*)

Passage 3: One such definition of academic discourse might be that it is the language spoken by people in the academy who had intellectual projects as students and chose a particular domain, the university, to carry out these projects. Like yourself, they did not imagine that just because a project was studied in a university setting it had to divorce itself from "real life." Like yourself, they brought a healthy skepticism to the arguments of others, a belief in certain principles, and a willingness to join in a conversation. That is, one way to imagine academic discourse is as the type of conversation produced by skeptics about real life—people who will not willingly believe what they are told; people who demand proof; and, finally, people who demand that their work have relevance for others; people who care about the neighborhoods around them.

Throughout this semester, you will be placed in the position of this type of academic. You will be asked to study a set of "materials" and to decide what they mean. You will be asked to decide whether the terms, theories, and opinions they express offer a coherent image or a competing dialogue. You will be asked to determine what should define this particular neighborhood. Most importantly, you will be asked to intervene in their definitions when you feel a better argument can be made. You will be asked to record voices that aren't being heard and to think about policies that could be created to ensure they are heard. That is, as a committed skeptic yourself, you will be expected to join in this conversation. To quote a former teacher of mine, you will be expected to make your mark. (Freshman Composition Syllabus)

■ ■ ■

Throughout this book, you have had quite few terms thrown in your direction, such as *traditional intellectual, organic intellectual, academic discourse, civic mission,* and *community partnerships.* You have been asked to integrate those terms (and the theories behind them) into a somewhat more known vocabulary, featuring terms such as *student, professor, classroom, curriculum, college,* and *university.* There has also been an implicit sense that an actual non-college-based community will become part of the mix as well, perhaps bringing in its own vocabulary, such as *cabs, streets, intersections, brown bags,* and *strange angels.* Somehow, you are meant to hold these different vocabularies and worldviews simultaneously in your mind.

Moreover, you might soon be asked to enact through actual partnerships a practice based on this multifaceted way of speaking. Here you might find yourself being asked to work with a community on a project that will require you to collaboratively build strategies and practices that can lead not only to individuals producing written works but also to the production of an actual text in print or online. You might also find that very few people involved in the project have undertaken such work in the past.

This chapter begins with "The Writing Machine" prompt because it represents the difficult work that lies ahead: the demand to produce a blending of these different ways of speaking and understanding the world. In its invocation of a machine, the prompt also indicates that there is a set of established tools that you can use to support a community partnership, strategies that are specifically geared toward students in a writing class. These tools can help you complete almost any type of writing-based community/university partnership project.

To help you understand and use those tools, this chapter lays out a theoretical study of a partnership between Adams College and a local community. Although Adams College is fictional, the events discussed are drawn from actual projects and real institutions. Indeed, this chapter features some of the work completed by students and community members within specific projects. Although the particulars of this imagined project may not relate to every aspect of the work you will do as a class, the hope is its narrative arc will demonstrate a broad picture of the "machinery" that goes into community/university writing partnerships, allowing you to pull out pieces that fit your specific demands.

To be clear, however, the scope of work detailed in this chapter transcends what is possible in any one course; this kind of work would actually take several years. (In this sense, the work described below is representative of the transformational partnership discussed in Chapter 5.) Even though the story encompasses a longer time frame than your class will likely allow, the tools and strategies discussed can still be used in your limited, sustained, or transformational projects. Just as a wrench can be used to tighten a wheel or build a car, so can these tools be used for your immediate purposes in a course or extended projects you initiate after college.

As such, the structure of this chapter is different from previous chapters. The instruction will be accompanied by a series of short narratives about how the strategies discussed played out at Adams College. In this sense, the chapter might feel more pragmatic, more useful, than other chapters. You will not be working through definitions, for instance. Still, as the story unfolds, you should pay attention to how the conceptual terms presented in previous chapters explain particular decisions within the story. After all, a tool—whether conceptual or actual—is of no use unless you know how to use it. That is true whether you are doing work in a classroom or a community.

ADAMS COLLEGE: A Case Study in Community Partnership

Adams College is located in a large city with a rich history of diverse neighborhoods, each with its own economic and cultural identity. Surrounding the city is a ring of farmland that has been the site of family farms for generation after generation.

Over the past forty years, however, the city and the farmland have experienced many of the global changes that have affected communities across the United States. Increasingly, traditional jobs have been moved to areas where wages are lower, and corporations have taken on a larger role in local farming than ever before. As new jobs enter the area, the education required for entry-level positions—usually a community college or university degree—is of an increasingly higher level than previously. And while many neighborhoods remain intact, many are also suffering from the region's transition from a tax base drawn from an industrial and farm economy to one based more on high-tech and service industry jobs. As a result, cuts have had to be made to city services and public schools. There is hope, however, that these new jobs will continue to enter the city, eventually allowing many public services to be restored.

Adams College is the largest nonprofit entity in the region. Originally started as a community college, over the last forty years it has grown into a regionally respected four-year college, awarding both undergraduate and graduate degrees. Although the college was originally intended for only local residents, its growing reputation has led students from across the country as well as international students to attend, which has diversified the student population. Throughout this growth, the college has remained committed to the local community. Recently, it initiated a "community partnership" initiative that asks all departments to consider how their disciplinary knowledge might support local neighborhoods (and the city as a whole) in building on the region's long-standing values while also supporting residents as they move through difficult economic changes.

Within the city, there is a community that has traditionally been called Portside—a neighborhood with one of the richest and most diverse histories in the city. While the city has maintained a strong Native American community, the last hundred years have seen an increase in people of European, African American, Latino, and now Eastern European lineage settle in the community. The neighborhood has also seen a decline in economic opportunity, as have many other neighborhoods in the city. Led by Adams College, a network of local, state, and financial organizations have come together both to support the history of diversity in the neighborhood and to revitalize its economy. Adams College has specifically encouraged writing classrooms to work with the residents, public schools, and nonprofit organizations in the community. From an initial interest in a partnership with a public school, a series of initiatives has resulted.

Initiating Public School Partnerships

Lincoln Middle School is approximately five miles away from the Adams College campus. As with most of the city's schools, budget cuts have reduced the number of teacher's aides in the classroom, which has decreased the individual attention paid to each student as well as led to a slight increase in in-school suspensions.

The principal and teachers at Lincoln Middle School hope that students from Adams College can help English teachers provide more attention to student writing as well as enable students to learn better academic habits. Wanting to start small, the first decision is to have the college students work with the school students who are in the in-school suspension program, turning what was a day of just sitting in a room into one of participation in an active writing center. The first step is for the college students to develop a set of activities for the school students that will both support their academic progress and address the immediate cause of the suspension. To this end, the college students create a series of writing prompts. (See p. 199 for sample writing prompts.)

Prior to going to class, the college students are given preparation in how to work with the middle school students as well as how to discuss the writing produced. Given that in-school suspensions usually last for several days, the goal is to have the suspended middle school student write and review the same piece of work throughout that period. Ultimately, the piece would be given to the principal, who could reduce the student's suspension based on the quality of the writing. Indeed, given the middle school students' enthusiasm, there is now talk of using this work to embed a stronger writing focus in an after-school tutoring program. The public school, college, class professor, and college students see their work as being a great success.

A tutor working with students in a community space in Somerville, MA. Melanie Stetson Freeman/Christian Science Monitor/The Image Works

Creating a Tutoring Program in Schools

As is implicit in the first part of the Adams College story, much of the work done in this project has to be completed through negotiation between the school, university, and academic department representatives. That will likely be true about your own partnership projects. In this way, your role as a student is more like that of a teacher's aide, helping to support or even run specific programs.

The key here, though, is that the work you will be asked to undertake is directly related to your education. It would be inappropriate, for instance, to ask you to manage a file system because that task would not engage you in work that can teach you about writing or community issues. Indeed, given the stress that most public schools face, there will be continual pressure for you to take on other work, such as small requests to quickly run an errand that could soon become your primary focus. As a result, you need to stay in constant touch with your teacher, who needs to be in touch with the school staff, to ensure that you stay committed to the task of tutoring students. Communication among all those concerned is a key element to your success.

Using Writing Prompts

When you first begin to work with a student, regardless of the eventual work to be done, it is important to have short pieces of writing for the student to complete. This exercise allows you to see the student's level of writing and allows the student to have a quick success in working with you. Writing prompts serve both purposes. Indeed, if you are working with the same set of students over the course of several weeks, which is usually the case in after-school programs, you might develop a series of writing prompts that are focused on the same theme, such as

Angele Seiley

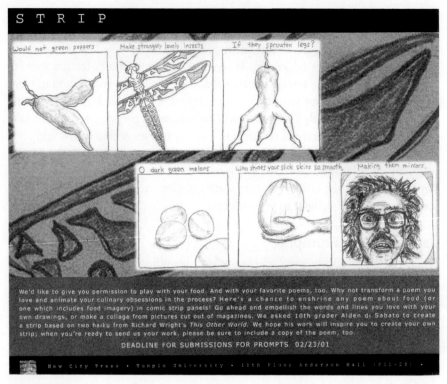

Angele Seiley

the environment or education. If students respond and revise a prompt each week, they will eventually have enough material to make the basis of a longer paper. In effect, they will learn how to slowly develop a full-fledged piece of writing.

When developing writing prompts, you want to make sure you begin by having students reflect on an immediate experience. Regardless of grade level, the prompt itself should be short, generally no more than four or five sentences. It should also be evocative of many different types of responses. Look back at the prompts that begin many of the chapters in this book. For the most part, they have no word-count requirements, no formatting requirements, and no outside research requirements. Their purpose is to prompt thinking, opening an area for investigation. Perhaps in later prompts you might be more specific; in general, though, writing prompts are generative, not conclusion-based, forms of writing.

When developing a prompt, design is also a key element. It is difficult to take a task seriously when it looks thrown together. Handing any student a photocopy with a couple of sentences on it says, "I put no time into this work, so you shouldn't either." Once you have the language for your prompt, think about what images, fonts, or cultural references you want to include to entice the reader to respond. Often, the care taken in designing the prompt helps encourage students to respond. So think hard about your audience.

Recipes for a brave new world

More than just a cooking guide, a recipe is a formula for a desired end.
We ask you to take any concept or idea and reinvent it through a recipe.
Create a moveable feast, explore new means of sustenance. Send us your
recipes for revolt, ecstasy, heaven, insomnia, faith, hygiene, the
sublime, superstition, civilization, birth, poverty, or exile—any recipe
will do, as long as it whets our appetite for new world living. We've
included a sample recipe on the back.

Deadline for Submissions for Prompts Friday Feb, 23 2001

Angele Seiley

Recipes for a brave New World

1 lb. rage
1/2c. impatience
1T. righteousness
1 large coup
100 downtrodden masses
a pinch of thickening plot
a dozen tyrants
assorted picket signs
the roar of the crowd
stamping of feet

Assemble downtrodden masses in rows.
Sprinkle generously with rage.
Add contents to a large coup.
Add thickening plot and simmer until
mixture boils. Fold in impatience and
righteousness. Remove picket signs from
their packaging and baste with the roar
of the crowd. Spread mixture liberally
over tyrants. Garnish with stamping feet.

Angele Seiley

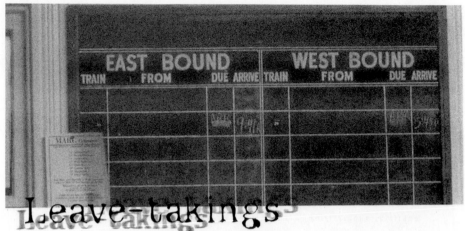

They's two trains running, none of 'em going my way

Two trains running, none was going my way

I'm gonna leave here walking on this very day.

"Frisco Whistle Blues"

Here comes your train . . . time to go. Gather up your things and get steppin'. Without leave-takings there would be no journeys, no arrivals, no reunions. Imagine your departure from the Celebration—was it joyous or sorrowful?—and let us know what you'll leave behind.

Contribute a response to this prompt and we'll include it in a book commemorating the 20th anniversary of the Celebration of Black Writing.

Submit your responses to:

August Tarrier, Editor
New City Press
10th Floor Anderson Hall
022-29
Temple University
Philadelphia, PA 19122

newcity@temple.edu
www.newcitywriting.org

Please submit your information

Name:

Address:

Email:

ART SANCTUARY

NEW
CITY
PRESS

Angele Seiley

Responding to Student Writing

A central part of the public school students' experience will be how you respond to their writing. In doing so, keep in mind that your role is to help students generate writing. For this reason, your first response to an individual student should always be positive. Start by pointing to a phrase or sentence and highlighting how well it captures an idea. Then move to the other sentences, asking the student for more detail based on your interest. For example:

- "I'd really like to hear more about this idea."
- "I don't know this part of the neighborhood. Could you tell me more about how it looks?"

You might have the student write the new sentences directly into the piece of writing, physically demonstrating that revision alters the shape and form of the first draft.

When you have gone through the entire piece, you might try to reduce your suggestions to two or three (no more than three) concrete actions the student can take, such as:

- "Let the reader know more about how the neighborhood looks."
- "Tell me more what you think about the idea of justice."

Write these comments at the bottom of the page, also adding a comment like "Can't wait to see what you do next."

Caution: You should avoid the topics of grammar and correctness. Discussion of grammar will almost immediately stop the student from writing and sharing ideas. Your primary goal is to generate text, and stopping to point out errors will hinder that purpose. It is also unclear whether pointing out an error outside the context of a rich and sustained discussion of language will actually produce much change. Instead, the best strategy is to wait until the student has worked through a series of prompts and chooses one to "finish," perhaps to share with parents or as a classroom reading.

Once the students have each revised their work several times and have become comfortable with it, ask them to consider how editing might make certain points more effective, dramatic, or powerful. Have a discussion based on how to make their sentences more persuasive to their imagined reader, whether a friend, teacher, or parent. This process will put the student in a position to decide which of the multiple strategies discussed best suits this piece.

Remember that your role is not a *grammar* teacher but a *writing* tutor. Only if the classroom teacher specifically asks you to focus on grammar should you approach this topic. (Even then, you should have a frank discussion with the teacher about whether you have the necessary knowledge and pedagogical training to talk about grammar so that the discussion does not diminish the work of the student or the structure of a particular piece of writing.)

ADAMS COLLEGE: Writing across the Classroom and Community

Given the success of the in-school suspension and after-school writing programs, Lincoln Middle School has decided that writing prompts and tutoring should now be embedded within a particular class, working with a single teacher. Part of this decision grew from a need to meet a new mandate that writing be taught "across the curriculum." (Such a mandate is actually occurring across the United States, making teachers who have never seen their primary role as writing teachers suddenly have to expand the type and scope of writing they teach.)

The particular focus on this project will be in the social studies class, which is the space in the curriculum where U.S. history is taught. The goal is to embed personal and research-based writing into the existing focus on the class, ultimately using writing to have students explore a particular issue and understand how different types of writing generate different types of knowledge.

At the outset of this project, Mr. Farrell, the public school teacher, visited the college class to go over the curriculum for the fall (roughly the span of time shared with the college class). He discussed the writing abilities of his students, their strengths in personal writing, and their difficulties in moving toward a more academic style of writing. He particularly noted the lack of immediate interest in U.S. history. As part of the meeting, Mr. Farrell and the Adams College students took specific texts and issues used in the class and generated possible areas of connection. Eventually, the theme of "freedom" was developed because it could be linked to issues of slavery in the United States, current situations of human trafficking, and global conflicts couched in terms of "spreading freedom."

At one point, one of the college students raised the point that "freedom" is a collective struggle, one that only gained meaning as more people joined in and fought for the idea. Indeed, there were probably many individuals who worked for and fought for their definition of freedom. With that in mind, the college students talked about how the topic is one that would have great resonance in the neighborhood given the high rate of current and former military service people there as well as its large migrant and immigrant communities. They suggested that the members of the community also be asked to respond to the prompts and that related college clubs and faculty be asked to read and engage with some of the community members' and public school students' writing. The hope is to produce a public forum for community dialogue.

With that in mind, a two-semester project was developed in which the college students and involved public school teachers create a series of prompts concerning freedom. The first-semester class worked with the students and community and developed materials focused on the topic of freedom. During the second semester, students will use these materials to create a public dialogue on the topic. To ensure continuity, both courses will be taught by the same professor. For the first-semester course, Adams College students will work individually with the middle school students and will also use their college connections to develop a database of possible respondents for student writing. Mr. Farrell also agreed to have students meet with the school's parent organization, which could reach out to the community to find individuals to write or read responses to the prompts. The goal was to create a series of writings that would capture how the community defines freedom. Once complete, a public reading would occur, followed by a community dialogue.

Creating a Multiple-Location Writing Project

By now you should have a sense of how a simple community project begins to grow and develop based upon student and community interest. Particular strategies within one project, such as writing prompts, begin to be used in other locations, such as classrooms. The original set of participants, students, begins to grow as the community learns of the work being done. And as this occurs, issues of how to present the work, what types of events can demonstrate the power of the writing being done, begin to enter the discussion. In the following section, the process and strategies of managing such growth are discussed. And fortunately, much of what you have already learned will be of great use in this work.

Writing Prompts for Classroom Purposes

As with the first project, the initial work in creating a multiple-location project is to generate a series of writing prompts that can be used by students. This case is trickier than the first, however, because now the students will have to respond to the curricular needs of a classroom. For that reason, it is important that you become familiar with the curriculum of the specific class as well as with any district-wide school standards. It will be important to have a conversation with the teachers about what particular standards they are focusing on within their classroom. You might also have them ultimately approve any prompt you develop. This step might seem to limit your creative freedom, but it will also give you a true sense of what it means to work in public education.

You might also want to think of the prompts as a series, as a way of preparing students to be able to make an extended argument. In this case, you might pose questions that imply (or require) research to generate an answer. Be mindful, however, that the students will rely primarily on existing classroom resources or the school library. Do not assume that access to the Internet will be available. Despite public rhetoric of a "wired world," that is not always the case in many public schools (or households, for that matter) across the United States.

As mentioned previously, the design of the prompt is equally important. You should see if there are any images that appear in the students' textbooks that might be used for a prompt. This will reinforce the connection between the prompt and the classroom, while simultaneously showing that the prompt's stance to this writing is not strictly "textbook" based. You might also, for instance, juxtapose images of the community with those in the textbook, graphically illustrating the type of connections you are hoping to achieve. When the prompts are complete, you will need to meet again with the teacher(s) and plan a schedule of when the prompts will be used, how many of the student responses to the prompts will be revised, and when the entire series of prompts will be completed.

Although these prompts are more classroom based than previous prompts, your method of response should stay essentially the same:

- Focus on the positive.
- Ask the student to continue to explore ideas and images.
- Have the student actively revise on the piece of paper in front of you.

Again, grammar lessons should probably be avoided or turned over to the classroom teachers.

An implicit part of this exercise is for students to understand what it means to write and respond to an actual reader. Instead of just their teacher, they will have a community looking at their writing; instead of just personal experience, they will probably be asked to integrate some research. Your role as a tutor is to ask them how their writing responds to this audience (Why did you write in a "school voice"? Why did you include a story from the neighborhood right after a

fact found in an encyclopedia?). Your role is not to give them the correct strategy; rather, it is to enable them to think about themselves as writing with a purpose. If you listen carefully, you will see that students of any age will often have a complex sense of what they are trying to accomplish. Once you understand their goals, you can draw from your own experiences as a writer to offer (not mandate) strategies that you have found useful in your writing.

CHECKPOINT ## Reading and Responding

Think about a time when you received very helpful feedback on a piece of your own writing, whether from a teacher, a tutor, or a peer. Consider the following questions:

- What was the feedback, and what about it did you find most helpful?
- Have you integrated that feedback into your writing for subsequent assignments and classes?
- How was this feedback different from less helpful feedback you have received on your writing at other times?

Finally, students might ask you directly why they have to use a school-based source (like an assigned reading). You have probably asked yourself the same question. In responding to the students, it might be best to ask them how evidence is used in their home community. How do they know when a story told is "true"? Then ask them how their teachers ask them to "prove their point" in class. That is, set up the discussion in terms of communities having different standards of evidence. By making the "academy" just another community, you move the discussion away from "academic intelligence" to "community practices." Although this process will not completely resolve the issue, it at least sets up a dynamic in which the way students argue outside of school is offered the same respect as argumentation in school.

One goal of this type of project is to give students an active audience to respond to their writing. The belief is that by making a classroom discussion or assignment the subject of community debate, you demonstrate the importance of classroom work. That is, the response to "Why are we doing this?" might be "We are taking part in a conversation being held in our classroom, our community, and our local colleges." Of course, no one answer will actually solve the fundamental "why" question, but this framing begins to position the students as potentially important contributors to a conversation that transcends their classroom. In this way, it is a thread that connects the students' insights to higher education and a civic identity. That is, it acknowledges them as intellectuals. In some ways, it is this recognition that is the bedrock of any such successful partnership. It will take real work from you to actually make these connections with individuals outside the classroom, however.

Connecting to the Community

One of the first challenges in creating a public forum for the students' writing is establishing a process that will enable the community to participate in both responding to the students' writing and contributing to the project themselves. Even the most dedicated of parents and community members will have a difficult time doing the work required of writing prompts, particularly if you ask them to commit to revision. They might also be nervous about their ability to write an extended response, even when they have extensive insights into the topic. For that reason, you might try some of the following strategies.

Fill in the Blank

Develop a "note card" prompt. On the front of a note card, explain the project and the importance of their response. On the back, put a key phrase, such as "Freedom is . . . " Ask the parents or other community members to complete that sentence in no more than ten words and put the note card in a "Prompt" box. Be sure that the prompt and the box are well designed. (Note: On the card, be sure to print that by submitting their writing, participants are authorizing its use in print and public forums. There will be more on copyright issues in Chapter 7.)

Develop a list of key places where the prompts and boxes might be left. Think of places that attract large numbers of people who will probably have time to respond, such as medical and dental offices, libraries, auto repair shops, and restaurants. Write a **goal statement**—a short script stating the goals of the project and describing how it is an alliance of the public schools and university. Practice the script in class. Choose a number of students to go to the key places and ask for permission to leave the prompt boxes, promising to provide prompts as needed and to collect the prompts. You might also promise to highlight the participation of these key places at the community dialogue.

If possible, you might also "table" the prompts. That means asking a local business with high-traffic volume, such as a grocery store, if you can put a table out with the prompts and ask customers to respond. Such tabling helps advertise the project and the community dialogue as well as get responses. It is best, however, if both students and community members, perhaps even a parent/student pair from the public school class, are involved in the tabling.

Audio or Video Responses

Because the community members are not required to write for the class, all these strategies can also be undertaken through the use of audio or video files. Their responses could be spliced together digitally as an opening "film" to begin the community event. In this case, tabling in high-traffic areas such as grocery stores or public libraries would probably work better than tabling in smaller businesses. It might also be possible to set up at certain gatherings, such as sporting events, places of worship, and public concerts, and ask individuals to respond. For these events, you would probably need the specific permission of the event coordinator. At the outset of each interview, you would also need to record each person speaking his or her name and granting permission to use the audio or video recording. (Copyright issues are covered more in Chapter 7.) Once you have that permission, these responses can be used at the public reading or community dialogue forum.

Community Leaders

Whether you use print or digital means, you should be sure that community leaders are contacted. Community leaders are individuals whose opinion is respected by the neighborhood, people whose commitment to the neighborhood has made them important voices in any neighborhood discussion. Such leaders can include

- Religious leaders
- Business owners
- Longtime residents
- Community activists

As part of this work, you will need to form a group of students to work with the teachers, parents, and community partners to discover these individuals and record their opinions on the topic being studied. At first this task may seem daunting; however, schoolteachers typically know who these individuals are, even if they might disagree with their viewpoints. Similarly, if you simply ask at your tabling event if there is someone you should be sure to contact, you will often hear the same set of names being suggested. Contact those individuals.

When contacting such individuals, it is important to show deep respect for their importance to the community. To a great extent, you are asking them to validate your project and put their prestige into your work. For that reason, your request should not be a drive-by experience. Instead, you should attempt to schedule a meeting with them with the primary goal of getting their input on the project. At the meeting, they will no doubt make many important suggestions about how to work with the community. (Consider the "Story of Self" workshop discussed in Chapter 5 about how sharing your own values and your belief in the project helps others trust your motives.)

At the end of that meeting, ask if they will consider taking part in the project by either sitting for an interview or providing a short response to the prompt (which you could offer to record rather than ask them to write). If they agree, offer a second meeting to do this work. (For strategies on interviewing individuals, see below.) Ideally, you will have two to four community leaders taking part in your project.

Connecting to College Students

A second hurdle of such a project is establishing a process that will encourage college students to participate. Here the issue will not necessarily be a fear of writing, although some might worry about their ability to talk to a community audience. Instead, the issue will be convincing them of the value of a project that, to them, will seem like a specific class assignment. It is at this moment that the strength of the community partnership becomes a valuable resource. Within this context, you might try some of the following strategies.

Student Organizations as Respondents

Most campuses are fortunate to have a variety of student organizations representing a diversity of interests. For many organizations, community outreach is a central part of their mission. With that in mind, have a small group in your class research which student groups, either through their mission statement or literacy programs, might be willing to respond to the student writing. Once you have this list, send a short e-mail to each group asking if members would be willing to provide written responses to the content of a set number of student papers; five is usually a good number.

When writing this letter, be sure to establish the following:

1. This project is not just for a class. It is an opportunity to take part in a university/public school/community literacy effort.
2. This event is public. Student organizations are more likely to participate if they understand the public nature of a project and know that their work will be read in a public forum.
3. They can respond through e-mail.
4. They must respond by a certain date. Nothing hurts a project more (or diminishes the enthusiasm of students) than a failure to receive a response.

Furthermore, although you will have gained experience in responding to writing, you can't assume that the student organizations will know the best way to encourage younger students. For that reason, it is useful to develop an outline or tip sheet to send along with the writing. Some tips you might include:

- Suggest that they address the writer by name as well as sign their own name.
- Suggest that they share some of their own experiences as students (think again about Ganz's point of establishing common boundaries).

▪ Make the point that they should *not* respond to any grammar issues, but only to the content of the piece. Explain that the teacher is going to address these issues. Again, you do not want to create a dynamic that squashes the enthusiasm of a young writer.

Finally, it is a good idea to send each piece of student writing to multiple student organizations. (Keep the original for yourself. Remove the student's last name from a photocopy and send that instead.) Casting a wide net almost certainly guarantees that you will get a response to the piece. Moreover, if you get a response that focuses negatively on grammar or is inappropriate for a younger student, you can choose not to use it. Most important, however, by including multiple groups and readers, you expand the dialogue, bringing in a wide variety of insights and opinions.

Note: You will need to get explicit permission from the university student respondents to use, quote, or read any materials they send to the project. You will also need the explicit permission of the public school students' teacher and possibly parents to circulate their students' writing. You should check with the school for its specific policies.

Attracting Social Media Responses

There is a strong likelihood that the students on your campus prefer to communicate through social media. With that in mind, your class might create a Twitter hashtag to send out to your peers asking them to respond to the same note card question provided to the community and later distill the best responses for use in the project. Your class might suggest that these responses can be images or words and mention that audio or video files would be welcome in addition to written responses. It might also be useful to create a meme image that could circulate across social media platforms (perhaps even beyond the specific region of your school) and generate responses to the note card question. A selection of these memes could also be part of your proposed public event.

Student Leaders

As noted above, each community has certain individuals whose opinion carries significance in any conversation. For this reason, following the same protocol used with community leaders, be sure to include student leaders. It is especially important to include those whose absence from the project would be noticed and, possibly, be read as a critique of the project.

Connecting to College Administrators and Faculty

It will seem odd to the community if faculty and administrators do not take part in the project. It will appear that the traditional intellectuals are either unconcerned or not interested in the voices of the local residents. For this reason, once you commit to a community dialogue, you need to ensure the participation of at least two or three such people.

Faculty

It is unlikely that you will be able to find college faculty to write responses to the younger students' writing; their primary focus will no doubt be on their own students. That does not mean that faculty should be excluded from the project, however. Instead, as a class, you should identify faculty members who through department affiliation or particular research interests have done work on the topic being explored by the class. Given that all faculty have at least department Web pages, this step could be as easy as doing a keyword search for your college or university and searching through the results.

Once you have developed a potential list of faculty, develop a letter (similar in strategy to the student organization letter) that explains the public nature of the project. Ask the faculty members if they would be willing to write a short response to the note card prompt or possibly agree to a short interview on the topic. Explain that their responses will be shared with the students, broadening how they might approach the topic.

As you get responses from community, student, and faculty leaders throughout the project, be sure to copy their materials so that you can present them to the public school classroom. This will allow the students to consider how the advice of those outside their specific class might inform their writing. After a period of group discussion, you can then move into your individual tutoring with a student, working in detail about how that other person's insights might be incorporated into the student's work.

If you find that certain faculty members are particularly engaged with the topic or project, you might ask them to attend the public reading, perhaps in the role of respondents to the discussion. Whenever a faculty member agrees, not only is a wider circle of participation throughout the project drawn in, but the faculty person can also share his or her research with the wider public. Although it is probably evident, you will need to make sure that any faculty participant understands how the project is based on a sense of respecting the community's intellectual insights.

Administration

Inviting faculty to participate in the project will send a signal to the community that the university is committed to a partnership, particularly if faculty members go to the community events related to the project. For this same reason, it is also important to include, when possible, figures from the college or university administration, such as the president, provost, and deans. Although the workings of any college are a bit mysterious, these administration figures are publicly recognized as important by both students and community members. It is worth some effort, then, to secure their involvement.

The easiest way to include administration figures is to ask them to draft a short statement on how they respond to the topic in general. In making your request, you will need to follow the same letter protocol discussed above. In this case, however, it is probably important to highlight your awareness of their busy schedules and estimate the amount of time you are asking from them. A written response to the topic could be as short as an e-mail response or a 5- to 10-minute interview that could take place in the person's on-campus office.

Remember that you are in effect asking them to endorse the project through their participation. That is also true with all the community, student, and faculty participants. For that reason, you should be prepared to explain how the project is structured, why it is based on a sense of equality among participants, and how each participant community (class, community, student organization, and faculty) will benefit from participating. Only as you provide solid answers to these questions will you gain the trust (and participation) of upper-level administrators.

Note: Strategically, it is probably best to secure the participation of students and faculty before asking administration. That way, you can show a broad base of support for the project, emphasizing that the project is real and therefore important enough to consider supporting.

Conducting Interviews: Frameworks and Strategies

By now it is probably clear that working with communities and attempting to record and distribute their insights will require developing strong interview skills. Having an interview strategy ensures that individuals without strong writing skills can be part of the work. An interview also provides a quick way to get the insights of individuals whose schedules are overloaded. When conducting interviews, though, keep the following practices in mind:

1. **Schedule the interview in advance.** Before the interview, provide the interviewee with an overview of the topics to be discussed.

2. **Prepare for the interview.** Preparing for the interview includes researching the specific topic to be discussed so that the person being interviewed does not have to spend time providing background. Also have a broad list of topics predetermined so that you cover all the relevant material. Knowing what needs to be discussed will not only ensure that the interview is effective but also lead to enhanced trust in you by the interviewee.

3. **Arrive on time.** Be sure to arrive on time and conclude the interview on time. It has often been said that time is our most valuable asset because we can never get it back. Keep that in mind when planning an interview.

4. **Ask for permission to record.** Before the interview begins, you will need to explicitly ask to record the interview (whether in audio or video form) if that is your intention. You should record this statement of permission.

You may not use any of the recorded material in any public context (except classroom discussion) until you have a signed "Permission to Print" document (see p. 240).

If you are interviewing individuals at a public location, as part of a series of short interviews at an event or as part of an extended project, you must provide them with a written statement about the project, how their recorded materials will be used, and whether they are giving you the right to use the interview for that purpose. (See Permission to Print p. 240).

5. **Keep to open-ended questions.** Open-ended questions allow space for the person being interviewed to establish what he or she sees as the most important way to address the interview. Within those broad topics, you might have a list of specific information that needs to be gained.

6. **Begin with a couple of personal questions.** Personal questions will help set the person being interviewed at ease. You can then move to more issue-based or policy-based questions.

Here is an example of an interview prep sheet.

Interview Prep Sheet for a Community Education Activist

- When did you first become involved in working on public school reform?
  - Did you attend a neighborhood public school?
  - Do you have kids in public schools?
  - Did a specific incident lead to involvement?
- What issues seem to be the most important to work on?
  - Classroom size?
  - Teacher experience?
  - Library access?
- What do you think of the most recent efforts to reform schools?
  - The No Child Left Behind Act?
  - Common Core standards?

Ideally, you have some sense of how the person might answer the first question and you would have research on the subtopics in the second and third questions.

Of course, what you do during the interview is just as crucial as preparing for it ahead of time. Always remember the following:

1. **Thank your interviewee.** It is best to begin the interview by directly thanking the person for his or her time, highlighting that you know he or she is busy. If you didn't do so previously, provide the interviewee with an overview of the topics to be discussed (which you actually should have already done when asking for the interview). You also need to directly ask if you can record the conversation, specifically stating that you will let the interviewee see any quotes prior to being used publicly. (If this interview is to be used in a publication, you should give an overview of the complete process.)

2. **Let your interviewee do the talking.** You want to ask short questions and prompt for more explanation if needed, but generally you want to remain quiet. That is, you want the interviewee to talk at length, not be constantly interrupted by follow-up questions. The more you let the person speak at the beginning, the more likely he or she will provide expansive answers throughout. You also find that the interviewee will draw connections that might not be evident to you.

3. **Trust your instincts.** Although it is important to have a strong sense of the direction the interview might take, it is also important to trust your instincts in the moment. If the interviewee keeps returning to a topic or theme, you should depart from your plan. Typically, if left to develop, these tangents add depth to the topic at hand.

4. **Really listen.** The ultimate success of any interview depends on whether the person answering your questions believes you are listening, so turn off your phone, sit leaning forward, and look at the interviewee while he or she is talking. That is, demonstrate that you are deeply interested in the person's answers. In fact, if you demonstrate that you believe these answers are important points to make, you will be surprised at the insight and eloquence that emerges. Everyone is an intellectual; you just have to remind people of this fact through paying attention to their words.

ADAMS COLLEGE: Creating a School/Community Dialogue

The goal of the first semester was to create a project in which the public school students' writing and ideas circulated beyond their classroom and to the communities and colleges that surround them. By now, with the semester drawing to a close, the students should have received feedback on their writing and heard audio or video interviews of important residents of their community (whether neighbors or academics). If these steps have been accomplished, significant work has been done. As members of such a course, the college students would have produced an important network, one that, with care, could expand the project even further.

There is still work to be done, though. Adams College and the school district imagined that the partnership would last longer than one college semester; they hoped that it would last the majority of the public school academic year. With that in mind, preparations had already been made to offer a second college course that worked with the emergent network of teachers, community members, and faculty to produce a public dialogue based on the work created by the public school students. To organize this event, however, new tools need to be added to the partnership toolbox.

Sponsoring Community Dialogue

At the outset, it is important to recognize that every community already has ongoing dialogues about issues in their neighborhood. In this sense, the community dialogue being sponsored by your project is another moment in that conversation—a potentially important moment, but one that occurs within a history. How your project presents the large amount of material generated by your project is therefore of key importance. As a group, you need to make the following decisions:

- What is it about your project that offers a unique insight into the topic?
- What structure for the event will best present that vision?
- What location best suits the event?
- What effect (long term or short term) do you want the event to have?

It might be useful to consider what factors will go into each decision.

What is it about your project that offers a unique insight into the topic? In answering this question, it is important to recognize your audience. The goal is to provide new information to the community, not to your professor or an academic field (although that might also have occurred). For that reason, it is important that you meet with your community partners to discuss how to frame the insights that the project might bring to the community dialogue. To a great extent, these partners should decide how to frame the event to best meet the needs of those in attendance. That does not mean that you are silent in these discussions. Instead, returning to the earlier discussion of humility, it means both recognizing the different levels of expertise about the community that mark the participants in your project and understanding your necessarily limited sense of community dynamics.

An example of a community dialogue at a public forum. Jim West/PhotoEdit, Inc.

What structure for the event will best present that vision? Assuming that your project was able to bring together public school students, teachers, community residents, college students, student organizations, professors, and college administrators, your work has already accomplished something important—a cross-constituency conversation among many differently situated individuals. In this way, the very nature of the project provides a model for what elements might go into a fully developed dialogue. Any structured event should attempt to represent the ways in which that conversation demonstrated equal respect to all involved.

With that in mind, you might decide as a class to start the event with a collage of different voices that took part in the project. Perhaps you start with an individual from each constituency reading his or her work or a digital presentation that brings together audio and video files (a strategy premised on technology being available to broadcast at the event). Rather than having a featured speaker, your class might decide to have a panel discussion, perhaps chaired by a community elder, with different constituencies presenting their take on the issue (you might need to tailor the idea based on the age of the public school students). Whatever the plan, it should have no more than five speakers and, typically, should last less than 45 minutes.

Regardless of any particular structure, it is important to leave ample time for dialogue. This opportunity for dialogue can be as simple as having an open microphone to which people can walk up and speak, perhaps with a 3-minute time limit. To ensure that each constituency has an opportunity to speak, you might mandate that the speakers rotate between resident and college speakers, differentiate by age (say under thirty and over thirty), or alternate between students and nonstudents. Whatever you choose, you need to be sure it causes no division in the room and ensures fair opportunity to talk.

You might also begin the event with a short writing prompt. Here you would pass out individual note cards with a central question to be considered. Participants would then write their response and, when dialogue begins, read their response to those in attendance. If someone is too shy to speak, the note card could be handed to a designated person who could then read it aloud. Having such a prompt to start the event tends to focus the issue and indirectly shift out tangential topics. Also, such prompts tend to spark conversation among participants, creating a spirit of dialogue from the beginning of the event.

The setup of the room can also encourage dialogue. It is a good idea to have the room arranged with table and chairs. An arrangement with chairs in a row, echoing a classroom, tends to reduce conversation and necessarily puts all the attention up front. This dynamic might work well for large lectures, but for a community event the room should demonstrate that the focus is communal. Tables and chairs spread around the room demonstrate this fact. Having speakers or panelists move through the tables when speaking also increases this sense of community.

With all these moving pieces, it is important to have a very strict schedule for the event and a timekeeper who can ensure that the schedule is followed. Typically, no public event should last more than 90 minutes, although people might choose to stay after for further conversation. A typical schedule might look as follows:

Introductions	5 minutes
Writing prompt	15 minutes
Collage presentation	10 minutes
Panel or group presentation	30 minutes
Common dialogue	30 minutes

It might go without saying, but there should be a central person, a moderator, who is responsible for moving the schedule along. This person's role is slightly different from that of the timekeeper, whose main job is to track time and hold up "Time's up" signs to speakers. The moderator has to have the trust of everyone involved and be able to step in to defuse any tense moments that might occur—and there will be tense moments. With that in mind, the person most suited for this role is a community elder, someone who can be trusted to know when to ask a speaker or participant to let others speak. The moderator will also be trusted to intervene and correct comments that might inadvertently misrepresent the community. As a class and in dialogue with your partners, significant time should be put into the decision on who will moderate the event.

What location best suits the event? One final set of decisions that needs to be made concerns the time and location of the event. If you imagine the primary purpose for this project to be to support student learning, it might make sense to have the event in a classroom, with the audience being just the students and one or two representatives from the partnership network. You would still need the many moving pieces from above, but the public stakes of the event would be low. If you believe the work produced by the project merits a larger audience, you might choose to have an event at the school on an evening when the school's parent organization is meeting or a parent/teacher conference is taking place. This timing will broaden the scope of the audience but still have the event occur within a very supportive environment in that parents will no doubt praise the work of their children. The first event would be scheduled for the day; the second two events would occur in the evening. For both you might want to offer some type of refreshments.

Depending on the age of the public school students involved, you might choose to hold the event at a public venue (YMCA, place of worship, recreation center) and actively invite people to attend. This approach will take significant work on your part because you will not have a built-in audience for the event. You will probably need to plan about four to six weeks in advance, network with organizations to advertise to their members, and perhaps make direct calls. The advantage of this type of event is that it represents the most authentic community because it will bring in individuals not attached to the project or project participants. The disadvantage, besides the work involved, is that you might need a strong moderator to keep the conversation on track. Such events typically have free refreshments.

Note: You will most likely need to secure permission for any event, whether held on school property or a local venue. In some cases—if you choose to use a public park, for instance—you might also need to secure a permit from the local government. For this reason, you should begin to look into these issues when you are choosing the location.

What effect (long term or short term) do you want the event to have? Many projects begin, do their work, and then stop, which is a completely fine model. If your work is part of a fully articulated community partnership, new projects will emerge that continue the dialogue and support among the different constituencies with whom you have worked. Still, as any project nears its conclusion, it is important to *consciously* decide what (or if) the project should do next.

Depending on the decision made, various strategies might be deployed. Here are four possible outcomes.

1. **The project ends.** In this case, the community dialogue would be the culminating event. At the end of the dialogue, it is important to have a party with the students, thanking them for their participation and saying good-bye. Nothing is worse than simply not showing up anymore without explanation. That attitude only reinforces the worst images of community/university partnerships. In addition, as a class, you need to assign students to write individual thank-you letters to individuals or organizations that supported this work. Beyond just exhibiting basic manners, you need to leave the participants feeling respected. Otherwise, when other college students approach these same supporters in the future, they will most likely decline to participate. Finally, your class might approach the campus newspaper or radio station to run a story on the project. This kind of coverage is particularly important if the project went well because it shows the possibility of such work to other students, faculty, and administrators.

2. **The project continues in the classroom.** Although the specific focus of the public school students' inquiry might be completed, your college class will have developed a set of materials that can be used by these public school students in the future. This product can be in textbook format or how-to format. For the former, you might collect all the materials (writing prompts; note card prompts; student, community, and college responses; historical research; extended pieces of academic writing) and put them together in a textbook fashion. That is, think about how placing the materials in a coherent order might allow students in future classes to study the work of your project and use it as a resource in the public school classrooms. This textbook can be as simple as a photocopied packet, perhaps with a table of contents, to as grand as bound book (see Chapter 7 for details about to do this work). By doing this work, you will have enabled future students to continue to reflect on this issue. As importantly, by making student work the object of study, you have begun to transform who counts as an intellectual in the room.

   Because you have also created a process that can be replicated using different research topics, you could also create a how-to booklet specifically designed for use by the public school students. To some extent, the first iteration of this project was led by your class in partnership with the school and community. It would be interesting to see how you could empower the public school students to take the lead in this work. Given your relationship with the school, you would have ample resources and experiences to help you consider how that might be done.

3. **The project continues in print or digital format.** As indicated above, one way to have the project continue in the schools is to produce a publication that can be used by students as a research tool or as a tool to replicate the project. As will be discussed in greater detail in Chapter 7, another way to organize a publication is as a text to be read by the larger community. Here the goal is to encourage further discussion and debate through the use of a widely distributed book.

4. **The project continues as a public forum.** Continuing as a public forum is the most difficult task to accomplish. Here your role as a class would be to help the partnership structure (the department in which the class is offered, the public school, and community partners) develop a memorandum of understanding that would ensure continuation of the community dialogue process for a set time period, usually a specific number of years. With this type of deep partnership structure, complicated issues such as course offerings and faculty schedules for both college and public school partners would need to be negotiated. Continuing as a public forum requires a firm commitment from the community partners to continue to respond to student writing, generate resident participation in public forums, and support wider conversations among the residents on the chosen topics. This work is best done outside of a specific class, usually by one to three students who are enrolled in an independent study or internship with a faculty member. Although such work is necessarily daunting, the labor involved will provide a deep education in the theories and practices of collaborative partnerships focused on literacy and community empowerment.

ADAMS COLLEGE: Creating a Community Writing Group

After the public forum, the Adams College faculty and Lincoln Middle School teachers were approached about how the partnership might support adult writers in the community. Many of the residents, it seems, have stories, poems, and memoirs and hope to get advice on how to develop them. Because that was not the original purpose of the partnership, the college had to decide how to best support such an effort. Eventually, the English department decided to create a course that would see its role as supporting community writers. That is, in addition to learning how to write effectively for the university, students in this class would learn the tools necessary to support writing within the local community. Ultimately, the course would ask students to consider the relationship between traditional and organic intellectuals. Indeed, the students' work that term will ask them to theorize and reflect on the meaning of the word *intellectuals*.

First, though, a community writing group had to be established.

The Mechanics of a Community Writing Group

Writing groups are formed as a result of self-motivated interest on the part of local residents or organizations that often want a context to have community writing discussed. You might work with an individual or with an organization that wants to initiate such a group. In either case, the process is essentially the same.

Establishing a Writing Group

If you are to help organize the writing group, be sure to work with your community partner to understand the motivation and purposes for this effort. You should also be very clear about your role in the group. More than likely, you are a short-term participant in a writing group that might continue for years. From the outset, then, you need to be clear about your commitment. It is completely okay to announce that your involvement is part of a class project that concludes at the end of the semester. You also need to state what interested you in *their* project and why you chose to take part in such a project during your college career. Members of the community will welcome and enjoy working with you if they see you as respecting and wanting to support *their* goals. One strategy to begin such a process might be to conduct Marshall Ganz's "Story of Self" workshop with the group (see p. 178).

Typically, writing groups do not happen organically. The way a writing group is set up is important if the group is to sustain itself, both as a collective effort and later as a possible community publisher (see Chapter 7). Although most writing groups can start out somewhat large, they usually settle into a set number of eight to ten participants. If you are working with an organization, an announcement will probably be sent out through the organization's established communication channels. If you are working with an individual or unaffiliated group of people, you will have to think about places where residents congregate and where they will see information, such as grocery stores, health centers, places of worship, libraries, and ball fields. If you have worked with a local school, the administration might be willing to include information about the proposed writing group in the students' "book bag" express or through the parent/teacher association. Based on recommendations of some of your community partners, you might also develop a list of individuals to invite to participate and telephone those persons directly.

When developing materials to invite participants, it is best to highlight the community effort. Do not print materials on college letterhead stationery or invoke the college as a funder or participant. Although this approach might attract some people, it will more likely dissuade many individuals from participating either because of a lack of confidence (it's a *college* writing program) or through concern about the college itself (it's the same old same old . . .).

Most important is that the writing group should *actually* be a local effort, which will ensure its sustainability whether the college stays committed to the group or not.

The materials themselves can be as simple as a flyer to as complicated as a brochure. Depending on whom you want to attract to the group, you will have to decide if a high-end production brochure would be as effective as a simple flyer. Although it is difficult to gauge how much a particular type of publication might cost in any region of the United States, a black-and-white flyer could most likely be printed for as little as 5 cents a copy and a two-sided brochure for about 10 cents a copy. Ideally, your community partner will have its own network through which to advertise the event, so it is probably not worth spending more than $50 on copies at this early stage of the project.

Remember, though, that with each announcement, you are sending a signal about who is welcome in the group, so be sure to make the group open to those you intend to invite. In all cases, the materials should stress that the group is a safe space to share writing. Participants do not have to be published writers. They do not have to be in the middle of a large writing project. They just need to enjoy writing and want to share this interest with others. It is this self-motivated interest that will allow the group to continue after your own participation ends.

Holding an Opening Meeting

A good opening tactic is to bring all those who respond to your flyers, brochures, and phone calls together for an informational meeting. At this meeting, your community partner should talk about the goals of the group, how it will be run (see below), and any plans for publication you might have. This talk, though, should be brief and last no longer than 10 minutes. Then, rather than ask individuals to introduce themselves, which can be a rote exercise, provide them with a writing prompt and ask them to work in pairs. This prompt might be a version of the "Story of Self" workshop, or it might ask participants to talk about their favorite piece of writing (either their own or by a published author). At the conclusion of the allotted working time, ask them to introduce themselves and read their work. This exercise will create an engaged and fun atmosphere. Be sure to invite every person present, but do not force anyone who is uncomfortable to read his or her piece. Either offer to read it aloud for them or just let them pass. Allow other participants to comment on the work, citing what is positive in the piece.

Once everyone has shared their work, end the formal meeting and let the participants mingle, possibly sharing any refreshments you have provided. Tell them that if they are interested in joining the group, they should complete a "group member" handout, on which they write their name, contact information, and available times to meet. Your work will be to find a common time for the largest number of individuals and to announce the next meeting time and location. This second meeting should usually be held within a week of the opening meeting. At that time, the group will decide how often to meet.

Meeting Place

Your community partner might never have attempted such a writing group project. With that in mind, it is useful to know that once established, writing groups need to meet at convenient times and places for the target participants. Groups that meet in the evening may find that people are reluctant to come out at night, for example; groups meeting in the daytime may clash with work obligations for some. To plan the second meeting, you will need to sort these schedules out; after that, the group will decide which option fits the collective needs of all those involved. Also consider various meeting places. Although it might be convenient to have the group meet on campus, that plan is ultimately unsustainable. It is best to use neutral spaces rather than someone's home as a meeting place. Sometimes a friendly restaurant or café will tolerate or even encourage a group to meet at its facility.

Ground Rules

The basic principles of writing groups are to ensure that people arrive on time and identify what they are going to read at the beginning of the meeting. *Be sure that the meeting starts on time.* Encourage people to exchange roles such as chairing the meeting and organizing refreshments; switching roles helps share responsibility. Take care of new members and ensure that they are introduced. In general, only community members should take on formal roles.

Reading Work in Groups

When participants are reading their work, some negotiation may be necessary. Longer prose pieces should be broken into 10-minute chunks if the other members are to be able to comment usefully. Some individuals' work may need to stretch over several meetings. Scripts may also need extra time so that people can read the parts aloud. Poems are usually best presented one at a time. Where possible, encourage authors to provide photocopies, which will enable people to exchange work and give more extensive feedback. Keep a record of what has been read by whom, and if people miss their chance to read one week, ensure that they are prioritized the next time. Offer voluntary writing tasks if people have difficulty knowing what to write about during any particular week.

Criticism and Feedback

Set a ground rule for constructive, not destructive, criticism. Allow all the comments in the group to be heard before the author responds to any of them. All comments are valid, but it may be useful for the chairperson to draw people out if they say only that they "liked" a piece. If work is to be published in a group publication, it should first have been aired in this way to be considered representative of the group's work. Offer voluntary deadlines for changes.

Your Role as a Student

Participating in writing groups as a student can be tricky. There can be an assumption by the group that you are "really a writer" or, conversely, that you "don't know enough to comment on a piece about the community." In either case, you should be careful not to assume a greater expertise than the group members. Although you *might* be more familiar with academic writing, you probably have less experience in community writing and in understanding the local community. It would be a mistake to value or judge the group members' writing according to academic genres.

Also, although your academic courses may have given you interesting questions to ask about how gender, race, and class are represented in writing, you need to embed those questions in the specific project of the community writer, who may or may not find them useful. You also need to express your ideas in your regular voice, not your classroom or academic voice. Finally, writing group discussion is not like academic debate. Rather than points being earned through strong critique, writing groups work from expressing what is best about a piece. The goal is to encourage writing, not to demonstrate your own knowledge.

Public Readings

Ultimately, members of a writing group want their work to be heard. One way your class can support the group is to help plan a public reading. Your class can find a venue, take care of logistics (microphone, seating, etc.), and create posters to advertise the event. Here you can also use your campus connections to teach students at your college about the local community. You might also consider having the writing group perform for individual classes that might be working on related issues. The invited college class can serve as an audience for the group members to practice performing their work, especially if reading publicly is new to some of them. If possible, your class might also videotape the event, creating a CD that can be distributed at local stores or events such as a community picnic.

One issue to consider when planning the event will be who will read their work. Will it be just residents, or will it include student participants? Will everyone read? If someone is too nervous to read, can another member perform the piece? Will there be an open mic for anyone who attends and wants to read? Each of these questions touches on the group's identity, its sense of itself as a community, and its relationship to the university. If possible, devote an entire group meeting to these logistics, allowing extended discussion of each issue. There are no correct answers except those that draw the greatest consensus from the group.

© iD8/John Birdsall/The Image Works

Working for Publication

After a writing group has been meeting for a while, it might be time to consider making a publication that presents its work to the community. Although details will be discussed in the following chapter, there are some initial areas to consider.

If it is the group's first publication, keep it simple and the costs low. For instance, make a photocopied, not bound, book. Print in black and white, not color. Restrict the number of words allowed for any piece selected. If costs are not kept down, the process of raising funds can make the entire process drag on, impede recruitment of new members, and result in a publication that no one is very interested in by the time it comes out.

Also find a way to include everyone. Allocate tasks such as finding a printer, negotiating distribution in local business, and so forth, to different participants. Two or three people might coordinate editing the pieces, but no changes should be made in someone's work without their permission and cooperation. Some authors may have to accept that material is unpublishable unless they make changes.

Successful publication depends on good marketing. Think first about how and where you will sell or distribute your work and in what quantity. If no funding is available, work out a price for the publication and subdivide the total among the group membership. Each member can be asked to contribute a sum and take away as many copies as this amount purchases at cost. In this way, the group always breaks even on its sales, and everyone is involved in distributing the publication.

ADAMS COLLEGE: Resting Points

At the outset, Adams College imagined establishing writing partnerships with a local school, beginning with a small writing exercise located in one program. As its work continued, other opportunities emerged that helped create a community dialogue and a community writing group. Each new writing effort emerged organically from the momentum of the project. Although the totality of the work now being undertaken is not unusual for many such community writing projects, students usually see only small pieces of the work. Indeed, such work can often be occurring across the community, with each group of residents working in isolation from other projects. As we will discuss in Chapter 7, one way to broadcast the writing being done — and develop partnerships among such efforts — is to publish and actively circulate this work.

As this chapter has shown, organic intellectuals gain power by having their words draw together different constituencies (students, teachers, community members) under the same set of values, enabling them to work together for a new vision of their community. The work of this chapter has been to provide the tools that make the opportunity for such a vision to be imagined.

And as will be discussed in the next chapter, written words are the basis but not the end of such imaginative work. They are a resting point before beginning again.

RUNDOWN Strategies for Community Writing Groups

Generating Writing

- Create prompts linked to school needs or ongoing community discussion.
- Respond to the content of writing.
- Avoid responding to grammar concerns.
- Find college- and community-based respondents.

To increase participant support for the project, make use of images, fonts, and design elements in the writing prompts to establish the importance of the project.

Establish quickly that your role is not to correct writing or comment on grammar; rather, it is to facilitate writing as a means for students to express their opinions.

Use campus-based student organizations to find non-school-based respondents.

Create guide sheets for how to respond to student writing.

Generating Audiences

- Offer multiple sites for individuals to participate in community writing projects.
- Develop numerous formats (print, digital, interview) to expand participation.
- Sponsor public forums to share written work.
- Create ongoing writing groups.

  Use public spaces, such as medical offices or grocery stores, to expand who can participate in the project.

  Meet with community and college leaders to discuss the project as well as discover a format (audio, print, video) that will allow them to participate.

  Frame any public event within the needs of the community, not the needs of a particular college class.

  Support the development of writing groups through providing organizational support, not through commenting on the writers' work.

Discussion Questions & Activities

1. Before the next class, find three documents written by partners in your community project. Bring these documents to class and collectively choose one paragraph from each. Then create small groups of four people each and complete the "Writing Machine" prompt at the start of this chapter. (If your class is not involved in a community project, use the texts provided in that prompt to complete this activity.)

2. Discuss how the terms *organic intellectual* and *traditional intellectual* inform the ways in which the writing projects discussed in this chapter are structured.

3. Even though Adams College is a fictional institution, the projects discussed are real. As you understand the goals of your college and the interests of the surrounding community, which of these projects would you choose to implement? Which project would you not implement? Why?

4. Although many projects are discussed in this chapter, there are no examples of college student writing, nor are there examples of how doing this work enabled

or supported the college students' writing goals. As a class, discuss how your class might assess the value of each project in terms of its students' own academic goals. What might they find valuable? What might they find not valuable?

5. Each project discussed had the possibility of being multimodal, blending print, audio, video, and digital platforms. At its core, however, each project also depended on face-to-face interactions. Discuss what it means to take one of those projects and have it exist strictly as an online digital community. How might this exposure expand the type of work created? How might it limit the type of participation allowed?

Community Events and Community Publishing

Writing Prompt: "Coming Home"

Home may be a place in your heart or in your memory. You may feel a sense of it only with certain people. Perhaps home is a physical place: a special room where only you are allowed, a place in the woods that only you know about, or a coffee shop where you are recognized. Perhaps you get home by praying, by walking, or by closing your eyes. Whether you have chosen your home or it has chosen you, define it; draw a map to your home. Based on your drawing, tell us about a time when you came home.

Response: "Old West Street" by Gary Bonaparte

From *Home: Journeys into the Westside*

old West St. before the 8-lane hi-way to nowhere.
poor sweet mean scared bold alive
families of outsiders
daring to persevere in a new culture

Gary Bonaparte/Gifford Street Community Press

Gary Bonaparte created "Old West Street" in a neighborhood meeting designed to support the creation of a community-based publishing project. The total writing prompt exercise probably lasted about 30 minutes. In truth, however, the insight required to craft those words and create that image is the result of Bonaparte's lifetime of experiences in his home community. In their very brevity, his words represent a powerful statement about a historic sense of belonging—and a sense of alienation from the larger city in which his community resides.

A major issue facing community/university partnerships is what to do with the artifacts produced. How can an individual piece of writing be used to foster a wider sense of community identity? How can it support the work of community-based organic intellectuals who need to speak and be heard by those with more decision-making authority, traditional intellectuals such as politicians, businesspeople, and educators? To return to a question posed in Chapter 1, how can individuals such as Gary Bonaparte and Mom Frasier have their ideas circulate and have influence on public issues? How can such writing become part of an effort to confirm that community values inform educational, cultural, and political decisions about a neighborhood?

Traditionally, university, business, and political leaders have large public relations machines that can ensure that their version of what should happen is printed in the newspaper, reported in the local press, and told to political leaders. That is not the case for many resident-based efforts. As the Adams College example demonstrates, however, community/university partnerships can produce a significant amount of writing, whether from an after-school program, a school-based writing center, or a community writing group. Because this writing represents a story about the community written and edited by the community itself, it presents a unique perspective. The community writers and partners often have a strong desire to have their voices circulate both in their neighborhood and in the larger communal context of the city, county, or region. They want an opportunity to affirm their vision of the values that shape their lives.

When community writing is created with a plan for the words to circulate widely, a community publication provides an important vehicle that can guarantee these voices gain an audience. Publications not only provide these voices with a concrete way to travel across their own community but also allow community writers to expand the venues in which their voices are heard—from neighborhood restaurants to university classrooms to city legislative hearings. Indeed, a central element of such publications is to work with community partners to answer three basic questions:

- *Who* is the intended audience for this work?
- *How* will it be presented?
- *Where* can this audience best be reached?

Indeed, once you start this discussion with your community partner, what might have been a typical classroom conversation about the imagined audience for a piece of writing—a central concern of writing courses—takes on very real consequences. It is no longer a hypothetical question; rather, it becomes enmeshed in larger project of supporting community-based organic intellectuals and their community.

When you undertake this type of partnership work, your identity shifts from being simply a "student" to being a strategic partner, with all the weight and seriousness such a role implies. Taking on the position of interacting with an actual public audience and advocating for a position might at first seem intimidating. Similar to the pragmatic strategies in Chapter 6, however, there are established practices you can use to support these efforts.

This chapter will suggest two principal strategies—a community picnic and a community publication—to distribute the writing produced by your specific community project. To show the continued development of a community/ university partnership, these specific projects will be placed within the continuing narrative of Adams College, highlighting how such work presents moments of both possible collaboration and conflict between the community and the college.

■ ■ ■

ADAMS COLLEGE: From Partnership to Publications

As the Adams College partnership project has developed, the community has developed a set of resources that have allowed it to foster a broad constituency of writers crossing generations and backgrounds. The community has, in effect, created a network of individuals dedicated to "telling the truth" of their neighborhood. They have even created a name for themselves, the Neighborhood Writers Collective (NWC). Lately, however, tension has developed because the NWC wants to use its writing as a way to confront individuals and organizations over their failure to respect certain community values or failure to provide adequate support to community causes. For example, local officials are supporting the building of national chain stores over local businesses, and the school board has decided to support privatizing some public schools. Although Adams College does not want to engage in such overtly political work, thereby changing the nature of the community partnership into one of advocacy, the members of one college writing class have collectively decided to become involved in the community's efforts, choosing to connect their labor power and academic skill to this new community effort.

After an initial meeting, the NWC, faculty, and college students decide to create a community picnic. They think that such an event will bring the community together in large numbers and provide an opportunity to share common concerns about the neighborhood. Perhaps it will also increase the number of individuals using writing to promote the interests of the neighborhood, making the picnic both a public forum and a springboard to the group's larger publication goals.

Creating a Community Event

Your community partner's motivation in choosing an event might be to highlight a particular neighborhood issue, such as landlord abuse, educational opportunities, or crime. With that in mind, the goal is to create an event that presents the community's vision of the issue in its own terms and in a format that represents its values. Whatever the topic, your collective work will involve creating an event, limited in time but broad in impact, that can draw in both residents and media outlets. Regardless of whether you are working with a small group or large partnership, here are some strategies to consider when undertaking such an event.

Working Closely with Your Community Partner

You will need to work with your community partner or partners to ensure that the event's purpose and educational goals are realized in a set of concrete actions. Because any action will necessarily be altered as implementation occurs, constant communication is a must. To that end, you might want to delegate one to three students who will consistently meet with the community partners to share updates on plans, materials being developed, and outreach to the intended audience.

Setting Goals and Work Plans for the Event

Although your community partner might have a broad idea for the event, holding a meeting to turn the goals into an initial set of plans is very useful. At this meeting, you can write a **work required plan**. For instance, if the goal is to highlight educational needs and resources in the community, the work required might include surveying neighborhood residents about their own educational background and what resources they would like to see brought into the neighborhood. You might also need to meet with local schools, literacy organizations, or vocational education centers to see what programs are offered.

Once you have brainstormed ideas, you can begin to determine what labor (student or resident) you can put into the event over what period of time. In this conversation, be sure to assign individuals to specific tasks with specific deadlines. By linking your goals to the labor that is actually available and to a schedule, you will be able to set a realistic plan for your event.

For a public event to be successful, you clearly need participants. As a partnership, you will have to decide who your target audience is. Again, work closely with your community partner on this issue. Although it might make sense to try to reach as many people as possible and advertise the picnic across the community, this strategy can be difficult because drawing large numbers is always a struggle. Instead, you might decide to invite residents who might be affected by the issue being resolved; in this case, you might invite students and participants at literacy programs across the community, parents of public school students, and others. By using this strategy, you will most likely be able to develop a list of individuals who will continue to work on the issue once the picnic is over.

Whatever the event, your decision for a target audience needs to be based on a dialogue with the community and a realistic sense of the labor available to generate participants.

You will probably need a permit for almost any event that does not occur on private property. Securing a permit is not an insurmountable obstacle, but it will have to be planned in advance and will most likely require funds. As such, you might decide that it is best to locate your event at a community partner's site. If your project involves working at a school, for example, you might be able to hold the event there; schools tend to be centrally located and typically have the resources to hold events inside in case of bad weather.

If none of your partners has a suitable location, you might approach other organizations in the community to host the event. To start, you will need to write a letter, possibly followed by a meeting, to the organization explaining your event's purpose, why you hope to host the event at that location, what the event will look like, and what the organization's actual commitment (in terms of resources, time, and labor) will be. *Remember that most organizations are over-committed, so if you ask for a lot of support, many might decline to participate.* You are also asking an organization to indirectly endorse your event by hosting it, so as with previous work you have done, be sure you can answer any concerns it might have about the event.

CHECKPOINT Asking for Approval

Imagine that you are a business owner being approached to host a public event. Write down five specific questions you might have for the group approaching you. What kinds of answers would make you most inclined to say yes? What kinds of answers would dissuade you from wanting to participate?

Public events should be structured to ensure the largest possible participation by the audience. Except for perhaps political rallies by major political figures, most audience members prefer dialogue to listening. To that end, whether it is a picnic or an open meeting, the following are useful strategies.

Writing Prompts

Have a short writing prompt prepared that everyone at the event will have an opportunity to respond to. These responses can be hung from a clothesline or on a wall. The more prompts that are displayed, the more individuals will gather to read them, which will increase the number of responses you get. The prompt should be structured around a key question that cuts to the core of your event (such as "What is a 'good' education?"). It should be printed on a card whose size indicates that short answers are acceptable, such as a note card, which will encourage individuals to

An example of a publicly displayed writing prompt. This prompt originated from Candy Chang, a New Orleans artist who transformed the side of an abandoned house in her neighborhood into a giant chalkboard on which community members could express what was important to them. Alex Wong/Getty Images

write a response and will eliminate the pressure to go into a depth that might scare off unsure writers. You might even put a word limit on the prompt to force creative responses and say, for instance, "In ten words or fewer, what is a 'good' education?"

Open Mic

An open mic event allows any individual who signs up to share his or her ideas about the event topic. As part of the event, you can invite certain individuals and organizations to be speakers to show that you value their work and have the support of a broad range of organizations. It is important to provide a sheet that details certain rules for the open mic, such as no profanity and no singling out local residents for criticism. Your community partner will be able to help draft these guidelines. It is also very important to have a community timekeeper who will know how to have residents conclude their comments if they exceed a predetermined time limit, usually 2 minutes.

Public Readings

As stated earlier, any community/university partnership will produce quite a bit of writing. Your event should feature this work. Ideally, you would have one or two readers from each element of the project—child/adult, school based/community based—read a short piece of their work. Usually, no one should read for more than 5 minutes. Fronting community writers in this way demonstrates the goals of your partnership. Once they have read, you might also invite others to read (announcing this opportunity prior to the event).

As with the open mic, you will need policies in place to ensure that the materials read are suitable for the audience and build (not diminish) a sense of community. You will also need to select a community member to be an emcee.

© David Bacon/The Image Works

Organization Tables

Depending on the nature of your event, you might allow neighborhood organizations working on the same issue to set up a table and pass out literature. Although it will mean some work for you, such as finding tables and making sure that organizations know about the opportunity ahead of time, it helps expand those involved in your partnership. The attendance of the organizations also works to indirectly validate your efforts, securing broader approval for your goals and community partnership.

Kids' Station

Children will be present at almost any event you hold. Rather than see them as a distraction, you should create an art table where kids can do crafts, draw, or paint. If you have the help, a resident or student can sit at the table and ask children to draw or paint in response to questions related to the theme of the event. (Be sure to use terms that kids will understand. For example, instead of "What is a 'good' education?" you could ask "What would the perfect school look like to you?")

As with the prompts, these drawings can also be hung or displayed during the event. In general, the more materials the event can generate and display, the more a communal feel will be generated and a collective sense of purpose created.

Volunteer Table

There should also be one table or space where your partnership is advertised and its work displayed. This visibility increases public knowledge about your work and the issues involved as well as provides other people from the community an opportunity to volunteer. It is this set of new volunteers who might bring exactly the skills you need to continue and expand your work.

For this table to be effective and draw interest, though, think about what type of flyers, brochures, and community writing will best represent your work. (Community publications will be discussed later in this chapter.) When making the flyers or brochures, keep in mind the design issues (you want to show that you are community based) as well as audience (you want to use language that will appeal to that audience, not to your professor). Also remember that any produced materials should be approved by your community partners.

Food

Whether your event is an actual picnic or another type of community meeting, the importance of food cannot be overstated. Beyond simply providing nourishment and energy to those attending, sharing food is a necessarily communal event, sparking conversation and dialogue. It is a key ingredient in a successful event.

How the food is obtained is equally important, and you need a community aspect to how it is part of the event. Ideally, you would develop a list of individuals who could offer to make and bring food to an event. (For our imagined picnic, you would need a large number of volunteers.) If that is not possible, you could write a letter explaining the event and take it to *local* businesses and ask them to donate. Because local businesses are often asked for donations, it is important that the request come from a resident, preferably a resident leader. Even if the size of your event disallows resident cooking or food donations and you have to go to the local corporate grocery store, make sure that some locally cooked food is offered at the event. It will signal a good intention and promote goodwill.

Follow-Up

At the conclusion of the event, you will need to write a thank-you letter to each organization or invited individual who participated. You should also have a final meeting with your community partner at which the event is assessed. Questions to be answered include the following:

- Did the event meet the stated goals?
- Did the materials provide sufficient information?
- Was there strong participation in the event?

In each case, you should begin with the positives (e.g., "Education was highlighted for a complete day in the neighborhood"; "We had a great turnout of both college students and community members") and then move on to what might have occurred differently (e.g., "Fewer speakers might have made the open mic more manageable"). You might end by discussing whether the event should be repeated annually. Such a conversation will be a barometer of the event's value because it will imply that those involved would commit to spending resources the following year.

ADAMS COLLEGE: Creating a Publication

The NWC community picnic was, to a great extent, a success. There was significant participation by the community, both through attendance and through written responses to the prompts. The open mic generated a lot of discussion and opinion about the need to increase education opportunities in the community. Unfortunately, not all the comments were as productive as hoped. Indeed, several speakers made suggestions that were at odds with the goals of the NWC and the community/university partnership, arguing against the value of community leaders having a strong voice in educational decisions with comments along the lines of "Leave such decisions to the teachers and the school district." It became clear that more work was needed to circulate community insights from the NWC (and its emerging list of volunteers and participants) than a one-day event could provide.

For this reason, the NWC has decided to create a book that can circulate across the neighborhood as well as across classrooms. The hope is that this publication will allow the NWC to show the powerful writing produced by "community intellectuals" as well as provide a counterweight to how the organization/partnership is being understood. To a greater extent, the purpose is to alter how the community is understood within the larger city and region. In addition, although Adams College still does not see itself as supporting overt activism, the administration believes the overall partnership benefits both residents' and students' literacy skills. The college has therefore decided to continue to work with the community and with the NWC in particular.

Writing classes will continue to support the partnership without, however, any Adams College funds being used to support the publications. Any proposed publications will have to be produced either very inexpensively or through fund-raising strategies. There is a sense, however, that this hurdle can be overcome. Indeed, it is believed by those involved that "the book" carries a status that offers increased legitimacy for the voices included; in some ways, the traditional tools of publishing are being used to support the status of everyday intellectuals. In some ways, this publication is the culmination of much of the work of the community/university partnership.

Creating a Community Publication

A common culminating project in community-based projects is a publication that highlights the writing, research, artwork, or photography—or a combination of such work—undertaken by participants. Many publications will be broadsheets (photocopies of text designed in word-processed documents) or smaller publications (brochures, flyers, handouts), but if you want the publication to be used in university, public school, or community classrooms, a more formal publication is usually necessary. Creating a community publication is not as difficult as it seems. Below is the information necessary to produce a publication out of a community project, with a specific emphasis on book production.

Setting Publication Goals

If you are going to publish about a non-campus-based community, your community partner needs to have a say in how the publication is framed, produced, designed, and distributed. (That is true even if the book is designed primarily for an audience of your fellow students.) Otherwise, you are repeating an unfortunate history of college faculty and students by ignoring or dismissing the community's knowledge and needs. You should work closely with your community partner to develop a framework for what should be included in the publication. For instance, if the publication is focused on residents, you need to collaboratively develop the list of whom to interview; if it is a book focused on community history, you need to collaboratively choose what locations, events, and individuals are included.

Fundraising to Meet Goals

Any publication goal has to be set within a budget. In the best-case scenario, your community partner or course instructor will have secured base funds to support a publication. Here, "funds" can mean both actual financial support and access to technology (such as photocopy machines) that can reproduce the publication. Even with these base funds, however, consider ways to supplement support for your work. Useful strategies include:

1. **Support from Local Businesses**   Depending on the nature of the publication, local businesses will often provide financial support if they are listed as a sponsor of the publication. Sponsorships typically range from $50 to $250. When asking for a sponsorship, you will need to develop a request letter stating the goal of the publication as well as a budget outlining how the funds will be used. It is also important to have your community partner make the request with you. (Indeed, the community partner must approve any plan to approach individuals, businesses, or organizations for funds.) After an initial inquiry through this letter, attempt to schedule a meeting at which you can further discuss the possibility of funding.

2. **Support from a Local Public School**   If your publication features writing by local school students (even if other types of writers are featured as well), public schools will often agree to purchase the publication for their libraries or, in certain cases, for particular classes. These requests can be made to both the principal of the school in which the students are enrolled and the school superintendent. (Note: Schools typically purchase any materials at a substantial discount. For that reason, a school will typically only pay for the cost of the publication. So, even though this strategy will ensure that your publication reaches school students, it will not pay for additional copies to be printed.) The strategy of approaching other organizations that have members published in the book might also produce similar types of funding for the publication.

3. **Support from Local Foundations**   Working with your community partner, you might research local foundations that support community development or literacy programs. (*Literacy* is a term often used to frame community writing projects.) Typically, local foundations have funds set up to support small projects on a request-by-request basis. For instance, a foundation might provide $500 to pay for a workshop for parents on healthy eating strategies for children. If your publication speaks to an issue of local concern, local foundations might provide some funding for the publication. Again, you need to work with your community partner to produce a funding request letter as well as to arrange to speak directly with someone at each foundation.

4. **Campus Fundraising**   It is also possible to develop strategies to raise funds on campus. Your class might sponsor a bake sale or online fundraising campaign, for instance. Campus offices might align with the interests of the publication, too. If the publication speaks to issues of diversity, for example, you could approach the campus office of multicultural affairs. Many campuses now also have community partnership offices that might support the publication. As with other requests, $50 to $250 is probably the most that will be provided. Before making any decisions, you should make sure that your community partner will support each request.

Ideally, prior to the beginning of the term, your community partner and your course instructor should have secured some base funding for any proposed publication project. Use of the above strategies, however, will help you learn how to raise the funds that will bring the project to fruition.

Generating Writing for the Publication

Academic books are traditionally written by recognized experts—traditional intellectuals. In this case, however, the true experts about the community are the residents—organic intellectuals. Their writing, then, should be central to the publication.

When starting a publication, assess what writing from your community partner already exists. This assessment will give you a base from which to determine how much additional work will be necessary to complete the publication goals. Work with your community partner to collect any participant writing—poetry, reports, essays, memoirs—that have been produced over the previous year. Discuss with the partner whether this writing meets the goals of the project. If no existing writing is available from community writers (or if more is required), try to form a writing group or conduct interviews of residents (see Chapter 6).

Permission to Print

Each participant (author, poet, photographer, etc.) featured in the book will need to sign a "permission to print" letter. In addition, if you want to publish images of any local school students featured in the book, you will need to secure permission from both the applicable school and the parents or guardians.

In gaining this permission, you will need to be explicit about the platforms through which the work will be published. Publishing a print book with local circulation is an entirely different situation from posting a video or audio recording online on sites such as YouTube or iTunes. Particularly, if you post online on a commercial site, you will need to research what permission requirements these sites might have as well as what uses you are giving the sites to the materials you uploaded. In some cases, you must have the individual sign the agreement demanded by the particular site you are using *prior* to actually uploading the material.

Given the complexity of publishing in multiple platforms, no one example can provide all the necessary information. No one template can capture the specific legal requirements of your particular location. It is always best to vet your letter with an expert prior to its use. The letter below, however, offers a template that can serve as the basis for seeking permission in any particular project.

Publication Agreement

This letter will serve as an agreement between (**name of community partner organization**) and (**interviewee/author name**), hereafter referred to as "author," to publish (**title of work**) in the forthcoming publication with the working title (**title**). The author also grants permission to include this work in any future editions of the publication.

The author understands and agrees to the following:

- Author will be given an opportunity to review the excerpt selected for publication.
- Published work may be used for promotional purposes.
- Author will not be compensated. Publication sales will be used by the two nonprofit organizations to offset the cost of its production.
- Each author will receive three (3) copies of the publication. S/he may purchase additional copies at 50% of the retail price.
- Where the publication appears online, on a non-profit or for-profit site, the author acknowledges receipt of the specific guidelines of that site's "usage" policy and authorizes (**name of community organization**) to upload his/her work to this site. The following are the only online sites to which the author's material may be uploaded without explicit permission by the author: (**list of class/community sites where the work will be published**).

No additions or alterations to this agreement will be considered. Please sign one copy and keep it for your own files, signing and returning the other to _____.

If you have any questions or concerns, please contact _____.

One final note: There will be projects in which you will interview individuals at public locations or at public events, usually with audio or video equipment. When conducting such interviews, you must get explicit permission to both record and use these interviews. For that reason, you might develop a version of the "permission to print" letter that they can sign (or record) as follows:

Public Interview Agreement

This letter will serve as an agreement between (**name of community partner organization**) and (**interviewee/author name**), hereafter referred to as "interviewee," to record an interview on (**date of interview**) on the topic of (**topic**) to be used in the following project: (**title, summary of project**). The author also grants permission to include all or excerpts of this interview in any printed/digital/audio products produced by the (**name of organization**).

The interviewee understands and agrees to the following:

- Interviewee will be given an opportunity to review the excerpt prior to its public use.
- Initial here if that right is waived: _____
- Interview may be used for promotional purposes for this project.
- Interviewee will not be compensated. Any income generated by produced public materials will be used by (**name of organization**) to offset the cost of its production.
- Where the publication appears online, on a non-profit or for-profit site, the interviewee acknowledges receipt of the specific guidelines of that site's "usage" policy and authorizes (**name of community organization**) to upload the interview to this site.
- The following are the only online sites to which the interview may be uploaded without explicit permission by the interviewee: (**list of class/community sites where the interview will be published**).

No additions or alterations to this agreement will be considered.

Signature

Date

If you have any questions or concerns, please contact _____.

Design

Early into this project, your class should identify who in the partnership has design skills—knowledge of software programs such as InDesign, Adobe Photoshop, or other publishing programs—as well as who has photography or illustration skills. These individuals should form a committee and develop several options for the design of the publication. This design team should find books whose style and graphic design they believe might fit the goals of your project. These books should be shared with the class and community partner to begin narrowing down design options, one of which will ultimately be chosen by the community partner.

If you are planning to actually print a book, the book should be a standard print size, such as 6 by 9 inches or 5 by 7 inches. Alternatively, the design might also call for standard letter-size paper (8½ by 11 inches) to be folded in half. Because this layout drastically cuts publishing costs, its use in community organization publications is very popular.

Editorial Decision Making

The central work of this project is to establish an editorial decision-making process to ensure that the community has a strong hand in the content and design of the final project. Both your class and the community partner should agree on this process in writing, and it should be referred to when making decisions. Among the issues to consider are the following:

- Who will make the initial decision on accepting or declining submitted materials to the book?
- In making these decisions, how important is it that the entire community be represented?
- How will the final decision over included materials be made?
- How will the final design of the book be approved?
- Will authors be paid, or will they receive free copies of the book?
- How will the contributions of the class be represented?
- How will the book be distributed?

In making these decisions, you need to be mindful of balancing the need for community control with the resources and labor available. Although it might seem correct to have the community partner make all decisions, there is a good chance the partner will not have the time to do so. The usual model is to have the class collect all the materials, make initial editorial decisions about content and design, and then present a range of options to the community partner—highlighting which pieces were not initially selected for publication. After feedback, a revised version is created, which is then resubmitted for final approval.

Throughout the process, there is often communication about certain pieces of writing or images, so conversations between you and the community partner continue. In fact, there should never be a moment when you are out of touch. The above process illustrates one way to manage everything.

The Question of Standard English

You will necessarily face the issue of standard English. Should the materials submitted for publication be dialect-free or not? Is it possible to include materials in languages other than English? This is a sensitive issue and should be decided in conjunction with your community partner, for whom you are producing the anthology. There is no correct answer on this issue. You do need to have a policy regarding standard English prior to beginning any interviews or editing of community writing so that all participants are aware of how their work will be approached.

You also need to have a discussion with any writer who decides not to standardize his or her "voice." Many community writers have never been published. They may not know how dialect-based writing—or even the content of their own writing—will be received. It is important to meet with the writer and discuss any possible controversies that might emerge from publishing that particular work in the book. Your goal is not to dissuade the writer from participating; rather, it is to allow the person to make a fully informed decision. (In some ways, this moment is the community-based version of writers having a right to their own language, which was discussed as it relates to students in Chapter 3.)

Print Publishing Considerations

Given that many community publications will have actual circulation in the community and beyond, how the book should be printed involves major decisions. The least expensive way to produce a publication is to create a WordPress or Blogspot site from which individuals can download a PDF of the book (PDF stands for portable document format). Here the strategy is to have different academic or university programs post the PDF on their sites. You could also develop multiple interactive features on the Web site, such as individual blogs by each author and a community feedback section, to allow for feedback and discussion about the book.

You might decide to also print bound copies of the book. Doing so can be as simple as making photocopies and stapling the photocopied pages together to create a 'zine or as complicated as producing an on-demand print product, which gives you a bookstore-quality publication in about ten days in almost any quantity needed. One of the benefits of a 'zine publication is its handmade quality. You can literally have all the partners come together and build the book collaboratively, designing and producing hard copies the same day.

While 'zine publications are handmade, and do not necessarily require software design knowledge, many projects will want to produce a book that can circulate in classrooms, organizations, and bookstores. Producing this type of end product requires several more steps. That said, if your project has someone with strong InDesign software knowledge, it is not necessarily more difficult. Typically, this person will be someone working for your community partner, although sometimes a student in your course might also possess this knowledge. Depending on the size of your actual publication,however, it may or may not be realistic—depending on the complexity of your actual publication—to ask a student to undertake the design work.

The end product represents what most individuals consider to be a book. To produce such a publication, the following steps are recommended.

Digital Book Files

In general, printers require book files to be submitted as application files via InDesign. They will also require that any images in the files be scanned at the highest resolution possible (usually at least 300 dots per inch, or dpi). Once you design the files, you can send them to the printer electronically. If you do not have anyone in the class or community partner organization who knows how to use InDesign, you might be able to send PDF files to certain printers. Early in the project, you should assign one student to research and analyze printing services in the area to find the one that best meets your needs.

International Standard Book Number (ISBN) and Bar Codes

If you decide to print a book, it is useful to include an International Standard Book Number (ISBN). School districts, local bookstores, and national chains often require that any publication used or sold by them have an ISBN account. Through the Web site bowkerlink.com, it is relatively easy to obtain an ISBN. Next, you will need to purchase a bar code (which you can also do through bowkerlink .com). When designing the book, the ISBN and bar code should be positioned on the back of the book (e.g., the back cover) in the bottom right-hand corner. If possible, do not embed the price of the book into the bar code.

On-Demand Printing

Unless you are printing more than five hundred copies for a guaranteed sale, avoid using large printing companies. On-demand printing companies can usually print a fifty-five-page paperback book with a full-color cover and photos inside for less than $6 per book. You can find a print-on-demand shop through an online search. Some may even be local, although that is not a requirement because the files will be transferred electronically. On-demand printing companies can produce as few as ten copies or as many as a thousand. They will often keep a copy of your files and will print them as needed (hence the name). On-demand printing is the most cost-effective way to produce bookstore-quality books.

Note: Remember that on-demand printing requires money. Be sure to account for it in your project budget. If the book will be printed outside your local community, remember to add shipping costs to the budget, too.

Printing Time Frame

If you are using a standard printer for a run of more than five hundred books, allow at least eight to ten weeks to receive bound copies of your book. This time frame makes traditional printing infeasible for most class-based projects. If your community partner wants to use such a printer, the class would work on the project up until the final files are ready for the printer. Then your community partner should make plans to send each of you in the class a copy of the printed book once it is complete.

If your goal is to have the publication completed prior to the end of the course, however, use an on-demand printing process. You only have to allot about ten days from the time you submit your document until it is in your hands.

Handmade publications, such as the 'zines described above, are quick to put together. With saddle-stapling down the middle, your stack of photocopies can be available for distribution immediately.

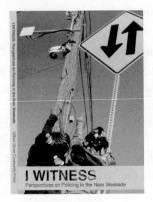

The covers of two community publications from the New City Community Press (left) in Philadelphia, PA, and Gifford Street Community Press (right) in Syracuse, NY.

New City Community
Press/Elizabeth Parks

Gifford Street Community
Press/Elizabeth Parks

Distribution

Questions about where and how books will be made available to the community as well as others should be addressed at the outset of the project. Although the actual distribution of the published book will probably fall outside of what can be accomplished during a one-semester class, it is vital to have a distribution plan. Indeed, part of the plan can be to decide if any class members would be willing to volunteer their time to distribute the book next semester.

Book Launch

It is hard to overestimate the power that new authors feel upon being published, particularly when there are few published authors in the community. To celebrate, your class should have a small publication event, perhaps at the community partner site, to launch your book. The event does not have to be elaborate, but it should include light snacks and beverages. Those featured in the book, along with their family and friends, should be invited to the event. You might also ask several contributors to the book to read excerpts of their work; depending on the setting, you might need to set up a microphone. This event is not meant to be an exercise in planning; rather, it will be a celebration of the important work you all accomplished.

A Final Note on Adams College

The story of Adams College has moved from an initial moment of a writing project in one school to the creation of a publication designed to foster a community-wide debate. Through its telling, however, you have been provided with real tools to become an effective community partner. You have seen what it means to be a member of a collective that enables a community to organize its stories, create texts that capture its vision, and circulate these products throughout the neighborhood, city, and region. Whether it is participating in a tutoring program, helping create a publication, or sponsoring a process that leads to a new organization, your work will have a public impact, affect real lives, and perhaps make a real difference. Earlier chapters discussed why such work should be part of a college writing course and the theoretical issues involved in moving outside your classroom, and later chapters provided a set of tools to use as you undertake this work. The next step is up to you.

RUNDOWN   Strategies for Community Events
and Community Publishing

Community Events

- The community partner should define the goal of the event.
- The event should feature many opportunities to participate and speak out.
- Local resources should be used when planning the event.
- Upon completion, the event should be assessed.

    Facilitate a workshop with the community partner to clarify the goal of the event as well as resources available (including labor) to ensure the event's success.

    As much as possible, any food or refreshments served should be homemade or from a local store.

    Create venues for participants to speak out with an open mic event or public writing prompt.

    Invite local organizations and leaders to demonstrate broad support for the goals of the event.

Community Publishing

- The community partner should define the publication's purpose and audience.
- Community writing should be central to the publication.
- The editorial and design processes need to be clearly stated.
- The publication's format should balance cost and distribution goals.

Work with the community partner to collect any existing writing and art and decide how much is suitable for the proposed publication; sponsor writing groups if more work is needed.

Discuss with community writers the impact of publishing their work, with specific emphasis on how their decisions about standard or dialect-based English might be received.

Design a first draft of the book, with several design options, to share with the community partner for feedback; revise in response to any feedback.

Explore different funding options to show to the community partner; then produce a funding strategy that will ensure broad production and distribution of the proposed book.

Discussion Questions & Activities

1. Before the next class, write a response to the "Coming Home" writing prompt at the start of this chapter. Share your response with your classmates.

2. At a certain moment in the Adams College partnership, the community believed it needed to take on an overtly political stance, advocating for specific goals and against specific community organizations. Adams College was uncomfortable with this stance. Do you believe that the college should have joined in the community advocacy efforts? Do you believe that students, as part of a class, should have to take part in such efforts?

3. Different forms of publications are discussed in this chapter, such as blogs, WordPress sites, 'zines, and books. Within the Adams College narrative, the residents chose the book form because they thought it was the most legitimate form of publication. Do you believe that to be the case? How has social media changed what it means to be seen as a "legitimate" publication?

4. The story of Adams College is intended to represent a fully realized community/university partnership. What did you gain from this story? What further questions do you have about this case study? Talk to fellow students and your instructor about how such a program might work in your own school's community. Identify what methods you think would—or would not—work and be prepared to explain why. What advice would you follow? What would you do differently?

Writing Place: Mapping Yourself onto Local, National, and International Communities

At this point, you have seen that the idea of *place* encompasses so much more than just a location. Place is a complex mixture of personal and public contexts, boundaries, and possibilities. As a jumping-off point for further discussion of place, here is a poem—presented in both Spanish and English—about the meaning of place and the crossing of boundaries.

"Indocumentado"

Solo,
Frente a luces ajenas
Oye otras voces calladas, distantes:
Este puente te lleva al olvido,
Te cambia de nombre.

Ya nada será tuyo,
Escucha el sonido del tren que se aleja,
El viento que roza la tarde.
Ya nada será tuyo
Y cuando vuelvas

Traerás en las uñas, en el tacto, en tu aliento,
Las sensación de haber visitado
El envés de tus sueños.
Ya nada será tuyo
Como lo fueron una vez los juegos de niño.
Aquellos jardines del pueblo,
El mismo recuerdo.

"Undocumented"

Alone,
Facing foreign lights
He hears whispered voices, distantly:
This bridge takes you to oblivion,
It changes your name.

Nothing will be yours now,
Listening to the departing train,
The wind rubbing against the evening.
Nothing will be yours now
And when you return
You'll bring under your fingernails, your touch, your breath,
The feeling of having visited
The underside of your dreams.
Nothing will be yours now
As were the games of childhood,
Those village gardens,
The same memory.

—Enrique Cortázar
From *Espejos y Ventanas/Mirrors and Windows:*
Oral Histories of Mexican Farmworkers and Their Families
Translation by Jimmy Santiago Baca

How do you know where you stand? This question is not as easy to answer as it first appears. The same street, for instance, can be seen as part of your neighborhood, your city, your region, and your country. It can be understood as part of your organic heritage or seen through the insights of your traditional education. Depending on your particular circumstances at a given moment, the question you are trying to answer, or the destination you are trying to reach, you will need to decide which of these criteria are the most important. Yolanda Wisher and Mom Frasier (see Chapter 1) were standing on the same set of streets, for instance, but they clearly read the meaning of those streets in very different ways.

Of course, it is not only personal perception that dictates the meaning of where we stand. The broader culture also determines how we interact with the space around us. As poet Enrique Cortázar notes above, crossing an international border can lead to oblivion if the receiving country does not want to recognize your existence. Indeed, crossing from one side of a school lunchroom to another and joining another group of students can often have the same (if more limited) effect of erasing our previous identity.

And then there are also moments when the broader culture removes a border in an attempt to expand the possibilities for movement. When a church and a mosque invite their members to attend an evening event, they open up new friendships and spark a common dialogue. Similarly, when government policies recognize the rights of disabled residents to accessible sidewalks and buildings, they expand how individuals can be active members in the community. Even at the moment of a personal decision, we might find ourselves part of this broader culture, such as when we walk up a ramp into our high school to vote for or against an immigration rights measure in our particular community. As you choose your path, then, you are also consciously (or unconsciously) crossing over and intermixing these personal, communal, and international geographies.

As you move forward, you might experience the exhilaration of a decision meshing perfectly with the geography—when the roads just appear to be built to move you forward, personally and collectively with others. Or perhaps you will experience a moment when your decision makes you an undocumented traveler running on the margins of a community, outside or underneath accepted geographic and cultural borders. Probably, though, you will be in that confusing middle space, having to navigate a terrain where you seem to be both within and outside of multiple boundaries, where most complicated decisions are made. Navigating this terrain, making these decisions, ultimately leads us all to create new pathways for ourselves and others.

It is at those moments when we are at the margins or when we see the problems with how borders have been constructed that we need to draw on the collective strength of those around us. If we live within a network of influences and forces, of restrictions and limitations, we also live within the possibility that collectively, as partners with others, we can move our neighbors, our community, and our country to redraw the current boundaries and open up a different set of possibilities for ourselves and others. Communal partnerships can alter the future of individual lives.

Indeed, this conceptual and material power to make such decisions—to blend our organic and traditional understandings, working collaboratively to chart a unique course and revise established boundaries—is a central component of a person's identity. That is, everyone has an inherent right to constantly serve as a compass for their own sense of values and, in the process, work collectively to create pathways that others might follow. Indeed, understanding the multiple geographies in which we exist, establishing a framework by which to make decisions, and understanding what it means to move forward individually and collectively represent the work of this chapter.

In taking on this work, you will read selections from a series of authors and activists, each of whom has grappled with geographic boundaries. As such, this chapter will allow you to engage with their ideas as you develop your own trajectory. More than just theorize about this work, however, you will also see that many of these authors created journeys, maps, and projects that enacted their sense of direction and their own moral code for navigating personal and public spaces. You will also have the opportunity to create such work for yourself; you will be able to move from theorizing to practice, with all the possibilities and problems such work involves.

References and notes for the readings can be found in the appendix on page 427.

NEDRA REYNOLDS

Reading Landscapes and Walking the Streets *and* Maps of the Everyday: Habitual Pathways and Contested Places

Courtesy of Nedra Reynolds.
Photo: Joannah Portman Daley

Nedra Reynolds is a professor of writing and rhetoric at the University of Rhode Island. Her work emerges from a focus on how individuals understand the space they inhabit; the two essay excerpts that follow are from her book *Geographies of Writing: Inhabiting Places and Encountering Difference.* She argues that although traditional and online maps can seemingly represent a community (the primary topic of "Reading Landscapes"), the geographic understanding of the residents is more nuanced and more attuned to local history (the primary topic of "Maps of Everyday"). Indeed, Reynolds demonstrates through both excerpts that depending on the government policies that have shaped who lives there, the community stories told about who lives there, and the individual experiences of residents, one street can carry multiple meanings. To understand a community means to understand one's unique interactions with these always-present multiple levels of meaning. Mapping a community cannot be separated from the cultural experiences one brings to such work. In this regard, understanding geography becomes a difficult and multilayered enterprise.

■ ■ ■

Geography is very much a *seeing* discipline, whose premises and proofs, methodologies and conclusions, stem from visual evidence.[1] The importance of seeing is a fundamental element, of course, of mapping or cartography—that is, the representation of space in two-dimensional or in digital forms, using lines and measurements and colors and textures. . . .

Geography's dependence on seeing is especially prominent in traditional cultural geography, a subdiscipline of human geography that first evolved from fears that the natural world was being eroded by modernization. Attributed to Carl O. Sauer and the Berkeley School, cultural geography evolved as a strong reaction against environmental determinism, an approach that reduced explanations of human beings or cultures to the physical attributes of the earth.[2] In his 1925 "The Morphology of Landscape," a methodological piece, Sauer traces the "chorologic interest" of geography to "the establishment of a critical system which embraces the phenomenology of landscape," a landscape that most definitely includes "the works of man as an integral expression of the scene."[3] As one of the first cultural geographers, then, Sauer argued against tendencies in human geography that made geography a study of spatial laws. In his argument for "a science that asked how individual landscapes came to take on their shapes,"[4] Sauer was primarily concerned with "areal differentiation," or what makes places unique.[5] . . .

Cultural geographers study the ways in which cultures are contested spatially and how identity and power are reproduced in the everyday, in mundane, ordinary landscapes. How do particular sites acquire meanings, and how do different subcultures use places and sites?[6] According to Linda McDowell, cultural geographers examine

> how the increasingly global scale of cultural production and consumption affects relationships between identity, meaning, and place. Attention is focused on the ways in which symbols, rituals, behaviors and everyday social practices result in a shared set or sets of meaning that are to greater or lesser degrees, place-specific. Thus a geographic perspective has become central to the cultural studies project more widely.[7]

Generally, cultural geographers want the construction of identity understood as a *spatial* process, but a process that resists a "one-to-one correspondence between the image and consumption of a place and its."[8] Indeed, cultural geographers influenced by Sauer have long resisted a one-to-one correspondence between the land and the culture—like that living on the Great Plains means being a farmer, or that living by the sea makes one a fisherman. Just because someone spends her whole life in one place, a neighborhood or house, doesn't mean that she has a resultant stable identity, or adopts the same habits as all of her neighbors, or uses all the same pathways. Being raised in Brooklyn or L.A. or Crabapple Cove doesn't mean having a stable identity, either, as recognizable as a sitcom rerun. Therefore, in their attempt to understand how identities are constructed in space, through experiences with place, cultural geographers insist on explicitly material notions of culture, not abstract ones.[9] . . .

Cultural geography resists explanations of culture divorced from materiality and derives, in part, from cultural materialism, via Raymond Williams (Jackson). For Williams, culture cannot be reduced to ideology, "narrowly conceived, because it is part of a social and political order that is *materially produced.*"[10] According to Jackson, Williams's concept of structures of feeling is particularly important for cultural geographers because it connects to the important geographical idea of "sense of place."[11]

In *Marxism and Literature*, Williams identifies structures of feeling as "meanings and values as they are actually lived and felt" and "specifically affective elements of consciousness and relationships."[12] Intended as a cultural hypothesis, structures of feeling can be used to understand, in particular, art and literature, a way of recognizing "their specific kinds of sociality."[13] Williams asserts that social forms become social consciousness "only when they are lived, actively, in real relationships."[14] Cultural geographers like Jackson are attracted to Williams's structures of feeling because experiences within landscapes or the built environment are often very much like responses to art and literature, and these responses are materially produced, not simply aesthetic. Cultural geographers want to claim, from Williams, that geography is lived, actively, in real relationships.

Jackson also sees structures of feeling as related to Bourdieu's concept of habitus. Habitus attempts to represent how social behaviors, habits, become so naturalized as to be inscribed onto the body, a result of "the sedimented history of particular practices"[15]: for example, an English professor who can't read without a pen in hand, or a seven-year-old ballet student whose legs and posture already show the signs of dance training, or someone abused as a child who often cowers at a raised hand or sudden movement. Practices and habits become inscribed upon the body, and many of these habits evolve from places, from where we hang out or from our usual haunts. . . .

As a set of embodied practices, habitus keeps us in our place, so to speak, or defines the tactics and strategies we rely upon for moving through the world. Modes of transport or preferred pathways are part of one's habitus, as are clothing and style, gestures and movement, accent and expressions. A person's sense of place, while a result of many layered effects, is quite directly related to her body in space. . . .

The *Flaneur,* Walking, and Ways of Seeing

With the rise of the modern city, new ways of seeing became possible; rather than sitting on a hillside gazing at the valley below, urban observers walk the streets, mixing with people from "all walks of life." Characterized by paradoxical spaces, confusion between public and private, and resulting identities in flux, the modern city becomes a text made up of both material and metaphorical elements, the *flaneur* its composer. In the histories and literatures of modernism, one of the most compelling street figures is that of the *flaneur,* urban rambler, or street prowler, known best through Charles Baudelaire and Walter Benjamin and more recently through Edmund White. I explore this figure as a way of representing both actual physical movement through the streets and ways of seeing in built environments.

Strolling through the literature of modernity, geography, urban studies, and critical theory, the *flaneur* embodies the spatial practices of walking as writing, writing as walking; his main focus is to absorb and render the city through writing. A writer, artist, and journalist who collects as he saunters, sketches as he watches, the *flaneur* organizes and juxtaposes material in various ways.[16] Forms of *flanerie*, this section argues, are important to claim for material and geographic rhetorics, for ordinary journeys of the everyday, those defined by images of the built environment and determined by pathways through the built environment. The rambler is a figure worth habilitating for material rhetorics and geographies of writing not because he *solves* something in our dilemmas about visual culture but because he embodies method.[17] Forms of *flanerie* stand for an approach to street life, a way of moving through the world, collecting, arranging, and remembering, dependent on seeing. . . .

10   Learning to see at street level might help us understand how it is that images are taking on certain functions formerly carried by language.[18] "Sequence," for example, becomes less important, but remembering where one is, in relation to other places, becomes more important. In geographical rhetorics, then, memory and arrangement become critical. Where do things go, and how can we keep track of them in different types of texts, not all of them organized by text running from left to right? How do memories of other texts or images influence arrangement? What visual representations of texts are lodged in readers' and writers' memories that affect their arrangements or "moves"—their pauses, clicks, page downs, or bouts of rereading? . . .

Material rhetorics invite a type of seeing and forms of movement that help writers or other composers pay more attention to how they navigate space, inhabit places, or encounter difference. "Learning to see," as some urban planners argue, can result in collaborative projects to restore neighborhoods, to reclaim buildings, and embrace community life. . . .

I learned a great deal about cultural geography, mapping, and streetwork from a small group of undergraduates in England as they took ordinary journeys of the everyday, often into contested places, and as they attempted to understand an unfamiliar place from the perspective of cultural researchers. Their experiences with encountering difference demonstrate the extreme limitations of traditional maps, which cannot include "the breeze [that] carries the smell of the lake, or the Swedish bakery, or grilling kielbasa."[19] Maps can never capture the operations of walking or the well-trodden paths: "Surveys of routes miss what was: the act of passing by."[20] The activities of passers-by—walking, wandering, or window shopping—are transformed, de Certeau says, into points on a map, and then "the trace left behind is substituted for the practice."[21] The geographical system of mapping, therefore, can transform action into legibility, "but in doing so it causes *a way of being in the world* to be forgotten."[22] Other forms of mapping might make experiences in space more legible or transferable, forms that come not only from cartography but also from stories and legends about places. . . . Mental maps and not just textual maps affect deeply our sense of place; mental maps are "written" through our identities and means of moving through the world.

■   ■   ■

Mental Mapping, Maps That Move

While print and electronic maps are the most familiar forms, "mapping" is increasingly used as a metaphor for charting, understanding, exploring, or organizing. Mental mapping and cognitive mapping are both terms used by educators and researchers to refer to a person's cognitive capacity to understand where things are in relationship to one another, sense of direction, or sense of distance. It's the ability to carry around in our heads organized information or images of cities, especially images that are "soaked in memories and meanings."[23] A form of imagined geography, mental maps hold the cognitive images in our minds about a place, a route, or an area. We have mental maps of our hometowns or the most familiar places of our childhoods; we have mental maps of our current neighborhoods or campuses. Based on these mental maps, many of us could give directions to a stranger or could sketch the way from A to B. . . .

Mental maps, however cognitively housed, are socially constructed. They are a particular form of "imagined geography" that illustrate the complex relationships between the social and the spatial. Most importantly, maps and spatial memory have been shown to relate to gender and class. This means they are not "cognitive" topics but social ones. The research of Peter Orleans from 1967 in Los Angeles provides the most striking example of this: asking residents of L.A. to share their mental maps of urban space, Orleans questioned a wide range of groups and then created composite maps from their responses.[24] Unsurprisingly, the higher the income and the whiter the neighborhood, the richer and more wide-ranging were residents' knowledge of L.A. White respondents from Westwood represented tourist areas and the coast, for example, while black residents in Avalon identified main streets leading to downtown, but other districts were vague entities. Finally, Spanish-speaking residents in Boyle Heights constructed the smallest mental maps of all, representing only the immediate area, the City Hall, and the bus depot.[25] In other words, leisure time, access to affordable transportation, and above all, feelings of empowerment and safety allow people to explore little-known regions and to broaden and deepen their own "mental maps" of a place or region.

Soja pins a fondness for mental mapping on secondspace epistemologies,

> immediately distinguishable by their explanatory concentra-
> tion on conceived rather than perceived space and their implicit
> assumption that spatial knowledge is primarily produced through
> discursively devised representations of space, through the spatial
> workings of the mind.[26]

Artists and architects, urbanists and designers can be found in secondspace, according to Soja, where "the imagined geography tends to become the 'real' geography, with the image or representation coming to define and order the reality."[27] Despite his criticisms, others believe that mental maps and a variety of forms of mapping can become vital tools in exploring people's understanding of space, or the cultural and social spaces that mark inclusions or exclusions: "Just as individuals need cognitive maps of their cities to negotiate their spatial environment, so we need maps of society to intelligently analyse, discuss and intervene in social processes."[28]

I rely in this chapter on overlapping versions of mapping to argue that mapping as a concept helps us understand the social production of space and people's experiences in space, but our concept of mapping must include the realandimagined and needs to be drawn from the actual experiences of sociospatial beings. Mental maps are drawn by people's experience in space and with specific places or locations—experiences that have everything to do with class, race, gender, age, mobility, and sexuality. Identity is constructed in place, via place, and I hope to build on that assertion both by qualitative research methodologies and through the rich literatures of cultural geography. . . .

In order to explore the relationship between the spatial and the social in a concrete and practical way, I interviewed eight students in a cultural geographies class at Leeds University about their experiences in Leeds, with getting around the city, with living and working there as students. My purpose was to explore the everyday material existence of university students in the "mundane land-scape" of the campus, the surrounding area, their housing, and the other places of their social and spatial lifeworlds. What places did these students see as contested, desirable, or dangerous? Which places did they avoid or feel excluded from? How are their experiences in space shaped by their identities as students, who are typically transient members of learning communities? In what ways do students—straddling the borders of a number of communities—describe geographically-constructed difference? My analysis of the interview transcripts suggests that an awareness of the workings of geographic exclusion helps us come to terms with the "invisible" types of difference that are the hardest to identify and understand. Geographies of exclusion[29] are worth far more of our attention as we attempt to understand the various ways in which difference is encoded. . . .

On a gray afternoon in February, taking my usual route from campus to
Headingley, I overheard one side of a mobile phone conversation, where a male
student said to his caller, "I'm walking through Hyde Park. . . . No, the dodgy
one. In *Leeds.*"

5

Hyde Park is most often associated with London, but that confusion is only one
of many layers of complicated meaning affixed to this place. I begin with Hyde
Park, the dodgy one in Leeds, because it emerged in these interviews as a place
marked by contestation and controversy, while it was also obviously a gathering
place and a playground. It served the functions that city parks fulfill—it was a
pleasantly green respite from the otherwise brick and stone environment—and it
was also perceived to be a dangerous place. As one geographer has noted, "Parks
are typical of those spaces that make the edge of the street ambiguous, that extend
the space the street signifies."[30] It was often filled with people using the space in
various ways; on a nice day, you could see dogs being walked, children on the
playground, older teens on the skateboard ramp or basketball court, pick-up football matches, and many people just passing through on their way to and from the
university or towards the Hyde Park bus stop on one edge of the park. However,
at dusk or after dark, it took on a different identity, and for women, at least, even
the streets surrounding the park take on a sinister quality.

For residents of Leeds, "Hyde Park" refers to both a park, with clear borders,
and a neighborhood, with boundaries less obvious. Hyde Park is both a clearly
bound green space, with playground areas and trees lining the sidewalks, and also
a residential area characterized by red-brick terraced housing, a shopping area,
and at least one major traffic artery (the Otley road). I often had to ask students to
clarify whether they meant Hyde Park as *park* or as neighborhood, and this distinction is just one layer of the contestations surrounding this space. On the city
of Leeds ward map, Hyde Park is part of the Headingley ward. One would have
to "know the area," in experiential ways, to distinguish the boundaries between
Hyde Park and other parts of the Headingley ward (including Headingley the residential and commercial district within the voting ward of Headingley).[31] Rates
for rentals, higher in Headingley, and the number of "ethnic" shops, higher in
Hyde Park, can serve to distinguish between the two areas.[32] On the northwestern edge of the university, the park serves as *a space in between* the campus and
some of the most student-populated neighborhoods in Leeds—streets that are
also more permanently occupied by a very diverse group of residents.

Hundreds of pedestrians and cyclists, making their way to or from the university, walk through Hyde Park, both as a shortcut to certain parts of campus and
to avoid or take a break from the busy and noisy main road. My first reaction to
it was a very pleasant one—after a mile of walking on an exhaust-fumed main
road, I welcomed a calmer green space. However, I was to learn later that Hyde
Park is considered by most students to be unsafe at certain times or in certain

situations. In addition, students consider Hyde Park the neighborhood to be, simultaneously, terrible, rundown, and full of character. Even though those I interviewed called it "student land," it is also presented in social geography lectures as one of the most ethnic areas in Leeds, occupied mostly by South Asians, many of whom run businesses: shops, taxi stands, takeaway restaurants. I want to write about Hyde Park here to illustrate how contested places can be. Hyde Park operates as a complicated signifier for the students I interviewed and supports the argument that even the most precise, sophisticated map cannot represent much about a place except where it exists in (geometric) relationship to other places.

My own understanding of Hyde Park, and all its contestations, comes from walking through the area a few days a week and from living in Headingley, adjacent to Hyde Park the neighborhood. But none of my experiences as a transient resident prepared me for the strong reactions most of the students I interviewed had towards Hyde Park or the strong associations or a particularly resonant sense of place.

10   When asked how she knew that Hyde Park was an ethnic area, Elaine replied, "I know about Hyde Park because we live round there, so we have to walk

Hyde Park cinema. © EDIFICE/Alamy Stock Photo

An overview of Brudenell Road in Leeds.
© PA Images/Alamy Stock Photo

through that." She doesn't pause to clarify what *"that"* is, but given her wording and tone, it is clearly distasteful (why didn't she say "we have to walk through *there*"?). Elaine also says: "I've been in Hyde Park in the middle of the night, and it's like oh my gosh I'm so scared." When I asked her whether she meant the park itself or the neighborhood, she said "both down there — there's always more ethnic minorities walking around than you see white people." Mitchell, who calls Hyde Park "definitely one of the ethnic areas," also specifically mentions "a lot of Asian shops like grocery shops and meat shops' Halal signs."

Sheila was the only student of the eight interviewed who lived in Hyde Park by choice: "I live in this area here — it's Hyde Park and it's definitely ethnic 'cause there's a lot of like Asian families that live in and around here; I've been there so I know." Since all of her friends live there too, Sheila is careful to distinguish between Hyde Park the neighborhood and Hyde Park the park.

I: Would you walk in Hyde Park, at night?

S: Hyde, the actual park? No, you never walk through Hyde Park, that's definitely a no-go area; I'll mark that one actually. . . . The actual park is not lit; it's really dark; actually the council should probably spend a bit of money on lighting. Of course I'd walk through at night but in a massive gang, I'm talking four plus. Walk through coming back home from the university union Old Bar and go home; I'd walk through there if there's more than four of us usually—usually if there's a lad as well but *never* just me and my friends walking in from the union, always round the side of the park, never through the park.

I: Even in the daytime you go around?

S: The worst time apparently for like student muggings or other incidents is around five or six o'clock at night when it's dark, so going home from uni, that's the time I usually go, between half five and seven at night I'm usually on my way home so then I would always go around the side.

I: And that's better lit?

S: It's better lit and there's just traffic and houses.

I: More people?

S: Yeah, there's loads of students walk down there; I mean 'cause it's terrifying when you're walking through the park and it's dark and someone comes from the opposite direction and you're oh no, and you realize that there's students so it's okay, and you think oh it's just students so they're legitimate, which is a bad thing to think anyway. [laughter]

Sheila's relief at seeing other students, which she admits is problematic, may illustrate the high ethnic population of Hyde Park. Even Sheila, who enjoys living in Hyde Park for its diversity, expresses her sense of relief at encountering other students at night—rather than, one assumes, other locals who may not be white.

Mitchell and Anna both talk about the contested claims to residency status or the about the contestation over who belongs in this neighborhood and who doesn't. Mitchell says,

> I know people who live in the Hyde Park area, and their next door neighbors who're Asian come round and knock on their door and say, "Why are you living here, this is an Asian area." So I think as well as white people saying it's is an ethnic or Asian area, Asians see it as an ethnic area themselves.

Anna relates her own experience as a visitor and nonresident:

A: Basically I went to a friend's house there [in the Hyde Park area], and we're all sitting in the lounge having a cup of tea or something, and these kids were climbing on the bars in front of the windows climbing across the bars [imitates them], "Oy mister, mister, give us this, give us that," and they [my friends] can't put any, any of their washing out, and there are literally—there are sort of bars over the windows to stop the kids coming in, and they're inside the house and that's their territory—soon as you step outside the house then it's almost like it's Asian people's territory, really, . . . so

I: They'll ask you things like—

A: What are you doing here, what are you doing here. If you're in the way, or if you're wanting to get past them, it's fine if . . . you, you know, keep yourself to yourself and you've been quite separate about it, but if you—if there's any attempt to mix in any sense then, that, you know, I'd be nervous about it, definitely, so you tend to sort of keep yourself to yourself and walk with your head high and hopefully no one will bother you.

Anna identifies in this passage what David Sibley, in *Geographies of Exclusion*, calls a liminal zone, spaces of ambiguity where the categories of inside/outside, public/private, or home/street become blurred or uncertain. Sibley asserts "for the individual or group socialized into believing that the separation of categories is necessary or desirable, the liminal zone is a source of anxiety."[33] If students are in their homes, they are "safe," but Anna's anxiety begins when she has to cross the threshold, enter the streets, and move through the neighborhood. . . .

The students I interviewed did not openly challenge others' claims that they didn't belong; they recognized that other residents were far more permanent, with more of a stake in the area. Some students were willing to admit that they didn't always make "good neighbors"; Mitchell talks about how students don't care for their houses (because they'll lose their security deposit anyway). Elaine, however, describes an "antistudent sentiment" that she claims is held by most locals: "The locals think that we come in and make loads of noise and create rubbish and get drunk and we're hooligans; and they've just got quite a lot of negative feelings against us."

Sheila thinks the antistudent attitudes result from a very limited form of contact between the two groups: the Asian businesses provide services to students, and students are interested in or dependent on the Asians only as "service providers." The students are consumers, and the businesses need them to survive.

> Yeah, the only thing I do dislike about [Hyde Park] a lot is the fact the community's so divided, students and you know, the Asian families and businesses. The only thing you ever come into contact with people for unfortunately is buying burgers from the takeaway or taxis; that's the only contact. [. . .] I think that students, well I know that students are really resented by the locals—cause we can really misbehave.

For the residents, students' economic clout often overrides residents' resentment of their noise and "hooligan" behaviors. Sheila remarks about how "welcomed" the students feel when they return to Leeds in September: "We come back and

15

the taxi drivers always say 'Oh I'm so glad to have you back.' You know, students do bring most of the money into the area and businesses, especially all the takeaways."

As Sibley says, "In the interaction of people and the built environment, it is a truism that space is contested but relatively trivial conflicts can provide clues about power relations and the role of space in social control."[34] It's impossible to tell how serious or how trivial some of these encounters were between students and the Hyde Park residents; however, it's clear that the mix of social differences, beyond "race" or "class," causes boundaries or borders to shift and slide; those unsure of their place use tactics, like Anna's, of "keeping herself to herself" in order to get through territory that belongs to others. . . .

These mental maps of Leeds illustrate that movement through the spatial world hinges upon contested places, geographies of exclusion, and (sometimes invisible) markers of boundaries. The images we carry around in our heads, even those that come from the reports of others, affect our willingness to explore or our choices of residential areas. Even if people move through certain areas or neighborhoods without fear of physical harm, they may feel uncomfortable or they may have minor confrontations about "who belongs there."

Investigating the "imageability"[35] of cities or areas contributes much to our understanding of the social production of space and people's experiences in space, and these are the forms of mapping that I want to claim as spatial practices of the everyday that can help us to re-imagine acts of writing as material and visual. In *Writing Women and Space*, Alison Blunt and Gillian Rose claim that mapping "is a distinctive form of spatial representation because it can be interpreted as visual and/or textual . . . . the spatial imagery of mapping can expose tensions between the dynamics of the visual and the written."[36] I would add, however, that mental mapping, where the real and the imagined or the physical and the emotional come together, adds yet another layer to mapping and its representations.

20   Mapping, then, in all of its overlapping forms, contributes to geographic rhetorics by insisting upon the realandimagined production of space and more complex ways of representing places and spaces. Along with walking—forms of *flanerie*—and dwelling . . . mapping forms part of the techne for geographic rhetorics, those that focus on moving through the world, encountering the rub of differences, the fissures and gaps in discourse, the borders and fault lines. Maps work metaphorically, but they also do rhetorical work: they provide information that influences action; they persuade users to try a new route or stick with the old one; and they communicate an image of a place that may or may not hold up. Maps, like all texts, function in the betweens of metaphor and materiality: cartography is a useful and profitable "skill" done with tools, but mental mapping is a swirl of memory and experience related to race, class, gender, sexuality, age, or abilities. A geographical rhetoric, then, would not ignore longitude or

latitude but would try to capture the layers of meaning and the *feelings* of residents or visitors or trespassers. Contested places like Hyde Park in Leeds are not easily "mapped," but as rhetoricians and educators, it is our responsibility to understand not only where our students come from but also what forms of fear or reluctance keep students locked in place.

Students' highly charged responses to certain places in Leeds and their reluctance to explore neighborhoods beyond "student land" highlights how difficult it is to move learners to have a meaningful encounter with difference. The next chapter turns to the cultural geography method of "street-work" to show how walking and mapping can help us to understand the complex ways in which space hides consequences from us and the ways in which one's "sense of place" is constructed. Like forms of mental mapping, street-work exposes the workings of geographies of exclusion: how the landscape, the built environment, the inhabitants, or the force of their own preconceptions and expectations can make people feel excluded or alienated from certain places. This bodes ill, I argue, for composition's growing enthusiasm for service learning and literacy projects if such project designs do not include an awareness of the sociospatial construction of difference.

Reading

1. How does Reynolds argue that geography is a visual enterprise?
2. How does she argue that mental maps differ from traditional visual maps?
3. How does Reynolds define the *flaneur* (para. 8 of the first selection)?
4. How does the work of the *flaneur* compare to the work of the geographer?

Inquiring

1. Reynolds makes two claims about geography: (1) It is a visual enterprise, and (2) our vision is shaped by our cultural experiences. When looking at a map, then, it is possible that individuals might understand a town's geography in different (and perhaps contradictory) ways. Also, a person's perception of that geography might not stay constant; a particular context or newly acquired experience might sway his or her visual understanding. Reynolds uses the term *habitus* to explain this connection between identity and architecture, between individual experience and developed landscapes. How do you respond to Reynolds's arguments? How might you draw the line between a person's experiential understanding of a space and the meaning of the space itself? Do you find *habitus* a useful term? Why or why not?

2. A student exists in a complicated space defined by his or her temporary status at a local school yet often living and shopping in a historically situated

neighborhood. Citing the insights of David Sibley, Reynolds writes that such a "liminal zone, spaces of ambiguity where the categories of inside/outside, public/private, or home/street become blurred or uncertain" (para. 14 of the second selection), can create complex choices on how to proceed at any given moment. Spend 5 minutes briefly writing about a moment you faced such ambiguity. Share this writing with your classmates. Do you see a common set of concerns among your classmates or a common set of strategies for handling such moments? When seen as a collective set of concerns and strategies, what conclusions can you draw about the student body's relationship with the surrounding community? What do you see as the reasons for this relationship?

3. Reynolds claims that the *flaneur* stands for "an approach to street life, a way of moving through the world, collecting, arranging, and remembering, dependent on seeing" (para. 9 of the first selection). In making this claim, she argues that individuals who inhabit this identity can learn about the community in which they travel and live through observation. How do you understand the methods used by the *flaneur* to learn about a community? What does he notice? How does he understand what he sees? What type of conclusions does he draw? Prior to the next class, spend some time walking through your campus and community and attempt to see these places as a *flaneur* would. Come to class prepared to share your insights. What were you able to learn through this method? How did it help you resee your school community? What types of understandings were not gained through this method? What could you not *see* but still thought was important to notice?

Composing

1. Reynolds recognizes that within each of us is a collage of identities, a blend of unique perspectives that are our source for understanding the meaning of a street corner or neighborhood. Create a list of all your different identities (e.g., *student, daughter, music lover, city dweller, parent, clerk*). Then choose one location that you pass through at least once a day. Write one paragraph from each of these perspectives, explaining how a particular identity understands this location. (You might try to write in the voice that particular identity might use.) Once you have completed this exercise, use it to analyze the validity of Reynolds's argument about habitus — about how identity and architecture intersect in the creation of meaning in a local neighborhood.

2. One of Reynolds's central points is that geographic borders are not just the result of concrete streets and map-designated boundaries. Geography is also a "cultural production," the result of collective experiences by a community often not represented on paper or Web page. This mapping can only be seen through the work of studying individual oral histories from a neighborhood and drawing

these experiences and viewpoints into relationships with one another, such as Reynolds begins to do in her book *Geographies of Writing*. For this paper, find a printed map (or create a map through an online mapping program) that provides a visual representation of the street on which you live. To see how this map represents your neighborhood, analyze the suggested map keys, colors used, and other information provided. Then interview several of the residents about your street. Using this information, write a short essay in which you explore the relationship between "maps" and "neighborhood experience." Use the essay to discuss not only how Reynolds might describe this relationship but also how your own research about your street might expand or critique her insights. As in Reynolds's work, refer to and discuss the interviews in your essay.

3. Reynolds points to the *flaneur* as one way to understand a local geography. In making this claim, she is choosing a historical figure from a period in which there were no social or digital media. Today, a person's experience of his or her local terrain is informed not just by walking the streets but also by smartphone apps, GPS programs, and social media such as Yelp, WalkScore, and Neighborhood Scout. Write a paper in which you attempt to redefine the methodology of the *flaneur* for the digital age. Demonstrate how this "i-*flaneur*" framework allows you to analyze your home or school community.

Connecting

Reynolds claims that neighborhoods have both a physical structure and a mental structure, based on resident memories. Paula Mathieu (p. 268) seems to make a similar claim, particularly when she stages the "homeless" bus tour to interrupt how people perceive the city. Write an essay in which you discuss whether Reynolds might or might not have her students take on similar projects; in other words, can the *flaneur* be a community activist?

PAULA MATHIEU

Writing in the Streets

Courtesy of Paula Mathieu

Paula Mathieu is an associate professor of English at Boston College. Her work focuses on the relationship between universities and communities, with a specific emphasis on how university partnership work often fails to benefit the community. She argues that the size of most universities makes them unable to bend their institutional structure to the specific needs of a local neighborhood. Rather than attempting to engage with the whole university, she argues for partnerships that are tactical: minimal in institutional interaction, deliberate in focus, and limited in time. Integrating her commitment to issues of homelessness, Mathieu develops community/university partnerships that highlight the need to address them ethically and responsibly.

In the following excerpt from her book *Tactics of Hope: The Public Turn in English Composition*, Mathieu discusses the creation of a tour by homeless advocates and her students designed to highlight the issues of homelessness in Chicago.

■ ■ ■

We can never predict the impact of our actions . . . But we need to believe that our individual involvement is worthwhile, that what we do in the public sphere will not be in vain.

—Paul Loeb

What does writing *do*? In a performative sense, what does any act of writing accomplish in the world—either practically, personally, or politically? This may be the most basic yet difficult question a writer or writing teacher asks.

A traditional view of writing instruction measures the relevance and efficacy of writing within institutional boundaries and frameworks: The purpose of writing instruction is to bestow skills that prepare students for the next class or writing challenge; the audience of student writing is usually the individual instructor or the academic community that the instructor represents. Within this logic, writing functions as a form of cultural capital and writing classes (and by extension a college degree) operate transactionally, by bestowing on students institutional accreditation that they will cash in, so to speak, in future classes or at graduation. The value of a writing class thus conceived lies at least partially beyond itself. The purpose and audiences of any writing assignment are incidental, because the payoff of a course lies more in its grade and in the rehearsal of writing conventions than through any events or projects that transpire within the class itself.

Many composition scholars oppose defining the parameters of a writing course in strictly institutional terms. Geoffrey Sirc, for example, critiques an orientation that he calls "Freshman English as Corporate Seminar," which he describes as writing courses that privilege preparation for work over "intensification of experience."[1] Patricia Harkin[2] characterizes the institutional function of freshman writing as the university equivalent of automobile insurance—it's something no student ever wants to purchase, but they do it anyhow . . . just in case they "need" it at some future moment. As the corporate seminar and auto insurance metaphors connote, viewing writing as a universal requirement that exists only to transact skills or status limits the purview of writing and writing classes to the institutional setting. While few would contest the value of equipping students with writing skills and conventions that will serve them throughout their academic and work careers, many writing instructors also seek a variety of pedagogical approaches that move beyond narrow institutional definitions of writing.[3] One of these pedagogical responses has been inviting students to engage in public writing, which many feel gives students more intrinsic motivations for their writing by seeing broader purposes or audiences for their work.[4]

In some classrooms, public writing might mean sharing work among students through peer workshops, collaborative work, or classroom circulation of finished works. In others, public writing means asking that students' work involve the streets, by gearing writing toward public purposes and extracurricular audiences. In these courses, writing may become less like auto insurance, but what does it becomes more like? When the purview of a writing class encompasses issues and concerns in the streets, what can public writing accomplish? And how do we know? . . .

Public audiences are often unreceptive or difficult to move; clear measures of success or completion are difficult to find. In her scholarship on public writing, Susan Wells explores the challenge of creating clear audiences and purposes: "Our public sphere is attenuated, fragmented, and colonized: so is everyone else's. All speakers who aspire to intervene in society face the task of constructing a responsive public."[5] Following Jurgen Habermas' *Structural Transformation of the Public Sphere*, Wells describes public discourse not as a type or genre of writing, but as "a complex array of discursive practices, including forms of writing, speech, and media performance" in which speakers and writers "come to the public with a weight of personal and social experience . . . [and] render those experiences intelligible to any listener."[6] . . .

Without the power of state agencies to command media attention, activist groups face additional difficulties when trying to gain access to the public sphere. Oscar Negt and Alexander Kluge's *The Public Sphere and Experience* (1993) disputes Habermas' idea that the public sphere is open to all. They describe the public sphere as aligned with the ruling classes and institutions, which stands in contrast to what they call "proletarian experience. " At the same time, though, Negt and Kluge argue that excluded groups cannot simply disconnect from this public sphere: "If the masses try to fight a ruling class reinforced by the power of the public sphere, their struggle is hopeless; they are always simultaneously fighting against themselves, for the public sphere is constituted by them."[7] Wells discusses Negt and Kluge in her discussion of public writing, claiming that "allusively . . . they suggest tactics for creating partial, temporary, and multiple public spheres."[8] This notion of tactical alternatives—multiple publics and counterpublics—is fruitfully pursued in the work of Michel de Certeau.

. . . De Certeau's work acknowledges both agency and limitations in his distinction between strategic and tactical power, an idea he extends to discourse as well. Strategic discourses, as he describes them, are official, emanating from institutions, media conglomerates, and state agencies. . . . Strategic discourses include utility policies, gas bills, application forms for state assistance, housing policy regulations, welfare, and Medicaid rules. They also include commonplace beliefs about poverty and the responsibility of individuals or state agencies to provide financial assistance.[9] Since strategic discourses emanate (or are circulated) from secured institutional spaces, according to de Certeau, their power is spatial and relatively stable.

Tactical discourses, on the other hand, are "determined by the absence of power"[10] and are calculated actions emanating from unofficial places that lack a propertied locus. Since this discourse is not issued systematically from a proper space, tactical discourse operates "within enemy territory" and without "the option of planning a general strategy." Thus tactical actions operate as "isolated actions, blow by blow."[11] They are located temporally (and temporarily), not spatially. Tactical discourse includes trickery, polemics, and tales of miracles. For example, de Certeau discusses how the Brazilian peasants of Pernambuco talk about their situation.[12] He sees their discourse as operating on two levels: the polemical level which acknowledges their lack of institutional power—"they always fuck us over"[13]—and a utopian level of play and possibilities, filled in this case with stories of miracles centered around Frei Damião. These miracle stories respond to the socioeconomic situation from the outside "with irrelevance and impertinence" in a discourse that one cannot prove, but must only believe. These utopian stories according to de Certeau, exist as another discourse alongside the analysis of facts, "as the equivalent of what a political ideology introduces into that analysis."[14]

The power of tactical discourse, since it responds to strategic power without a stable spatial nexus, is temporary and fleeting. The effects of tactical discourse are not easily measurable in the short term and their overall effects are not always clear. . . .

To further explore public writing as tactical, I turn to a [story] from a writing group I ran at a Chicago street newspaper for two and a half years.

10

Not Your Mama's Bus Tour

Creating a theatrical tour of Chicago guided by homeless writers, for which we expected the public to pay $25, was a strange and silly idea in many ways. The possibilities for failure were many. The group had never attempted a project for which specific writers *had* to be present. At our public readings, interested writers just turned up, and we always had sufficient numbers. In this tour, we would have a specific cast with ongoing performance demands. No one was sure if we could—or would want to—accomplish them. Despite the risks, this seemed like an important public project for several reasons: (1) It was a concrete way to link the writers' stories with Chicago's city space in a format that would allow a powerful face-to-face interaction with a live audience. Unlike writing an article for a newspaper that people might or might not read, imagining an audience for the play was clearer for writers, because this audience would be physically present. (2) The bus tour could provide the writers with a public platform for raising political and social issues that affected their lives yet were beyond their individual control. Around that time, the group was especially concerned about citywide gentrification and Chicago's push toward a tourist economy, and how these priorities led to service cuts and decreased housing availability for low-income areas of the city. The bus tour was designed to co-opt (and parody) the city's tourist aims and provide a serious, yet humorous, counter-discourse to it. (3) Since we imagined a paying public for the tour, we planned to pay the writers/actors for their rehearsal and performance time. In this way, the writers would not have as many material constraints when choosing to work on this project. (4) This project would require the writers to hone a wide range of skills—writing for a public audience, proficiency with computers (to write and edit scripts), the ability to commit to a project and arrive on time, public speaking and performance skills, and the ability to collaborate on an ambitious project.

The tour came together quickly. With the help of a Dutch theater director and Chicago's Neighborhood Writing Alliance, our group planned to put a storytelling bus on the road within six weeks, to prove to ourselves that we could do it and to see if the public liked the idea. During the first three weeks, the writers scripted possible scenes, working from prompts I prepared. In the next three weeks we worked with a giant map of the city to determine which scenes were artistically and geographically possible, mapped a course, rehearsed scenes, raised money, found a bus, publicized the project, talked with reporters, and sold tickets. Our cast of a dozen homeless or formerly homeless writers-turned-actors kept to a rigorous rehearsal schedule. The writers negotiated a group agreement with the organization for payment for their writing and rehearsal and performance time.

The process was hectic and energizing. None of us was really sure that we could actually pull the project together. There were so many potentially crippling problems—actors not showing up, poor weather, lack of public performance permits, not to mention the possibility that the public would not respond well, or at all, to the event. We jokingly posted on the wall our ten biggest fears, naming and laughing at them as a way to take away their power. Days were spent editing and rehearsing scenes, while nights were spent driving through the city, planning the route, and timing distances from place to place.

On a warm and clear night in August 2000, a yellow school bus filled with press, friends, and supporters paused momentarily before driving northbound on Michigan Avenue toward Grant Park, the scene of the 1968 Democratic Convention riots, and the location of the first scene of Not Your Mama's Bus Tour. Curly, one of the two tour guides, announced the following to the 44 passengers on the bus:

> Ladies and gentleman, I'd like to welcome you aboard tonight and go over a few rules. According to the National Transportation Safety Board, we are required to tell you that:
>
> This is not a Gray Line, Blue Line, or Happy Face Tour.
>
> At 7:07 we will not strain our necks at Navy Pier to look at some McFerris Wheel and pay $14.95 for a sandwich named after a city 767 miles away.
>
> At 7:18 we will not entomb ourselves in a stomach-turning elevator climbing to the 104th floor of the Sears Catalogue.
>
> At 7:29, we will not pass Go or City Hall, where Richard sits only because his father sat all over this city.
>
> At 7:38 we will not even discuss corporatized cows or public ping-pong.
>
> At 7:57, we will not contemplate John Hancock in any form. The name alone indicates just how obscene it is.
>
> And finally at no time during this tour will we stop at any McDonalds, let alone some Rock 'n Roll McDonalds, for a way-too-boring double-cheeseburger combo super-sized, as if there isn't already enough wiener envy in this city.
>
> This is Not Your Mama's Bus Tour, but depending on your mama, this may be her kind of ride. Welcome aboard.

This introduction set the tone of the performance as both play and critique. Through humor and word play, Curly's introduction made it clear that this tour would show a different kind of Chicago to audience members, yet it would not be one lacking humor or pleasure.

Over the next two hours, the bus made six stops around Chicago: Grant Park, scene of the 1968 Democratic Convention riots; Maxwell Street, the birthplace of Chicago blues and a historic immigrant gateway and marketplace, now all but demolished due to the expansion of the University of Illinois at Chicago; a Gold Coast apartment building, where one writer had once been taken in by friends; the street corner where Gregory Becker shot Joseph Gould; Orchestra Hall, where one of the writers had performed at age 17 in an Irish dance troupe; and Malcolm X College. While the bus drove from place to place, the passengers heard stories told by two tour guides, as well as poetry, songs, and music. At each location, the passengers got off the bus and watched a scene based on a story from a writer's life.

Anaya, who was struggling with student-loan debt, performed her scene in front of Malcolm X College, one of several Chicago city colleges. Because she was nervous about the public exposure this event might bring, she was reluctant to disclose too much information about herself. We worked together to create a scene in which she could share certain information with the audience without feeling too exposed. We struck upon the form of a game, creating cards listing several topics about her life—some were areas she was willing to discuss and others were not. As the crowd exited the bus just at sunset, Anaya stood in a paved open courtyard, as a huge sign reading "Malcolm X College" was lit high above her head in the background. She smiled a radiant smile, sporting long braids and a bright purple jacket. Once everyone was gathered closely around her, she spoke:

> Hello everyone and welcome. You can call me Anaya. Anaya only. I am homeless. There are many stories I could tell you about my life and some things I don't want to talk about. So let's play a little game. To do so, I need two assistants. (She then chose two audience members.) On these cards are subjects related to my life—Family, God, Age, Childhood, Malcolm X College, Sex, Exercise, Drugs, Relationships, Recovery House, and Mental Health. If you choose a topic I am willing to talk about, this is the sound you'll hear. (To the first volunteer, she says) Please give us a sound! (Person makes a sound.) Thank you, let's give her a big hand. And if you've chosen a topic I am NOT willing to talk about, this is the sound you'll hear. (To the second volunteer she says) Please give us a different sound. (Other person makes a sound.) And two more rules: no pictures and no questions. Let's play.

15

When someone selected the card "Malcolm X College," the audience heard the following:

> I am standing just twenty steps from the door of Malcolm X College. But it might as well be 20 miles. Six thousand dollars in student-loan debt separates me from Malcolm X or any other college. How long would it take you to pay off this debt? For some people it might be two years, a year, two months, two weeks, or even one day. For me, it's been five years, and I still haven't made a dent. I have worked homeless and gone to school homeless. How can a girl who loves education and longs to go to college make her way when the earth trembles and the ground beneath her begins to shake?

Anaya's scene was interspersed with both polemical and utopian fragments, including singing, poetry, and monologue sharing personal information like the fact that she had never used drugs, was mentally healthy, wanted to wait until marriage for sex, and was a devout Christian.

At the end of the scene, she explained the game to the audience by saying, "I used to say yes to any request, providing any information, regardless of whether I wanted to or not. But now, I can say no. I am not my experiences, I am not my debt, and I am not my past. You can call me Anaya."

In this scene, Anaya was able to speak about the role debt was playing in her life, to educate the audience, without feeling a sense of shame or apologizing. For those few minutes, she literally controlled the game, and she reveled in the moments when audience members chose cards, such as "Age" or "Family," and she held up her laminated sign, "I don't want to talk about it." And in the moments she did share, she gained a sense of confidence that evolved over the length of the performances. Her previous reluctance to speak gave way to memorable performances, where she played with the audience while allowing them to assemble a partial tapestry of her life. Her game subtly played with the public's voyeuristic interest in the poor. The audience *had* to ask questions, and Anaya was in the role of saying yes or no, controlling the audience's desire for information.

This was just one example of the element of parody in the performance. The writers and I had agreed that the audience should not find the tour lacking in humor or artistic pleasure. Many scenes had nothing to do with homelessness at all, because the writers wanted the audience to see that being homeless was just one aspect of their lives; it didn't explain who they were or encompass their identities. Thus music, both recorded and live, dancing, poetry, and humor were all elements of the tour.

20   Later in the tour, the bus wound its way through Chicago's medical district, described by Curly as "the largest concentration of hospitals in the city, which

ironically sits just east of the neighborhood in the city where the fewest residents have health insurance." He dryly added, "Well, at least they have a nice view of the hospitals." He went on to describe the procedure for seeing a dentist at the county hospital (for those lacking health insurance), which he described as "the only place in the world where people run to, and not away from, the dentist." The "Toothless Olympics," as Curly called it, was a process that begins with a qualifying phone call at 7 A.M. one day. The next day everyone lucky enough to get through on the phone waits outside a locked door, and when it opens they race down a series of hospital hallways to try to beat out the "69 other tooth-achin' qualifiers" to arrive at a desk, get a number, and wait several hours on "a hard-ass bench" to see a dentist—to have the tooth pulled. "That's right," the guide told the audience in an authoritative and reassuring tone. "The only dental care available at County is getting a bad tooth pulled. No fixings, no fillings, just pulled. So, remember everyone, don't forget to brush!" At that point, the maso-chistic song "Dentist" from *Little Shop of Horrors* boomed through the bus, while a cast member cheerfully passed out toothbrushes to passengers.

Through moments like these, the writers shared a view of the city and its bureaucratic procedures for dealing with poor people that most audience mem-bers had never seen, yet did so in a playful rather than heavy-handed way. And since the audience and actors were physically present together—in an un-air-conditioned school bus in August—this allowed for dialogue between writers and audience. One of the tour guides, for example, always asked whether any-one in the audience had ever been inside Cook County Hospital. During the dress rehearsal, when the casts' family and friends were aboard, many affirmative hands went in the air. Once the paid performances began, no hand ever went up. The tour gave audience members a glimpse into life at the county hospital. And by handing everyone a toothbrush, the guide suggested that they too might find themselves on a "hard-ass bench" someday, waiting for a free tooth pulling.

For its final scene, the bus stopped in front of Chicago's Orchestra Hall, where Maggie would be selling newspapers, awaiting our arrival. She refused to ride with the other actors in a car just in front of the bus, assuring us that she would be waiting at the scene when we arrived. Every night the tour guides and I would sweat out the moments before the bus pulled up to the spot, fearing she might not be there. Gee, Curly's co-guide, would even tell audiences, "Maybe we'll see Maggie; sometimes she's out here selling newspapers," just in case she wasn't there. Then there would be a pause as Gee looked for her, a pause that seemed to me to last forever, though in reality it was never more than a moment or two. "There she is," he ended up saying every night. The audience filed out and gath-ered around Maggie, as she stood on a busy sidewalk downtown on Michigan Avenue. My laptop and portable speakers were quickly rushed out to provide musical accompaniment. Radiant at sixty, with colorful headscarves and several shirts and skirts, Maggie commanded attention. With a portable microphone, the guide introduced her and asked her why this location was special. Every night

her explanation differed somewhat, but it always included her memory of dancing onstage at Orchestra Hall as part of an Irish Dance troupe when she was 17.
She usually said, "We did a four-handed reel that night, but since I am alone
here tonight, I'll dance a jig for you all." At that, my computer started an mp3
file of "Irish Washer Woman," and Maggie danced a jig with the lightness and
brio of a teenager. Through her words and dance, Maggie transformed from a
self-described "bag lady" to a joyful presence that captivated the crowd each
night. People far beyond our paying audience stood around to watch and listen,
so she regularly danced for hundreds. My hope was that her performance — as
well as the rest of the tour — communicated to the audience that much history,
talent, and beauty reside in the people that one might see homeless on the
streets.

Our group staged six two-hour tours over the course of three weeks. Local
media covered the event, including local TV news coverage, print stories in seven
newspapers including the *Chicago Tribune* (Chicago's largest daily paper), top
coverage on a local theater website, performances recorded by two documentary
filmmakers, and reports by two radio stations, including a 20-minute interview
and news piece on the local NPR affiliate. The reviews were all positive. One
reporter called the project a mixture of "Chicago history, street theater and can-
dor."[15] Another described it as bringing "an unconventional history lesson to
life through street theater. At times, it is also a poetry slam, a jam session, and
a sing along."[16] The headline from the theater website said, "This bus'll school
ya . . . ."[17] All the shows sold out, and the public responded warmly to the tour
and to the actors. Audiences lingered after the performances, asking questions of
the cast, and getting autographs. People called and emailed words of gratitude
and praise. Of the twelve cast members, none missed a performance and almost
no one missed a rehearsal, an unprecedented reality in the two-and-a-half-year
history of our group.

Tactical discourse was the realm of the StreetWise Writers Group. Unable to
equal or overturn the powerful strategic systems scripting their lives, the group
created projects in various polemic and utopian forms — calculated pot shots,
poetry, humor, critique and parody — as tactical responses to the systems framing their lives. Not Your Mama's Bus Tour parodied the present strategic power
of the city and offered glimpses of possible other realities. During the weeks of
rehearsals and performances, all the group members were committed to — and
pushed each other toward — the impossibly funny and strange idea of a traveling
theatrical bus tour narrated by singing, dancing, and speaking homeless people.
The project temporarily rewrote the strategic mandates affecting the writers' lives.
Twenty people of different ages, races, and economic groups worked together
toward one vision of a yellow school bus. The writers negotiated their own work
conditions. They were paid a living wage to share their wisdom and perform life
stories, taking people to the actual city spaces where they occurred. More than

150 members of the paying public heard stories about living with debt, police brutality, discovering sexuality, and finding hope. Twelve homeless writers/actors received pleasure, good experiences, and a job for six weeks. They honed their writing skills in creative and engaging ways to directly and immediately address a public audience. And indirectly, the writers responded to the powerful records and institutions framing their lives. At its best, perhaps this fleeting experience allowed the writers and producers a glimpse of a different life, where work is a meaningful act of creation. Perhaps it gave everyone involved a bit of hope, to keep struggling and keep risking.

The tour attempted to upset conventional expectations about Chicago, bus tours, and homeless people. Unable to directly change the city spaces denied to the poor, the cast literally co-opted the city for two hours a night and turned it into an impromptu performance space.

Lacking the stable nexus from which to continue the bus tour in the long term, the project's power was tactical—short-term, with a beginning and ending point. There was friction within the nonprofit about how quickly the project came together and the writers' right to negotiate their own work terms. The organization's director threatened repeatedly to cancel the show and, in the end, only reluctantly let it go forward. During the first scene of our last performance, police arrived and threatened to tow the bus away for not having secured permits to allow people to gather. An attorney advised us that if the tour were to continue, we could be sued for playing music without paying royalty fees. The tactical possibilities of this wonderful project eventually began giving way to the strategic realities of laws, permits, and organizational dissent.

The end of this project also marked the end of my three-plus years at that organization. Our writing group continued in a similar form after I left, and a revised version of the tour has continued for several summers. After the performances, however, even the most well-intentioned audience members returned to their comfortable homes, while Anaya still faced her debts; a tooth that could be filled today is still pulled at Cook County Hospital. As a tactical project, this tour created flurries of press and moments of energy. But as de Certeau suggests, the effects of tactics are not clear or permanent. They must operate within temporal restrictions. Structural realities do not readily disappear.

Yet, despite the fact that this project did not have a clear outcome, it was still a meaningful act of creation. One performer described the time of the play as one of the happiest moments of her life. Another said, "This is real. In a world that is increasingly unreal or virtual, that's important." Another said, "It's art, and that's why it's important." After nearly three years working with the StreetWise Writers Group, I began to understand the hopeful aspect inherent in tactical writing. The writing of the group, especially in this project, was never a means for something else—a better job, a grade, a more just world. While many of the writers wanted to change their lives, get a better job, or change the

25

world, all were aware of the slim likelihood that our articles or projects could accomplish that. Certainly, the writing always had an eye on someplace else: on a better future. Underneath it all was hope, a hope that maybe enough writing, publishing, and bus tours might change the world. Hope stirred the projects and prompted discussions and writing, but the work was an end in itself. In this group, public writing was a meaningful act of community. Writing was never a transactional means to something else. The pleasures of the collaborations, shared meals, discussions, and quiet moments of writing were enough, for that week. But how the group's writing changed any readers or the writers is unknown and even unknowable. . . .

Classroom Public Writing as Tactics of Hope

The writing projects described in this chapter represent just a handful of experiences of a few activists and financially marginalized people; the purposes, audiences, and means of circulation of these writers would likely differ from that of writers working in large nonprofit institutions or with greater access to economic and social power. Their tactical writing serves specific rhetorical aims in specific times and places. Based on these examples, I would like to explore, in the remainder of this chapter, possibilities for classroom public writing as tactical acts of hope.

The Outcomes of Public Writing Are Mysterious and Unknowable

30   Viewing public writing by those without claims to mainstream power as tactical acknowledges writing as powerful in mysterious, uncontrollable, and playful ways. Rather than understanding writing as a clear transacting process, a tactical view marvels in the potentiality of writing while acknowledging the limits of its power. To view public writing otherwise asks students either to practice simulated documents that never enter the public realm at all (such as a letter to the editor that isn't sent), or to send out writing into the world without much rhetorical calculation about where or how it might make a splash. Without an appreciation of the unpredictable nature of public writing, dutiful students might be disappointed by their forays into the public sphere. A tactical view of public writing incorporates the unpredictability of the outcome as part of the process.

To incorporate an understanding of the tactical nature of public writing into a class, one could take time to introduce students to an understanding of how social change occurs and the role writing plays in that process. Paul Loeb's *Soul of a Citizen* is an excellent source to use with students to interrogate and understand processes of social change. Historical case studies can also be useful. For example, reading about the suffrage movement in the United States creates an awareness of the need for patience and persistence in assessing the transforming power of words and public appeals. Many of the landmark appeals for women's suffrage date back to the Seneca Falls Conference in 1848, yet the 19th Amendment, which granted women the right to vote, was not passed until 1920. Two now-canonized suffragists, Elizabeth Cady Stanton and Susan B. Anthony, died nearly two decades before American women earned the right to vote, but their speeches and written texts were key to that movement. This example, and countless others through history—including the anti-apartheid movement in South Africa, nuclear disarmament, and the anti-Vietnam War movement—show that the rhetorical power of words within a movement toward social change often requires a historical view to assess. As part of asking students to engage in public writing, it is useful to begin with a historical understanding of how public discourse has and continues to change the world.[18]

Tactical Writing Focuses on Projects, Not Problems

Tactical writing employs a project rather than a problem orientation. A problem orientation operates from a negative space, in that it seeks to solve a problem, ameliorate a deficit, or fix an injustice. There is a transactional quality to it—if the problem is not solved or the injustice ended, the work will be deemed unsuccessful. A problem orientation runs the risk of leaving participants overwhelmed, cynical, and feeling weak. A project orientation, however, privileges creation and design. Projects respond to problems but determine their own length, scope, and parameters, instead of being defined by external parameters. . . . The *StreetWise* writers didn't take on homelessness directly, but through projects like the bus tour indirectly made things happen that *might* change the reality and perceptions of homeless people in their city.

The writing class can be imagined as an ideal time and space for public-writing *projects,* as a creative space in which interesting projects happen during the course of the semester. Geoffrey Sirc, in *English Composition as a Happening,* critiques composition's epistemic turn for causing the field to lose sight of the avant-garde elements of composing, thereby losing a vision of the writing classroom that allows "the inhabitants a sense of the sublime, making it a space no one wants to leave, a *happening* space."[19] While Sirc might view my interest in public writing as far removed from the avant-garde compositions of artists like Marcel Duchamp and Jackson Pollock on which Sirc's work focuses, I believe we share a desire to create writing classes that become exciting pedagogical writing spaces in themselves, without needing to appeal to an extrinsic result, exchange, or skill.

What kind of tactical public-writing projects can work in the classroom? Any examples I offer will not be determinative, in that each local space, class, and teacher will need to discover what kinds of projects would be engaging or relevant. Much of the most exciting work in composition today, however, shares a desire to reframe the classroom as a writing-project space. Michael Blitz and C. Mark Hurlbert's *Letters for the Living,* for example, describes writing courses where students write books alone or in semester-long writing partnerships with students at another campus. Nancy Mack[20] asks her working-class writing students to create multigenre research projects detailing some aspect of their background or home community. Derek Owens in *Composition and Sustainability* works with his students to explore and document stories and histories about local places—hometowns, haunts, and hangouts—as a way to participate in a public discussion about the health and sustainability of places. What these projects share is a focus on creating meaningful and innovative texts that work beyond themselves within the communities of the classroom and within the families and neighbors of the writers as well. Other writing projects that come to mind include oral history projects,"[21] public or campus events, or campaigns. Projects can also evolve through collaboration with activist groups, community organizations, or local nonprofits. . . .[22]

Tactical Writing Invites Collaboration and a Long Vision

35   Semesters are short, but the lives of public campaigns are long. How can the two work together? A tactical view of writing makes collaboration, both in the classroom and with local groups, an important way to turn writing classrooms into project spaces that can tap into larger movements. As any public writer or activist knows, any event, rally performance, public debate, or newspaper issue comes about through the cooperation of many people and an ongoing agenda. And through those moments of cooperating on a project larger than oneself, one can find a great deal of pleasure and meaningful exchange. By cocreating with other people, one can find, in Loeb's words, "a sense of connection and purpose nearly impossible to find in purely private life."[23]

Students themselves are often great sources of information about key local and national issues. Student groups have recently been at the forefront of anti-sweatshop movements and other projects for global justice. In a writing course, if you choose an issue-related project in which all will have to participate, you run the risk of turning off students who either don't agree with or are not interested in the issue. If, however, you simply ask individual students to "go out" and "find a public issue" that they "care about," the risk is that they will never participate in either the pleasures or frustrating mystery of public writing in any communal or collaborative way. What I try to do in my classes is to create one or two projects that relate to ongoing issues familiar to me, and to allow students to participate in those or to choose something of their creation. I don't think any one approach is best; rather, it's important to know the pitfalls of any collaboration and make an informed decision accordingly. For students anxious to see the effect of their public writing, the requisite long vision for tactical projects might prove disappointing. If the collaboration reaches beyond the bounds of a classroom, one needs to assess realistically what kind of support or help a semester's worth of college students can provide to your campus or to a local community group. In this aspect, general guidelines are not useful, since the local needs and demands are key.

Writing instructors can play a key role in helping semester-long projects tap into ongoing campaigns. New class projects can extend or build on projects from past semesters. If an instructor has ongoing relationships with local writers or activist groups, new projects can develop as needs change. I say more about the role of the teacher/writer/scholar in the streets in the concluding chapter.

Tactical Writing Embraces the Imaginative to the Mundane to the Silly

I have learned . . . that engaging in public work means doing many things at once—one day writing ritualized appeals for funding to state institutions or foundations and the next writing an article, poem, or press release. Forms vary widely, as do the rhetorical needs of the writing tasks. When asking students to write publicly in a classroom, we can draw on a wide range of rhetorical forms, from the imaginative to the ritualized. Writing a press release, an appeal to a judge, a grant proposal, a recommendation letter, a poem to be read at a public picnic, a newspaper article, an editorial—each of those acts of public creation places different rhetorical demands on a writer and creates different effects in the world. A tactical approach to public writing allows the rhetorical demands to dictate form, formality, and content. For example, in a research writing course I once taught on the topic of globalization, students first wrote academic research papers and then collaborated to revise their individual work into a class website about their concerns for the future. Each writer had to decide, in consultation with his or her peers, how to revise individual research into forms that would make sense and connect with an unknown audience on the Web. One writer, for example, transformed her research on the environmental impact of computer manufacturing into a quiz for visitors to the site. Another student turned his exploration into the effects of NAFTA on unionized workers like himself into a funny poem entitled "Afta NAFTA, what's next?" (In these and other tactical writing projects, questions of form also include visual design, especially if websites, books, fliers, or other public documents are created.)

As forms range, so does the level of seriousness and play. At times, as the *Real Change News* example shows, dedication, research, and journalistic balance can win the day. In tactical writing, however, humor often prevails by having a "subversive effect on the dominant structure of ideas."[24] Even *Real Change* works to use games and humor in certain key ways to get their messages across. Their website (http://www.realchangenews.org) includes an interactive game, entitled "Hobson's Choice: The Game You Just Can't Win." Players enter a simulated world of homelessness and are faced with a fixed number of choices at each turn, and each decision leads to consequences that can improve or worsen the player's plight. For example, when faced with having no place to stay, a player might select "Sleep in your car" as an option, which leads to the following consequence: "Too bad, you're in Oregon where it's illegal to sleep in your car. Now you're in jail." If the player selects the choice "Call your lawyer," the response might be, "Too bad, poor people can't afford lawyers. You're still in jail."

40   The less reliable access writers have to institutional power, the more likely their exercises of tactical power will employ jokes and humor as "attacks on social control."[25] In a classroom, teachers, students, and situations will dictate if and in what ways humor, games, or play are relevant, but tactical writing projects should be open to such possibilities.

Tactical Writing Has Clear Exigency, if Not Always a Clear Goal

As a project orientation suggests, writing projects succeed if they manage to create something that has energy. Tactical writing rarely transacts or accomplishes anything concretely.[26] The class, the project, the thing itself, should always have clear hopes and purposes while letting go of specific goals.

. . . The various projects of the *StreetWise* writing group, and the past ten years of *Real Change News* are just [two] examples of the many ongoing public writing projects operating in the streets of our cities and towns. These writers draw from a range of rhetorical stances and appeals—anger to parody to balanced journalism—in order to use writing to intervene in public ways. They organize their work around various projects: a rally, the week's issue of the paper, a public reading, an open house, a public discussion of an issue, a trial, a bus tour. Each individual writing project is temporary but not isolated, in that it is a part of a movement or a campaign larger than itself. Each project garners energy and then ends, but during the process it is alive and engaged with the world. These public writing projects are tactical, and rely on hope and goodwill to go forward. They don't claim systemic change in and of themselves.

Seeing writing as a transacting tool (to credentialize or influence) frames writers as subjects who need to gain power in order [to] achieve something else. Seeing writing as a tactical act of hope acknowledges that power is something that all people, even the socially marginalized, already have. Tactical power is real, but it is unreliable, constrained, and its effects are often unclear. Claiming that power through acts of public writing is insufficient. It is an act of hope.

Reading

1. How does Mathieu define the difference between strategic and tactical ways of acting?

2. How does she define the purpose of Not Your Mama's Bus Tour? Is it strategic or tactical?

3. How does she understand the goals of community-based writing projects? Are they strategic or tactical?

4. How does she understand the value of such community-based work for students?

Inquiring

1. Mathieu argues for the value of tactical projects. She claims that this type of strategy is best suited to those who do not have the resources to create a broad-based protest movement for their particular issue. In some ways, tactical is the precursor, the original moment, from which larger struggles are to be based. To make her point, Mathieu discusses the political power of homeless individuals to redefine the "streets" and "landmarks" that make up the geography of the city. Discuss the examples she provides of their writing and activism. Based on your discussion, what does she mean by *tactical*? How do writing and publishing support such tactical work? How do you understand the value of such work for dispossessed groups to gain recognition for their causes?

2. For Mathieu, community writing and publishing play important roles in altering public opinion. She argues that certain publications, when connected to organized struggles, can interrupt our popular understanding of marginalized individuals in our local communities. Rather than being defined negatively by those in power, these individuals become part of the city's cultural and political geography on their own terms, with their own agenda. As an example of such work, Mathieu points to a homeless writers' group that publishes in *Streetwise*, a newspaper that focuses on homelessness. In her full book, she provides the following example of this writing:

"A Day of Selling Streetwise"
Robert Dillard

Sunday: I was out selling papers on Diversity and Clark. The time was about 5:00 when this gentleman walked up to me and asked, "What are you selling?" I said, "Streetwise." Then he said, "I can't stand that paper, or you. Why don't you go somewhere else? The world would be better if people like you weren't out here everyday."

He was a white guy, about as tall as me (about six feet), wearing a T-shirt, gym shoes (it was kinda cold but he had on a T-shirt). Talked like he had a real nice education—he wasn't no bum.

I didn't respond. I kept saying to myself, I'm not going to let this guy make me mad. I just let him keep doing his thing. Then he said, "It's a stupid paper, it takes a stupid person to stand out in any kind of weather trying to sell a stupid paper like this. Don't you have anything better to do?"

I responded, "Yes, instead of me standing out here selling my paper, I could be at home writing my book. And by the way, if you don't mind, sir, I'd like to put you in my book. The name of my book is *The World as I See It.* May I have your name please."

He said, "No way."

I said, "I'll just call you Mr. John Doe. But I will put you in the book, because of the way you talk to me. And you kind of opened my eyes about what I want to say about the world as I see it."

He said he didn't care and he walked off. I told him, "Have a good day and God go with you." (Mathieu, *Tactics of Hope: The Public Turn in English Composition*, 2000, p. 36)

How does the selected piece attempt to intervene in popular understandings of homelessness? Why might the publishers of *Streetwise* consider such essays to be effective? What might they believe is the potential power of community writing to alter public opinion?

3. Although Mathieu talks about the tactical power of community writing, she also provides an example of community performance. In particular, by having homeless individuals narrate a different history of the community's streets and buildings, the bus tour was an attempt to alter the way in which local residents understood the meaning of their city. Here the tactic was to interrupt ways of speaking that masked the experiences of those who lacked the power to be heard and thus create a new cultural geography. In making her argument, Mathieu also argues that the project's participants gained increased power. As you think about tactical interventions in public narratives, do you believe such an effort would be effective? How would you describe the power provided to individual participants in this project? What do you see as the long-term effect of this individual's power? The long-term effect of this tour?

Composing

1. Mathieu argues that there is a disconnect between the public understanding of homelessness and the actual individuals described by that category. Much of her work is dedicated to dismantling such misunderstandings to represent a deeper complexity on this issue. In this way, Mathieu is attempting to create an understanding—a new cultural geography to guide individual responses to, and collective planning about, homelessness. Such work involved both tactical actions and institutional partnerships. Use Mathieu's framework to write an

essay in which you discuss how to alter the public perception of this issue in your local neighborhood or campus. (This exercise will probably require some research on how your local environment is already responding to this issue.) In your essay, also discuss how Mathieu's framework informed your proposed plans. How might the specific needs of your particular project inform or revise her general framework? Her sense of tactics?

2. In writing about the bus tour, Mathieu connects the activity of writing for a public audience to an increased power by the community member, citing how invoking community insights allows the writer to gain some control over the public representation of his or her life. Mathieu even implies that the individuals found a collective power in working with one another. Write an essay in which you describe the meaning and importance of this community-informed individual and collective power. Why does Mathieu find this work to be so important for community writers? Now consider the power typically gained by students in a writing classroom. Is there a role for their community knowledge in the classroom? How would you describe the typical relationship between a student's individual power and collective power in the classroom? What do you understand as the goals of Mathieu's vision of a community writing classroom in reframing how and why students learn to write?

3. Throughout her article, Mathieu invokes the importance of tactical thinking when undertaking community-based projects. Each of the tactical projects, however, occurs within a network of larger organizations that are equally committed to changing the cultural geography of the issue at hand, homelessness. Write an essay in which you discuss the relationship between these two types of effort, tactical and institutional. What are the strengths and weaknesses of each? Using this framework, how would you describe the ideal relationship between a university, a community, and a community writing class? How would you describe the different roles of these partners in remapping popular opinion on an issue?

Connecting

Mathieu's book is called *Tactics of Hope*. By using this title, she links the specific practices of individuals to aspirations for a better life, individually and collectively. Jesús Villicaña López's journey across the border (p. 286) might be seen as one such tactic of hope. Write an essay in which you discuss whether the language of tactics and strategies provides an effective tool for analyzing López's experience. Does such language fully capture the hopes that led López to cross the border? Does it provide a road map for the hopes of others who follow?

JESÚS VILLICAÑA LÓPEZ

I Left Moroleón at Daybreak, with Great Sadness

Photo by © Mark Lyons

Espejos y Ventanas/Mirrors and Windows: Oral Histories of Mexican Farmworkers and Their Families, the book from which this essay is taken, is the result of a five-year effort to represent the Mexican mushroom-picking community in Kennett Square, Pennsylvania. In particular, the goal of the project was to provide a public vehicle for the community to redefine its public image in the midst of public debates over immigration. To that end, *Espejos y Ventanas* represents the lives of recent and long-term Mexican residents, farmworkers and their children, both school-age and college students. What emerges is a history of a community struggling to keep its heritage while integrating in U.S. culture. It is a community laboring under trying conditions but attempting to build an economic future.

In the following essay, Jesús Villicaña López discusses crossing the U.S. border as a teenager, beginning to work in the mushroom industry, and his advice to those also considering crossing the border. Like all the stories in *Espejos y Ventanas*, López's story was originally printed in both English and Spanish; the English version is reproduced here.

■ ■ ■

My decision to come here caught me by surprise. The truth is that I hadn't really thought about coming here. But as I grew up I looked around and the idea came to me that I had to find a way to better myself so that someday I could start my family. And then an uncle of mine and a cousin helped me decide if I wanted to come here, no? They were already here in the United States.

My mom was against my coming because I was still very young. I came here against her will, so to speak, because she didn't like the idea that I would be so far away from them. She told me to think very carefully about things: if I felt able to move away from them and come here to confront new challenges, new things in life, then I would be living a life I wouldn't even be able to imagine. I would be far from my family, from my home, from my country, without knowing anybody or knowing where I would end up or who would come to visit me. In the end, I made the decision on my own because I wanted to find a new way of life or a future for myself. I wanted to be self-reliant and also to help my family—my mom and my siblings. I have four siblings, all younger than I: my sister is 8 years old and I have one brother who is 14 and another who is 12. Because I am the oldest, I have a great responsibility to be with them, to protect them and my mom. It's my duty to give them the best, to create opportunities for them so that they can get ahead. I am responsible for showing them how to live life.

Unfortunately, my father is sick. He lost his memory—he doesn't remember anything. He's like, traumatized, or something. He's around 40 and is gradually losing his intellect. His illness is sapping his abilities little by little—his mind and his body. Even though my father has no memory, I think that he knows that I am here. I don't know if I can express it very well, but I think he must have some strong feelings for me. In other words, it's like I can feel what he feels, but I don't know how to describe it.

My mother works in the city of Moroleón in a tortilla shop—she makes sandwiches and cooks. She is paid 100 pesos a day, about $10. Almost all of what my mom made went toward buying things for us and she also paid for our studies. If she made around 500 pesos [$50] a week, about 200 of that she gave to us to spend outside of school or to go out to a party or something like that, right? I admire my mother very much because in spite of being a woman, she held the family together without depending on anyone, with nothing more than her own strength, her will, and her work. Because we are very poor there in Mexico.

In Mexico, we lived in a stone house patched with clay that had a dirt floor—it was tiny, with only one room for the entire family. We made our living growing corn and beans to eat—this is a staple food of the region. Most of the time my grandparents grew the food since my mother insisted that I go to school. She wanted me and my brothers to improve our lives and she believed very strongly that school was the best route to do that. But I helped my grandparents when I wasn't in school and on the weekends. I tried very hard to do my best, to put a lot of passion into my work. I know that school is very useful, but I didn't have the resources to continue my studies and neither did my mom or my grandparents. So I decided to leave school and come up here. I believe that by doing this work here in the US, I can help my brothers and sister get ahead in life and provide them with a better education, a career, so that they won't have to make the same sacrifice that I made when I came here for them. I send my family four or five times as much as they used to earn each month. Every three or four weeks I send around $1000 to Mexico.

My trip North was very—how can I explain it?—it wasn't a very happy trip, but it was something I had to endure in order to go on. I had to face dangerous situations, like crossing the border, sleeping under the moon at night, and then in darkness in the forest. I was afraid that if I were to go out, some strange animal might come to kill us. There were all sorts of dangerous animals in the forest—snakes, bears, things like that.

I left Moroleón for the North at daybreak, with great sadness. I was with a group—my uncle and some friends of his, all older. I was the only young person in the group. The night before I left I tried and tried to get to sleep so that I could leave easily in the morning, but I couldn't sleep the whole night. I stayed up all night with my mom and then it was time for me to prepare to leave. My uncle came to the house and said that they had come for us. I left with my suitcase and then, with the blessing of my mother, I climbed into the car and we left. Crying, with great sadness, we left our families and the village where we lived behind.

We left focused on our future, with the intention of finding a new way of life and confronting new problems. But, then, at the same time, it was a risky and very dangerous adventure. Friends had preceded me to the North and they told me that I was going to experience the adventure of a lifetime. They talked about what was in store for me—crossing rivers, escaping from different animals, climbing mountains, and making my way through the cacti. They said that in the desert there would be times when we wouldn't have enough food or water for maybe six, seven or eight days. In fact, the main thing we carried with us was water because it is true what they say—that water is life.

We crossed the border with a *coyote* that my uncle had found. This *coyote* wasn't bad—in fact, he was kind. He helped us and went through everything with us, until we reached the border. My trip cost 1,500 Mexican pesos—$150—and later, when I had already arrived here at the border, I asked my relatives here in the United States for another $1,500 to come from the border up here to Pennsylvania. Yes, it's a lot of money, but as I told you, I have friends here—uncles, aunts, cousins. In five months I finished paying back the money that was raised for me.

10   I left my town on August 6th and I arrived here on North American soil on August 13th. There were around 17 of us; about six were from my group, from La Ordeña. When we arrived at the border we came through a wooded mountain range in Arizona. It was cool, with many tall trees that blocked the sun. I entered the forest and started to walk for a long time. We walked all afternoon and all night and suddenly it started to rain and we continued walking in the rain. At night we rested and slept for maybe three hours—say, from midnight to 3:00 A.M. We walked the whole day and we rested for a short while to eat. We also slept sometimes during the day. Then I arrived at a town called Phoenix. Some of the others got separated from us—we went through the mountains and they went

through the desert—but we all arrived at a designated time at the same hotel in Phoenix. When I got to the hotel, I found all the different groups gathered together in small rooms. And they had locked us in and we didn't sleep. Finally, at daybreak they fed us.

It's true that I was hungry during the trip; we had some food, but it wasn't enough. We survived, thank God. The main thing was that we carried water—it was more important than food. We were lucky to go through the mountains because there were fresh-water streams where we could fill our gallon jugs.

When I was in the forest, I happened to see two bears—they were small, but I was scared that the mother was around. I saw a snake—it crossed my path and I got scared and ran away. Also, there were caves in the middle of the forest. The government had put up boards, like wooden signs with a skull and crossbones, that prohibited entrance to the caves because there might be toxic materials inside. We continued on and we didn't even look at the caves.

When we were crossing the border, I saw the border patrol, but they didn't see us. I could see them at night from far away on the highway. When we crossed the highway, they were passing by, but they didn't see us. I didn't see them face to face. It wasn't my turn for them to catch me.

I didn't have too many problems during the crossing because I was accustomed to walking and running—I played sports. Some of the others had a hard time—they were tired and exhausted. Some weren't able to walk or climb the mountains, but I kept moving forward. I tried to help my uncle at times: I carried some of his gear because he wasn't accustomed to walking so much. He even told me that it seemed like I had come before because I didn't have any problems. I was advised before the trip that I would have to learn to separate the good from the bad and I was able to discern the difference for myself, so—thanks to that—I was overcoming difficulties and helping the rest of the people on the trip.

The whole trip took six days—three days walking in the mountains and three days there in Phoenix at the hotel waiting for my cousins to send me $1,500 so I could leave Phoenix and come here to Philadelphia. With this money the *coyote* got his pay for bringing us to the United States and he bought us a plane ticket to come from Phoenix to Baltimore. After arriving in Baltimore, we took a taxi to Kennett Square.

I am one of the younger people in the camp, but there are others younger than I—some are friends and one is my cousin, who is 14. When I first came here the truth is that I felt an enormous fear inside of me, since I didn't know where I was and I knew no one except my uncle, who came with me. At night I felt this profound loneliness because I was in such a big place without knowing anybody. At first my uncle lived with me in the same camp, but after a while he left and went to work in another place. In a few months, another uncle came and is here with me. He gives me advice about how to get along with the others here, so that everyone can be friendly. My uncle is my guiding light.

15

Actually, I was very surprised at the conditions here in the camp. When I left Mexico, I thought that I was coming to a place where we were going to be, well, free, with a big living space. But when I got here, I realized that it wasn't that way—it was a small place where many of us were cramped together. At times we really have to make an effort to get along, since there are so many of us—we are 16 now, and in the summer there will be 20. The camp is one long room, an open dormitory, without separate bedrooms. Each of us has our own space where we sleep, but there is no real private space. We make sure to respect each other's things, though. With so many people living together, there are bound to be conflicts sometimes, but we know that we have to try to avoid them. If someone tries to attack you, you just have to put up with it.

In the kitchen, there are two groups that cook—eight people in each group. When I first came, I didn't know how to cook, but as time passed I ventured into the kitchen, watching how they made the food, and I latched onto what they could teach me about cooking. Now I know how to cook. Most of the time we cook basic Mexican food, like beans, soup, and roasted or grilled meat. Each person from the group has to know how to cook and to wash his own clothes and keep his personal space clean. Even though the boss hires two people to clean the camp, the truth is that the conditions aren't very suitable—the place needs to be fixed up because it's pretty rundown. Awhile back, the State inspected the camp and they told our boss that he had to fix it up—like put a new roof on and paint it. They said if the repairs weren't done we would have to vacate.

I get up faithfully at daybreak, at 2:00 in the morning. Before I leave for work I eat a little. If I want to, I can rest one or two days a week, but since I'm not that tired, I figure I should put more energy into work. I work seven days a week, 12 or 13 hours a day. Some days, when there isn't much work, I might be done by 8:00 in the morning. Today, I worked until 4:00 in the afternoon—13 hours. The only thing that affects you is lack of sleep because you have to wake up so early. That's the one bad thing about harvesting mushrooms—you wake at dawn and are nearly always sleep deprived.

20   It's piecework—they pay me by the box—so if I want to make more money, I have to force myself to try to harvest more mushrooms. They ask you to pick an average of six boxes an hour—they pay $1.00 a box. Each box holds ten pounds of mushrooms. There are times when I fill eight or ten boxes an hour—so I pick 80 to 100 pounds of mushrooms each hour. There are weeks when there is a lot of work, which means you get a bigger check. And when there are very few mushrooms you leave early and don't earn much. When there's no work, you make $100 or $200 a week, but when there's work, most workers get $500. Me, I've gotten four-hundred-dollar checks. After working awhile, it's not that hard anymore—you get used to picking mushrooms.

When I first started to work in the mushroom plant, it was very difficult for me to learn to pick mushrooms. You have to harvest the mushroom by cutting it with a knife and it was hard for me to get a good grip on the knife, so I kept dropping the mushrooms after I cut them. Sometimes I cut myself and even now I still do, but not so often. When we cut ourselves, the wounds aren't so deep—they are only scratches and we keep on working. Now when I cut myself I don't worry, since my fingers are used to it.

The bosses don't pay much attention to the health of the workers. At the company, for example, we don't even have a medicine cabinet. If one of us had the misfortune to take a fall or cut ourselves, we would have to resort to driving ourselves to the hospital or demanding that the boss help us. At first when I was working on the upper mushroom bed I was afraid to walk because I was way up high. But I'm no longer afraid. Sometimes people do slip and fall, but usually they're OK. Once my cousin fell and ended up missing several weeks of work, but he had health insurance. I don't have insurance.

There are lots of chemicals that cause irritation or rashes, but the bosses say that there is no problem. I remember that when I first started working here, they had me sign a contract—they gave me a list of what I should do before coming to work and after leaving. Like, I should take a bath, or I should wash my hands before I eat.

In my free time, I go out with friends to the stores or something or I hang out with them in the house, chatting or watching TV. There are different cable channels. I like to watch sports—I often spend Saturday and Sunday watching the soccer teams with everyone. My favorite team is "America" from Mexico City. During the time that I have been here, I haven't gone out much—most of us are not accustomed to going out. We're somewhat isolated because we're not familiar with how to travel in this country, to go to the city or other places. . . .

The most difficult thing about living here is that you're not close to your family and loved ones. That's what you think about most—your family, your brothers and sisters, your relatives, the people you love the most. I miss my family in Mexico, but I've been here just a short time, so I don't feel that I'm very far away from them. Also, I talk to them every week on the telephone, which makes me feel close to them. And they write to me. In her letters, my mother tells me to take care of myself, to save my money, to put passion into my work and to avoid getting into scrapes. She reminds me of what she taught me well—to choose my friends wisely.

When I talk to my mother on the phone, she tells me to save my money so that I can get ahead and to think about making a house for myself someday. I want my house to be in the town where I grew up, in La Ordeña. My dream is to try to save a lot of money here and someday go back to Mexico and get a house. I'd like to get married, have children and live happily, to just live my life.

I would like to say something to all the people who might think that being here in the United States is easy. I want them to know it isn't that way because you don't necessarily know what you're up against. You think you will come here and find happiness, a new world full of marvels—but it isn't that way. You will face tremendous loneliness with a great many problems, large and small. And you have to be responsible for yourself instead of expecting to rely on others.

I would advise all who are thinking of coming here to think carefully about things. First, think about what you will do when you are here, who might accompany you on your trip, and if you are mentally and physically prepared, if you are strong enough to face your personal and social problems. Because if you are not prepared to face life, to face new challenges, it will weigh very heavily on you over time. Often it is misfortune that makes us unable to bear this burden and that gets us into trouble. And everything that you hoped for when you came here can turn out quite differently than you planned. You can succumb to temptation, like alcohol or drug addiction, and all the desires and dreams that you came here with can so quickly disappear into oblivion. If a person comes with desire, with interest, and if he knows why he's coming, what he's coming to and what he intends to accomplish here, then, yes—it's worth it.

[In the fall of 2003, Jesús' father died. Jesús was not able to return to Mexico for his burial. In the Spring of 2004 his mother, two brothers and sister moved into their new three-room house in La Ordeña—paid for with the $10,000 that Jesús had sent home.]

Reading

1. How does López define his reasons for coming to the United States?

2. How does he describe his living conditions once he arrived at the mushroom farm?

3. How does he describe his daily life at the mushroom farm?

4. How does he talk to those considering coming to the United States?

Inquiring

1. López tells the story of his border crossing from Mexico to the United States. Thinking about the totality of his experience, what does the border mean to him? To his family? To his community? How would you describe your own relationship to the Mexico-U.S. border? Thinking about the collective experience of you and your classmates as well as that of López, what conclusions can you draw about the meaning of *national borders*?

2. As López crosses the Mexico-U.S. border, he witnesses a series of workplaces and meets many types of workers. As a class, make a list of all the different types of workers mentioned in the story. How do these workers help explain the economic dynamic between the United States and Mexico? What do these occupations tell us about the significance of borders in the working lives of individuals?

3. One way to read López's story is that it has a happy ending. The editorial note at the end of his story implies that his family is better off for his labors in the United States. As a class, discuss whether you believe that to be the case. What evidence does the story provide to support such an argument? What elements of the story might complicate such a reading? In other words, how do you think López (as well as the editors of the collection) want you to understand his story?

Composing

1. Although López's journey might appear to be different from your own experience, in truth we have all had to cross borders throughout our lives. These borders might be geographic, personal, or economic. Each represented their own challenges; each required that we shift our relationship to our family, home community, and, possibly, nation. Write an essay in which you discuss an important moment when you crossed a border. Be sure to highlight how this crossing fundamentally altered your identity within a particular community. As you look back on this experience, to invoke López, would you tell the reader it was worth it? Would you have advice for others attempting to make such a border crossing?

2. Certainly one of the editors' goals in making *Espejos y Ventanas*, the book from which López's story is taken, was to intervene in public representation of Mexican farmworkers. As you read López's story, what would you describe as their strategies? Why would they choose, for instance, to feature his story? What are they trying to argue about Mexican farmworkers? Then consider recent coverage by one news outlet on immigration from Mexico. How do certain media outlets define the border and the farmworkers who cross it? How do the media characterize the farmworkers' presence in the United States? As you place this coverage next to that of *Espejos*, do you believe producing narratives by individuals such as López is important? If you do, how would you describe the effectiveness of such stories to inform public debate?

3. Numerous maps provide an image of the Mexico-U.S. border as well as the different states and cities within those countries. Such maps, however, rarely represent the journey of Mexican farmworkers from one country to another. Take an existing map of the Mexico-U.S. border (print or digital) and represent López's journey from his home to the city of Kennett Square, Pennsylvania. In charting his journey, you will need to consider what landmarks to represent, what images to provide, and what "map keys" are necessary for the reader to find the map useful in understanding his journey. In effect, you will have to decide what use you want the map to serve: a guide for future Mexican farmworkers, for border police, for immigrants' rights activists, or for opponents to

immigration legislation. Having done this work, write an essay in which you discuss whether creating a visual representation of López's journey allowed you to make a different type of argument. For instance, do arguments made through visual materials allow you to reach different audiences? Do they allow for a different type of emotional or intellectual appeal to the reader? What do you see as the benefits or drawbacks of this type of argument compared to López's written narrative?

Connecting

López provides a detailed discussion of what it meant to cross the border from Mexico to the United States. In doing so, he provides a geography for those who have not experienced the journey. Nedra Reynolds (p. 253) is also a geographer. It is not clear, however, what she might say about López's geographic description. Write an essay in which you discuss how Reynolds might analyze López's narrative. What might she notice? What might she revise? How do you respond to her analysis? Does it capture what is important to you about López's narrative?

Projects for Chapter 8

The following are group and class projects. You should talk to your instructor about which projects you will complete in your course.

PROJECT 13 Listening to the Voice of Experience

Reynolds's theory (p. 253) and López's narrative (p. 286) share a common belief in the power of local knowledge to inform our general understanding of an area. Indeed, for each author, local experience was used to highlight the absences or gaps in official documents or public debate. The authors' insights helped demonstrate how any geography, any mapping of a terrain, must be understood within residents' experiences. Such experiences are not often made public or placed in the public record, however.

For this assignment, you will, as a class, create an audio tour. Begin by researching a common tour offered on your campus or in your community. It could be anything from an admissions tour for interested students to a cultural tour of a particular neighborhood. If possible, get copies of the materials that participants are provided as part of the tour. As a class, discuss what it might mean to represent the everyday experience of individuals who live in (or pass through) this area not as tourists, but as residents. Choose six or seven locations. Split into teams and undertake one of the following strategies:

1. If there is a single community that is associated with that location, develop a series of short (45- to 90-second) audio clips that describe what that location means to those individuals (i.e., students if a campus tour; residents if a neighborhood tour), citing important moments that occurred there and highlighting what such moments mean to its history.

2. If there is an existing dynamic between students and residents at a certain location, be sure to interview both types of individuals. Ask them, what the location means to them and to each of their communities. Create a series of short (45- to 90-second) audio clips of these experiences that demonstrate how the different sets of individuals share or conflict on the meaning of that location.

When the audio clips are complete, as a class decide how to organize the tour (i.e., the order in which each place within that location will be visited) and then order the audio files accordingly. The class should choose a title for the project and write (and then record) an introduction to the audio files that details the tour's purpose. Finally, a musical theme should be chosen to play at the beginning, between audio clips, and at the conclusion of the audio tour. The entire class should then listen to the tour and offer revisions and suggestions.

Once the audio tour is completed, decide as a class how public you wish to make it. You might, for instance, simply seek a small set of volunteers to take the tour and give you their response. You might work with your university paper and ask a reporter to write a short story about the tour and link it to the paper's Web site. Through that site, you could track blog responses. You might also ask the local newspaper to do the same. As you track the responses—whatever strategy you've chosen—be prepared to discuss how this experience demonstrated the importance (or lack of importance) of local knowledge in understanding your college and community.

PROJECT 14 Becoming Visible

This chapter includes readings by authors who are concerned about the ability of "maps" to represent the power relationships within a community accurately. Reynolds (p. 253), for example, demonstrates how maps cannot capture the relationship between residents and students. Expanding on this idea, Mathieu (p. 268) writes about the experiences of the homeless that were not part of the "public geography." López (p. 286) demonstrates how even clear borders, such as a national border, can't represent the intricate relationships existing within that border's local communities.

Although each of these authors speaks about communities geographically distant from many of us, our own college or local communities are not immune to similar criticisms. Any definition of a community leaves out or maps over alternative definitions. For this project, you will create a campaign to make public a population or issue that needs a greater presence on your campus or in your community. In crafting materials for this campaign, explore the strategies used by the authors in this chapter—personal memoir, community publication, public tour, research documents—and see if any of them would be useful to you. Once you have a campaign strategy, you will need to produce the actual materials, producing enough of each proposed document for the class to be able to understand its utility to the campaign as a whole. You will also need to produce one written document suitable for publication in a campus publication or public Web site.

Once your campaign materials are complete, present your campaign to the class. As a group, discuss what you have learned about the possibility or difficulty of intervening in official or popular frameworks, ones that do not give enough attention to your issue. Also be sure to recognize how one piece of writing, by itself, is unable to shift public perception. Explain how your particular campaign must be part of a general effort to shift opinions and suggest partners who might support your goals.

PROJECT 15 Performing Citizenship: Crossing and Collaborating on the Border

Borders are sites of tension. López (p. 286) faced starvation and danger crossing the border. Mathieu (p. 268) documented what happens when individuals, such as the homeless, fall outside of accepted cultural borders; they vanish from our public perception. Indeed, Reynolds (p. 253) demonstrated how many of the tensions within a community around unspoken borders are never discussed and never become the object of investigation and intervention. Although your college or community may not have such dramatic examples of border tension or exclusion, it is probably not free from such moments.

Indeed, one theme in the readings was to make such tensions visible, drawing out different experiences for the sake of dialogue. The works of Mathieu and López are the hallmarks of such efforts. As a class, choose a location either on or off campus that has a contested border—a site where different populations, identities, or opinions are attempting to integrate a variety of backgrounds, heritages, or cultural backgrounds—such as a college cafeteria where students appear to intentionally sit according to personal heritage or background, a community health center that is witnessing a change in the population it serves, or a church that has welcomed recent immigrant populations into its congregation. It should also be a location where some (if not most) members of the class have some personal connection, such as living by the site or having to cross over this border daily. Over seven to ten days, do one of the following projects:

1. Have a group of students with a connection to the site interview individuals who can speak to the tensions existent in that location. The goal should be to get a wide range of opinions while representing the different constituencies involved. These interviews should be recorded and transcribed and then brought to class. (See pp. 213–15 for interview and permission protocols.)

2. Have a group of students research any media coverage about the site. Include community publications, blogs, and other local newspapers as well as mainstream newspapers. As a group, choose a range of incidents that you believe capture the tensions in that area. Choose specific quotes from media sources or featured community voices, while understanding that their words might have been taken out of context.

Based on these collected materials, the class as a whole should prepare a 10-minute script that enacts the border tensions of that location. The goal is not to present a solution, a resolution, but rather a representation of the tensions.

Once the script is created, record the audio—having class members read the parts. You might also decide to create a video montage to accompany the audio file. This presentation is your completed play.

At this point, the class can either ask a local campus publication to post the video on its Web site, asking students to respond, or contact campus groups that might be willing to respond to the video. As you receive their responses, discuss how your efforts to discuss a border issue was received by your peers. Did the video move debate past the types of arguments represented in the video? Why or why not? In addition to the video, what additional work would be necessary to facilitate a productive discussion? Or to invoke López, what beyond the telling of his story, in a book dedicated to making a more nuanced sense of argument possible, needs to be done to alter border conflicts?

PROJECT 16 *From Our Eyes*: A Community Tour Book

Brighton is a tourist community in England. As in most such cities, there are "standard tourist" sites that people visit. These visitors helped support the local economy, but not equally. Many of the long-standing "mom-and-pop" stores—as well as entire communities—rarely benefited from their tourist dollars. With this fact in mind, community members created their own Brighton map, a map that told the city's history through the eyes of long-term residents. To do this, the community set up writing stations at sites seen as important to them—bakeries, parks, homes, etc. Residents wrote down their memories. All of this work was collected into a book and published as a "tourism" guide.

You might not be at a tourist destination. You are, however, in a community that has set ways of traveling—by foot or car—that probably separate residents into distinct parts of the community. These distinctions are the invisible borders that Reynolds speaks of in her work. For this project, you will prepare and distribute a publication with a community partner who is interested in drawing more individuals to the community. Collaboratively decide how you want the community to be portrayed and what collective beliefs will both represent the values of the community and attract visitors. Then develop writing prompts for residents to respond to in writing or through audio recordings for use at certain chosen sites. It might take several weeks before you have enough material to use in your publication.

Once the materials have been collected, work with your community partner to develop a short publication (an extended brochure or chapbook) that can be printed inexpensively. (For the long-term sustainability of the project, it is important to keep costs in mind.) Once the publication is printed, develop a plan to distribute the publication in areas that currently attract significant foot and automobile traffic. If you have recorded interviews, you can also develop an audio tour book. For that product, distribution includes advertising—perhaps in partnership with business organizations, nonprofit organizations, and local news-papers—as well as creating a means for individuals to download the audio files.

Try to schedule the completion of this publication so that there is suffi-cient time in class to track the success and response to it. It could be useful to plan its publication around an important holiday or community event because people will already be exploring or discovering new aspects of the larger com-munity at that time.

For strategies on writing prompts, see pages 199–202; for publication per-mission, see pages 240–41; and for print publishing considerations, see pages 244–46.

PROJECT 17 *Crossing Borders*: A Community Publication

In many ways, López's story (p. 286) is an attempt to bear witness to the hard-ships faced by immigrant farmworkers. In this way, López shares an affinity with the work of Mathieu (p. 268) in that both authors believe in the need to "speak truth to power." Although they each speak from different positions (individual, professor) and through different means (community publication, scholarly publication, newspapers, community tours), each imagines that the personal experience of those involved carries significant importance within public debates.

For this project, you will work with your community partner to define an issue—either in the immediate neighborhood or in another local area—that needs increased visibility. In particular, it should be an issue in which the experi-ence and insights of local residents have not been sufficiently heard or respected. In collaboration with your partner, develop a list of individuals who should be heard on this topic, because of either their status in the community or the particu-lar population they represent (such as young adults). Work with each individual to develop a one-paragraph statement on his or her stance on the issue at hand.

NOTE: There is no need to consolidate the opinions of those interviewed into a consistent message. The goal of this project is to demonstrate the nuanced understanding already existing in the neighborhood on the issue as a means to advocate for increased resident participation. For although there is probably not a unified opinion on the issue within the community, the commu-nity members are probably unified in the belief they should be heard.

Once these paragraphs are completed, work with your community partner to design a series of posters and postcards that do the following:

1. Highlight the personal testimony of the resident affected by the issue.
2. Provide research data that support the individual's testimony.
3. Feature an image that reflects the position articulated by the above information.

4. Provides information on where the reader of the materials can participate in a discussion on this issue; it will most likely be a meeting or forum sponsored by your community partner.

The goals of the poster are to highlight the community's experience of the issue, validate this understanding, and advertise a place and time where the reader can take action on the issue.

Once you have finished the materials, develop a series of sites where the posters can be posted or the postcards distributed. Your community partner will most likely be the best resource for these sites. Make sure to develop a way to track the response at each site as well as the overall effect of the campaign. For instance, you might keep track of the postcards distributed at each site as well as track the number of actual phone calls or e-mails received about this issue. As a culminating event, plan a community forum with your partner that will allow the issue to be discussed publicly.

As a class, discuss the success (or lack of success) of your poster or postcard campaign in drawing people to participate in the issue.

For strategies on interviewing, see pages 213–15; for publication permission, see pages 240–41; for publication design, see pages 242–43; and for event-planning strategies, see pages 233–34.

PROJECT 18 Building Community

One theme of this chapter has been the concept of border crossing, whether the crossing is economic, political, or personal. The ability of borders to be both permeable and permanent has been the foundation of many of the readings. This project provides a way to articulate some of the issues discussed in these readings.

With your community partner, discuss some of the borders that community residents constantly confront. Borders could mean either the literal act of crossing a national border, if the community has a strong migrant population, or cultural borders, if some in the community are having a difficult time gaining broader acceptance. Having chosen the border, develop a list of fifteen to twenty individuals whose personal narrative could speak to these tensions. After the community member has secured the participation of these persons, undertake the following work:

1. Develop a key set of common questions that you will ask each individual.

2. Create teams of one student/one community member (if possible) to conduct the interviews.

3. Assign each team at least one interview to conduct.

4. Have each team practice interviewing by asking each other the questions.

5. Arrange a time for the interview and record the interview as an audio file.

Once the interviews have been conducted, they will need to be transcribed, work that is usually assigned to the student partner. Plan one week for this process. To catch any gaps, misquotes, and the like, read the transcript out loud to at least one other student.

Each team should then edit the transcripts together. Here the goals are to reduce redundancies and consolidate the interviews into one strong narrative. This work is best done initially by the team and then shared with others involved in the project. Once the community/student collective has approved the edited transcript, it *must* be shared with the person interviewed for revisions and changes according to that individual's concerns and clarifications.

As with Project 5's publication, discussed above, the collective needs to design the book and develop a distribution strategy. Again, keeping the costs of the publication low will help ensure its continued use. You might also decide to link the publication to a Web site where audio files of the interviews or more extensive narratives can be accessed. The extensive nature of this project will probably make it difficult to track the circulation of the publication during your actual class. You might, however, build in a reporting structure whereby your community partner will send out an e-mail two months after publication asking about its use in the community.

For strategies on interviewing, see pages 213–15; for publication permission, see pages 240–41; for publication design, see pages 242–43; and for print publishing considerations, see pages 244–46.

Writing Networks: Creating Links Online and Offline

What does the word *network* mean to you? Is it a verb or a noun? Is it something that exists in real life or online? Is it somehow all of the above? The selections in this chapter explore how both in-person and digital networks function and can how they can enrich people's lives and work. As a starting-point, here is a short story about how calling upon an online network helped to enable real-world political progress.

I woke up that day of the 12th February to an invitation on Facebook. A group calling for an uprising in Libya inspired by the huge success of Egypt and Tunisia's revolutions. "This was a joke" I said and I went randomly inviting friends to join. And some of my friends' reaction was removing me off the Facebook friends list. A word of mouth was circulating in Libya, the Facebook page and the possibility of an uprising was the core conversation in every café and gathering in Libya. None had expected a major event, and those who did said it most probably would be as big as previous incidents such as the mini revolutions Libya went through in 2000 and 2006.

A couple of days passed and as I was talking over the phone to my friends in Benghazi, I was advised to be there in case things get serious. At the beginning I saw no point for traveling to Benghazi but after hearing a few of my friends say, this would be a historical moment whether it succeeds or fails, I decided to go. Just the fact that you can be in the streets in

Libya holding up signs asking for reforms in the government was something Libyans never experienced or dreamed to do in Libya before.

[*Mass protests emerge in Libya, specifically in front of the National Court House.*]

As I was standing there and chatting with some of my friends. I saw Mohamed Nabous. He told me he was going home to bring a satellite Internet system to the court in order to connect to Al Jazeera. He wanted to go live on the air to show the world what was really happening in front of the court of Benghazi. At that time, no proper videos were broadcasted, only some amateur camera phone videos. He was trying to find other people to come with him to carry the satellite Internet. We got into a pickup truck.

It took us almost 45 minutes to do so, [but] we all carried the heavy dish [onto the truck bed]. . . . I sat in the front with the driver and the other guys went in another car. All I could see at that time was a helicopter. It was flying over the same area as Mohamed's house, and I was concerned they were taking pictures from that helicopter. I thought *What if they have a machine gun over there?* As we were driving and getting closer to the court, I was trying to calm myself down, but couldn't help but worry, *What if we were stopped by the police or the army?* I told the driver to let me do the talking if we were stopped. We made up a story together and decided we would tell them that this satellite we were carrying was just a normal TV dish and that we are making a delivery. I would tell them I was a technician. After all they wouldn't recognize that it is different. *How would they know?* As we were getting closer to the city, the streets were empty, and the only thing you could see was the smoke of the burning buildings. We arrived safe to the court that was my mission of the day. People were happy to see the satellite. Finally the world would witness our happiness. I felt so proud to be part of this small mission.

—**Ibrahim Yousif Shebani, "Libya: The Revolution in Four Days"**
From *Revolution by Love: Emerging Arab Voices*

▪ ▪ ▪

There is a utopian feel to the Internet or, really, to social networks in general. These resources are cast as creating an open forum, a democratic space, where anyone can be heard. And it is true that when forming their opinions on issues, most people now have access to some of the world's greatest libraries, research documents, and historical collections. The possibilities seem limitless. Most of us, however, do not exist simply online; we also exist in networks of friends and family. Our lives are intertwined with the fate of our neighbors, our cities, and our region. When we sit down at a computer or pull out our smartphone, we are drawing together all these networks, forming and re-forming them, with every touch of the keyboard keys or a conversation with the person sitting next to us.

What are we to make, then, of our place in this series of interlocking networks, this constellation of connections and bridges to people and places? The difficulty in answering this question is, of course, the requirement for nuance. It would be too simple to claim that we "control our destiny" or that we are "cogs in the machine." Our networks provide us the ability to move across different locations (intellectual and actual) as well as create barriers—that is, moments when being connected to a person or place actually limits our access to resources. It is the difference, to some extent, between owning a computer and using it at home and versus having to go to an Internet café to access the Web. You can move your goals forward in either case, but one is surely an easier pathway than the other. Understanding how to shift the balance, manage, or create new networks, provides an individual a window into how the larger culture enables or disables the aspirations of individuals or communities.

So while the term *network* is currently cast in a glow of optimism among many digital-culture advocates, this chapter takes a slightly different angle. The authors featured here pose the question of why networks exist, what it means to actually exist within them, and how they foster (or fail to foster) opportunity. Finally, these authors question how the digital media networks being created support or expand our previous networks. Do they radically alter what networks can produce socially and politically? (Think of Shebani's story above.) Or do they simply further consolidate the power differences already in place? The answers to these questions are more subtle than you might imagine. And for that reason, they offer a rich conversation in which to enter and form your own opinions.

You will do more, however, than simply develop your opinions. As someone who already exists within networks—and, as a result of your course work, may have begun broadening your network within your college and community—you already have some experience in shaping their purpose. This chapter will draw on your experience and the insights of the authors in this chapter to propose specific projects. Through these projects, you will be able to enact your new understanding, support or create new networks, and in the process gain experience in what it means to push the rhetorical hope of networks into democratic practice.

References and notes for the readings can be found in the appendix on page 427.

The Whole Is Great

© Paul Schnaittacher Photography

Nicholas Christakis is a professor of sociology and a professor of medicine at Yale University, and James Fowler is a professor of medical genetics and a professor of political science at the University of California, San Diego. Their collaborative work focuses on how human networks shape a person's emotions, friendships, and even participation in larger political structures. Indeed, they argue that networks are a genetic necessity, providing the increased cognitive and labor power that enable human progress. As such, Christakis and Fowler are particularly interested in how the invention of the Internet supports, distorts, or expands the power of human networks. The intersection of genetics and the Internet is a key area of their research.

In the following excerpt from their book *Connected: The Surprising Power of Social Networks and How They Shape Our Lives*, the authors make their argument about the necessity and value of human networks.

■　■　■

Babylon, the first city to be built after the great mythical flood, was one in which, the book of Genesis tells us, humanity was united: "And the Lord said, 'Behold, the people is one, and they have all one language . . . and now nothing will be restrained from them, which they have imagined to do.'"[1] And the first thing that the unrestrained residents of Babylon imagined to do was to build a tower so immense that it would reach the heavens. Genesis recounts that God punished the people by destroying the tower, giving them multiple languages, and scattering them across the earth. This story illustrates the folly of hubris, and we usually focus on the polyglot consequences. Often overlooked, however, is the fact that the Babylonians were punished not so much by being given different languages but, rather, by becoming disconnected from one another.

By banding together, the citizens had been able to do something—build the tower—that they could not have done alone. Other stories from the Bible allude to the power of connections but put a more positive spin on what connected humans can do. When Joshua and the Israelites arrived at the gates of Jericho, they found that the walls of the city were too steep for any one person to climb or destroy. And then, the story goes, God told them to stand together and march around the city. When they heard the sound of the ram's horn, they "spoke with one voice"—in a kind of synchronization like *La Ola*—and the walls of Jericho came tumbling down.

Observations about connection and its implications are ancient, in no small part because theologians and philosophers, like modern biologists and social scientists, have always known that social connections are key to our humanity—full of both promise and danger. Connections were often seen as what distinguished us from animals or an uncivilized state.

In 1651, the English philosopher Thomas Hobbes engaged in a thought experiment in which he described the prototypic condition of human existence. In a "state of nature," he supposed in his famous work *The Leviathan*, there is *bellum omnium contra omnes*, a "war of all against all." There is anarchy. It is, in fact, Hobbes who observed that the "life of man [is] solitary, poor, nasty, brutish, and short."[2] Hobbes's use of *solitary*—which is often, unaccountably, clipped from the phrase—suggests that a disconnected life is full of woe.

5 　 Given these grim circumstances, Hobbes theorized, people would have chosen to enter into a "social contract," sacrificing some of their liberty in exchange for safety. At the core of a civilized society, he argued, people would form connections with one another. These connections would help curb violence and be a source of comfort, peace, and order. People would cease to be loners and become cooperators. A century later, the French philosopher Jean-Jacques Rousseau advanced similar arguments, contending in *The Social Contract* that the state of nature was indeed brutish, devoid of morals or laws, and full of competition and aggression. It was a desire for safety from the threats of others that encouraged people to band together to form a collective presence.

This progression of human beings out of such an ostensibly anarchical condition into ever larger and ever more ordered aggregations—of bands, villages, cities, and states—can in fact be understood as a gradual rise in the size and complexity of social networks. And today this process is continuing to unfold as we become hyperconnected.

The Human Superorganism

The networks we create have lives of their own. They grow, change, reproduce, survive, and die. Things flow and move within them. A social network is a kind of human superorganism, with an anatomy and a physiology—a structure and a function—of its own. From bucket brigades to blogospheres, the human superorganism does what no person could do alone. Our local contributions to the human social network have global consequences that touch the lives of thousands every day and help us to achieve much more than the building of towers or the destruction of walls.

A colony of ants is the prototypic superorganism, with properties not apparent in the ants themselves, properties that arise from the interactions and cooperation of the ants.[3] By joining together, ants create something that transcends the individual: complex anthills spring up like miniature towers of Babylon, tempting wanton children to action. The single ant that finds its way to a sugar bowl far from its nest is like an astronaut stepping foot on the moon: both achievements are made possible by the coordinated efforts and communication of many individuals. Yet, in a way, these solitary individuals—ant and astronaut, both parts of a superorganism—are no different from the tentacle of an octopus sent out to probe a hidden crevice.

In fact, cells within multicellular organisms can be understood in much the same way. Working together, cells generate a higher form of life that is entirely different from the internal workings of a single cell. For example, our digestion is not a function of any one cell or even one type of cells. Likewise, our thoughts are not located in a given neuron; they arise from the pattern of connections between neurons. Whether cells, ants, or humans, new properties of a group can emerge from the interactions of individuals. And cooperative interactions are hallmarks of most major evolutionary leaps that have occurred since the origin of life—consider the incorporation of mitochondria into eukaryotic cells, the agglomeration of single-cell organisms into multicellular organisms, and the assembly of individuals into superorganisms.[4]

Social networks can manifest a kind of intelligence that augments or complements individual intelligence, the way an ant colony is "intelligent" even if individual ants are not, or the way flocks of birds determine where to fly by combining the desires of each bird.[5] Social networks can capture and contain information that is transmitted across people and time (like norms of trust, traditions of reciprocity, oral histories, or online wikis) and can perform computations that aggregate millions of decisions (such as setting a market price for a product or choosing the best candidate in an election). And networks can have this effect regardless of the intelligence of the individual members. Consider, for example, that the way humans laid a rail network throughout England in the twentieth century resembles the way fungi (another species that forms superorganisms) collaboratively explore a patch of ground in the forest in order to exploit and transport resources by creating a network of tubes.[6] Fungi can even "collaborate" to find the best path through mazes into which they have been placed by human experimenters.[7]

Social networks also have a memory of their own structure (staying intact even if people come and go) and their own function (preserving a culture even when people come and go). For example, if you join a trusting network of people,

10

you benefit from that trust and are shaped by it. In many cases, it is not just that the people in your network are more trusting, or even that their trusting behavior engenders trust in you; rather, the network facilitates this trust and changes the way individuals behave.

Like living creatures, networks can be self-replicating. They can reproduce themselves across space and time. But unlike corporeal organisms, networks can, if disassembled, reassemble themselves at a distance. If every person has a memory of whom he or she is connected to, we can cut the connections and move all the people from one place to another, and the network will reappear. Knowledge of one's own social ties means that the network can reemerge even though no single person knows how everyone else in the network is connected.

Networks are also self-replicating in the sense that they outlast their members: the network can endure even if the people within it change, just as cells replace themselves in our skin, computers are swapped out on a server farm, and new buyers and sellers come to a market that has been located in the same place for centuries. In one study of a network of four million people connected by their phone calls, researchers showed that, paradoxically, groups with more than fifteen interconnected people that experienced the greatest turnover endured the longest.[8] Large social networks may in fact require such turnover to survive, just as cell renewal is required for our bodies to survive.

These observations highlight another amazing, organism-like property: social networks are often self-annealing. They can close up around their gaps, in the same way that the edges of a wound come together. One person might step out of a bucket brigade, but then the two people he was connected to will move closer to each other, forming a new connection to fill in the gap. As a result, water will continue to flow. In more complicated, real-life networks, it seems likely that the very purpose of redundant networks ties, and of transitivity, is precisely to make the networks tolerant of this kind of loss, as if human social networks were designed to last.

15   Like a worldwide nervous system, our networks allow us to send and receive messages to nearly every other person on the planet. As we become more hyperconnected, information circulates more efficiently, we interact more easily, and we manage more and different kinds of social connections every day. All of these changes make us, *Homo dictyous*, even more like a superorganism that acts with a common purpose. The ability of networks to create and sustain our collective goals continues to strengthen. And everything that now spreads from person to person will soon spread farther and faster, prompting new features to emerge as the scale of interactions increases.

It's Neither Yours nor Mine

The social networks we create are a valuable, shared resource. Social networks confer benefits. Alas, not all people are in the best position to capture these benefits, and this raises fundamental questions of justice and public policy.

Social scientists call such a shared resource a *public good*. A *private good* is one the owner can exclude others from consuming, and one that, once consumed, cannot be consumed again. If I own a cake, I can prevent anyone else from eating it, and once I eat it myself, there is none left for anyone else. A public good, in contrast, can be consumed without harming the interests of others, and without reducing others' ability to use it. Think of a lighthouse. One ship making use of the light to avoid colliding with the rocks does not prevent another ship from doing the same. Public radio, Fourth of July fireworks, and municipal water fluoridation are other examples of public goods. Not all public goods are man-made, of course. Think of the air. One person breathing does not make anyone else have less air, nor does it prevent anyone else from breathing.

Other public goods are less tangible even than light or air. Think of civic duty. As Alexis de Tocqueville argued in the early nineteenth century, if everyone feels the obligation to maintain a civil society, to act in a trustworthy way, and to volunteer for the nation in times of attack, then all citizens can benefit from these traditions and norms. And the benefit to one person does not reduce the benefit for others.

But public goods are difficult to create and maintain. It often seems that no one has an incentive to care for them, as a breath of not-so-fresh air in any polluted city demonstrates. Hence, public goods often arise as by-products of the actions of individuals acting with some self-interest. A shipping company or port authority that builds a lighthouse to safeguard its own ships ends up safeguarding all ships.

Some public goods get better the more they are produced. A classic example of a particular kind of network good is a telephone or fax machine. The first person to get a fax machine finds that it is worthless because there is no one to fax anything to. However, as more and more people acquire fax machines, they become more and more valuable. A similar—if more abstract—example of a network public good is trust. . . . Trust is most valuable when others are also trusting; and being trusting in a world of free riders is very painful. But many other human behaviors and beliefs increase in value in this way. For example, the positive effects of religiosity on well-being is higher in countries where average religiosity is higher.[9] Like fax machines, religion is more useful if others also believe, in part because religion works to enhance well-being by fostering social ties.

The social networks that humans create are themselves public goods. Everyone chooses their own friends, but in the process an endlessly complex social network is created, and the network can become a resource that no one person controls but that all benefit from. From the point of view of each person in the network, there is no way to tell exactly what kind of world we inhabit, even though we help create it. We can see our own friends, family, neighbors, and coworkers, and perhaps we know a little bit about how they are tied to each

20

other, but how we are connected to the network beyond our immediate social horizon is usually a mystery. Yet, as we have seen time and again, the precise structure of the network around us and the precise nature of the things flowing through it affect us all. We are like people on a crowded dance floor: we know that there are ten people pressed up against us, but we are not sure if we are in the middle or at the edge of the room or whether a wave of ecstasy or fear is spreading toward us.

Of course, not all networks create something that is useful, valuable, and shared, let alone something that is positive. When we say "good" we really just mean any old thing: pistols and poisons are goods too. And networks can function as conduits for pathogens or panic. Indeed, social networks can be exploited for bad ends. . . . Violence spreads in networks, as does suicide, anger, fraud, fascism, and even accusations of witchcraft.

The interpersonal spread of criminal behavior is an illuminating example of a bad network outcome. One persistent mystery about crime is its variation across time (fluctuating from year to year) and space (varying in adjoining police precincts or jurisdictions). For example, in Ridgewood Village, New Jersey, there are 0.008 serious crimes per capita, whereas in nearby Atlantic City, there are 0.384—a nearly fiftyfold difference. This variation seems too great to be explained by some kind of disparity in the costs and benefits of crime, or even in observable features of the environment or the residents, such as the availability of after-school programs or educational attainment. So what explains the difference? Much evidence suggests that it is partially due to the reverberation of social interactions: as criminals act in a given place and time, they increase the likelihood that others nearby will commit crimes, so that even more crimes occur than would otherwise be expected.[10] And the groups over which these effects extend can number in the hundreds.

A detailed study of these effects by economist Ed Glaeser and his colleagues also shows that certain crimes spread more easily than others, just as one would expect if social influences were more important than local socioeconomic conditions. People are much more likely to be influenced to steal a car when someone else does than to commit a burglary or robbery, and influence is even weaker for crimes like rape and arson. The riskier or more serious the crime, the less likely others are to follow suit (though there can be frenzies of murder too, as in the Rwandan genocide). Moreover, as a further illustration of the social nature of crime, nearly two-thirds of all criminals commit crimes in collaboration with someone else.[11]

25   While we are not aware of any experimental efforts to foster crime by exploiting social contagion, there have been experiments to study less extreme unethical behaviors. At Carnegie Mellon University, a group of students were asked to take a difficult math test. In the middle of the room, researchers placed a confederate who at some point visibly cheated on the test. When students witnessed the cheater's

behavior, they too began to cheat.[12] Especially relevant, though, was the discovery that cheating only increased if the cheater was a person to whom the other students felt connected. If the cheater wore a plain T-shirt, students were more likely to cheat than if he wore a T-shirt from the University of Pittsburgh (Carnegie Mellon's local rival institution).

The Spread of Goodness

In spite of these potential negative effects, we are all connected for a reason. The purpose of social networks is to transmit positive and desirable outcomes, whether joy, warnings about predators, or introductions to romantic partners. To some extent, the transmission of bad behaviors and other adverse phenomena (like germs) are merely side effects that we must endure in order to reap the benefits of networks; they are grafted onto an apparatus that was built, evolutionarily speaking, for another, more beneficial purpose.

To be clear, we are not suggesting a linear progression across history or evolutionary time from anarchy to state to utopia. But we do believe that there is a utopian impulse to form networks that has always been with us. We gain more than we lose by living within social networks, and this drives us to embed ourselves in the lives of others. The natural advantages of a connected life explain why social networks have persisted and why we have come to form a human superorganism.

Crucial traits and behaviors that lie at the root of—and that nourish—social connections have a genetic basis. Altruism, for example, is a key predicate for the formation and operation of social networks. If people never behaved altruistically, never reciprocated kind behavior, or, worse, were always violent, then social ties would dissolve, and the network around us would disintegrate. Some degree of altruism and reciprocity, and indeed some degree of positive emotions such as love and happiness, are therefore crucial for the emergence and endurance of social networks. Moreover, once networks are established, altruistic acts—from random acts of kindness to cascades of organ donation—can spread through them.

Charity is just one example of the goodness that flows through networks. About 89 percent of American households give to charity each year (the average annual contribution was $1,620 in 2001), and fund-raising efforts often seem designed to capitalize on processes of social influence and notions of community embeddedness. Appeals are commonly organized so that people you feel connected to rather than strangers call you to ask for money, such as graduates of your college or relatives of your friend with cancer (of course, it is cheaper to use such volunteers too). Bikeathons and walkathons are organized to engender a sense of community among those participating and to encourage direct contact between participants and the friends and neighbors who sponsor them. And organizations from hospitals to Boy Scout troops to small towns employ a kind of thermometer that is publicly displayed and that tracks charitable giving to their cause, implicitly saying, Look, all these other people gave money; now how about you? Indeed, surveys of people who have given money to diverse causes find that roughly 80 percent did so because they were asked to by someone they knew well.[13]

In one demonstration of the spread of prosocial norms, economist Katie Carman studied charitable giving (via payroll deductions to the United Way) in 2000 and 2001 among the seventy-five thousand employees in a large American bank operating in twenty states. She found that employees gave more when they worked next to generous colleagues. Carman acquired detailed information about the employees' connections at work and their specific locations in bank offices. In a clever exploitation of the most mundane piece of information imaginable—the mail codes used to deliver letters and parcels to areas within bank buildings—she was able to identify groups of people ranging in size from one to 537, with a median size of just nineteen people. She studied what happened to employee giving if they were obliged to move from one location in the bank to another. She found that when people were transferred from a location where others did not give much money to a location where they did, every $1.00 increase in the average giving of their nearby coworkers resulted in a $0.53 increase in their own contribution.[14] There are, of course, several possible mechanisms for this influence: one person could provide information about how to give, could pressure the other to give, or could simply act as a role model for giving.

While Carman's work suggested the person-to-person spread of altruistic norms, our own experiments illustrate the surprising pay-it-forward properties of altruism. We know that if Jay is generous to Harla, Harla will be generous to Jay, but if Jay is generous to Harla, will Harla be generous to Lucas? We devised an experiment to evaluate the idea that altruism could spread from person to person to person. We recruited 120 students for a set of cooperation games that lasted five rounds. In each round, students were placed in groups of four, and we adjusted the composition of the groups so that no two students were ever in the same group twice. Students were each given some funds, and they could decide how much money to give to the group at a personal cost, and then at the end of each round we let them know what the others had done.

When we analyzed their behavior, we found that altruism tends to spread and that the benefits tend to be magnified. When one person gives an extra dollar in the first round, the people in her group each tend to give about twenty cents more in the second round, even though they have been placed in completely new and different groups! When a person has been treated well by someone, she goes on to treat others well in the future. And, even more strikingly, all the people in these new second-round groups are also affected in the third round, each giving about five cents more for every extra dollar that the generous person in the first round spent. Since each group contains three new people at every stage, this means that giving an extra dollar initially caused a total increase in giving by others of sixty cents in the second round and forty-five cents in the third. In other words, the social network acted like a matching grant, prompting an extra $1.05 in total future giving by others for each dollar a person initially chose to give.

Whether people behave altruistically is also determined by the structure of the social network. One ingenious experiment documented a "law of giving" at an all-girls school in Pasadena, California.[15] The investigators asked seventy-six fifth- and sixth-grade girls to identify up to five friends; this allowed investigators to draw the girls' social networks and ascertain which girls were each girl's friends, friends of friends, friends of friends of friends, and so on. They had the girls play the dictator game . . . , and each girl was asked how much she would share from a $6 sum with each of ten other girls who were listed by name. The girls were most generous with their friends, and the amount given declined as social distance increased. On average, the girls offered their friends 52 percent of the $6, friends of friends 36 percent, and friends of friends of friends 16 percent. The best predictor of how much each girl gave was not any measured characteristic of either the givers or the recipients—such as whether either girl was tall or short, had many or few siblings, or wore glasses or braces. Instead, it was the degree of separation between the giver and the receiver.

This is one way that popularity is beneficial. If you are in the center of a social network, you are more likely to be one, two, or three degrees removed from many other people than if you were at the periphery of the network. Consequently, you can earn a centrality premium if good things (like money or respect) are flowing through the network. More people are willing to act altruistically toward you than toward those at the margins. When all the rounds of the game among the schoolgirls were completed, the most popular girls earned four times as much as the least popular. The ability of social networks to magnify whatever they are seeded with favors some people over others.

A pair of experiments with college undergraduates added a few wrinkles to these results.[16] One elicited information about the close friends of 569 undergraduates residing in two large college dormitories in 2003. The other involved 2,360 students using Facebook in 2004. The students were less and less generous to people farther away in the network and were no more generous to people beyond three degrees of separation than they were to total strangers. The college students were also more likely to act altruistically, and to give generously, to social contacts with whom they shared many friends in common. Katrina is more likely to act altruistically toward Dave if they share Ronan and Maddox as friends than if they just share Ronan.

Moreover, the motivation to give to friends that subjects did not expect to interact with again was twice as strong as the motivation to give to strangers that subjects expected to have further interactions with. Put another way, we would rather give a gift to a friend who will never repay us than to give a gift to

35

a stranger who will. The reason is that we give to sustain the network, and it is the network itself that we value. Our social ties repay us for our gifts. Generosity binds the network together, but the network also functions to foster and determine generosity.

This study of college students confirmed a final, crucial point: in real-life interactions, . . . cooperators tend to hang out with other cooperators, and there is homophily in the inclination to be altruistic. Altruistic and selfish undergraduates each had the same number of friends, on average. But altruistic people were embedded in networks of other altruistic people.

Haves and Have-Nots: Social Network Inequality

Today it is common to focus on inequalities in our society that appear to arise from race, income, gender, or geography. We pay attention to the fact that people with better education generally have better health or more economic opportunities, that whites may enjoy advantages that minorities do not, and that where people live affects their life prospects. Politicians, activists, philanthropists, and critics are driven by the recognition that we do not all appear to have equal access to societal goods and that the pattern of access is often manifestly unjust. In short, we live in a hierarchical society, and our sociodemographic characteristics stratify and divide us.

But there is an alternative way of understanding stratification and hierarchy that is based on how people are positioned with respect to their connections. *Positional inequality* occurs not because of who we are but because of who we are connected to. These connections affect where we come to be located in social networks, and they often matter more than our race, class, gender, or education. Some of us have more connections, and some fewer. Some of us are more centrally located, and some of us find ourselves at the periphery. Some of us have densely interconnected social ties and all our friends know one another, and some of us inhabit worlds where none of our friends get along. And these differences are not always of our own doing because our network position also depends on the choices that others around us make.

40   Not everyone can tap the public goods that are fostered and created by social networks. Your chance of dying after a heart attack may depend more on whether you have friends than on whether you are black or white. Your chance of finding a new job may have as much to do with the friends of your friends as with your skill set. And your chance of being treated kindly or altruistically depends on how well connected others around you are.

Social scientists and policy makers have neglected this kind of inequality, in part because it is so difficult to measure. We cannot understand positional inequality by just studying individuals or even groups. We cannot ask a person where he is located in the social network as easily as we can ask him how much money he earns. Instead, we must observe the social network as a whole before we can understand a person's place in it. This is not a trivial problem. Thankfully, . . . the advent of digital communications (e-mail, mobile phones, social-network websites) is making it easier to see networks on a large scale without necessarily surveying individuals at great expense. Correlating people's network centrality with their mortality risk, their transitivity with their prospects of repaying a loan, or their network position with their propensity to commit crimes or quit smoking offers new avenues for policy intervention.

But in an increasingly interconnected world, people with many ties may become even better connected while those with few ties may get left farther and farther behind. As a result, rewards may flow even more toward those with particular locations in social networks. This is the real digital divide. Network inequality creates and reinforces inequality of opportunity. In fact, the tendency of people with many connections to be connected to other people with many connections distinguishes social networks from neural, metabolic, mechanical, or other nonhuman networks. And the reverse holds true as well: those who are poorly connected usually have friends and family who are themselves disconnected from the larger network.

To address social disparities, then, we must recognize that our connections matter much more than the color of our skin or the size of our wallets. To address differences in education, health, or income, we must also address the personal connections of the people we are trying to help. To reduce crime, we need to optimize the kinds of connections potential criminals have — a challenging proposition since we sometimes need to detain criminals. To make smoking-cessation and weight-loss interventions more effective, we need to involve family, friends, and even friends of friends. To reduce poverty, we should focus not merely on monetary transfers or even technical training; we should help the poor form new relationships with other members of society. When we target the periphery of a network to help people reconnect, we help the whole fabric of society, not just any disadvantaged individuals at the fringe.

Reading

1. How do the authors define the term *superorganism* (para. 7)?

2. How do they argue for the social benefits of social networks?

3. How do they distinguish between a "public" good and a "private" good?

4. How do they define *positional inequality* and its relationship to social networks (para. 39)?

Inquiring

1. "The Whole Is Great" makes some strong claims about the necessity and values of different kinds of human networks (online or on the ground). At times, Christakis and Fowler imply that human networks are a genetic necessity and

an evolutionary triumph. Assuming this implication is true, what evolutionary needs can you imagine being met by human networks? Do the authors (or you) believe these needs are also being met by social media networks? How might they be serving the same, different, or new needs?

2. Christakis and Fowler use the term *human superorganism* to explain some of the power of networks. They draw an analogy to ant colonies, where the sum of the ants' work is greater than any particular ant's understanding. This increased cognitive and physical ability is the hallmark of networks. What are the specific qualities of such superorganisms? What can such superorganisms accomplish for humans? Why would the authors believe such superorganisms are fundamental to human survival?

3. "The Whole Is Great" ends on an optimistic note. Having earlier argued that networks can maintain and distribute values across its members and citing examples such as how trust can be maintained even as members change, Christakis and Fowler argue that a focus on networks can produce social change. In effect, this argument minimizes the negative effects of networks and how crime or socially harmful values can also spread; the authors claim these consequences are just a "side effect" of networks. As a class, consider what evidence you could use to support or refute this claim. Can human networks be characterized as essentially good?

Composing

1. By the end of this extract, Christakis and Fowler have argued for how every individual exists within a social network. They do not provide a rationale for any particular network, however, nor do they provide an example of how an individual's relationship with others within a network might be organized. In other words, why might one person be more central within a network than another person, or how might one type of person be more central than another based not only on individual qualities but also on social economic position? Christakis and Fowler do not explain how individual networks are both unique to a person and part of a larger social fabric. For this assignment, make a map of one of the networks in which you exist (friends, family, online community, etc.). As the mapmaker, you will need to decide who and what are part of that community, how it should be displayed, and what values those connections bring to your network. Unlike Christakis and Fowler, however, you will need to make a key for your map, explaining how to read it. (For instance, you might use yellow lines to indicate a more positive relationship and blue to indicate a troubled relationship.) After making your map, write a short essay in which you discuss Christakis and Fowler's argument that networks can transmit values. Using your own mapped network, explore whether you support or question their arguments.

2. Christakis and Fowler write that the "purpose of social networks is to transmit positive and desirable outcomes, whether joy, warnings about predators, or introductions to romantic partners" (para. 26). This statement expresses a powerful sentiment, certainly one that most everyone would wish to be true, but do such sentiments match the historical record? Certainly, a counterargument could be made by invoking Jim Crow laws in post–World War II in the United States (which enforced segregation in the southern United States) or even by invoking the sheer fact of World War II. A more immediate example might be cyberbullying, a practice that feeds on social networks and that pushes some young people to suicide. Write an essay in which you reply to Christakis and Fowler's statement. What evidence from history supports their claim? What evidence refutes it? If you disagree with their claim that the purpose of social networks is to "transmit desirable outcomes," what happens to other foundational aspects of their argument? That is, are humans supposed to exist in networks?

3. Christakis and Fowler state that not all networks promote socially productive values nor do all networks provide equal resources to individuals. They are careful to avoid claiming that the values or resources within a network can be determined by simply examining issues of race, class, or gender, however. Although any person's particular ability to progress toward their goals might be limited within his or her own network (such as a person's ability to attend college), the reason for this limit cannot be simply placed on these categories. Instead, the authors argue for a model that attempts to value individual effort within the constraints of any network. It is unclear what such a model might look like in practice, though. For this assignment, research and write about the "human superorganism" networks within which you existed prior to coming to college. How did your network support or constrain your progress toward college? What connections or support did it offer? What did it fail to provide? How might such a model help you understand the power and possibilities of networks beyond categories of race, class, and gender? How might such a model confirm the importance of such categories?

Connecting

Christakis and Fowler claim that networks are almost a genetic necessity and that, on average, they produce beneficial social effects. Consider the case of WikiLeaks (p. 340). How might this project (and the reasons for its existence) test (or expand) Christakis and Fowler's belief about networks? What might it allow you to say about the relationship between a biological necessity and socially created networks?

JAMES PAUL GEE AND ELISABETH R. HAYES

New Kinds of People
and Relationships

Courtesy of James Gee   Photo by ASU

James Paul Gee is the Mary Lou Fulton Presidential Professor of Literacy Studies at Arizona State University, and Elisabeth Gee (formerly Hayes) is the Delbert and Jewell Lewis Chair in Reading and Literacy at Arizona State University. In their collaborative work, they explore the ways in which digital culture has altered (and at points empowered) oral and written communication. In particular, they discuss how the Internet has fostered new types of relationship that exist principally online, exploring the ways in which these new relationships can shift concepts of identity, friendship, and personal networks.

In the following excerpt from their book *Language and Learning in the Digital Age*, the authors discuss the difference between relationships with weak ties and those with strong ties in a digital age.

■ ■ ■

Strangers

. . . One function of language is to communicate social bonding versus social distance. In this chapter, we will expand on this idea and consider how digital media are changing our social relationships, particularly whom we consider to be strangers and intimates.

. . . Strangers are one problem that nearly all cultures face. In a small village or in a small band of hunters and gatherers, there were usually no strangers, so there was no problem with how to interact with them. But in more complex social groups there are strangers. How should we speak to them?

Cultures, and even individuals within larger cultures and societies, differ in how they choose to talk to strangers.[1] Think about what you would do if you were standing next to a stranger at a bus stop for some time. Some people will talk to the stranger and use informal, friendly language near the bonding end of the bonding–distance continuum. They do this, perhaps, to show the stranger that they do not represent a threat. A potential problem is that the stranger may either not want to treat the speaker in such an informal and friendly way or, on the other hand, may take the bonding too seriously and think that the speaker really means more friendship than he or she actually intends. The speaker may only be using "small talk" socially to lubricate a potentially uncomfortable situation.

Other people choose either more formal, polite, distancing language or choose to stay silent and not talk at all to the stranger. In this case, a potential problem is that the stranger may feel threatened if not addressed at all or may resent being addressed, or may be offended by formal, distancing talk, expecting a more friendly overture. That's the trouble with strangers. We do not know the social "rules" they expect to be followed and they do not necessarily share the "rules" by which we operate.

Part of what complicates matters is that people across and sometimes within cultures differ in how they wished to be treated.[2] Some people have a stronger need for acceptance and bonding than others. They feel insulted if left out and not included. Such people are said, by sociologists, to have stronger "positive face needs" than "negative face needs."

Other people have a stronger need for not being imposed upon than others. They feel insulted or bothered if people interact with them or make requests of them, or otherwise attempt to include them, without their explicit permission or without knowing them well. Sociologists say such people have stronger "negative face needs" than "positive face needs."

Everyone has both bonding needs and needs to be respected and not to be imposed upon. All people have both positive (a need to be included and involved) and negative (a need to be left alone and not imposed upon) face needs. But people differ in which of these needs are stronger for them or stronger for them in different contexts.

The problem with strangers is more complex in modern urban societies where many different sorts of people are in close proximity. We can be too polite (distant) when people expect us to be friendlier. We can be too friendly when people expect us to be more polite and distant. We can talk when they do not want or expect us to talk. There are many opportunities for insulting people. The problem with strangers becomes yet more complex with digital media.

Strong and Weak Ties

We have, what have been called, "strong ties" to people we know well, because we see and relate to them often. We have, what have been called, "weak ties" to people whom we do not know well, because we do not see and relate to them often.[3]

10   There are good and bad aspects of both strong and weak ties. The people to whom we have strong ties are more likely to give us help and support when we need it. That is a good thing about them. The "bad" thing is that these are people with whom we share a good deal of knowledge and background. Such people are not often a source of truly new and rare information for us.

The people with whom we have weak ties are not close to us and not likely to "be there" for us if we need them. They owe us nothing. That is the bad part. However, these are people with whom we share much less knowledge and background. Such people are much more likely to know something we do not already know and give us new or rare information. That is the good part.

Consider a working-class man who lost his job in a bad economy. The people with whom he has strong ties are unlikely to know about new jobs that he does not already know about. Indeed, many of them may have also lost their jobs. They already will have shared all they know with each other.

However, if this man has weak ties with people he does not know well—that is, if he has some contact with people outside of his normal social network—these people may know about jobs and possibilities he and his friends do not already know about. Perhaps they know about a job in a new field outside the man's neighborhood and can even give the man a name and contact number.

In stable times where change is slow, weak ties are not that important. But in fast-changing and unpredictable times, weak ties are crucial. They may be the only way we can get fast-changing information in order to cope and survive.

15   For most of human history, people had strong ties with other people much like themselves, people with whom they lived closely and shared a culture. In modern cities, people can and do come to have strong ties with other people from different social and cultural groups, through much interaction and because they live or work near each other.

Digital media have greatly changed the nature of strong and weak ties.[4] They have greatly complicated both the perils and possibilities of strangers. Thanks to digital media, everyone in the digitally connected parts of the world, in a sense, lives next to each other. People can be strangers and intimates at one and the same time. This has never been possible in history before.

Literacy already opened up this possibility. People could have long-term correspondences (via letters) with someone else across the globe. They may never have met in person and they may have known little about each other personally. However, in such cases, writers often shared professional, religious, or class affiliations. The affordances of digital media were necessary to make "intimate strangers" a reality on a large scale.

Strong Weak Ties and Intimate Strangers: A World of Contradictions

Digital media are, in part, like literacy, a delivery system for language. However, they create conditions in which language has never before been used. For most of human history, people did not have strong ties (interact regularly) with people whom they did not know well or who were, in fact, strangers. They did not expect to get a great deal of new and rare information from their intimates and close friends. At the same time, they did not expect to get help and support from people they did not know well. Now all this has changed.

Let's consider a little story. It's the early days of *World of WarCraft*, a game we will just call *WoW*. *WoW* is an extremely popular massively multiplayer video game. Players team up with other players to engage in quests (e.g. finding things and fighting things). At any one time, on a given server, thousands of real people will be playing the game together. Even if you are not playing directly with other people in a group, you can run into them at any time in the big wide world of *WoW*. What other people do can affect what you do (e.g. what they do may help or hinder you). You can, if you wish, talk to these other people any time you want, and even ask them for help or just socialize with them.

When people play *WoW* they are represented in the game by an avatar, a virtual character that need not bear any physical resemblance to the player. The avatar for a 50-year-old white male may be, for instance, a blue female night elf. When players interact, no one knows who they are, their nation, age, race, or gender, unless they are using voice chat (players often type to each other) or they choose to divulge such information.

WoW is now the most popular massively multiplayer video game in the world. When *WoW* first launched, a player whose avatar was named Allele began to play the game. Like many others, the player-as-Allele played hundreds of hours and became quite adept at the game. He often encountered another player, whose avatar was named Band. They quested together at times and with other people. They often talked, at first knowing nothing about each other except that they were both elves. Eventually they talked about their real identities and what they did in the "real world."

Allele was a white man in his fifties, living in the United States. Band was an Albanian man in his twenties. Allele ran successful technology start-ups in Silicon Valley and Band worked for a struggling technology company in Albania. Allele sent Band some software and gave him technical advice, both of which helped Band's company. Band, in return, bought a very special sword in *WoW* and gave it as a gift to Allele, who used it to gain more power and status in the game.

In one sense, Allele and Band had strong ties. They interacted regularly, came to know a good deal about each other, shared personal information, and used bonding language with each other. Yet they were "strangers" in the sense that they had never seen each other and shared little background and culture.

20

In another sense, Allele and Band had weak ties. They came from different worlds and often shared new and rare information with each other. Indeed, they were a typical "weak tie" source of such information for each other. Yet they also offered each other the sort of free support and help that we expect only from friends, people to whom we have strong ties.

25   There is a real paradox or contradiction here. Allele and Band's tie was both strong and weak. They benefited from both strong and weak ties. We can say that they had a "strong weak tie," which sounds like a contradiction—and it is—but a contradiction that happens through digital media all the time all over the world.

The strong weak tie between Allele and Band seems like a good thing. We are more worried when a strong weak tie arises on the Internet between an old man in one place and a teenage girl in another, for example. Like all effects of technology, strong weak ties can be good or bad depending on context and circumstances.

New Kinds of Relationships? New Kinds of People?

The whole idea of who a person is, as well as who is or who is not a stranger or an intimate, is changing thanks to digital media. When two people have interacted in a game like *WoW* as much as Allele and Band, are they friends? Do they really know each other? What is the difference between Allele (a character in the game, but controlled by a human), the fifty-something white male playing Allele (a person in the real world), and that fifty-something white male choosing to communicate and act in certain ways when, and sometimes only when, he is playing as Allele?

Let's turn to another story. Here another fifty-something white man is playing *WoW* with his forty-something wife. They both have attractive (albeit blue) female elf avatars. While they are playing they encounter a male elf character who asks them if they are male or female in "real life." The man replies that they are sisters, one fifteen, one seventeen, playing together. The male elf, who claims to be a teenage boy, starts to flirt with the fifty-something man, eventually offering to play the game with "her" every day.

The man has no idea how to respond to such flirtation. He has never experienced such a thing in real life, having never been an attractive teenage girl. He remembers the power teenage girls seemed to have when he was a teenage boy. He has always wondered about that power and what it felt like to have it. He asked his wife how to respond as a teenage girl and with her help was soon chatting and joking with the boy. He was amazed by the experience of something that was, in a sense, literally impossible.

30   Of course, the teenage boy could have been an old man or woman or anyone else. This story will seem "creepy" to many readers. The question relevant to our discussion is, though, what does this anecdote tell us about these people as "real"

people? Did the man discover something "real" about himself, or about human relationships, whether good or bad? Do such experiences, afforded by digital media, allow us to become "new people" in any sense?

Here is yet another story. *Second Life* is a massively multiplayer virtual world, rather than a game. It is a virtual world that is designed and built by its own players. It contains a great many different environments in which people do everything from creating artwork to working as bartenders to participating in political organizations. Much of what people do involves socializing with each other. In *Second Life* people have avatars, as in *WoW*, and these avatars can look like any sort of human or many non-human creatures.

Our story is about one avatar that became popular in *Second Life*.[5] Many people felt that the person controlling this avatar, whoever he or she "really" was in "real life," was a fascinating, friendly, and good person. Many people wanted to interact with the person and sought the person out.

The "person" controlling the avatar was not one person. It was five patients in a long-term care facility. These were people who had spent their lives in this facility because of severe deformities. A nurse controlled their common avatar and they made decisions together about what the avatar should say and do. These were people who, in the outside world, were feared and shunned. In *Second Life*, they were sought out and valued. They had never before experienced what it was like to be treated as valuable, "normal" people, to be valued for who they were and not what they looked like. They loved playing *Second Life*.

In *Second Life* these people were valued for "who they were" and not what they looked like. But let's think a minute about what that means: they were "themselves," something they could not be in "real life," only when they were a single avatar representing five people! Who was this "one" person (a popular one)? We really are talking about something that has never happened on earth before. For most of human history, one's fate was eternal and there was no second chance at life. But these people have broken, albeit in a small way and only for a moment, the skein of fate. This is, indeed, the stuff of the gods.

Literature

We misled you. We said that the play with identities and relationships we have been discussing was unique to digital media. We said this because, at its current scale and global reach, it is true. But something similar can happen with literature, though the ability of literature to set free new identities eventually was "tamed" by the institution of school. We wonder if the ability of digital media to set free new identities will eventually be tamed by institutions.

Consider what once was called "the canon." The canon was the list of great literature by writers like John Milton, William Shakespeare, and Jane Austen. Today, the very idea of a canon is controversial. Interestingly, both conservatives and liberals agree that canonical literature (the so-called "Great Books")

35

is indoctrinating. The right wing applauds the work the canon can do to align people with what it sees as universal values, values that it sees as already its own. The left wing decries this same thing, claiming that the values embedded in the canon are, far from being universal, just a historically and culturally specific instantiation of the values of certain Western, "middle-class" white people, people who wish to use the canon to enshrine their values and perspectives as superior.

Both views show a woeful ignorance of, and even a certain disdain for, how many people in the past (especially many poor people, people who rarely get invited into academic debates about the canon) actually read and used canonical works like those of Homer, Shakespeare, Milton, Carlyle, Arnold, Austen, Emerson, and a great many others. Many a woman, nonwhite, or poor person actually read canonical works as empowering texts that made them challenge the class hierarchy of their societies and the ways in which schools, churches, and rich people upheld this hierarchy in their own favor.

Jonathan Rose's massive tome, *The Intellectual Life of the British Working Classes,* is full of stories from the eighteenth through the twentieth century of women, poor people, and nonwhite people who interpreted canonical literature as representing their own values and aspirations and not those of the wealthy and powerful. For example, Mary Smith (b. 1822), a shoemaker's daughter, who stated that: "For long years Englishwomen's souls were almost as sorely crippled and cramped by the devices of the school room, as the Chinese women's feet by their shoes," said this about reading Shakespeare, Dryden, and Goldsmith:

> These authors wrote from their hearts for humanity, and I could follow them fully and with delight, though but a child. They awakened my young nature, and I found for the first time that my pondering heart was akin to that of the whole human race. . . . Carlyle's gospel of Work and exposure of Shams, and his universal onslaught on the nothings and appearances of society, gave strength and life to my vague but true enthusiasm.[6]

The left wing may say that Mary Smith was conforming to the dictates of the elites in her society without knowing it and mistakenly taking their values to be her own. But the only people who were duped by the canon were the right-wing elites who thought it uncritically represented their viewpoints and the left wing who agreed with them. Mary Smith interpreted what for us is "high literature" but for her was "popular" literature to say that even the daughter of a shoemaker was the equal, in intelligence and humanity, of any rich person.

40   Why did Mary Smith read canonical works as affirming her humanity and rights to equality in a hierarchical society? She identified *herself* with the

characters and viewpoints in these books. She projected herself into them. She didn't distance herself from the hero because he was a male and a king in a Shakespeare play, however much she might have wanted and certainly deserved female heroes. She saw herself as projected into that powerful monarch. Perhaps sometimes when she read Shakespeare, she was a king and other times a queen. Perhaps sometimes when she read Shakespeare, she was not a traditional monarch at all but a monarch shoemaker with the dignity and the human worth of a traditional monarch. Perhaps sometimes, she was all these and more. Remember, she was not just taking on the life of a virtual character in the book or play. She was also projecting herself into that character, creating something that both she and Shakespeare made, neither one of them alone.

Neither the right nor the left wing wrote the scripts for the plays in Mary Smith's mind, no matter how influenced she, like all of us, was by the political and cultural factors of her time. Shakespeare was deeply influenced by his own times, but he wrote original scripts nonetheless. So did Mary Smith. Mary Smith read books that today's students find boring, with the excitement that today's students find in video games, because, perhaps, she read them at least in part much like those students sometimes play video games, actively, critically, and projectively; that is, she projected herself into the text so that a king or queen became her "avatar" in the text.

In the end, Mary Smith and many more like her believed that canonical literature, far from representing the values of wealthy elites, undermined their values and showed them for the hypocrites they were. The message Mary Smith got from such literature was that she was at least their equal and in all likelihood their better.

Conservatives and liberals who argue over the canon tend to act as if people like Mary Smith will read such books and either want to emulate their "betters" (the right-wing perspective) or passively accept the inferiority ascribed to them by the elite (the left-wing view). The Mary Smiths of the world need do no such thing. These people already know that they are thinking, worthy beings. They sometimes see in canonical literature examples of who and what they could be, if others in society ceased to disdain them.

Do we think there is some definitive list of "Great Books"? By no means. For us, the canon is and was never a closed list. Any book is canonical if it lends itself to the powerful projective work in which Mary Smith engaged and leads people to desire not more hierarchy, but more opportunities for the display of human worth and the greater development of human capacities for all people. A work is canonical, for us, if it gives people, in Kenneth Burke's[7] phrase, new and better "equipment for living" in a harsh and unfair world.

In this sense, works like Ralph Ellison's *Invisible Man* and Gloria Naylor's *Mama Day* are canonical for us and many other people. There are a good many books written by women, nonwhite people, and poor people that never got on

45

the "official" canon as a list, due to the workings of racism and patriarchy, but are most certainly, in our terms, canonical.

Traditional canonical works, like those of Homer, Shakespeare, Milton, and Dryden, function today quite differently than they did in Mary Smith's day. Smith's society denied her any sort of schooling that gave her access to these books. In fact, her society felt it inappropriate for a shoemaker's daughter to be reading such books. She picked them up anyway with defiance, and saw in them resonances with herself that just further proved her own intelligence and worth.

Schools, by and large, have tamed the canon. They have made it into the stuff of tests, multiple-choice answers, and standardized responses. Everyone now, finally, has access to the canon at a time when schools have rendered it toothless. Young people today have access to far more texts, images, and diverse media of far more kinds than even the wealthy of Mary Smith's time. Milton's *Paradise Lost* played a very different role in the textual ecology of Smith's world than it does for a young person today. For her it was a precious book, hard won through a great deal of physical labor (to buy it, if she didn't borrow it) and mental labor (to read it seriously). For a young person today, the book is cheap to buy and the school tells them how to read it in the "right" way (or get a poor grade).

This is no plea for reading Milton, though we are sure many people still get a great deal out of traditional canonical literature when they read it of their own choosing, usually outside of school. There is plenty of evidence that people today still read and watch many things that serve some of the same purposes that canonical literature did for Mary Smith.[8]

Video games are a new form of art. They will not replace books; they will sit beside them, interact with them, and change them and their role in society in various ways, as, indeed, they are already doing with movies. (Today many movies are based on video games and many more are influenced by them.) We have no idea yet how people "read" video games, what meanings they make from them. Still less do we know how they will "read" them in the future. It won't do to start this investigation by assuming they are dupes of capitalist marketers, though of course, some of them very likely are. But there will always be Mary Smiths out there who use cultural products, whether "high" or "low," for good purposes.

Reading

1. How do Gee and Hayes define the advantages and disadvantages of "weak ties" (para. 10)?

2. How do they define the advantages and disadvantages of "strong ties" (para. 11)?

3. How do they argue that social media expand the possible identities of its users?

4. How do they believe social media "freedom" could be brought into the classroom?

Inquiring

1. Gee and Hayes argue that interactions between people were historically characterized by weak or strong ties. The advent of the Internet, however, has created a new category, the "strong weak tie." Most of their examples of such ties are drawn from multiplayer video games. As a class, spend time discussing the meaning of the term *strong weak tie* and then develop a list of other types of interactions that could be characterized as strong weak ties. Are they all Internet based? If so, how might this fact affect the strength of Gee and Hayes's argument? If not, how might the term be useful when trying to understand other aspects of society?

2. *WoW* and *Second Life* are spaces where individuals can assume new identities, creating avatars that may or may not represent who they are in real life. Indeed, Gee and Hayes cite the case of an adult male who claims, through his avatar, to be a teenage girl. The individual does not, however, invent a new way for teenage girls to respond, relying instead on advice from his wife on how to behave. Can we therefore say that individuals such as the man in question have truly taken on new identities? Or have they merely taken on a preexisting social role? What is the relationship between the values of online games and real-life values? Is it something new, or is it a repetition of existing beliefs? Draw on your own relevant experiences (if you have them) to help justify your argument.

3. By the end of the essay, Gee and Hayes draw a comparison between the freedom of video games, which allow you to assume a character in a game, and the possibilities of "canonical literature," which, citing Burke, they define as a text that provides "new and better 'equipment for living' " (para. 44). They argue, however, that school has erased this possibility of "freedom" or "better 'equipment for living' " by mandating a particular type of reading for canonical literature. Do you agree with this point? As classrooms begin to study online video games, do you think these games could suffer the same fate?

Composing

1. While considering the ways in which digital media have allowed individuals to expand their sense of identity—opening spaces to create and act on alternatives senses of self—Gee and Hayes also wonder if this possibility "will

eventually be tamed by institutions" (para. 35). Their example of such a "taming" is students' response to the canon. Write an essay in which you articulate what the authors see as the potential for digital media. How do they see it changing the very definition of our self-identity? Find an example of a situation in which there is a battle between the possibilities of digital media to open up identity (perhaps around issues of gender or sexuality) and institutions attempting to shut this possibility down. What kinds of forces are informing this debate? How do you respond to such forces?

2. Gee and Hayes write that weak ties were not as important when change happened slowly, but now, they say, "in fast-changing and unpredictable times, weak ties are crucial. They may be the only way we can get fast-changing information in order to cope and survive" (para. 14). Analyze this statement. Do you agree with the authors? Write an essay in which you support or dispute this claim by examining your own online network for its strong and weak ties.

3. At different points in the essay, Gee and Hayes claim that "digital media are, in part, a delivery system for language. However, they create conditions in which language has never before been used" (para. 18). Write an essay in which you articulate why the authors believe their claim to be true, citing their examples as support. Having done this work, address whether you find their arguments convincing. Do you believe the way language is used now is profoundly different than in the past? If so, what do you believe it means for how communities operate? Can we speak of "local communities" in a digitized world?

Connecting

Gee and Hayes claim that social media have expanded the types of relationships available to individuals. On the whole, they argue, this expansion has been a social good. It is now possible for individuals to have wide networks of support, for instance, even though they may not share the same physical space. Pirate radio, described by Matt Mason (p. 329), is also an example of a type of social media community. Write an essay in which you explore how Gee and Hayes might understand the phenomena of pirate radio and the ethics supporting it. How might the example of pirate radio expand or alter their understanding of the effect of "new kinds of people and relationships"?

MATT MASON

The Tao of Pirates

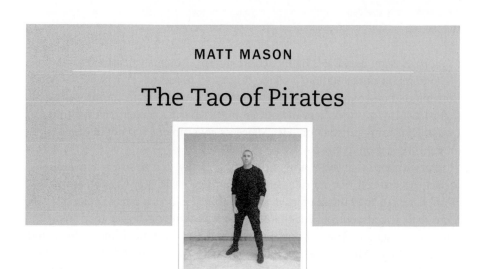

Photo by Jamie James Medina

Matt Mason is a writer and creative executive. He is the former chief content manager at BitTorrent and has worked in pirate radio and as a club DJ in London. He also helped found *RWD*, a magazine focused on music and culture. His work represents a study of how music, technology, culture, and politics intersect in the digital age. In particular, Mason is interested in how digital culture creates new possibilities for individual freedom and alternative communities. For that to happen, however, individuals have to adapt a "pirate" ethos, using tools and property that are not their own, to place endless pressure on mainstream business and culture to open spaces for innovation.

In the following excerpt from his book *The Pirate's Dilemma: How Youth Culture is Reinventing Capitalism*, Mason discusses the development of pirate radio and how it transformed (and was transformed by) mainstream culture.

■ ■ ■

Drift a few miles east from Harwich, a town on the southeastern coast of England, into the murky salt waters of the English Channel, and you'll see two hulking concrete towers jutting out of the briny deep. At the base of these columns, the wreckage of a sunken ship languishes on the seabed like some drowning Atlas supporting their weight. Eighty-five feet above, on the towers' twin summits, rests a gigantic rusting platform lashed by decades of wind and rain. It was built during World War II, complete with living quarters that housed hundreds of British troops and an arsenal of antiaircraft guns that picked off the Luftwaffe descending on London. This embattled structure was known as Fort Roughs before it was decommissioned in 1946 and left to rot on the high seas by the British government. Nobody predicted the coming of Major Paddy Roy Bates.

Former army man Bates happened upon Fort, Roughs when he was running Radio Essex, a pirate station broadcasting rock 'n' roll to the United Kingdom from another one of four identical sea forts in the area. But the problem was that this particular fort stood less than three miles off the mainland, still within the United Kingdom's jurisdiction. Her Majesty's government was not amused. They ordered the station to close.

Bates realized that these rules didn't apply farther out to sea, at Fort Roughs. In fact, he realized that *no* rules applied farther out to sea. On Christmas Eve 1966, Bates stormed the sea fort, evicted with brute force a pirate station already there, and seized control. But this time he was thinking bigger than just running a radio station. The self-appointed Prince Roy; his wife, Princess Joan; and their son, Prince Michael, declared their decaying bounty an independent sovereign nation in accordance with international law, and the Principality of Sealand was born.

Prince Roy set about transforming the crumbling fort into the world's smallest state, hoisting a flag and adding a helipad. The British did nothing to prevent the population of Sealand (at the time, three, and since then, rarely north of five) from minting their own coins and stamps, issuing passports, and handing out regal titles. In fact, you can become a lord or a lady of Sealand via eBay for £18.95 plus postage.

5   "Sealand was founded on the principle that any group of people dissatisfied with the oppressive laws and restrictions of existing nation-states may declare independence in any place not claimed to be under the jurisdiction of another sovereign entity," the Bates family proclaimed. And so began one of the most bizarre stories in British (or Sealandish) history.

Strange tales from Sealand regularly made headlines over the years. In 1968, shots were fired at a passing navy vessel (that may or may not have been trying to invade). Bates landed in court, but the English judge took the position that Sealand was indeed outside the United Kingdom's territorial waters. In 1977 it *was* invaded by a posse of German and Danish conspirators, but the Bates family regained control and fended them off in a war the size of a large bar fight. Sealand has long attracted legions of shady characters looking to set up casinos, brothels, and other such illicit enterprises safe from national laws. Sealand passports (many of them forgeries) have turned up in the possession of unsavory characters around the world; one was found with the body of Gianni Versace's assassin in Miami.

The micronation made international headlines in 2000 when a company called HavenCo struck a deal with the "royal family" to build a heavily armed offshore data sanctuary to house "sensitive" information anonymously, outside the reaches of governments, lawyers, ex-wives, and other prying eyes. Gambling sites, file-sharing networks—really, anyone trying to escape state surveillance or the tax man—were welcome. The only data HavenCo won't house is anything to do with child porn, spamming, or terrorism.

Sealand wasn't just the world's first man-made sovereign state, but also the first global capital of Internet anarchy. The second-craziest Bates family in the world turned a pirate station into a renegade, pirate nation.

Sealand may be the first and only sovereign territory founded by a pirate DJ, but it's far from being the only country built on pirate culture. In fact, pirates have been the architects of new societies for centuries: they have established new genres of film and music and created new types of media, often operating anonymously and always—initially, at least—outside the law. They overthrow governments, birth new industries, and win wars. Pirates create positive social and economic changes, and understanding piracy today is more important than ever, because now that we all can copy and broadcast whatever we want; we can all become pirates.

No sea fort required.   10

Copyrights and Wrongs

So who exactly is a pirate?

A. That guy who sells bootleg DVDs on the corner;

B. Some dude with a beard and a parrot who might mug you if you go boating;

C. A guardian of free speech who promotes efficiency, innovation, and creativity, and who has been doing so for centuries.

The correct answer is all of the above. A pirate is essentially anyone who   15
broadcasts or copies someone else's creative property without paying for it or obtaining permission.

First things first: some acts of piracy are quite simply theft. Every year industry loses billions to piracy. Companies suffer, artists and creators lose earnings, and people lose their jobs.

But although intellectual property rights seem right and piracy clearly seems wrong, the opposite also can be true. One man's copyright terrorist is another's creative freedom fighter: many forms of piracy transform society for the better.

Another pirate nation that began in a fashion similar to Sealand is the United States of America. During the nineteenth-century Industrial Revolution, the Founding Fathers pursued a policy of counterfeiting European inventions, ignoring global patents, and stealing intellectual property wholesale. "Lax enforcement of the intellectual property laws was the primary engine of the American economic miracle," writes Doron S. Ben-Atar in *Trade Secrets*. "The United States employed pirated know-how to industrialize." Americans were so well known as bootleggers, Europeans began referring to them with the Dutch word "Janke," then slang for pirate, which is today pronounced "Yankee."[1]

Trace the origins of recorded music, radio, film, cable TV, and almost any industry where intellectual property is involved, and you will invariably find pirates at its beginnings. When Edison invented the phonographic record, musicians branded him a pirate out to steal their work, until a system was created for paying them royalties. Edison, in turn, went on to invent filmmaking, and demanded a licensing fee from those making movies with his technology. This caused a band of filmmaking pirates, among them a man named William, to flee New York for the then still wild West, where they thrived, unlicensed, until Edison's patents expired. These pirates continue to operate there, albeit legally now, in the town they founded: Hollywood. William's last name? Fox.

20 When cable TV first came about, in 1948, the cable companies refused to pay the networks for broadcasting their content, and for more than thirty years operated like a primitive illegal file-sharing network, until Congress decided that they, too, should pay up, and a balance was struck between copyright holders and the pirate TV broadcasters.

If copyright laws had stopped these pirates in their tracks, today we might live in a world where America looked more like a giant Amish farm. We would have no recorded music, no cable TV, and a selection of films on a par with an economy airline seat. The pirates were on the wrong side of the law, but as Lawrence Lessig expounds upon in his book *Free Culture*, in hindsight it's clear their acts were important. By refusing to conform to regulations they deemed unfair, pirates have created industries from nothing. Because traditionally society has cut these pirates some slack and accepted that they were adding value to our lives, compromises were reached and enshrined in law, and as a result new industries blossomed.

Could it be that the guy bootlegging DVDs on the corner is still forcing the film industry to become more efficient, even today? HDTV billionaire Mark Cuban seems to think so, arguing that consumers *should* be able to view a film "how they want it, when they want it, where they want it." His company chose to simultaneously release Oscar-winning director Steven Soderbergh's film *Bubble* in cinemas, on DVD, and on HDTV on the same day in 2006. "Name any big-title movie that's come out in the last four years. It has been available in all formats on the day of release," Soderbergh told *Wired*. "It's called piracy. Peter Jackson's *Lord of the Rings, Ocean's Eleven*, and *Ocean's Twelve* — I saw them on Canal Street[2] on opening day. Simultaneous release is already here. We're just trying to gain control over it."

The history of piracy repeats itself. By short-circuiting conventional channels and red tape, pirates can deliver new materials, formats, and business models to audiences who want them. Canal Street moves faster than Wall Street. Piracy transforms the markets it operates in, changing the way distribution works and forcing companies to be more competitive and innovative. Pirates don't just defend the public domain from corporate control; they also force big business and government to deliver what we want, when we want it. . . .

Rock the Boat

The gap between pirate radio stations in the United States and Europe is almost as wide as the Atlantic itself. In the United States most pirates have traditionally been fun, quirky operations run by hobbyists, who come on air for a few hours at a time and close down after a few days or weeks.[3] But in Europe, pirate radio is big business. Stations operate around the clock, generating new strains of music and occasionally boatloads of money. Many pirates have even become brands in their own right, selling merchandise and setting up spin-off ventures.

This difference was a result of Europe's failure to catch on to the potential of commercial radio. And this failure forced Europeans to take to the seas, taking advantage of the fact that it was perfectly legal to broadcast from international waters.

The first legendary European stations weren't on ships at all. In 1929 Radio Normandie began broadcasting to northwestern France and southern England from an opulent villa in the French town of Fécamp. Radio Paris transmitted from an antenna hoisted atop the Eiffel Tower,[4] and in 1933, from a country so small the letters of its name won't fit inside it on most maps, came Radio Luxembourg. Radio Luxembourg boasted what was the world's single most powerful radio transmitter, which not only allowed it to legally blanket its own tiny homeland but also to reach out to the United Kingdom, France, Germany, and many other parts of Europe where commercial radio was contraband, and where pop music couldn't be heard on the radio. It was the largest commercial station in Europe by the 1950s, with millions of listeners. Some Europeans claim they learned to speak English just by listening to Radio Luxembourg, but the station's first language was rock 'n' roll, and soon enough the whole continent would be fluent.

The legal loophole highlighted by Radio Luxembourg was the gateway to a lucrative new radio market. Quickly others realized that if they were transmitting from outside of nation-states where commercial radio was illegal, they could still legally broadcast to European audiences and sell commercials. The pull of this new rock 'n' roll music and the potential revenue to be made from advertising were like buried treasure to entrepreneurs around the world, who quickly found their sea legs and began to take to the waters in droves.

Offshore radio exploded in the 1960s, with stations such as Radio Caroline (started by a young Irishman named Ronan O'Rahilly, who for a time also managed some band called the Rolling Stones), Radio Sutch (founded by British pop star/politician Screaming Lord Sutch, operating from another disused sea fort), Radio London (housed on a secondhand U.S. minesweeper and funded by a consortium of Texas businessmen), and at least thirty others patrolling the English Channel transmitting the latest hits to millions of listeners in London and beyond. The rock group the Who even recorded their 1967 album *The Who Sell Out* as if it were transmitted live from Radio London. But despite what the Who thought, the British government had decided that these particular kids weren't all right, and legislated heavily against the pirates the same year, making offshore broadcasting illegal and scuppering almost all of them.[5]

25

The BBC launched a pirate copy of Radio London, called Radio 1, whose mission, according to Bill Brewster and Frank Broughton in *Last Night a DJ Saved My Life*, was "to take the last breath of wind out of the pirates' sails." Some of the original pirates, including Caroline, continue to fight on, many now reincarnated on digital and satellite frequencies. For the most part, the English Channel was returned to the relative calm of ferries, fishing boats, and our friends on Sealand. But although the pirates had lost this particular naval battle, it turned out they'd already won the war.

Coming Up from the Streets

30   Rather than stopping the pirates, legislation forced them back onto land, where they hit the ground running. This community of pirate entrepreneurs and DJs had revolutionized radio and European society, helping to bring rock 'n' roll, the top-forty charts, and the very idea of pop music to the people. The British music industry recognized this as commercial radio took off in the 1970s, and rewarded many of them handsomely for their services. Former Radio London and Caroline DJs such as Jimmy Savile, John Peel, and Tony Blackburn were hired by BBC Radio 1, and went on to become household names in the United Kingdom. And as the first generation crossed over and went legit, a new underground was forming in cities across the Continent.

Instead of exposing themselves on the open seas, this new breed of pirates began to operate cloaked in the anonymity of urban sprawl. Switching over to the FM band, pirates in the 1980s and '90s serviced a new generation of radio listeners in London, Paris, and beyond, listeners more interested in sounds such as soul, hip-hop, house, garage, and techno drifting over from the United States. The powers that be can detect a pirate's homemade antenna, usually tacked to the top of a tower block, but the studio connected to this antenna by a less powerful (and undetectable) microwave signal, hidden in the concrete labyrinth of a city grid, is difficult to track down. Transmitters are found and confiscated, but studios are harder to find, and stations earning revenue from putting on raves and selling advertising[6] can afford to replace lost antennae, sometimes within hours. This game of cat and mouse continues to keep pirates operating across the planet today.

The estimated 150 pirate stations on the FM dial in the United Kingdom[7] act as musical petri dishes—they have spawned new genres and cultures for decades, and attract as much as 10 percent of London's radio audience. Acid house, hard-core, drum 'n' bass, U.K. garage, grime, and dubstep are just a handful of now worldwide underground movements that developed in this way. Pirate radio is an incubator where new music can mutate. Initially, the new strains of music it produces are seen as too risqué for the mainstream to touch, but once this music reaches a critical mass in popularity, anthems from the pirates start hitting the pop charts, pirate DJs become crossover celebrities, and the scenes created by these stations grow into cottage industries and worldwide exports. . . .

The Tao of Pirates

Pirates highlight areas where choice doesn't exist and demand that it does. And this mentality transcends media formats, technological changes, and business models. It is a powerful tool that, once understood, can be applied anywhere.

Successful pirates adapt quickly to social and technological changes, but this is true of all entrepreneurs. What pirates do differently is create new spaces where different ideas and methods run the show. Some create their own media formats, as DJ Fezzy did with AM radio. Others manipulate formats that already exist to create new choices, as Hollywood did when it created an alternative unlicensed film industry, or as the pirates today bootlegging Hollywood are doing, giving you the option of watching new movies at home (albeit filmed secondhand on a camera phone).

Thinking like a bootlegger can take you in new directions. If you have an idea, but the infrastructure to get it out there does not exist, you may have an opportunity to create your own. Finding a space to get your idea across is as important as having the idea itself. If the idea is good, growing an audience won't be difficult. It's this audience that gives pirates their power.

Lao-Tzu, the founder of Taoism, famously said that when leaders lead well, people feel that they did it themselves and that it happened naturally. Pirates are experts at leading communities in this way, bringing people products, services, and sounds they didn't know they couldn't live without. Once these new ideas are broadcast, they unavoidably create a Pirate's Dilemma for others in that market. Should they fight these pirates, or accept that there is some value in what they are doing, and compete with them?

On one side, regulators may argue that pirate stations are illegal and damaging to holders of radio licenses. But radio listeners may ask "Why isn't there a legal station playing music like this when so many people clearly want to hear it?" Artists may protest that "the pirates play and support my records, when the mainstream stations and stores won't, and as a result I actually sell more."

The actions of pirates raise questions, and when they do something society finds useful, it creates productive discussions that often lead to changes in the law, which result in social and economic progress. If democracy is about creating processes that allow people to empower themselves, then pirates are clearly the perfect catalysts for such processes.

Pirate stations in London create this momentum by empowering the DJs who play the music. These DJs are so passionate about the music they play, most pay a monthly subscription fee to the station owner just to play on the radio at

35

all, not to mention risking their liberty for the privilege of creating shows and content that give them and the station credibility. When they strike a chord with their audience, the community spirit of the listeners is also harnessed. This community intimidated the British government so much that they didn't start trying to close down the offshore stations until they had created the state-sponsored pirate Radio 1 to appease the millions of music fans they knew they would anger. . . . The Internet community that believes file-sharing networks are vitally important to culture and innovation have never stopped opening new p2p networks as fast as the authorities try to close them down. A good idea is powerful only if people are willing to get behind it. By giving a community a new space that was not previously available to them, you can empower them, and they in turn will propel your idea forward. . . .

The Three Habits of Highly Effective Pirates

40   From the birth of America to the birth of the Internet, it is often left to pirates to chart the winds of change and plot better courses for the future. When pirates start to appear in a market, it's usually an indication that it isn't working properly. When governments and markets recognize the legitimacy of what these pirates are doing, their activities are enshrined in new laws, creating a new order that serves society better.

We live in a new world where things we used to pay for, such as music, movies, and newspapers, are now available for free. But things that used to reproduce for free, such as seeds and pigs, have to be paid for. This is a world where we all need to understand the finer points of the pirate mentality:

1. **Look Outside of the Market**
   Entrepreneurs look for gaps in the market. Pirates look for gaps *outside of* the market. There was no market for Hollywood films before William Fox and friends. There was no market for commercial radio in Europe before pirate DJs. Pirates have proved that just because the market won't do something, it doesn't mean it's a bad idea.

2. **Create a Vehicle**
   Once pirates find a space the market has ignored, they park a new vehicle in it and begin transmitting. Sometimes this new vehicle becomes more important, or as Marshall McLuhan put it, the medium becomes the message. The platform that pirate DJs created was more important than rock 'n' roll. The idea of the "blog" had a much greater impact than the picture of Cary Grant dropping acid on Justin's Home Page.

3. **Harness Your Audience**
   When pirates do something valuable in society, citizens support them, discussion starts, and laws change. It is the supporters that pirates attract

that enable them and their ideas to go legit. Kiss FM got a license thanks to its listeners. Roh Moohyun became president thanks to citizens using the pirate mentality on his behalf. Entire nation-states are supporting pill pirates to save lives.

Power to the Pirates

Piracy has gone on throughout history, and we should encourage it. It's how inefficient systems are replaced.

Wherever you tune in, somewhere you will find a pirate pushing back against authority, decentralizing monopolies, and promoting the rule of the people: the very nature of democracy itself. The pirate mentality is a way to mobilize communities, drive innovation, and create social change. By thinking like pirates, people grow niche audiences to a critical mass and change the mainstream from the bottom up. They've toppled more inefficient corporate pyramids than they've invented styles of music, and as long as there are people or choices not being represented in the marketplace, there will always be pirates pushing the envelope. Margaret Mead famously said, "Never doubt that a small group of thoughtful, committed citizens can change the world. Indeed, it's the only thing that ever has." Pirates are some of the most committed citizens we've got.

Many pirates aren't just copying the work of others. Some give this work new meaning by broadcasting it somewhere else. But as we shall now see, there are pirates reinventing the work of others entirely, using a process that gives them a unique perspective, a powerful tool we can all use to create change.

Reading

1. How does Mason define the term *pirate*?
2. How does he define the "Pirate's Dilemma" (para. 36)?
3. How does he define the habits of "highly effective pirates" (paras. 40 and 41)?
4. How does he argue for the social value of pirates?

Inquiring

1. Mason imagines the pirate as an interloper in existing networks, actively opening up those networks' resources for the larger public. At the same time, he positions the pirate as existing in a hacker network as well. How would you describe the ethics that inform a pirate's behavior in both networks? Does there seem to be a moral code that guides the pirate's actions? Can we even speak of a moral pirate?
2. Throughout his essay, Mason provides many examples of when pirates used technologies invented by others for their own purposes. His examples range from individuals developing pirate radio to countries developing their wealth

through the ideas of others. He claims, however, that "some acts of piracy are quite simply theft" (para. 16). As a class, discuss how Mason draws this distinction between piracy and theft. Is the difference as simple as he implies? Why or why not?

3. Prior to pirate radio, music was produced, circulated, and valued according to an existing network of values—values in which everyone participated. Piracy changed these behaviors. It could be argued that a piece of writing, like a scholarly argument or student paper, also exists within networks—that is, within an existing world where there are also accepted rules of behavior. What might it mean to adopt a pirate ethos as a writer? How would it change our standard conceptions of quotation and citation? Could one author publish portions of Stephen King's or Maya Angelou's work under his or her own name? Would plagiarism exist in a world of "pirate writing"? How might writers benefit from living within the borders of a nation like Sealand?

Composing

1. In discussing *The Tao of Pirates*, Mason quotes Lao-Tzu, saying that "when leaders lead well, people feel that they did it themselves and that it happened naturally" (para. 36). Mason goes on to argue that pirates are skilled in leading communities in just such a way, allowing people to resee how digital technology might reshape our daily lives. Write an essay in which you discuss whether the ethics of pirates, designed to open up digital networks, are in fact effective for communities, either local or national. What might it mean to how communities establish productive networks for those involved?

2. Mason argues that pirates are ultimately good for capitalism and good for our society. He believes that legal structures, such as copyright, allow companies not to have to innovate to stay in business; thus, our culture stays static, and the larger culture is unable to benefit from the possible uses of emergent technology. Pirates "liberate" technology, forcing companies to respond and ultimately incorporate the results of such piracy into their operations. Write an essay in which you examine Mason's arguments about the usefulness of pirates. Consider what type of change pirates ultimately produce within a specific context, such as music. What is the social good that results, and who benefits? What existing digital or on-ground community networks does pirates' work ultimately support or disrupt? Who do you see as ultimately benefiting from their actions?

3. Almost without exception, all Mason's pirates are men. He includes little discussion of how other gender identities have attempted to hack into existing social media technologies to create alternative uses for these tools and thus provide resources to networks that might want to use them to gain a larger public voice. Write a paper in which you both articulate Mason's concept of the

pirate—the goals and possible effects of such efforts—and then discuss how adding in an alternative gender identity might change this concept. Research one such effort, such as Double Union or Mz. Baltazar's Laboratory. Use your discovered "nonmale gender" pirate project as a way to make concrete your theoretical sense of what might change. Be clear about where this project both supports and expands Mason's argument (in other words, avoid simply turning this new project into a counterexample).

Connecting

Mason argues that piracy has a productive purpose in that it shakes up existing institutions, forcing them to be more nimble, more responsive, and more open. One of the most significant acts of "piracy" since the 1990s has been the work of WikiLeaks (p. 340). Write an essay in which you discuss whether Mason would endorse the work of WikiLeaks. Then discuss whether you find such acts of piracy justifiable. Put another way, when (if ever) are such acts of piracy against the government justifiable?

About WikiLeaks

WikiLeaks is a not-for-profit media organization founded by Julian Assange. The goal of WikiLeaks is to provide a resource to individuals who wish to leak classified business or government documents for use by journalists. To make this possible, WikiLeaks has created a drop box that can collect materials while ensuring anonymity through cutting-edge encryption technology. Since its inception in 2006, WikiLeaks has published documents related to topics such as Guantanamo Bay, the Iraq war, and the Copenhagen climate change agreement. It has received the 2008 Economist New Media Award, the 2009 Amnesty International Human Rights Reporting Award (New Media), and numerous other international awards. WikiLeaks has also been nominated for the Nobel Peace Prize in six consecutive years.

The following selection is an excerpt of the WikiLeaks mission statement and "About" section of its Web site dated from May 7, 2011. To view the full WikiLeaks Web site, go to wikileaks.org.

■ ■ ■

What Is WikiLeaks?

WikiLeaks is a not-for-profit media organisation. Our goal is to bring important news and information to the public. We provide an innovative, secure and anonymous way for sources to leak information to our journalists (our electronic drop box). One of our most important activities is to publish original source material alongside our news stories so readers and historians alike can see evidence of the truth. We are a young organisation that has grown very quickly, relying on a network of dedicated volunteers around the globe. Since 2007, when the organisation was officially launched, WikiLeaks has worked to report on and publish important information. We also develop and adapt technologies to support these activities.

WikiLeaks has sustained and triumphed against legal and political attacks designed to silence our publishing organisation, our journalists and our anonymous sources. The broader principles on which our work is based are the defence of freedom of speech and media publishing, the improvement of our common historical record and the support of the rights of all people to create new history. We derive these principles from the Universal Declaration of Human Rights. In particular, Article 19 inspires the work of our journalists and other volunteers. It states that everyone has the right to freedom of opinion and expression; this right includes freedom to hold opinions without interference and to seek, receive and impart information and ideas through any media and regardless of frontiers. We agree, and we seek to uphold this and the other Articles of the Declaration.

How WikiLeaks Works

WikiLeaks has combined high-end security technologies with journalism and ethical principles. Like other media outlets conducting investigative journalism, we accept (but do not solicit) anonymous sources of information. Unlike other outlets, we provide a high security anonymous drop box fortified by cutting-edge cryptographic information technologies. This provides maximum protection to our sources. We are fearless in our efforts to get the unvarnished truth out to the public. When information comes in, our journalists analyse the material, verify it and write a news piece about it describing its significance to society. We then publish both the news story and the original material in order to enable readers to analyse the story in the context of the original source material themselves. Our news stories are in the comfortable presentation style of Wikipedia, although the two organisations are not otherwise related. Unlike Wikipedia, random readers can not edit our source documents.

As the media organisation has grown and developed, WikiLeaks been developing and improving a harm minimisation procedure. We do not censor our news, but from time to time we may remove or significantly delay the publication of some identifying details from original documents to protect life and limb of innocent people.

We accept leaked material in person and via postal drops as alternative methods, although we recommend the anonymous electronic drop box as the preferred method of submitting any material. We do not ask for material, but we make sure that if material is going to be submitted it is done securely and that the source is well protected. Because we receive so much information, and we have limited resources, it may take time to review a source's submission.

We also have a network of talented lawyers around the globe who are personally committed to the principles that WikiLeaks is based on, and who defend our media organisation.

Why the Media (and Particularly WikiLeaks) Is Important

Publishing improves transparency, and this transparency creates a better society for all people. Better scrutiny leads to reduced corruption and stronger democracies in all society's institutions, including government, corporations and other organisations. A healthy, vibrant and inquisitive journalistic media plays a vital role in achieving these goals. We are part of that media.

Scrutiny requires information. Historically, information has been costly in terms of human life, human rights and economics. As a result of technical advances particularly the internet and cryptography—the risks of conveying important information can be lowered. In its landmark ruling on the Pentagon Papers, the US Supreme Court ruled that "only a free and unrestrained press can effectively expose deception in government." We agree.

We believe that it is not only the people of one country that keep their own government honest, but also the people of other countries who are watching that government through the media.

10   In the years leading up to the founding of WikiLeaks, we observed the world's publishing media becoming less independent and far less willing to ask the hard questions of government, corporations and other institutions. We believed this needed to change.

WikiLeaks has provided a new model of journalism. Because we are not motivated by making a profit, we work cooperatively with other publishing and media organisations around the globe, instead of following the traditional model of competing with other media. We don't hoard our information; we make the original documents available with our news stories. Readers can verify the truth of what we have reported themselves. Like a wire service, WikiLeaks reports stories that are often picked up by other media outlets. We encourage this. We believe the world's media should work together as much as possible to bring stories to a broad international readership.

How WikiLeaks Verifies Its News Stories

We assess all news stories and test their veracity. We send a submitted document through a very detailed examination a procedure. Is it real? What elements prove it is real? Who would have the motive to fake such a document and why? We use traditional investigative journalism techniques as well as more modern technology-based methods. Typically we will do a forensic analysis of the document, determine the cost of forgery, means, motive, opportunity, the claims of the apparent authoring organisation, and answer a set of other detailed questions about the document. We may also seek external verification of the document

For example, for our release of the Collateral Murder video, we sent a team of journalists to Iraq to interview the victims and observers of the helicopter attack. The team obtained copies of hospital records, death certificates, eyewitness statements and other corroborating evidence supporting the truth of the story. Our verification process does not mean we will never make a mistake, but so far our method has meant that WikiLeaks has correctly identified the veracity of every document it has published.

Publishing the original source material behind each of our stories is the way in which we show the public that our story is authentic. Readers don't have to take our word for it; they can see for themselves. In this way, we also support the work of other journalism organisations, for they can view and use the original documents freely as well. Other journalists may well see an angle or detail in the document that we were not aware of in the first instance. By making the documents freely available, we hope to expand analysis and comment by all the media. Most of all, we want readers know the truth so they can make up their own minds.

The People Behind WikiLeaks

WikiLeaks is a project of the Sunshine Press. It's probably pretty clear by now that WikiLeaks is not a front for any intelligence agency or government despite a rumour to that effect. This rumour was started early in WikiLeaks' existence, possibly by the intelligence agencies themselves. WikiLeaks is an independent global group of people with a longstanding dedication to the idea of a free press and the improved transparency in society that comes from this. The group includes accredited journalists, software programmers, network engineers, mathematicians and others.

To determine the truth of our statements on this, simply look at the evidence. By definition, intelligence agencies want to hoard information. By contrast, WikiLeaks has shown that it wants to do just the opposite. Our track record shows we go to great lengths to bring the truth to the world without fear or favour.

The great American president Thomas Jefferson once observed that the price of freedom is eternal vigilance. We believe the journalistic media plays a key role in this vigilance.

Anonymity for Sources

As far as we can ascertain, WikiLeaks has never revealed any of its sources. We can not provide details about the security of our media organisation or its anonymous drop box for sources because to do so would help those who would like to compromise the security of our organisation and its sources. What we can say is that we operate a number of servers across multiple international jurisdictions and we do not keep logs. Hence these logs can not be seized. Anonymization occurs early in the WikiLeaks network, long before information passes to our web servers. Without specialized global internet traffic analysis, multiple parts of our organisation must conspire with each other to strip submitters of their anonymity.

However, we also provide instructions on how to submit material to us, via net cafes, wireless hot spots and even the post so that even if WikiLeaks is infiltrated by an external agency, sources can still not be traced. Because sources who are of substantial political or intelligence interest may have their computers bugged or their homes fitted with hidden video cameras, we suggest that if sources are going to send WikiLeaks something very sensitive, they do so away from the home and work.

A number of governments block access to any address with WikiLeaks in the name. There are ways around this. WikiLeaks has many cover domains, such as https://destiny.mooo.com, that don't have the organisation in the name. It is possible to write to us or ask around for other cover domain addresses. Please make sure the cryptographic certificate says wikileaks.org.

Banking Blockade

20   WikiLeaks has published the biggest leaks in journalistic history. This has triggered aggressive retaliation from powerful groups. Since 7th December 2010 an arbitrary and unlawful financial blockade has been imposed by Bank of America, VISA, MasterCard, PayPal and Western Union. The attack has destroyed 95% of our revenue. The blockade came into force within ten days of the launch of Cablegate as part of a concerted US-based, political attack that included vitriol by senior right-wing politicians, including assassination calls against WikiLeaks staff. The blockade is outside of any accountable, public process. It is without democratic oversight or transparency. The US government itself found that there were no lawful grounds to add WikiLeaks to a US financial blockade. But the blockade of WikiLeaks by politicized US finance companies continues regardless.

As a result, WikiLeaks has been running on cash reserves for the past eleven months. The blockade has cost the organization tens of millions of pounds in lost donations at a time of unprecedented operational costs resulting from publishing alliances in over 50 countries, and their inevitable counter-attacks. Our scarce resources now must focus on fighting the unlawful banking blockade. If this financial attack stands unchallenged, a dangerous, oppressive and undemocratic precedent will have been set, the implications of which go far beyond WikiLeaks and its work. Any organization that falls foul of powerful finance companies or their political allies can expect similar extrajudicial action. Greenpeace, Amnesty International, and other international NGOs that work to expose the wrongdoing of powerful players risk the same fate as WikiLeaks. If publishing the truth about war is enough to warrant such aggressive action by

Washington insiders, all newspapers that have published WikiLeaks' materials are on the verge of having their readers and advertisers blocked from paying for their subscriptions.

The UN High Commissioner for Human Rights has openly criticized the financial blockade against WikiLeaks, as have the UN Special Rapporteur on the Promotion and Protection the Right to Freedom of Opinion and Expression and the Inter-American Commission on Human Rights Special Rapporteur for Freedom of Expression. The blockade erects a wall between us and our supporters, preventing them from affiliating with and defending the cause of their choice. It violates the competition laws and trade practice legislation of numerous states. It arbitrarily singles out an organization that has not committed any illegal act in any country and cuts it off from its financial lifeline in every country. In Australia, a formal, US triggered investigation into our operations found that WikiLeaks and its founder Julian Assange have no case to answer. In the US, our publishing is protected by the First Amendment, as has been repeatedly demonstrated by a wide variety of respected legal experts on the US Constitution. In January 2011 the US Secretary of the Treasury, Timothy C. Geithner, announced that there were no grounds to blacklist WikiLeaks. There are no judgements, or even charges, against WikiLeaks or its staff anywhere in the world.

The most powerful players in the banking industry have shown themselves to be a politicized arm of Washington. This collusion has occurred outside of any judicial or administrative process. The reach of these companies is global and violates the most basic principles of sovereignty. In Europe, VISA and MasterCard together control 97% of the card payment market. Alternatives have been aggressively opposed by VISA and US embassies. The European Central Bank announced plans in 2008 to introduce a European card system. A similar 2010 proposal in Russia together with a bill banning individualized VISA transaction records from going to the US were met with intervention by the US Embassy in Moscow. VISA calls itself the world's largest currency, but every transaction is controlled by the VISA corporation and the groups that influence it. VISA is a national security problem and a threat to state sovereignty. No state, individual or organization has full economic autonomy or privacy if they rely on VISA. It is able to provide significant intelligence on not only individual behaviour and economic relationships but on large sections of the entire microeconomy and the movement of labour.

The Bank of America is one of the principal promoters of the WikiLeaks financial blockade; it is also the creator of VISA, which until 1976 was called the "Bank Americard". In February this year, it was revealed in detail that the Bank of America had commissioned, through Washington lawyers Hunton & Williams, a consortium of three US intelligence contractors, including HBGary, to propose a systematic US $2 million/month multi-pronged attack to hack and smear WikiLeaks. HBGary was referred to the bank's lawyers by contacts within the US Department of Justice. The correspondence and proposals, which include plans to target journalists and lawyers supporting WikiLeaks, are now public. An extract from the proposal to sabotage WikiLeaks can be found on page 16 of plan 6:

- **Feed the fuel between the feuding groups.** Disinformation. Create messages around actions of sabotage or discredit the opposing organizations. Submit fake documents and then call out the error.

- **Create concern over the security of the infrastructure.** Create exposure stories. If the process is believed not to be secure they are done.

- **Cyber attacks against the infrastructure to get data on document submitters.** This would kill the project. Since the servers are now in Sweden and France putting a team together to get access is more straightforward.

- **Media campaign to push the radical and reckless nature of WikiLeaks activities.** Sustain pressure. Does nothing for the fanatics, but creates concern and doubt among moderates.

25   In order to ensure our future survival, WikiLeaks is now forced to temporarily suspend its publishing operations and aggressively fundraise in order to fight back against this blockade and its proponents. We have commenced pre-litigation action against the blockade in Iceland, Denmark, the UK, Brussels, the United States and Australia. We have lodged an anti-trust complaint at the European Commission and expect a decision by mid-November as to whether the European Competition Authority will open a full investigation into the wrongdoing of VISA and MasterCard.

Reading

1. How does WikiLeaks define its purpose?
2. How does WikiLeaks verify the validity of the documents it posts?
3. How does WikiLeaks invoke other international organizations or declarations to justify its purpose?
4. How does WikiLeaks claim to be different from other intelligence organizations?

Inquiring

1. To say that WikiLeaks is a controversial network is to state the obvious. Much of the controversy comes from its mission statement. Discuss whether you agree with the statement's analysis of current political culture and its stated need to intervene in that culture. Even if you find yourself agreeing with

WikiLeaks' analysis of current political culture, do you support its strategy of releasing documents?

2. WikiLeaks is dedicated to political transparency. How does the organization's mission statement represent the foundation's identity? The partnerships that allow it to continue? Is there information that you believe should be provided but is missing? If so, why might that be the case? In other words, does WikiLeaks meet its own standard of openness?

3. WikiLeaks is a controversial network. As a class, discuss what it might mean to be a public supporter of its work. What, for instance, would it mean to wear clothing with the WikiLeaks insignia on campus? In your community? What type of risks might you face? Or is the notion of being at risk for supporting such a political project incorrect? Which networks do you think would support a political stance in support of WikiLeaks? Which networks might challenge it?

Composing

1. One stated goal of WikiLeaks is to provide the information that will allow the public to fully understand the actions of their governments. The belief is that only by having such information can the public decide whether to support (or attempt to change) existing policies. The question is whether WikiLeaks' efforts have actually produced such results. Spend time exploring the full WikiLeaks Web page, finding documents that speak to a specific political event or action taken by the U.S. government. Research how political figures and mainstream media were discussing that event at that time. Consider whether the WikiLeaks documents provide an important insight into these government actions. Having done this work, attempt to assess the importance of political networks such as WikiLeaks. What do you see as their role in fostering openness in political debates?

2. WikiLeaks makes a point of stating that major banks and credit card companies have decided not to process any payments to its site, effectively cutting off the ability of most individuals to support the project. This "banking blockade" can be understood as an attempt to remove WikiLeaks from commerce networks and thereby isolate the organization. Research why this blockade was put in place. Do you believe financial institutions and governments are justified in attempting to isolate WikiLeaks from such networks? What should be the criteria for implementing such barriers? Are there other organizations you also believe should face such sanctions? If so, which ones, and why?

3. Networks exist online and on the ground. In both cases, it is the personal and collective supports provided by the network's participants that ensure its continued existence. Rhetoric is a key element in convincing people of the value of such supports. Rhetoric provides the conceptual landscape and articulates the inherent values of the network. Examine the rhetoric of the

WikiLeaks document featured in this chapter. Does the language used describe its mission, its actions, and its sense of its place in the world? How would you characterize the tone? What it means to join WikiLeaks' efforts? If you were a rhetoric consultant for WikiLeaks, what advice might you give the organization about how to expand its network of support? Could it gain increased membership? Or is the project of WikiLeaks so objectionable to so many that no rhetorical polishing could broaden its support?

Connecting

WikiLeaks challenges the belief that the government should be able to withhold information from its citizens — arguing there are almost no instances where this should be the case. Gee and Hayes (p. 318) argue that social media allows for a freedom of identity that is often diminished by the role students are expected to take as readers, as students in the classroom, where freedom is replaced with a sense of responsibility to the book being read. Write an essay in which you discuss Gee and Hayes's sense of freedom and responsibility in relationship to WikiLeaks' sense of these terms. Does the ability to share information, allowing anyone to play the role of government insider, need to be tempered by a responsibility to institutional needs and government secrecy?

Projects for Chapter 9

The following are group and class projects. You should talk to your instructor about which projects you will complete in your course.

PROJECT 19 A University WikiLeaks

A central motif of this unit has been the ability of social media to disrupt existing networks of communication, whether political communication, such as WikiLeaks, or entertainment communication, such as music. As a class, analyze a particular channel of communication in which, collectively, there is a sense that inadequate or incorrect information is being distributed. Perhaps it is the student government's decision-making processes or the university food service's policies on purchasing local food. Then develop a Web site in which individuals can provide documentation that makes overt how these decisions are made. Be sure to develop a rationale for the page and explain its purpose, necessity, and operating practices. Think through the ways information might be submitted anonymously and how you will explain the need for such anonymity for these individuals.

Having done this work, develop a strategic plan for how you might gain such information, who might be your contacts, and what type of materials your contacts might provide. Create a plan for reaching out to one such individual and prepare a list of the materials needed to make this contact happen. Role-play the initial meeting in class. Based on this practice session, discuss how the strategy might have to change to be successful.

As a class, answer the following questions: Would you enact this university-based WikiLeaks? Why or why not? What are the risks involved? Why are you willing or not willing to accept such risks? How does this project speak to the power of existing networks?

PROJECT 20 A Gaming Classroom

Social media, it can be argued, dramatically expand an individual's ability to create an open-ended identity, one in which the personal and communal connections enable actions and conversations that previously were unimaginable. At the same time, according to Gee and Hayes, classrooms are shutting down the way students can invent their identity and enact a full sense of self. It is the difference between fully enacting yourself as an avatar in a game and being assigned a preexisting role in a static environment.

It is tempting to imagine a classroom infused with avatar-type practices. It is equally unclear, however, what this new classroom might actually look like. Break into small groups of about four people per group. Choose one class that does not use any social media in which one group member is currently enrolled. As a group, redesign one assignment for that class that fully integrates social media, networks, and gaming into its design. How does this design change the imagined identity of the student? How does it change what it means to do work in that field?

Have each group share its revised classroom assignment. When taken collectively, what type of work is allowed in these classrooms? Do you believe it is the type of work that should mark a university education?

PROJECT 21 Media Networks

Most college campuses have a central newspaper, usually supported by a combination of student fees, administrative support, and advertising. Existing more on the margins, however, are usually publications that typically try to alter or expand the types of issues that frame student debate and conversations. They range from issue-based to identity-based publications. Lacking the resources of larger central publications, these smaller publications often have a difficult time gaining mainstream influence.

For this project, make a list of these smaller publications at your own university. Break into groups, creating one group for each publication. Use the research methods discussed in this chapter about mapping networks to research the connections and links in which your assigned publication exists. Compare this network to the goals of the publication's mission statement (often on the inside front page of a publication or denoted as such on its Web page). Develop a list of additional individuals or organizations that should be associated with the publication. What strategies might make these connections possible? What changes might the publication have to make to secure these connections?

Have each group share its analysis and plans. Use these plans to discuss the difficulties of expanding existing networks to gain more resources. Note: Your class might also extend this work by approaching each publication, interviewing staff on their needs in terms of expanding their networks, and then developing a plan. Speak with your instructor about this possibility.

PROJECT 22 Networking Action

A consistent theme in this chapter's readings has been the multiple networks in which we all exist. Each nodule within each network supports or works against how we hope to move through society. Understanding the scope of our networks, then, can enable us to see both what resources are available to us and what resources we need to acquire. For this project, you and your community partner will conduct a three-hour meeting that will use this framework to do a "power" analysis that will analyze the organization's ability to achieve one particular project. Having done this work, you and your community partner will then guide the organization through the process of linking those resources to the project.

To do this work, you should undertake the following tasks:

A. Meet with the leadership team of your community organization and decide which project (of its many efforts, no doubt) is a top priority and could benefit from a power analysis.

B. Schedule a meeting in which as many individuals involved in the project can attend as possible. Invite immediate actors in the project as well as any other individuals who have been involved or whom you and your community partner would like to have involved. Schedule at least two hours for this meeting.

C. Begin the meeting with a Ganz "Story of Self" workshop (see p. 178). The primary question is, "What brought you to work on this project?"

D. Provide an overview of the proposed project, clearly stating its importance and relevance to the neighborhood.

E. After the Ganz workshop, provide each individual with a blank sheet of paper and several markers of different colors. Ask each person to create a "map" of his or her resources for this project on one side of the piece of paper. Highlight that time, labor, friends, connections, and so forth all count as resources. Give them 5 to 10 minutes to complete this step.

F. Now ask them to list all the resources that are needed but they can't bring to the project on the opposite side of the paper.

G. Lead a discussion in which you begin by mapping out which resources are most important to the project and who in the group can provide them. You might draw this map as a series of concentric circles.

H. Ask each person to list the resources that are needed but they do not have. See which of these resources have already been provided. Brainstorm how these resources might be acquired.

I. Translate your "concentric circle of resources" into a timeline that details which resources are needed at different points; then ask those who possess these resources to volunteer (ask them exactly how much they can volunteer). This timeline should be done on large pieces of paper and be taped to the wall.

J. Once the plan is complete, ask those who volunteered to sign the plan, pledging their work and support.

K. End the meeting by setting up the next meeting and possibly asking the group to retell its "Story of Self," but this time revising it to express the new collective vision.

PROJECT 23 Literate Lives

Much of the work in this chapter has involved thinking about how literacy is the result of (and exists within) larger institutional networks. For this project, you will develop a publication that provides models of how community members can link with existing educational resources to improve their school and vocational literacies. You will work with your community partner to develop a list of the type of literacies that will most benefit the community, such as computer literacy, school literacy, and health literacy. Once you have completed this list, develop a list of individuals representative of the entire community who are seen as having each literacy.

Then, as a class, develop a set of interview questions that will enable the people to talk about how they developed this literacy. What personal, familial, communal, and organizational networks did they access? How did they learn to access these networks? Transcribe and edit their interviews collaboratively with each participant and as a class. Once the community member has approved the edited copy, research information on all the communal or organizational networks cited in the interviews. Find their mission statements, addresses, hours, and other relevant information about the group. Make sure to have all the necessary information so that someone else could easily access those services.

Working with your community partner, develop a small publication that can be circulated throughout the community to provide this information to residents. As a related project, create an online version of this publication that provides direct links to the organizations listed.

For strategies on interviewing, see pages 213–15; for publication permission, see pages 240–41; for publication design, see pages 242–43; and for print publication considerations, see pages 244–46.

PROJECT 24 Pirate Radio

As Mason argued in this chapter (p. 329), pirate radio was a response to existing radio's failure to provide a broad enough range of musical choices, whether these choices were based on a lack of emergent musical trends being featured or the personal tastes of an individual. Existing media, it seemed, were not up to the job. Piracy was needed.

Perhaps your community partner feels a similar lack of attention to its interests or a failure to recognize emergent populations or needs within a community. The question to decide with your partner is what type of social or digital media will best broadcast the organization's message. What resources does it have or need to ensure that whatever is created will be sustained and not be, as is often the case, a one-shot intervention in mainstream local media?

To this end, do the following:

1. Meet with your community partner to decide which issue facing the community is both the most pressing and the most underreported by local mainstream media.

2. Create a YouTube channel dedicated to this issue that features materials from the community perspective.

3. Create a series of prompts that ask residents to respond to this issue. Create enough prompts and make their subject matter broad enough so that they can be used for other projects. Ultimately, the community organization will have to take over this work.

4. Work with your community partner to develop a list of locations where residents congregate. Think of places that attract large numbers of people who will probably have time to respond, such as medical and dental offices, libraries, auto repair shops, and restaurants. You might also choose locations where individuals meet weekly, such as religious institutions or sporting events. Ask if these places will allow you to set up a video camera there once every four weeks and invite individuals to respond to the prompts. Create a schedule of when each location will be visited, which student will work the camera, and which student might help individuals respond to the prompts.

5. For the initial visits, students and community members should go to the location together and encourage individuals to respond to the prompt. (Be sure to get each individual's permission to post his or her material on YouTube.)

6. Working with your community partner, decide when these prompt responses will be posted. In making this decision, take into account the labor needed to record, edit, and post the videos. You also need to be sure that someone in the organization can handle the technical aspects and edit the videos, making sure that the prompt question is featured, either through print or audio means. As an example, you might decide to post the videos on Sunday mornings and ask aligned religious institutions to announce each installment.

7. As a class, develop a letter to send to local network television stations, local and campus radio stations, and local newspapers announcing the creation of this YouTube channel. Also create materials to advertise the channel in the community, highlighting how individuals can submit their own videos or take part in a prearranged session. Because some of the locations used

earlier (e.g., medical offices) will not want to open their facilities to the general public, you might need to find public venues such as libraries and community halls for the prearranged sessions.

8. If possible, assist with the YouTube channel for one month, including taping, editing, and advertising the pirate channel to mainstream media and community members.

9. Before the end of the term, work with the community partner to assess what is working well, what needs improvement, and what tasks need to be completed over the next three months.

For strategies on prompts, see pages 199–202; for publication permission (regarding the YouTube site), see pages 240–41; for publication design, see pages 242–43; for print publication considerations, see pages 244–46; and for strategies on reaching out to local businesses for support and space to interview residents, see pages 239–40.

Writing Identity: Moving in and across Boundaries

As this book has made clear, identity plays a crucial role in shaping how we move through the world—as individuals, as members of communities, and as writers. As a jumping-off point for the readings in this chapter, which will ask you to explore your own ideas about identity, below is a poem written by a student about the many facets of her identity and how she is perceived—and sometimes mis-perceived—by others.

Perhaps you have seen her
Rushed and flustered
Belittled and beaten down
Forcing smiles
With strained politeness
Biting her tongue?

Perhaps you have mocked her
"Ignorant profession"
A server attending to your needs
Her trite existence
With meager means—
A lifestyle unlike your own

Perhaps you pity her
"Oh look she's pregnant!"
"And so young!"

Quick, ring check—
"at least she's married . . ."
Poor baby.

Or perhaps you are her
Struggling, hardworking
A college student with honors
A writer with potential
A happily married woman
An excited mother-to-be

Perhaps if you saw me
As more than a server
Grant me the credit I merit
Dispose of your pity and mockery—
Recognize the resemblance?
Could I be you?

—Danielle Quigley, "Server"

From Pro(se)letariets: The Writing of the Trans-Atlantic Worker Writer Manifesto

■   ■   ■

Look at yourself in the mirror. How do you understand the image in front of you? What is that image's relationship to the objects that surround it within the reflection, the objects that frame your body? How might such objects speak to your familial, cultural, or ethnic heritage? How might they explain you?

Now imagine that reflected image as one in a series, one moment in a collection of family photos or yearbook pages. How does its meaning change? What if the image were tagged and distributed across a range of social media sites, possibly turned into a meme, with folks endlessly adding punch lines that change its import? How would you understand the possible connections among all these repeating images, each link seemingly casting a new sense and purpose to the physical body captured in the mirror?

When confronted with such a seemingly endless proliferation of possible meanings, it might seem comforting to slip into a singular sense of identity—seeing ourselves as representing only one particular heritage or social group and making our self a unitary figure. Such a move, however, would be out of step with the current moment — a moment when we are witnessing an emergent sense of body politics that is premised on multiplicity, on a person's ability to inhabit many potential identities at once, both online and on the ground. It is a moment when we can build a new way of speaking that seeks to validate these multiplying connections within and among ourselves, authorizing a sensibility that provides the broadest sense of identity for all involved.

For ultimately, how we define our bodies directly affects how we relate to those around us. Any individual decision about "who we are" and what rights our bodies might claim from society is necessarily made in relationship to the collective "we," forcing us take a stand about how we consider those who walk next to us on the street or appear next to us in a series of "tagged" photographs. We are always part of the body politic. We are always part of a collective set of decisions not only on local issues, such as how a classmate is treated, but on global issues as well, such as our responsibility to refugees and victims of war. We must constantly decide which bodies should (or should not) be brought into society's cultural and economic safety net. Not only must we consider the body we see in the mirror; we must also consider what other bodies should be seen as part of our community and deserving of our attention.

Taking part in this emergent conversation marks the work of the authors and projects in this chapter. Here you will join a discussion among a series of authors and activists, each of whom has grappled with how to understand the body as both individually and collectively defined. As you read their works, you will see that many of these authors actively pushed to expand both the conversation about and the limits of the "body" and in so doing created new ways of speaking and acting upon which others could build. You will be able to use their insights to develop your own sense of how the body relates to the body politic. Once this work is complete, you will have the opportunity to move from theorizing about bodies to actual material practices, with all the possibilities and problems such work involves.

This chapter asks you to consider how our visual perception of "bodies" carries with it personal and political consequences. It asks you to locate yourself and your identity within myriad contexts, attempt to learn which connections ensure the greatest agency for all involved, and then actively work to make those imagined connections a reality.

References and notes for the readings can be found in the appendix on page 427.

WESLEY YANG

The Face of Seung-Hui Cho

Courtesy of Wesley Yang

Wesley Yang is a contributing editor at *New York* and *Tablet* magazines. He also has written on contemporary culture for *n+1* magazine, from which the following piece is drawn.

In this essay, Yang discusses his resemblance to Virginia Tech gunman Seung-Hui Cho, who shot and killed 32 people and wounded 17 others in the largest mass murder in American history at the time. Yang uses his physical similarities to Cho to explore the social problems faced by young men with a certain kind of physiognomy.

■ ■ ■

The first school shooter of the 1990s was an Asian boy who played the violin. I laughed when I heard an account of the rampage from my friend Ethan Gooding, who had survived it. Ethan forgave me my reaction. I think he knew by then that most people, facing up to a real atrocity, as opposed to the hundreds they'd seen on TV, didn't know how to act.

Ethan had left New Providence High School in central New Jersey for the progressive utopia of Simon's Rock College of Bard in Great Barrington, Massachusetts. Simon's Rock was a school for high school juniors and seniors ready for college-level work, a refuge for brilliant misfits, wounded prodigies, and budding homosexuals. Ethan was a pretty bright kid, brighter than me, but mostly he was a budding homosexual. One day in gym class at New Providence, Ethan made a two-handed set shot from half-court using a kickball while dressed in buttercup-yellow short-shorts and earned the nickname "Maurice." This was not a reference to E. M. Forster's frank novel of gay love, but to Maurice Cheeks, the great Philadelphia 76ers point guard. The unintended resonance was savored by those few of us who could discern it. Ethan had a striking pre-Raphaelite pallor set off against flaming red cheeks and lips with the puckered epicene aspect that speaking the French language too young will impart to a decent American mouth. None of this in itself meant, necessarily, that he was going to become gay, but then—well, he was.

Gay-bashing was less of a hate crime back then and more of a patriotic duty, particularly in a race-segregated, heavily Catholic suburb like New Providence. At Youth & Government, the YMCA-sponsored mock legislature attended by suck-ups with Napoleon complexes, the "governor" from our school introduced a bill to "build an island of garbage off of the Jersey Shore" where we could "put all the homosexuals." We all chortled along, none more loudly than the closet cases in our midst. It was the kind of place you wanted to flee so badly that you trained yourself to forget the impulse.

But then there was a place called New York, only a half hour's drive away. We made our first anxious forays into New York City nightlife, Ethan and I and Jasper Chung, the other Korean kid from my high school (himself a governor of the mock legislature, and also a closet homosexual). We tried to get into the back room of the Limelight, where the real party was happening. "Try to look cute," Ethan told me, brushing my hair with a concerned, appraising look. Then he sucked in his cheeks, which I guess was his way of looking cute, or at least making his face less round. It would be more than a decade and a half before I learned what a smile could do for you (it is one way to hold at bay the world's cruelty), so I made a fish-eyed grimace in emulation of David Gahan of Depeche Mode. They never let us into the back room.

Those were the wild Peter Gatien days, when the place was still bristling with drugs and prostitution, most of which managed to pass us by. But we were assailed by a phalanx of sweaty, shirtless Long Island beefcake. Ethan would, to my frightened astonishment, meet other guys, and go off into a dark corner with them, and leave me to fend for myself, which I was not equipped to do. I'd get dehydrated and wear an anxious scowl. I would attempt some rudimentary sociological and semiotic reading of the scene that swirled all around me. I couldn't relax.

Not that I was myself homosexual. True, my heterosexuality was notional. I wasn't much to look at (skinny, acne-prone, brace-faced, bespectacled, and Asian), and inasmuch as I was ugly, I also had a bad personality. While Ethan was easing himself into same-sex experimentation, I was learning about the torments and transports of misanthropy. "That kid," I remember overhearing one of the baseball players say, "is a misfit." No one ever shoved my head in a locker, the way they did the one amber-tinted Afghani kid, or P. J., the big dumb sweet slow kid, and nobody ever pelted me with rocks, as they did Doug Urbano, who was fat and working class (his father was a truck driver, and sometimes, when he lectured us about the vital role that truck drivers play in the American economy—they really do, you know—he was jeered). But these judgments stayed with me.

Jasper once told me that I was "essentially unlovable." I've always held that observation close to my heart, turning to it often. It's true of some people—that there's no reason anyone should love or care about them, because they aren't appealing on the outside, and that once you dig into the real person beneath the shell (if, for some obscure if not actively perverse reason, you bother), you find the real inner ugliness. I knew lots of people like that—unloved because unlovable. Toward them I was always cold. Maybe I held them at arm's length to disguise from myself our shared predicament. And so, by trying to disguise something from yourself, you declare it to everyone else—because part of what makes a person unlovable is his inability to love.

One day we were hanging out with Ethan in Jasper's room over winter break. Ethan was telling us all about Simon's Rock, and—this might be an invented memory; it feels real, yet I can't rely on it; the very feeling of reality makes me distrust it—Ethan told me that I reminded him of this weird Asian guy at his school, whom he then proceeded to describe. Ethan, cherubic complexion not-withstanding, could actually be pretty mean. He was proud of his ability to wound with a well-chosen phrase coined in an instant, which is not to say that I didn't aspire to the same facility. It's just that he really had it. In any case, Wayne, my double, was an Asian boy ill at ease in the world and he had a chip on his shoulder. His father had been an officer in the Taiwanese air force, and his mother had been a Suzuki-method violin teacher. For a time, Wayne had been among the best violinists in the world in his age group. He was headed along the familiar track of Asian American assimilation. By the time he arrived at Simon's Rock, he had other things to prove.

The gay guys liked to tease Wayne and intimate that he might be one of them. It was good-natured ribbing, gentle to the extent that it was not tinged with gay malice; and who could begrudge them their share of malice—a little or a lot—given the world they were entering? On top of everything else, an incurable illness spread by the kind of sex you were already having or else aching to have was killing off a whole generation of your predecessors. You could get a rise out of Wayne, and he deserved it: here he was at this place where people were finally free to be who they really were, and who he really was turned out to be someone who didn't want other people to be free to be who they were. He had fled Montana only to discover his continuing allegiance to its mores. And who knows, conceivably he was even a bit bi-curious. "How tough are you?" Wayne's friends used to ask him, egging him on. "I'm tough!" he would shout.

10   By now the story of Wayne Lo has been well told, though he has not become a figure of American legend. (His certified authentic "murderabilia" drawings

were fetching just $7.50 on his website at the time his jailers shut it down.) On Monday, December 14, 1992, a package arrived for him in the mail from a North Carolina company called Classic Arms. It contained 200 rounds of ammunition that Wayne had ordered using his mother's credit card. The school's dean held the package, and, after questioning Wayne about what was inside it (Wayne assured him that it was a Christmas gift), gave it back to him. Liberals! They'll hand over the ammunition that their enemies will use to kill them.

Ethan told his version of the story to Jasper and me over hamburgers at the A&W Restaurant at the Short Hills Mall. Wayne had started hanging out with some other students who wanted to rebel against the orthodoxy of difference at Simon's Rock. They listened to Rush Limbaugh and joked about killing people. They were suspicious of Jews and blacks and homosexuals and . . . did they make an official exception for Asians? Wayne wrote a paper proposing a solution to the AIDS crisis: Kill them all. He lacked the imagination to come up with the island of garbage disposal. Then, according to psychiatrists hired by his defense, Wayne was overtaken by a "somatic hallucination"—not heard, but directly experienced in his body—of God urging him to punish the sinners of Simon's Rock.

It was a more innocent time, in a way. The Berlin Wall had come down. Crime rates were beginning the historic fall they were to make during the 1990s. American soldiers were ensconced in the Persian Gulf, having recently kept the armies of Saddam Hussein from entering the land of the two holy places. People didn't know about school shooters back then. They still thought that Asian men were happy to be (as Ethan liked to call us) the Other White People. Or even, as many people were suggesting, the New Jews. And for the most part, Asian people were happy—and are. I mean, maybe they were nerds, maybe they were faceless drones, but did anybody know they were angry? What could they be angry about? They were getting rich with the rest of America—and reassuring everyone of our openness and our tolerance for everyone prepared to embrace the American dream.

Lo went around the campus with the Chinese-made SKS Carbine rifle that he bought in a neighboring town. He shot and killed two people and wounded four others. Had his rampage not ended prematurely when his rifle repeatedly jammed (cheap Chinese junk), he might have set a record that no one was going to best. Instead, he called the police and negotiated his surrender.

The perpetrator of the largest mass murder in American history was an Asian boy who wrote poems, short stories, a novel, and plays. I gazed at the sad blank mug of Seung-Hui Cho staring out at the world on CNN.com—the face-forward shot that was all the press had before they received Cho's multimedia manifesto, mailed on the day of the shootings, with its ghastly autoerotic glamour shots (Cho pointing gun at camera; Cho with a hammer; Cho pointing gun at his head). I felt, looking at the photo, a very personal revulsion. Millions of others reviled this person, but my own loathing was more intimate. Those lugubrious eyes, that elongated face behind wire-frame glasses: *He looks like me*, I thought.

15   This was another inappropriate reaction. But the photo leapt out at me at a funny time in my life. I had come to New York five years earlier, to create a life for myself there. I had not created a life for myself there. I had wanted to find the emerging writers and thinkers of my generation. I had found the sycophants, careerists, and media parasites who were redefining mediocrity for the 21st century. I had wanted to remain true to myself as a writer, and also to succeed; I wanted to be courageous and merciless in defense of the downtrodden, and I wanted to be celebrated for it. This was a naïve and puerile desire and one that could not be realized—at least not by me, not in this world. It could not be done without a facility (and a taste) for ingratiation that I lacked. It could not be done without first occupying a position of strength and privilege that I did not command—because, as Jesus said, to him who hath, more will be given; nor without being enterprising and calculating in a way that I wasn't—because, as Jesus went on to say, to him who hath not, even that which he hath will be taken from him. It seemed to me that every kind of life, and even the extinction of life, was preferable to the one that I was living, which is not to say I had the strength either to change my life, or to end it.

And then to be confronted by that face. Because physiognomy is a powerful thing. It establishes identification and aversion, and all the more so in an age that is officially color-blind. Such impulses operate beneath the gaze of the supervisory intelligence, at a visceral level that may be the most honest part of us. You see a face that looks like yours. You know that there's an existential knowledge you have in common with that face. Both of you know what it's like to have a cultural code superimposed atop your face, and if it's a code that abashes, nullifies, and unmans you, then you confront every visible reflection of that code with a feeling of mingled curiosity and wariness. When I'm out by myself in the city—at the movies or at a restaurant—I'll often see other Asian men out by themselves in the city. We can't even look at each other for the strange vertigo we induce in one another.

Let's talk about legible faces. You know those short, brown-toned South American immigrants that pick your fruit, slaughter your meat, and bus your tables? Would you—a respectable person with a middle-class upbringing—ever consider going on a date with one of them? It's a rude question, because it affects to inquire into what everyone gets to know at the cost of forever leaving it unspoken. But if you were to put your unspoken thoughts into words, they might sound something like this: Not only are these people busing the tables, slaughtering the meat, and picking the fruit, they are the descendants of the people who bused the tables, slaughtered the meat, and picked the fruit of the Aztecs and Incas. The Spanish colonizers slaughtered or mixed their blood with the princes, priests, scholars, artisans, warriors, and beautiful women of the indigenous Americas, leaving untouched a class of Morlocks bred for good-natured servility and thus now tailor-made to the demands of an increasingly feudal postindustrial America. That's, by the way, part of the emotional undertow of the immigration debate, the thing that makes an honest appraisal of the issue impossible, because you can never put anything right without first admitting you're in the wrong.

So: Seung-Hui Cho's face. A perfectly unremarkable Korean face—beady-eyed, brown-toned, a small plump-lipped mouth, eyebrows high off his eyelids, with crooked glasses perched on his nose. It's not an ugly face, exactly; it's not a badly made face. It's just a face that has nothing to do with the desires of women in this country. It's a face belonging to a person who, if he were emailing you, or sending you instant messages, and you were a normal, happy, healthy American girl at an upper second-tier American university—and that's what Cho was doing in the fall of 2005, emailing and writing instant messages to girls—you would consider reporting it to campus security. Which is what they did, the girls who were contacted by Cho.

First, you imagine, they tried to dissuade him in the usual way. You try to be polite, but also to suggest that you'd actually prefer that your correspondent, if he could, you know, maybe—oh, I don't know—*Disappear from your life forever? How about that?*—and you had to do this subtly enough not to implicate yourself in anything damaging to your own self-image as a nice person, but then not so subtly that your correspondent would miss the point. When Cho missed the point, the girls had to call the campus police. They did not want him arrested, and they did not press charges. They just had to make clear that while Cho thought he was having one kind of encounter (a potentially romantic one), he was in fact having another kind of encounter (a potentially criminal one), and to show him that the state would intervene on their behalf if he couldn't come to terms with this reality. And so, the police didn't press any charges, but they did have a man-to-man talk with Cho, and conveyed to him the message that it would be better if he cut it out.

Seung-Hui Cho's is the kind of face for which the appropriate response to an expression of longing or need involves armed guards. I am not questioning the choices that these girls made; I am affirming those choices. But I'm talking about the Cho that existed before anyone was killed by him—the one who showed proficiency in beer pong at the one fraternity party his roommates took him to, and who told his roommates he had a girlfriend named Jelly who was a supermodel from outer space; who called one of his roommates to tell him that he had been on vacation with Vladimir Putin; and who emailed Lucinda Roy, director of the Creative Writing program, seeking guidance about how to submit his novel to publishers. "My novel is relatively short," he wrote. "It's sort of like Tom Sawyer, except that it's really silly or pathetic, depending on how you look at it."

20

Of course, there are a lot of things that Cho might have done to change his social fortunes that he declined to do. Either out of incompetence, stubbornness, or plain old bat-shit craziness, Cho missed many boats that might have ferried him away from his dark fate. For one, he could have dressed a little bit better. He might have tried to do something with his hair. Being a little less bat-shit crazy couldn't have hurt. Above all, he could have cultivated his taste in music. He was "obsessed with downloading music from the Internet," the press reported, putting a sinister cast on something that everyone of a certain age does. But the song he continually played on his laptop, driving his roommates to distraction, wasn't some nihilistic rhapsody of wasted youth. It wasn't Trent Reznor of Nine Inch Nails saying he wanted to fuck you like an animal, and it wasn't the thick lugubrious whine of James Hetfield of Metallica declaring that what he'd felt, and what he'd known, never shone through in what he'd shown.

No, it was the cruddiest, most generic grunge-rock anthem of the '90s, Collective Soul's "Shine." "Shine" came out in 1994, and you only had to hear the first minute to know that whatever was truly unyielding about the music Nirvana spawned by breaking punk into the mainstream was already finished. The song cynically mouths "life-affirming" clichés noxious to the spirit of punk rock, but then these are not, given the situation, without their own pathos. You could picture the Cho who stalked around campus not saying a word to anyone, even when a classmate offered him money to speak, coming home in silence to listen to these lyrics repeat in an infinite loop on his laptop, and even, one day, to write them on his wall:

> Teach me how to speak
> Teach me how to share
> Teach me where to go
> Tell me will love be there (love be there)

> Whoa-oh-oh-oh, heaven let your light shine down.

"You were the single biggest dork school shooter of all time," opined one internet chat board participant, and it was hard to disagree. Cho was so disaffected that he couldn't even get the symbols of disaffection right. In the fall of 2005, when he made the mistake of instant-messaging girls, Cho was also attending Nikki Giovanni's large creative writing class. He would wear reflector glasses with a baseball cap obscuring his face. Giovanni, who believed that openness was vital to the goals of the class, stood by his desk at the beginning of each session to make him take off the disguise. He later began showing up with a scarf wrapped around his head, "Bedouin-style," as Giovanni put it. When the attendance sheet was passed around, he signed his name as a question mark.

The class set Cho off, somehow—maybe because he had enrolled in the hope that his genius would be recognized, and it was not recognized. He began snapping pictures of female classmates with his cellphone camera from underneath his desk. Eventually, many of the seventy students enrolled in the class stopped coming. That's when Giovanni went to Lucinda Roy and insisted that Cho be barred from her workshop. She refused, in the words of one article about it, to be "bullied" by Cho.

"He was writing, just weird things," Giovanni told the *New York Times*. "I don't know if I'm allowed to say what he was writing about. . . . He was writing poetry, it was terrible, it was not like poetry, it was intimidating."   25

Giovanni's personal website has a list of all her honors and awards and another page for all the honorary degrees she has earned—nineteen since 1972—and a brief biography that identifies her as "a world-renowned poet, writer, commentator, activist, and educator," whose "outspokenness, in her writing and in lectures, has brought the eyes of the world upon her." Oprah Winfrey has named her one of her twenty-five living legends. "We are sad today, and we will be sad for quite a while," the 63-year-old eminence told the convocation to mourn Seung-Hui Cho's victims. "We are not moving on, we are embracing our mourning."

It's a perfectly consistent picture: Giovanni the winner of awards, and Giovanni the wise and grandmotherly presence on *Oprah*. But if you knew more about the writing of Nikki Giovanni, you couldn't help but wonder two things. What would the Nikki Giovanni of 2007 have made of a poem published by the Nikki Giovanni of 1968, and what would the Nikki Giovanni of 1968 have made of the Nikki Giovanni of the present? The Nikki Giovanni of 1968 wrote this:

Nigger
Can you kill
Can you kill
Can a nigger kill
Can a nigger kill a honkie
Can a nigger kill the Man
Can you kill nigger
Huh? nigger can you
kill
Do you know how to draw blood
Can you poison
Can you stab-a-Jew
Can you kill huh? nigger
Can you kill

Back then Giovanni was writing about a race war that seemed like it really might break out at home, even as the country was fighting what she saw as an imperialist war in Vietnam. Black militancy was something that many people admired, and many more felt sympathy toward, given the brutal history of enslavement, rape, terrorism, disenfranchisement, lynching, and segregation that blacks had endured in this country. And so you wonder what would have happened if, for instance, Cho's poems (and thoughts) had found a way to connect his pain to his ethnic identity. Would Giovanni have been less intimidated if she could have understood Cho as an aggrieved Asian man, instead of an aggrieved man who happened to be Asian? Or if he were black and wrote the way he did? Or if he were Palestinian and managed to tie his violent grievances to a real political conflict existing in the world? (Can you bomb-a-Jew?) Giovanni knows black rage, and she knows the source of women's bitterness. We all do. We know gay pride. We know, in short, identity politics, which, when it isn't acting as a violent outlet for the narcissism of the age, can serve as its antidote, binding people into imagined collectivities capable of taking action to secure their interests and assert their personhood.

Cho did not think of himself as Asian; he did not think of himself ethnically at all. He was a pimply friendless suburban teenager whom no woman would want to have sex with: that's what he was. And it turned out that in his imagination he was a warrior on behalf of every lonely invisible human being in America. This was his ghastly, insane mistake. This is what we learned from the speech Cho gave in the video he mailed to NBC News. For Cho, the cause to fight for is "the dorky kid that [you] publicly humiliated and spat on," whom you treated like "a filthy street dog" and an "ugly, little, retarded, low-life kid"—not just Cho, not just his solitary narcissistic frenzy, but also that of his "children," his "brothers and sisters"—an imagined community of losers who would leave behind their status as outcasts from the American consensus and attain the dignity of warriors—by killing innocent civilians.

Cho enclosed his speech, too, in the NBC packet, as "writings."

> You had everything you wanted.
> Your Mercedes wasn't enough,
> you brats,
> your golden necklaces weren't enough, you snobs,
> your trust fund wasn't enough . . .

> You have vandalized my heart,
> raped my soul
> and torched my conscience.
> You thought it was one pathetic, bored life you were extinguishing.

> I die like Jesus Christ,
> to inspire generations of the weak and defenseless people.

Cho imagines the one thing that can never exist—the coming to consciousness and the joining in solidarity of the modern class of losers. Though his soft Asian face could only have been a hindrance to him, Cho did not perceive his pain as stemming from being Asian: he did not perceive himself in a world of identity politics, of groups and fragments of groups, of groups oppressing and fighting other groups. Cho's world is a world of individually determined fortunes, of winners and losers in the marketplace of status, cash, and expression. Cho sees a system of social competition that renders some people absolutely immiserated while others grow obscenely rich.

When I was at Rutgers I knew a guy named Samuel Goldfarb. Samuel was pre- maturely middle-aged, not just in his dimensions, which were bloated, and not just in his complexion, which was pale but flushed with the exertion of holding himself upright—sweat would dapple the groove between his upper lip and nose—but above all in something he exuded, which was a pheromone of loneliness and hostility. Samuel had gone off to Reed College, and, after a couple of years of feeling alienated in that liberal utopia, he had returned east. Samuel was one of the students at Rutgers who was clearly more intellectually sophisticated than I. He knew more, he had read more, and it showed. He was the kind of nominal left-winger who admired the works of Carl Schmitt before many others had gotten onto that trend, and he knew all about the Frankfurt School, and he was already jaded about the postmodernists when others were still enraptured by the discovery of them. In addition to being the kind of leftist who read a Nazi legal theorist to be contrarian, Samuel was also the kind of aspiring academic so contemptuous of the postmodern academy that he was likely to go into investment banking and make pots of money while jeering at the rest of humanity, because that was so much more punk rock than any other alternative to it. He identified his "lifestyle"—and of course he put that word into derisive quote marks when he used it—as "indie rock," but Samuel's irony had extra bite to it, real cruelty and rancor, that was tonally off-kilter for the indie rock scene, which, as it manifested itself at Rutgers, was taciturn to the point of autism, passive-aggressive, and anti-intellectual, but far too cool and subdued for the exertions of overt cruelty.

You saw a look of sadness and yearning in Samuel's face when he had subsided from one of his misanthropic tirades—there was no limit to the scorn he heaped on the intellectual pretensions of others—and it put you on guard against him. What you sensed about him was that his abiding rage was closely linked to the fact that he was fat and ugly in a uniquely unappealing way, and that this compounded with his unappealing rage made him the sort of person that no woman would ever want to touch. He seemed arrayed in that wild rancor that sexual frustration can bestow on a man, and everything about his persona—his coruscating irony, his unbelievable intellectual snobbery—seemed a way to channel and thus defend himself against this consuming bitterness. He was ugly on the outside and once you got past that you found the true ugliness on the inside.

And then below that ugliness you found a vulnerable person who desperately needed to be seen and touched and known as a human phenomenon. And above all, you wanted nothing to do with that, because once you touched the source of

30

his loneliness, there would be no end to it, and even if you took it upon yourself to appease this unappeasable need, he would eventually decide to revenge himself against a world that had held him at bay, and there would be no better target for this revenge than you, precisely because you were the person who'd dared to draw the nearest. This is what you felt instantly, without having to put it into words (it's what I felt, anyway, though it might have been pure projection), the moment you met Samuel. For all that he could be amusing to talk to, and for all that he was visibly a nice guy despite all I've just said, you were careful to keep your distance.

Samuel used to complain about declining academic standards. He said that without much work he was acing all of his classes. This was a way of exalting himself slightly while mostly denigrating others, which made it an exemplary statement of his, but it was also a suspect statement, since no one had asked. One day, while I was in the history department's front office, I noticed a plastic crate full of hanging folders. In one of those folders, I found my own academic transcript in its entirety. Then I looked for Samuel's. Like mine, it was riddled with Ds and Fs. And while what Samuel had said about academic standards and his own aptitude was surely true, it was also true that he had lied—and I suppose I understand why. If your only claim to self-respect was your intellectual superiority, and you had more or less flunked out of Reed College because of the crushing loneliness and depression you encountered once you realized that liberal utopia wasn't going to embrace you as it did the willowy, stylish high school outcasts who surrounded you—and if your grades weren't much better at Rutgers (a pathetic public university, even though you hated Reed more), you might be forced to lie about those grades, because they were the public face of all you had left—your intellectual superiority—and even after all you'd endured, or maybe because of it, your public face still mattered. Unaware that the contrary evidence was there for anyone to check (it should not have been) or that a person inclined to check it existed (I should not have looked), you would assume that you could tell this lie without being caught.

I mentioned this incident to a mutual acquaintance, who proceeded to tell Samuel, who accused me of making up lies about him, and turned me into the great enemy of his life—he was clearly looking for one—which was too bad and a little disconcerting, because, as I explained to him, he and his grades had never meant anything to me. And yet I had only read two transcripts, his and mine, mostly because I suspected, correctly, that he was telling lies. Samuel had been wronged by me, and it would have been right for me to apologize, but I had some hostility of my own, so instead I told him that he was ugly on the outside, but even uglier on the inside, and that he meant nothing to me, and his enmity counted for nothing to me. And this was true. I had recognized him as a person with whom I had some mutual understanding—overlapping interests and, most of all, overlapping pretensions—but I never wanted him as a friend. The image this whole affair calls up is the scene in *Born on the Fourth of July* in which two paraplegics in wheelchairs start wrestling around in anger, and then tip each other into a ditch by the side of the road, and fall out of their wheelchairs, and roll around on the ground in the dirt, from which they are unable to lift themselves.

I saw Samuel Goldfarb at a coffee shop near Union Square about a year ago. He was chatting up the Eastern European counter girls. You could tell that he was a regular. He had put on a lot of weight and lost more of his hair, and his skin had lost none of its sebaceous excess. He had really become, at 32 or 33, the ruined middle-aged man that he already seemed on the cusp of becoming in youth. He seemed like a nice, harmless guy, but then you could still discern loneliness and sexual desperation clinging to him, though it had lost some of its virulence. I was glad to see his resignation. And I knew that he was probably very rich, and I felt weirdly good on his behalf to know that if he had to be lonely, if he had to be one of the millions of sexually null men in America—and for all I knew, he could have studied the Game and become a world-class seducer in the intervening years, though it seemed unlikely ("Hey guys—quick question for you—do you believe in magic spells?"—I couldn't see it)—at least he could be rich.

Lack of money had taught me the value of money. I had learned that when I didn't have it—and by this I mean, really having none of it, as in, like, nothing, which was most of the time—I would become extremely unhappy. And that when I did have it, even a little bit of it, which was rare, my despondency was assuaged, and I became like a dry and dwindling houseplant that would rally and surge up from out of its dolor when watered. I deduced from this pattern that what I needed to do was find an occupation that would pay me a salary—it was amazing to think how long I had gone without one—and then I would have money all the time, and then I would be, if not happy, at least OK. And to come to this realization seemed a little bit like the moment in *1984* when Winston Smith decides that he loves Big Brother, but then even more than that it just felt like growing up and it felt like life. And so I figured that Samuel was fine; and while I was very far from fine, I thought someday I'd catch on to something and I'd eventually be fine too.

And maybe I still will, at that.

A friend of mine wrote a book about online dating. She talked to hundreds of people about their experiences. Online, you become the person you've always known yourself to be, deep down. Online, you're explicit about the fact that you are paying for a service, and you're explicit about the fact that what you're paying for is to get what you really want, and what you're paying for is the ability to remove that annoying bit of residual romantic nonsense that gets us into annoying situations in life where we have to face up to the fact that we are rational profit maximizers in nothing so much as those intimate areas where we pretend to be otherwise. And so, people on the dating sites disclose what they really want, and also what they really don't want.

This friend talked to one man from Maryland who put up his profile on Match.com one night a few years back. This man had good reason to think he would do well on the site. He made more than $150,000 a year; he was white; he was over six feet tall. The next morning, he woke up and checked his account. Over the course of the previous night, he had gotten many responses. How many responses had he gotten? How well could he expect to do, being a man able to check off, without lying, boxes that certified that he made more than $150,000 a year, that he was six feet four inches tall, and that he was white? How well do you think he was going to do on that site where people disclosed what they really wanted out of life and also what they really didn't want?

40   He had gotten six thousand responses in one night. The fact was that if there was something intriguing or beautiful about that man—and there's something beautiful about us all, if you look deeply enough—someone was going to take the trouble to find it out, and they'd love him for that thing, not because he was six feet four inches tall, and not because he made more than $150,000 a year. You'd find out about his love of truth and poetry, to the extent that it existed, or at least his ability to make you laugh, or his own ability to laugh at things that made you laugh too—things on TV. You could watch TV together. Because the thing you wanted to do was to find true love and have that true love coincide with everything else that you wanted from life, so that you could have all the benefits of one kind of ease, and all the moral credit that others had to win by forgoing that kind of ease (but you could have it all, so why not?), and so you were going to put yourself in a position to do that. And you weren't going to answer the ads of anyone with beady lugubrious eyes in a forlorn, brown-tinted face, and if that person wrote you a message, you weren't going to write him back, and you'd probably even, if it seemed like it was necessary, block all further emails from that person. And you'd be right to do that. You'd be behaving in the way that any rational person in your situation would behave. We all agree that the rational thing to do is to shut every trace of that person's existence out of your view. The question, though, is—what if it's not you shutting out the losers? What if you're the loser whom everyone is shutting out? Of course, every loser is shutting out an even more wretched loser. But what if, as far as you know, you're the lowest person at the low end of this hierarchy? What is your rational move then?

You wake to find yourself one of the disadvantaged of the fully liberated sexual marketplace. If you are a woman, maybe you notice that men have a habit of using and discarding you, pleading their own inconstancy and premature emotional debauchery as a sop to your wounded feelings. If you are a man, maybe you notice that the women who have been used and discarded by other, more highly valued men are happy to restore (for a while) their own broken self-esteem by stepping on you while you are prone, and reminding you that even a society of outcasts has its hierarchies. Indeed, these hierarchies are policed all the more ruthlessly the closer to the bottom you go.

For these people, we have nothing but options. Therapy, selective serotonin reuptake inhibitors, alcoholism, drug addiction, pornography, training in mixed martial arts, mail-order brides from former Soviet republics, sex tours in Southeast Asia, prostitution, video-game consoles, protein shakes and weightlifting regimens, New Age medicine, obsession with pets or home furnishings, the recovery movement—all of which are modes of survival as opposed to forms of life. Each of these options compensates for a thing, love, that no person can flourish without, and each, in a different way, offers an endlessly deferred resolution to a conundrum that is effectively irresolvable. You could even say that our culture feeds off the plight of the poor in spirit in order to create new dependencies. You might even dare to say that an undernourished human soul—desperate and flailing, prone to seeking voluntary slavery in the midst of freedom and prosperity—is so conducive to the creation of new markets that it is itself the indispensable product of our culture and our time, at once its precondition and its goal.

There's a familiar narrative we all know about high school losers. It's the narrative of smart sitcoms and even edgy indie films. The high school loser grows up, fills out, goes to Brown or RISD, and becomes the ideal guy for every smart, sensitive, quirky-but-cute girl with glasses (who is, in turn, the female version of the loser made good). The traits that hindered him (or her) in one phase of life turn out to be a blessing in another, more enlightened phase, or else get cast aside. For many people, this is an accurate description of their experience—it is the experience of the writers and producers of these stories.

In the indie film version of Seung-Hui Cho's life, the escort Cho hired a few weeks before his massacre wouldn't have danced for him for fifteen minutes in a motel room and then shoved him away when he tried to touch her. Not every one of the girls he tried to talk to would have recoiled in horror from him. Something would have happened in that film to remind him, and us, of his incipient humanity—that horribly menaced and misshapen thing. He would have found a good-hearted person who had perhaps been touched in some way by the same hysteria—and don't we all know something about it?—that had consumed Cho's soul. And this good-hearted girl or boy would have known how to forgive Cho for what he couldn't forgive himself—the unbearable, all-consuming shame of being ugly, weak, sick, poor, clumsy, and ungifted.

We know that Cho had dreamt of this indie film ending. He had been dreaming of it for a long time. In the spring semester of 2006, he wrote a story about a boy estranged from his classmates: "Everyone is smiling and laughing as if they're in heaven-on-earth, something magical and enchanting about all the people's intrinsic nature that Bud will never experience." But eventually the boy meets a "Gothic Girl," to whom he breaks down and confesses, "I'm nothing. I'm a loser. I can't do anything. I was going to kill every god damn person in this damn school, swear to god I was, but I . . . couldn't. I just couldn't."

45

Cho's short story about the Gothic Girl should have ended, but did not, with this declaration. Instead, he and the girl steal a car and drive to her house, where she retrieves "a .8 caliber automatic rifle and a M16 machine gun," and the story concludes when she tells the narrator, "You and me. We can fight to claim our deserving throne."

In real life, there was no Gothic Girl, no *me* to Cho's *you*, no other willing actors—whether sympathetic, heroic, or equally violently deranged—to populate the self-made movie of his life.

Having failed to make it as a novelist—he really did send a book proposal to a New York publisher—Cho decided to make a film. This was a familiar trajectory, with a twist. He was going to collaborate with all the major television networks on it. In the days before his date with a self-appointed destiny, Cho was spotted working out in the college gym. He wanted his scrawny arms and chest to appear more credibly menacing than they were. How many of those men working their arms to the point of exhaustion were driven by the vain notion that they could improve their sexual prospects in the process? Cho had no such illusions. He was preparing a spectacle for the world to witness on TV, and he needed to look the part.

Reading

1. How does Yang define "identity politics" (para. 27)?
2. How does Yang define his own identity?
3. How does Yang discuss racial politics on college campuses?
4. How does Yang demonstrate the benefits of tolerance on college campuses?

Inquiring

1. Yang's essay highlights what he takes to be his physical resemblance to the school shooters at Virginia Tech and Simon's Rock College as one way to understand each incident. Indeed, he uses this resemblance to make strong claims about how Asian identity was (and is) perceived within college culture, moving, in effect, from his body to college's body politic. How would you describe his evidence for these claims? Do you find his conclusions convincing? Could you (or would you want to) use this method to describe your own college's understanding of different student identities?

2. One of Yang's central points about the Virginia Tech shooter was that although Seung-Hui Cho was popularly perceived as "Asian," his self-perception was that of a bullied loner, an outcast. Yang wonders whether embracing a form of identity politics might have given Cho a productive venue to vent his frustration, perhaps pushing him off his path toward violence. Maybe a different understanding of how to "read" his individual body as part of a larger heritage

might have led to different results, a more collective resistance to marginalization. Does Yang's definition of identity politics match your understanding of the possible value of identity-based politics? Is that your understanding of the possible value of identity-based politics? Do you believe such a strategy might have helped Cho? Do you believe such a strategy would be useful to other students struggling with their place in college?

3. There is a standard comment after jokes about a recent tragedy: "What, too soon?" This question might reasonably be asked about Yang's piece, in which he uses the horrific school shooting at Virginia Tech to reflect on his own identity. In the essay, Yang's tone moves from ironic to serious, with jokes sprinkled among the details. What do you make of his use of the Virginia Tech shootings to explore questions of identity? Was it necessary to choose this historical event to make his argument? How does such use diminish or increase the meaning of this event for the larger body politic?

Composing

1. One way to read Yang's piece is as an attempt to create a web of connections between his physical appearance and a series of cultural attitudes. Using this associative network, Yang then attempts to draw a set of conclusions about the relationship between physical appearance and the actions of others—actions that are often cruel or simply horrific. Write an essay in which you try to capture Yang's method. What are his research strategies and sources? How does he use these materials to connect attitudes and actions? Try using this method to understand how your own physical appearance positions you within your school and the larger culture of your local community. (If possible, think of some specific moments you can explore in detail.) Having done this work, assess the validity and usefulness of Yang's method. How might you build on or amend his analytical strategies? What alternative method might you suggest?

2. Yang attempts to provide an explanation for the Virginia Tech massacre: Cho's identity as an "outcast" ultimately trumped his Asian identity, shutting off the avenue of identity politics to vent his frustrations and leaving him instead to act as a violent representative of "outcasts." In making this argument, Yang consistently invokes and analyzes images of individuals, events, and cultures, yet he provides very few actual images in his piece. It is an essay about *images* written in *words*. For this assignment, use any social media tool with which you are familiar to create a digital image–based presentation featuring a nonverbal soundtrack that you believe represents why the Virginia Tech massacre occurred and what you take to be the meaning of the event. Once this project is complete, write a separate short essay to explain how you linked Cho and his victims to larger cultural arguments about the values that should inform the college campuses.

3. Implicit in Yang's piece is an argument for tolerance. He pointedly critiques the young women who dismissed Cho as a potential suitor based on his appearance and highlights the acceptance of his own gay friend as an alternative response. His piece does not, however, actually articulate what a new type of tolerance might entail; his views remain at the level of anecdote. For this assignment, develop your own theory of tolerance on a college campus. In producing this piece, be sure not to use truisms or clichés; also be sure to avoid assuming that the ethical basis for your appeal will be evident to the reader. Instead, attempt to clarify, in as detailed a fashion as possible, what it might mean to allow a complex sense of bodily identity to be respected and encouraged on college campuses.

Connecting

Yang seems to stake out a positive vision of identity politics. In her writing, however, Waite (p. 375) argues for a sense of self that seems to transcend traditional identity politics—I am Black; I am Queer—for a more multiple sense of identity. Write an essay in which you place Yang and Waite in a discussion about the value of identity politics on a college campus and then state your own position on this issue.

STACEY WAITE

Selections from Butch Geography

Courtesy of Stacey Waite

Stacey Waite is a published poet and an assistant professor of English at the University of Nebraska–Lincoln. Her poetry explores the relationship between identity and gender, and she often asks her readers to put aside easy assumptions for a more complex sense of how these terms interact. In her work, simple terms like *male* and *female* become less a set of clear-cut definitions and instead become terms that coexist and cross over each other as individuals chart their way through daily life. Waite has been described by critics as one of the "most dazzling and culturally relevant of living poets" and has been the recipient of numerous awards, including the 2004 Frank O'Hara Prize and the 2008 Snowbound Prize, as well as a National Society of Arts and Letters Prize.

In the following poems from her collection *Butch Geography*, Waite explores cultural assumptions about a stable and singular gender identity.

■   ■   ■

On the Occasion of Being Mistaken for a Boy by the Umpire
in the Little League Conference Championship

> I had learned quickly how to spit
> through the jail-like bars of the catcher's mask
> so looking back I can't say as I blame the umpire
> who, after seeing me spit and punch my glove,
> could only draw one conclusion:
> "You got your cup on, right son?"
>
> And almost everyone hears him, and I
> want my father to stand up, like he does, and yell,

"What the hell are you looking at, bub!"
10   or "Bad call, blue!" But instead there's a hush,
and I forget the signs for curve balls, fast balls,
and screw balls, and all I can think about is no balls,

no little ten-year-old balls to match my spit
and mitt-punching. My mother pretends
to clean up orange peels and the boys yell
from the infield, "It's a girl, we got a girl as catcher."
He doesn't know what to say so follows up "Alrighty"
with a quick "Play ball." But I can't squat now,

I think everyone is looking at my no balls.
20   They're all watching the girl with no balls.
I'm watching her, too. She knows better
than to cry so spits again. She learns
to live in halves, to, as her father says,
"Save it for the field." She snaps,
"What are you blind, Ump?" and digs
her plastic spikes into the fresh dirt.

Kimberly

Kimberly is the girl who played hopscotch on the blacktop.
I threw crickets at Kimberly on field trips.
Kimberly wouldn't have been caught with her shirt off
at the public pool, wouldn't have shaved her face
in the third grade, or called them "bad ass poppa wheelies."
My mother wanted to name me Kimberly.

I might have made better decisions about my hair
or done more sit-ups. I might have waited
to have sex with a man, thought it something special.
10   I might have drawn something more appropriate
for the refrigerator door. I might have practiced
spelling my name over and over in cursive.
Kimberly, I should have been Kimberly.
I would have felt some loyalty to a name like that.

On the Occasion of Being Mistaken for the Delivery Boy by Two Members of the Girls Youth Soccer League at the Marriot Hotel

I am at the door, pizza in hand
like Galileo with the globe.

I can hear them giggling
from behind the door, their footsteps
pitter-pattering. It is probably
their first time ordering pizza alone.
Tipping the driver will be
a sweet new power for them.

I feel the eye pressed against
the proverbial peephole.   10
"Pizza guy's here," she says.
"And he is so cute."
I pull my red Mama Angelina's
hat over my eyes, which are
far too feminine and blue,
and when the door swings open,
I am at the gate of a new heaven:

I am the cute delivery boy who,
after he is spotted by neighborhood fathers,
is kept away from daughters such as these.   20
They want me to join them,
to pull up a badly upholstered chair
and share the pepperoni pie radiating wet
heat through its bottom like an engine.

I stay for a glorious hour,
tell stories about the band
I never played in, tell them
the guitar has just always come
natural to me — I am self-taught, I say.
I can play anything you want to hear by ear.   30
Shauna is the one of them I love,
her calves carved out like crescent moons
as she props her Adidas sneakers atop
the television, which is blaring
Prince's greatest hits on MTV.

"Can you play guitar like him?" she asks.
And I think on the question of Prince,
his small erotic body, his long hair falling
around his shoulders like a black scarf.
I lie and say, "I think Prince is a sissy."   40

I never said I played this role well.
Truth is, I made a bad delivery boy
and felt shame fall over my body
when Shauna pressed her mouth
against my cheek and called me
"a hottie." And when she asked me
where the band was playing next,
I said Detroit. And when she asked me
where I was headed from the hotel,
50   I said back to work. The truth is,
I played classical guitar on Sundays
for my grandmother, who called me
her "little Czechoslovakian Princess."

The truth is, I couldn't go back to work.
Truth is, I couldn't go home again either.

About Ben

When I was fourteen, I had a girlfriend named Janie. She was from Smithtown, three miles west of my own small town where I was a Z. Cavaricci–wearing, suburban junior high-schooler who spent her Friday nights at the Commack Roller Rink with teased hair and hot-pink skate wheels. But not with Janie. To Janie, I was Ben . . . Axl Rose–looking, piano-playing, poem-writing Ben with long brown hair and peach fuzz above the lip. She loved me. She loved the way I sang "Stairway to Heaven" on her answering machine and wore a bulky black leather jacket. "I want to see you with your shirt off," she says. "You are probably so defined," she says. And Janie doesn't know how she's on to something, how
10   definition rests itself tightly rolled in the socks I have zipped into the crotch of my big brother's Wranglers. Janie says I have a gentle kiss, says her brother will kick my ass if he finds out we are "frenching."

I am afraid I had to leave her though, one Saturday evening outside the Sports Plus Entertainment Hall. I had to leave her standing there beneath the blinking green ticket sign. She was asking too many questions and the little bullets beneath the ace bandage wrapped around my chest were ready to fire forth and I knew it. "But we kissed," Janie says. I tell her I can't help it. My parents are making me move to Manhasset, which is a good thirty minutes away. I ask her for the photo her friend Emily took of me smoking at Caleb Smith Park. She must
20   have no evidence of Ben. I tell her I don't want the photo to be painful for her. She refuses to give it over. I tell her I will call but I don't, can't risk it. The phone is dangerous when my father picks it up while I am talking to Janie. "Stacey, I need the phone," he might say. And what would happen to me then, sitting in

those Z. Cavariccis with that hair and creating the life of Ben. Ben's father, after all, had died. His mother was a waitress and his stepfather hit him. Ben had it hard. Ben only had one other girlfriend before, named Lisa. She was short and had braces but Ben didn't mind. Ben was sensitive, didn't care about things like looks. Ben wrote long beautiful poems about not so beautiful girls. Ben did have a cousin named Stacey. Ben tells Janie she might see her sometime and she will know the girl is his cousin because they look exactly alike. Ben is meticulous,   30
covers all the bases. And when he walks away from her that Saturday, he dies a little, even at fourteen. He dies because he has lost everything.

On the Occasion of Being Mistaken for a Man by the Cashier in the Drive-Thru Window at a Wendy's in Madison, Wisconsin

When a woman does it, I feel more like a man.
Simone at the Wendy's drive-thru makes me feel
more like a man when she says, "Out of ten, Sir?"
and leans her breasts atop the little shelf, smiles
at the folding windows. "You have gorgeous hands,"
I say. I can't even see her hands, but tonight
I have license to compliment, to tell Simone
I have never seen more delicate hands.

In a perfect world, I wouldn't tell Simone I was
an "anatomical female" until our fourth date.   10
I would include this in the same sentence I tell her
my grandparents speak Slovak and my brother
is a restaurant owner. And Simone would sway in
and kiss my neck and say, "Isn't that interesting?"
Over dinner with her parents, her father would
not forget to ask me about my brother, about
whether we could all go out for a free meal.

In a perfect world, Simone's voice is a cocoon,
an agent of transformation, and Simone is a
drive-thru queen who gives us all permission   20
to stop dividing like cells, to stop her from leaving me
on our fourth date and never speak a word about me.

XY

The doctor, who speaks slowly, after spending quite a few moments by himself in his gray office, says there is a strong possibility I am "chromosomally mismatched," which cannot be determined now unless I pay for the test. But the test

is not necessary due to the fact that I am "out of the danger zone." The danger zone is puberty, he says, when "women like me" are at risk for developing genital abnormalities. I think back to myself at thirteen, staring at my body. And I think it might have made sense to me somehow, if my clitoris had grown like a wild flower and hung its petals between my thighs, which were plumping up in that adult woman way. The doctor is careful with me, knowing how my
10   being XY makes me a bad example of a woman: an XY woman is an ex-woman, whose blood has been infected by Y—the testosterone an uprising, a fire in her blood.

The doctor looks mostly at his chart. He wants me to disappear, to put back in order his faith in the system of things. He wants me to react correctly, to be ashamed. I sit nervously in the paper robe, which covers only the front of my naked body. The cold laboratory air drifts up through the gown. My nipples harden like the heads of screws. He doesn't know he's given me a second chance at my body: I think about the man I could have been. I make a list of names and settle on "Michael," after my father, who did not love me. I imagine the girls in
20   high school I would have been able to love. Michael could have saved me from all of this, from the sound of my voice, from the years of wearing that church dress, which was someone else's skin. Michael is the easier version of me. When the doctor leaves, I shove his crumpled paper gown in the crotch of my briefs. I cover my chest with the eye chart and try to look for Michael. But he is not able to be seen. He is out emptying the trash at the curb. He is in me in that way a man is in a woman.

Fixing My Voice

When Dr. Reardon says he can "fix my voice,"
he means he will give me shots of estrogen,
which will surge through my body like electric shocks
and send the hair on my chin and stomach running
for cover. He doesn't want me to be warm.

He doesn't want to listen to my large truck voice
fill his office like the soy milk bursting up
from the bottom of his morning coffee.
He wants me to be an affirmation.

10   He wants me perched on his plastic table
with smooth naked legs, singing hymns
in the voice of a woman who needs him
in order to recover some piece of herself

that has been swallowed by the jaws of testosterone,
opening and closing hard like the doors of angry lovers.
He doesn't exactly know that he hates me —
the feeling is more like gender indigestion,

how the sound of my voice keeps rising
up in his throat. And he can't rid himself
of the image of my lover, who stretches out   20
nude in our bed and presses her hand
to my chest saying,

"talk to me, please, talk."

From Laramie

I can't look
at the fences.
My body
takes a leave
of absence
before turning
into wildfire.
Signs litter
the open road.
The wind   10
has the trees
in a holdup
until they
let go
of the rain,
which slips
through
the branches
With such
simple rage.   20

For Tomboys

When the neighborhood kids realize you are not a boy,
run — head-tucked, arm-pumping, leg-burning run.

Don't hang around the soccer field to see what they might do.
Don't wait for any of them to press your body against a tree

while the others pull down your pants. Don't wait for reactions,
hoping they still choose you as team captain, still share their water.

Don't freeze up. Don't urinate in fear or shame. Try to forget
scoring your third goal of the afternoon. Forget Shannon Wallace

smiling in your direction, how the boys on your team high-fived,
10 forget that your hands and their hands smacked with sweat

like a kind of boy religion, that the soccer field was boy church,
until the neighborhood kids realize you are not a boy. Run.

Run hard. Run through the bushes—no matter how thick or thorned,
run like you're chasing down the offense, run away from the gold chain

dangling from Vinny Aiello's neck, the crucifix reflecting
the relentless sun. Run from the burning field, run away

from them circling you in the wooded pines, their fingers arrows
in your pounding chest. Run now. For your life. Run.

The Clownfish

How they change is a mystery,
and takes only a few hours,
shimmering with color against
the backdrop of the coral reef,
hiding in crevices for safety.
Sometimes from male to female,
sometimes female to male,
sometimes spending their clownfish lives as neither gender,
10 sometimes as hybrid, as both.
The scientists call it "sexual
plasticity." The scientists say
the clownfish and their ray-finned
friends change their genders
to *maximize fertility*. But
fuck the scientists. They're clownfish after all, making gender
into their honking rubber noses.
Perhaps their genders are a thousand
20 clowns emptying out of a clown car.
Perhaps it's all for a great laugh,
or a great grief, or a great love.

But make no mistake, the scientists
would like to stop them. One fish-
gender specialist in New Hampshire
has been trying for years to stop
the black sea bass from going
through their FTM sex changes.
He wants "more successful breeding."
But the fish won't quit. And "it just gets   30
worse in captivity," he says, leaning
against the tank in his lab coat.

It's clear he's grown fond of them,
the sea bass pressing their spongy
bodies against the glass, pushing at
the boundary between the water
and the threat of the open air.

Letter from Thomas Beattie to the Media
after Bassey Ikpi

This is me, pregnant, all man-chest
and man-chin, resting above a protruding
man-belly, bursting with the burden of baby birth.

This is me, pregnant, feet strapped up
in stirrups at the obstetrician, my legs
unshaven, my gender a *both-at-once*
in the face of fragile certainty.

There was a time you did not know me,
a time your safe sense of this or that
held you at night like an old blanket.   10
I do realize I've broken you.
I do realize I've sent you into a frenzy.

But this is me, pregnant, carrying a new life
in my man-body, pushing a baby through my
man-vagina, which I kept for such an occasion,
its hair coarse and thick with testosterone surge.

And you loathe me, even Oprah shifts in her chair:

> *But how could you . . .*
> *But how will you . . .*
> *But won't it be . . .*   20

This is me, pregnant, and there you are
with your God made this
and your God made that.

What you really know when you see me
is that God made a pregnant man. You know
God made gender a plaything. God made
gender a tire swing, some monkey bars.
God made gender an infinite playground.

This is me, pregnant, and I just might give birth
30   to a whole world, a whole nation of gender-fuckers
rising out from my inevitable and impossible womb.

Reading

1. How many (and by what) terms does Waite describe her identity in her poems?
2. How does Waite understand the relationship between her social and biological identity?
3. How does Waite understand the term *gender*?
4. How does Waite want her gender identity to be understood by others?

Inquiring

1. Waite portrays herself as consistently misidentified by people, whether they be baseball umpires or high school girlfriends. Indeed, one way to read her poetry is as an attempt to capture the complexity of her experience, providing a road map for others to achieve a more nuanced sense of personal identity and creating the possibility for a better response by individuals and the larger culture. As a class, discuss some of the moments when Waite was misidentified (either by accident or by her own choosing). How would you characterize these responses to Waite? Naive? Hostile? Accepting? What do you understand as Waite's way to respond to such moments?

2. After a series of poems in which Waite positions herself as intentionally on both sides of the male/female divide, often taking on the identity of a straight man or a lesbian woman, she writes a poem revealing that she has an extra Y chromosome. This genetic marker disrupts the standard biological definitions of *man* and *woman*. Why do you believe she includes this fact about her biology? Is it just because it is a fact about her? Or does she use this fact to justify her gender role play? How does the fact of this extra chromosome inform her theory of gender identity?

3. Throughout her poems, Waite discusses moments when she represents herself as having a singular identity to girlfriends, employees, and, in one instance, a room full of pizza-buying girls. How do you understand these moments? Do these actions reflect the political and cultural context of the body politic at that time? Has public opinion about "trans-identities" changed to make other actions possible? How do such moments demonstrate Waite's larger argument about gender identity?

Composing

1. Waite has several poetic prompts she consistently invokes throughout *Butch Geography*, such as "Dear Gender" and "On the Occasion of Being Mistaken for . . ." It could be argued that this repeated emphasis demonstrates how these issues are a consistent presence in her life. Waite is not alone in her struggle to understand and respond to gender expectations. Everyone faces this issue. For this assignment, choose one of those two prompts. Use its title and structure as a means to explore the boundaries of your own identity within the gender expectations of your college and larger society. How have these cultural attitudes informed your sense of self? Do you rest comfortably within or actively push against these expectations? Having done this work, write a short essay in which you discuss what values within our cultural geography should guide the definition of gender identities.

2. Waite takes on many identities in her poetry, such as a baseball player, delivery man, loving daughter, and caring boyfriend, among others. In the process, she attempts to invent (or invoke) a new way of speaking that draws all these moments together to explain how to read her gender, her body. Write an essay in which you explore Waite's use of language to describe her gender. Do you accept the necessity for such a new bodily rhetoric to talk about who we are? What might it mean about your own sense of identity if you adopted Waite's understanding of how identity works? Would you find this alternative way of speaking valuable for yourself or for the larger culture?

3. Waite's motivations for writing *Butch Geography* are no doubt complex. She brings together concerns about poetics, aesthetics, gender, personal experience, and cultural politics. It is an open question, however, whether Waite imagines her work as a manifesto—a statement of a broad theoretical and activist paradigm that she hopes others will join—or as a personal statement—one whose primary meaning is to herself. Write an essay in which you examine her goals. How would the meaning of her work be affected if it were read simply as a personal statement? What type of writing or direct action might result if you read her work as a proposal for a new understanding of gender identity? In other words, what insights and actions should follow reading Waite's vision of a "butch geography"? Do you support these actions? Why or why not?

Connecting

Waite argues that a gender identity is ultimately more than female or male, that there are categories between those two genders. Anzaldúa (p. 387) also seems to argue that a single body can inhabit simultaneous identities. Both authors seem to want to see identity as something that can be multiple, containing seeming contradictions. Write an essay in which you explore their understanding of identity, ultimately stating whether or not you find their work useful for how you understand your own identity.

GLORIA ANZALDÚA

Tlilli, Tlapalli/The Path of the Red and Black Ink *and* La Conciencia de la Mestiza/Towards a New Consciousness

Photograph by Margaret Randall

Gloria Anzaldúa was a poet, cultural critic, memoirist, and feminist/queer scholar. At all moments, her writing was concerned with issues of the borderland, of identities that cross multiple categories, and of the multiple languages needed to fully represent them. For this reason, her writing is rich in heritage and complex in structure. *Borderlands/La Frontera: The New Mestiza*, from which the following two essays are drawn, uses two variations of English and six variations of Spanish. It blends cultural criticism, poetry, and memoir. During her life, Anzaldúa received numerous awards, including the National Endowment for the Arts Fiction Award and the American Studies Association Lifetime Achievement Award. Since her death in 2004, the Society for the Study of Gloria Anzaldúa and a poetry prize have been created in her honor.

In the following excerpts, Anzaldúa discusses the meaning and possibilities inherent in a "borderland" identity.

■　■　■

"Out of poverty, poetry;
out of suffering, song."
—a Mexican saying

When I was seven, eight, nine, fifteen, sixteen years old, I would read in bed with a flashlight under the covers, hiding my self-imposed insomnia from my mother. I preferred the world of the imagination

387

to the death of sleep. My sister, Hilda, who slept in the same bed with me, would threaten to tell my mother unless I told her a story.

I was familiar with *cuentos*—my grandmother told stories like the one about her getting on top of the roof while down below rabid coyotes were ravaging the place and wanting to get at her. My father told stories about a phantom giant dog that appeared out of nowhere and sped along the side of the pickup no matter how fast he was driving.

Nudge a Mexican and she or he will break out with a story. So, huddling under the covers, I made up stories for my sister night after night. After a while she wanted two stories per night. I learned to give her installments, building up the suspense with convoluted complications until the story climaxed several nights later. It must have been then that I decided to put stories on paper. It must have been then that working with images and writing became connected to night.

Invoking Art

In the ethno-poetics and performance of the shaman, my people, the Indians, did not split the artistic from the functional, the sacred from the secular, art from everyday life. The religious, social and aesthetic purposes of art were all intertwined. Before the Conquest, poets gathered to play music, dance, sing and read poetry in open-air places around the *Xochicuahuitl, el Árbol Florido*, Tree-in-Flower. (The *Coaxibuitl* or morning glory is called the snake plant and its seeds, known as *ololiuhqui*, are hallucinogenic.[1]) The ability of story (prose and poetry) to transform the storyteller and the listener into something or someone else is shamanistic. The writer, as shape-changer, is a *nahual*, a shaman.

5   In looking at this book that I'm almost finished writing, I see a mosaic pattern (Aztec-like) emerging, a weaving pattern, thin here, thick there. I see a preoccupation with the deep structure, the underlying structure, with the gesso underpainting that is red earth, black earth. I can see the deep structure, the scaffolding. If I can get the bone structure right, then putting flesh on it proceeds without too many hitches. The problem is that the bones often do not exist prior to the flesh, but are shaped after a vague and broad shadow of its form is discerned or uncovered during beginning, middle and final stages of the writing. Numerous overlays of paint, rough surfaces, smooth surfaces make me realize I am preoccupied with texture as well. Too, I see the barely contained color threatening to spill over the boundaries of the object it represents and into other "objects" and over the borders of the frame. I see a hybridization of metaphor, different species of ideas popping up here, popping up there, full of variations and seeming contradictions, though I believe in an ordered, structured universe where all phenomena are interrelated and imbued with spirit. This almost finished product seems an assemblage, a montage, a beaded work with several leitmotifs and with a central core, now appearing, now disappearing in a crazy dance. The whole thing has

had a mind of its own, escaping me and insisting on putting together the pieces of its own puzzle with minimal direction from my will. It is a rebellious, willful entity, a precocious girl-child forced to grow up too quickly, rough, unyielding, with pieces of feather sticking out here and there, fur, twigs, clay. My child, but not for much longer. This female being is angry, sad, joyful, is *Coatlicue*, dove, horse, serpent, cactus. Though it is a flawed thing—a clumsy, complex, groping blind thing—for me it is alive, infused with spirit. I talk to it; it talks to me.

I make my offerings of incense and cracked corn, light my candle. In my head I sometimes will say a prayer—an affirmation and a voicing of intent. Then I run water, wash the dishes or my underthings, take a bath, or mop the kitchen floor. This "induction" period sometimes takes a few minutes, sometimes hours. But always I go against a resistance. Something in me does not want to do this writing. Yet once I'm immersed in it, I can go fifteen to seventeen hours in one sitting and I don't want to leave it.

My "stories" are acts encapsulated in time, "enacted" every time they are spoken aloud or read silently. I like to think of them as performances and not as inert and "dead" objects (as the aesthetics of Western culture think of art works). Instead, the work has an identity; it is a "who" or a "what" and contains the presences of persons, that is, incarnations of gods or ancestors or natural and cosmic powers. The work manifests the same needs as a person, it needs to be "fed," *la tengo que bañar y vestir.*

When invoked in rite, the object/event is "present"; that is, "enacted," it is both a physical thing and the power that infuses it. It is metaphysical in that it "spins its energies between gods and humans" and its task is to move the gods. This type of work dedicates itself to managing the universe and its energies. I'm not sure what it is when it is at rest (not in performance). It may or may not be a "work" then. A mask may only have the power of presence during a ritual dance and the rest of the time it may merely be a "thing." Some works exist forever invoked, always in performance. I'm thinking of totem poles, cave paintings. Invoked art is communal and speaks of everyday life. It is dedicated to the validation of humans; that is, it makes people hopeful, happy, secure, and it can have negative effects as well, which propel one towards a search for validation.[2]

The aesthetic of virtuosity, art typical of Western European cultures, attempts to manage the energies of its own internal system such as conflicts, harmonies, resolutions and balances. It bears the presences of qualities and internal meanings. It is dedicated to the validation of itself. Its task is to move humans by means of achieving mastery in content, technique, feeling. Western art is always whole and always "in power." It is individual (not communal). It is "psychological" in that it spins its energies between itself and its witness.[3]

Western cultures behave differently toward works of art than do tribal cultures. The "sacrifices" Western cultures make are in housing their art works in

10

the best structures designed by the best architects; and in servicing them with insurance, guards to protect them, conservators to maintain them, specialists to mount and display them, and the educated and upper classes to "view" them. Tribal cultures keep art works in honored and sacred places in the home and elsewhere. They attend them by making sacrifices of blood (goat or chicken), libations of wine. They bathe, feed, and clothe them. The works are treated not just as objects, but also as persons. The "witness" is a participant in the enactment of the work in a ritual, and not a member of the privileged classes.[4]

Ethnocentrism is the tyranny of Western aesthetics. An Indian mask in an American museum is transposed into an alien aesthetic system where what is missing is the presence of power invoked through performance ritual. It has become a conquered thing, a dead "thing" separated from nature and, therefore, its power.

Modern Western painters have "borrowed," copied, or otherwise extrapolated the art of tribal cultures and called it cubism, surrealism, symbolism. The music, the beat of the drum, the Blacks' jive talk. All taken over. Whites, along with a good number of our own people, have cut themselves off from their spiritual roots, and they take our spiritual art objects in an unconscious attempt to get them back. If they're going to do it, I'd like them to be aware of what they are doing and to go about doing it the right way. Let's all stop importing Greek myths and the Western Cartesian split point of view and root ourselves in the mythological soil and soul of this continent. White America has only attended to the body of the earth in order to exploit it, never to succor it or to be nurtured in it. Instead of surreptitiously ripping off the vital energy of people of color and putting it to commercial use, whites could allow themselves to share and exchange and learn from us in a respectful way. By taking up *curanderismo*, Santeria, shamanism, Taoism, Zen and otherwise delving into the spiritual life and ceremonies of multi-colored people, Anglos would perhaps lose the white sterility they have in their kitchens, bathrooms, hospitals, mortuaries and missile bases. Though in the conscious mind, black and dark may be associated with death, evil and destruction, in the subconscious mind and in our dreams, white is associated with disease, death and hopelessness. Let us hope that the left hand, that of darkness, of femaleness, of "primitiveness," can divert the indifferent, right-handed, "rational" suicidal drive that, unchecked, could blow us into acid rain in a fraction of a millisecond.

Ni cuicani: I, the Singer

For the ancient Aztecs, *tlilli, tlapalli, la tinta negra y roja de sus códices* (the black and red ink painted on codices) were the colors symbolizing *escritura y sabiduría* (writing and wisdom).[5] They believed that through metaphor and symbol, by means of poetry and truth, communication with the Divine could be attained, and *topan* (that which is above — the gods and spirit world) could be bridged with *mictlán* (that which is below—the underworld and the region of the dead).

> Poet: she pours water from the mouth of the pump, lowers the handle then lifts it, lowers, lifts. Her hands begin to feel the pull from the entrails, the live animal resisting. A sigh rises up from the depths, the handle becomes a wild thing in her hands, the cold sweet water gushes out, splashing her face, the shock of nightlight filling the bucket.

An image is a bridge between evoked emotion and conscious knowledge; words are the cables that hold up the bridge. Images are more direct, more immediate than words, and closer to the unconscious. Picture language precedes thinking in words; the metaphorical mind precedes analytical consciousness.

The Shamanic State

When I create stories in my head, that is, allow the voices and scenes to be projected in the inner screen of my mind, I "trance." I used to think I was going crazy or that I was having hallucinations. But now I realize it is my job, my calling, to traffic in images. Some of these film-like narratives I write down; most are lost, forgotten. When I don't write the images down for several days or weeks or months, I get physically ill. Because writing invokes images from my unconscious, and because some of the images are residues of trauma which I then have to reconstruct, I sometimes get sick when I *do* write. I can't stomach it, become nauseous, or burn with fever, worsen. But, in reconstructing the traumas behind the images, I make "sense" of them, and once they have "meaning" they are changed, transformed. It is then that writing heals me, brings me great joy.

To facilitate the "movies" with soundtracks, I need to be alone, or in a sensory-deprived state. I plug up my ears with wax, put on my black cloth eye-shades, lie horizontal and unmoving, in a state between sleeping and waking, mind and body locked into my fantasy. I am held prisoner by it. My body is experiencing events. In the beginning it is like being in a movie theater, as pure spectator. Gradually I become so engrossed with the activities, the conversations, that I become a participant in the drama. I have to struggle to "disengage" or escape from my "animated story," I have to get some sleep so I can write tomorrow. Yet I am gripped by a story which won't let me go. Outside the frame, I am film director, screenwriter, camera operator. Inside the frame, I am the actors—male and female—I am desert sand, mountain, I am dog, mosquito. I can sustain a four- to six-hour "movie." Once I am up, I can sustain several "shorts" of anywhere between five and thirty minutes. Usually these "narratives" are the offspring of stories acted out in my head during periods of sensory deprivation.

15

My "awakened dreams" are about shifts. Thought shifts, reality shifts, gender shifts: one person metamorphoses into another in a world where people fly through the air, heal from mortal wounds. I am playing with my Self, I am playing with the world's soul, I am the dialogue between my Self and *el espíritu del mundo*. I change myself, I change the world.

Sometimes I put the imagination to a more rare use. I choose words, images, and body sensations and animate them to impress them on my consciousness, thereby making changes in my belief system and reprogramming my consciousness. This involves looking my inner demons in the face, then deciding which I want in my psyche. Those I don't want, I starve; I feed them no words, no images, no feelings. I spend no time with them, share not my home with them. Neglected, they leave. This is harder to do than to merely generate "stories." I can only sustain this activity for a few minutes.

I write the myths in me, the myths I am, the myths I want to become. The word, the image and the feeling have a palpable energy, a kind of power. *Con imágenes domo mi miedo, cruzo los abismos que tengo por dentro. Con palabras me hago piedra, pájaro, puente de serpientes arrastrando a ras del suelo todo lo que soy, todo lo que algún día seré.*

20
Los que están mirando (leyendo),
los que cuentan (o refieren lo que leen).
Los que vuelven ruidosamente las hojas de los códices.
Los que tienen en su poder
la tinta negra y roja (la sabiduría)
y lo pintado,
ellos nos llevan, nos guían,
nos dicen el camino.[6]

Writing Is a Sensuous Act

Tallo mi cuerpo como si estuviera lavando un trapo. Toco las saltadas venas de mis manos, mis chichis adormecidas como pájaras al anochecer. Estoy encorvada sobre la cama. Las imágenes aletean alrededor de mi cama como murciélagos, la sábana como que tuviese alas. El ruido de los trenes subterráneos en mi sentido como conchas. Parece que las paredes del cuarto se me arriman cada vez más cerquita.

Picking out images from my soul's eye, fishing for the right words to recreate the images. Words are blades of grass pushing past the obstacles, sprouting on the page; the spirit of the words moving in the body is as concrete as flesh and as palpable; the hunger to create is as substantial as fingers and hand.

I look at my fingers, see plumes growing there. From the fingers, my feathers, black and red ink drips across the page. *Escribo con la tinta de mi sangre.* I write in red. Ink. Intimately knowing the smooth touch of paper, its speechlessness before I spill myself on the insides of trees. Daily, I battle the silence and the red. Daily, I take my throat in my hands and squeeze until the cries pour out, my larynx and soul sore from the constant struggle.

Something to Do with the Dark

> *Quien canta, sus males espanta.*
> —*un dicho*

The toad comes out of its hiding place inside the lobes of my brain. It's going to happen again. The ghost of the toad that betrayed me—I hold it in my hand. The toad is sipping the strength from my veins, it is sucking my pale heart. I am a dried serpent skin, wind scuttling me across the hard ground, pieces of me scattered over the countryside. And there in the dark I meet the crippled spider crawling in the gutter, the day-old newspaper fluttering in the dirty rain water. 25

> *Musa bruja, venga. Cúbrese con una sábana y espante mis demonios que a rempujones y a cachetadas me roban la pluma me rompen el sueño. Musa, ¡misericordia!*
>
> *Óigame, musa bruja. ¿Por qué huye uste' en mi cara? Su grito me desarrolla de mi caracola, me sacude el alma. Vieja, quítese de aquí con sus alas de navaja. Ya no me despedaze mi cara. Vaya con sus pinche uñas que me desgarran de los ojos hasta los talones. Váyese a la tiznada. Que no me coman, le digo, Que no me coman sus nueve dedos caníbales.*
>
> *Hija negra de la noche, carnala, ¿Por qué me sacas las tripas, por qué cardas mis entrañas? Este hilvanando palabras con tripas me está matando. Jija de la noche ¡vete a la chingada!*

Writing produces anxiety. Looking inside myself and my experience, looking at my conflicts, engenders anxiety in me. Being a writer feels very much like being a Chicana, or being queer—a lot of squirming, coming up against all sorts of walls. Or its opposite: nothing defined or definite, a boundless, floating state of limbo where I kick my heels, brood, percolate, hibernate and wait for something to happen.

Living in a state of psychic unrest, in a Borderland, is what makes poets write and artists create. It is like a cactus needle embedded in the flesh. It worries itself deeper and deeper, and I keep aggravating it by poking at it. When it begins to fester I have to do something to put an end to the aggravation and to figure out why I have it. I get deep down into the place where it's rooted in my skin and pluck away at it, playing it like a musical instrument—the fingers pressing, making the pain worse before it can get better. Then out it comes. No more discomfort, no more ambivalence. Until another needle pierces the skin. That's what writing is for me, an endless cycle of making it worse, making it better, but always making meaning out of the experience, whatever it may be. 30

My flowers shall not cease to live;
my songs shall never end:
I, a singer, intone them;
they become scattered, they are spread about.

—*Cantares mexicanos*

To write, to be a writer, I have to trust and believe in myself as a speaker, as a voice for the images. I have to believe that I can communicate with images and words and that I can do it well. A lack of belief in my creative self is a lack of belief in my total self and vice versa—I cannot separate my writing from any part of my life. It is all one.

When I write it feels like I'm carving bone. It feels like I'm creating my own face, my own heart—a Nahuatl concept. My soul makes itself through the creative act. It is constantly remaking and giving birth to itself through my body. It is this learning to live with *la Coatlicue* that transforms living in the Borderlands from a nightmare into a numinous experience. It is always a path/state to something else.

In *Xóchilt* in *Cuícatl*[7]

35   She writes while other people, sleep. Something is trying to come out. She fights the words, pushes them down, down, a woman with morning sickness in the middle of the night. How much easier it would be to carry a baby for nine months and then expel it permanently. These continuous multiple pregnancies are going to kill her. She is the battlefield for the pitched fight between the inner image and the words trying to recreate it. *La musa bruja* has no manners. Doesn't she know, nights are for sleeping?

She is getting too close to the mouth of the abyss. She is teetering on the edge, trying to balance while she makes up her mind whether to jump in or to find a safer way down. That's why she makes herself sick—to postpone having to jump blindfolded into the abyss of her own being and there in the depths confront her face, the face underneath the mask.

To be a mouth—the cost is too high—her whole life enslaved to that devouring mouth. *Todo pasaba por esa boca, el viento, el fuego, los mares y la Tierra.* Her body, a crossroads, a fragile bridge, cannot support the tons of cargo passing through it. She wants to install "stop" and "go" signal lights, instigate a curfew, police Poetry. But something wants to come out.

Blocks (*Coatlicue* states) are related to my cultural identity. The painful periods of confusion that I suffer from are symptomatic of a larger creative process: cultural shifts. The stress of living with cultural ambiguity both compels me to write and blocks me. It isn't until I'm almost at the end of the blocked state that I remember and recognize it for what it is. As soon as this happens, the piercing light of awareness melts the block and I accept the deep and the darkness and

I hear one of my voices saying, "I am tired of fighting. I surrender. I give up, let go, let the walls fall. On this night of the hearing of faults, *Tlazolteotl, diosa de la cara negra,* let fall the cockroaches that live in my hair, the rats that nestle in my skull. Gouge out my lame eyes, rout my demon from its nocturnal cave. Set torch to the tiger that stalks me. Loosen the dead faces gnawing my cheekbones. I am tired of resisting. I surrender. I give up, let go, let the walls fall."

And in descending to the depths I realize that down is up, and I rise up from and into the deep. And once again I recognize that the internal tension of oppositions can propel (if it doesn't tear apart) the *mestiza* writer out of the *metate* where she is being ground with corn and water, eject her out as *nahual,* an agent of transformation, able to modify and shape primordial energy and therefore able to change herself and others into turkey, coyote, tree, or human.

I sit here before my computer, *Amiguita,* my altar on top of the monitor with the *Virgen de Coatlalopeuh* candle and copal incense burning. My companion, a wooden serpent staff with feathers, is to my right while I ponder the ways metaphor and symbol concretize the spirit and etherealize the body. The Writing is my whole life, it is my obsession. This vampire which is my talent does not suffer other suitors.[8] Daily I court it, offer my neck to its teeth. This is the sacrifice that the act of creation requires, a blood sacrifice. For only through the body, through the pulling of flesh, can the human soul be transformed. And for images, words, stories to have this transformative power, they must arise from the human body—flesh and bone—and from the Earth's body—stone, sky, liquid, soil. This work, these images, piercing tongue or ear lobes with cactus needle, are my offerings, are my Aztecan blood sacrifices.

40

■ ■ ■

*Por la mujer de mi raza
hablará el espíritu.*[9]

José Vasconcelos, Mexican philosopher, envisaged *una raza mestiza, una mezcla de razas afines, una raza de color—la primera raza síntesis del globo.* He called it a cosmic race, *la raza cósmica,* a fifth race embracing the four major races of the world.[10] Opposite to the theory of the pure Aryan, and to the policy of racial purity that white America practices, his theory is one of inclusivity. At the confluence of two or more genetic streams, with chromosomes constantly "crossing over," this mixture of races, rather than resulting in an inferior being, provides hybrid progeny, a mutable, more malleable species with a rich gene pool. From this racial, ideological, cultural and biological cross-pollinization, an "alien" consciousness is presently in the making—a new *mestiza* consciousness, *una conciencia de mujer.* It is a consciousness of the Borderlands.

Una lucha de fronteras/A Struggle of Borders

Because I, a *mestiza*,
continually walk out of one culture
and into another,
because I am in all cultures at the same time,
alma entre dos mundos, tres, cuatro,
me zumba la cabeza con lo contradictorio.
Estoy norteada por todas las voces que me hablan
simultáneamente.

The ambivalence from the clash of voices results in mental and emotional states of perplexity. Internal strife results in insecurity and indecisiveness. The *mestiza's* dual or multiple personality is plagued by psychic restlessness.

5   In a constant state of mental nepantilism, an Aztec word meaning torn between ways, *la mestiza* is a product of the transfer of the cultural and spiritual values of one group to another. Being tricultural, monolingual, bilingual, or multilingual, speaking a patois, and in a state of perpetual transition, the *mestiza* faces the dilemma of the mixed breed: which collectivity does the daughter of a darkskinned mother listen to?

El choque de un alma atrapado entre el mundo del espíritu y el mundo de la técnica a veces la deja entullada. Cradled in one culture, sandwiched between two cultures, straddling all three cultures and their value systems, *la mestiza* undergoes a struggle of flesh, a struggle of borders, an inner war. Like all people, we perceive the version of reality that our culture communicates. Like others having or living in more than one culture, we get multiple, often opposing messages. The coming together of two self-consistent but habitually incompatible frames of reference[11] causes *un choque*, a cultural collision.

Within us and within *la cultura chicana*, commonly held beliefs of the white culture attack commonly held beliefs of the Mexican culture, and both attack commonly held beliefs of the indigenous culture. Subconsciously, we see an attack on ourselves and our beliefs as a threat and we attempt to block with a counterstance.

But it is not enough to stand on the opposite river bank, shouting questions, challenging patriarchal, white conventions. A counterstance locks one into a duel of oppressor and oppressed; locked in mortal combat, like the cop and the criminal, both are reduced to a common denominator of violence. The counterstance refutes the dominant culture's views and beliefs, and, for this, it is proudly defiant. All reaction is limited by, and dependent on, what it is reacting against. Because the counter-stance stems from a problem with authority—outer as well as inner—it's a step towards liberation from cultural domination. But it is not a way of life. At some point, on our way to a new consciousness, we will have to leave the opposite bank, the split between the two mortal combatants somehow healed so that we are on both shores at once and, at once, see through serpent and eagle eyes. Or perhaps we will decide to disengage from the dominant culture, write it off altogether as a lost cause, and cross the border into a wholly new and separate territory. Or we might go another route. The possibilities are numerous once we decide to act and not react.

A Tolerance for Ambiguity

These numerous possibilities leave *la mestiza* floundering in uncharted seas. In perceiving conflicting information and points of view, she is subjected to a swamping of her psychological borders. She has discovered that she can't hold concepts or ideas in rigid boundaries. The borders and walls that are supposed to keep the undesirable ideas out are entrenched habits and patterns of behavior; these habits and patterns are the enemy within. Rigidity means death. Only by remaining flexible is she able to stretch the psyche horizontally and vertically. *La mestiza* constantly has to shift out of habitual formations; from convergent thinking, analytical reasoning that tends to use rationality to move toward a single goal (a Western mode), to divergent thinking,[12] characterized by movement away from set patterns and goals and toward a more whole perspective, one that includes rather than excludes.

The new *mestiza* copes by developing a tolerance for contradictions, a tolerance for ambiguity. She learns to be an Indian in Mexican culture, to be Mexican from an Anglo point of view. She learns to juggle cultures. She has a plural personality, she operates in a pluralistic mode—nothing is thrust out, the good the bad and the ugly, nothing rejected, nothing abandoned. Not only does she sustain contradictions, she turns the ambivalence into something else.

She can be jarred out of ambivalence by an intense, and often painful, emotional event which inverts or resolves the ambivalence. I'm not sure exactly how. The work takes place underground—subconsciously. It is work that the soul performs. That focal point or fulcrum, that juncture where the *mestiza* stands, is where phenomena tend to collide. It is where the possibility of uniting all that is separate occurs. This assembly is not one where severed or separated pieces merely come together. Nor is it a balancing of opposing powers. In attempting to work out a synthesis, the self has added a third element which is greater than the sum of its severed parts. That third element is a new consciousness—a *mestiza* consciousness—and though it is a source of intense pain, its energy comes from continual creative motion that keeps breaking down the unitary aspect of each new paradigm.

En unas pocas centurias, the future will belong to the *mestiza*. Because the future depends on the breaking down of paradigms, it depends on the straddling of two or more cultures. By creating a new mythos—that is, a change in the way we perceive reality, the way we see ourselves, and the ways we behave—*la mestiza* creates a new consciousness.

10

The work of *mestiza* consciousness is to break down the subject-object duality that keeps her a prisoner and to show in the flesh and through the images in her work how duality is transcended. The answer to the problem between the white race and the colored, between males and females, lies in healing the split that originates in the very foundation of our lives, our culture, our languages, our thoughts. A massive uprooting of dualistic thinking in the individual and collective consciousness is the beginning of a long struggle, but one that could, in our best hopes, bring us to the end of rape, of violence, of war. . . .

El camino de la mestiza/The Mestiza Way

Caught between the sudden contraction, the breath sucked in and the endless space, the brown woman stands still, looks at the sky. She decides to go down, digging her way along the roots of trees. Sifting through the bones, she shakes them to see if there is any marrow in them. Then, touching the dirt to her forehead, to her tongue, she takes a few bones, leaves the rest in their burial place.

15

She goes through her backpack, keeps her journal and address book, throws away the muni-bart metromaps. The coins are heavy and they go next, then the greenbacks flutter through the air. She keeps her knife, can opener and eyebrow pencil. She puts bones, pieces of bark, *hierbas*, eagle feather, snakeskin, tape recorder, the rattle and drum in her pack and she sets out to become the complete *tolteca*.

Her first step is to take inventory. *Despojando, desgranando, quitando paja.* Just what did she inherit from her ancestors? This weight on her back—which is the baggage from the Indian mother, which the baggage from the Spanish father, which the baggage from the Anglo?

Pero es difícil differentiating between *lo heredado, lo adquirido, lo impuesto.* She puts history through a sieve, winnows out the lies, looks at the forces that we as a race, as women, have been a part of. *Luego bota lo que no vale, los desmientos, los desencuentos, el embrutecimiento. Aguarda el juicio, hondo y enraizado, de la gente antigua.* This step is a conscious rupture with all oppressive traditions of all cultures and religions. She communicates that rupture, documents the struggle. She reinterprets history and, using new symbols, she shapes new myths. She adopts new perspectives toward the darkskinned, women and queers. She strengthens her tolerance (and intolerance) for ambiguity. She is willing to share, to make herself vulnerable to foreign ways of seeing and thinking. She surrenders all notions of safety, of the familiar. Deconstruct, construct. She becomes a *nahual*, able to transform herself into a tree, a coyote, into another person. She learns to transform the small "I" into the total Self. *Se hace moldeadora de su alma. Según la concepción que tiene de sí misma, así será.*

Que no se nos olviden los hombres

> *"Tú no sirves pa' nada—*
> you're good for nothing.
> *Eres pura vieja."*

"You're nothing but a woman" means you are defective. Its opposite is to be *un macho.* The modern meaning of the word "machismo," as well as the concept, is actually an Anglo invention. For men like my father, being "macho" meant being strong enough to protect and support my mother and us, yet being able to show love. Today's macho has doubts about his ability to feed and protect his family. His "machismo" is an adaptation to oppression and poverty and low self-esteem. It is the result of hierarchical male dominance. The Anglo, feeling inadequate and inferior and powerless, displaces or transfers these feelings to the Chicano by shaming him. In the Gringo world, the Chicano suffers from excessive humility and self-effacement, shame of self and self-deprecation. Around Latinos he suffers from a sense of language inadequacy and its accompanying discomfort; with Native Americans he suffers from a racial amnesia which ignores our common blood, and from guilt because the Spanish part of him took their land and oppressed them. He has an excessive compensatory hubris when around Mexicans from the other side. It overlays a deep sense of racial shame.

The loss of a sense of dignity and respect in the macho breeds a false machismo which leads him to put down women and even to brutalize them. Coexisting with his sexist behavior is a love for the mother which takes precedence over that of all others. Devoted son, macho pig. To wash down the shame of his acts, of his very being, and to handle the brute in the mirror, he takes to the bottle, the snort, the needle, and the fist.

20

Though we "understand" the root causes of male hatred and fear, and the subsequent wounding of women, we do not excuse, we do not condone, and we will no longer put up with it. From the men of our race, we demand the admission/acknowledgment/disclosure/testimony that they wound us, violate us, are afraid of us and of our power. We need them to say they will begin to eliminate their hurtful put-down ways. But more than the words, we demand acts. We say to them: We will develop equal power with you and those who have shamed us.

It is imperative that *mestizas* support each other in changing the sexist elements in the Mexican-Indian culture. As long as woman is put down, the Indian and the Black in all of us is put down. The struggle of the *mestiza* is above all a feminist one. As long as *los hombres* think they have to *chingar mujeres* and each other to be men, as long as men are taught that they are superior and therefore culturally favored over *la mujer;* as long as to be a *vieja* is a thing of derision, there can be no real healing of our psyches. We're halfway there—we have such love of the Mother, the good mother. The first step is to unlearn the *puta/virgen* dichotomy and to see *Coatlalopeuh-Coatlicue* in the Mother, *Guadalupe*.

Tenderness, a sign of vulnerability, is so feared that it is showered on women with verbal abuse and blows. Men, even more than women, are fettered to gender roles. Women at least have had the guts to break out of bondage. Only gay men have had the courage to expose themselves to the woman inside them and to challenge the current masculinity. I've encountered a few scattered and isolated gentle straight men, the beginnings of a new breed, but they are confused, and entangled with sexist behaviors that they have not been able to eradicate. We need a new masculinity and the new man needs a movement.

Lumping the males who deviate from the general norm with man, the oppressor, is a gross injustice. *Asombra pensar que nos hemos quedado en ese pozo oscuro donde el mundo encierra a las lesbianas. Asombra pensar que hemos, como femenistas y lesbianas, cerrado nuestros corazónes a los hombres, a nuestros hermanos los jotos, desheredados y marginales como nosotros.* Being the supreme crossers of cultures, homosexuals have strong bonds with the queer white, Black, Asian, Native American, Latino, and with the queer in Italy, Australia and the rest of the planet. We come from all colors, all classes, all races, all time periods. Our role is to link people with each other — the Blacks with Jews with Indians with Asians with whites with extraterrestrials. It is to transfer ideas and information from one culture to another. Colored homosexuals have more knowledge of other cultures; have always been at the forefront (although sometimes in the closet) of all liberation struggles in this country; have suffered more injustices and have survived them despite all odds. Chicanos need to acknowledge the political and artistic contributions of their queer. People, listen to what your *jotería* is saying.

25   The *mestizo* and the queer exist at this time and point on the evolutionary continuum for a purpose. We are a blending that proves that all blood is intricately woven together, and that we are spawned out of similar souls.

Reading

1. How does Anzaldúa define a *mestiza* consciousness?
2. How does she define the *mestiza* consciousness's primary struggle?
3. How does writing in multiple languages express this consciousness?
4. How does Anzaldúa's writing attempt to demonstrate the "consciousness of the borderlands"?

Inquiring

1. In discussing her identity as a writer, Anzaldúa states, "The writer, as shape-changer, is a *nahual*, a shaman" (para. 4 of the first selection). Later,

when describing the shamanic state, she describes how her "awakened dreams" are really about "shifts" between realities, between genders, where "one person metamorphoses into another in a world where people fly through the air, heal from mortal wounds. I am playing with my Self, I am playing with the world's soul, I am the dialogue between my Self and *el espíritu del mundo*. I change myself, I change the world" (para. 17 of the first selection). Given these statements, what do you imagine Anzaldúa believes to be the work of the writer? How might taking on this sense alter your own writing? What might it mean about learning to use language to speak publicly on issues important to you, to change the world?

2. Anzaldúa writes about her hybrid identity, her ability to shift between the multiple cultures in which she exists. One way in which this hybridity is made evident is in the multilingual nature of her text, which features both English and Spanish. Unlike some similar texts, however, Anzaldúa does not offer translations of either language. Clearly she must have known that many of her readers would be unable to read both languages. As you understand her project, why do you think she made this decision? Would you have made a similar decision? Why or why not?

3. The selection from *La conciencia de la mestiza* attempts to create an alternative to current forms of public debate over the values of different cultural heritages—a form of debate characterized by a stance/counterstance model. Although acknowledging the need to critique existing forms of oppression, Anzaldúa argues that "a counterstance locks one into a duel of oppressor and oppressed; locked in mortal combat, like the cop and the criminal, both are reduced to a common denominator of violence" (para. 8 of the second selection). As a class, trace what Anzaldúa believes to be the values of Western culture, particularly its framing of Mexican/Latino history and heritage. How does her position as a *mestiza* writer offer something different from a counterstance to Western culture? What productive alternative does Anzaldúa see herself as offering?

Composing

1. When defining her identity as a writer, Anzaldúa draws on the multiple heritages in which she participates: Mexican, lesbian, feminist, and *mestiza*, to name a few. She also makes a point of inflecting her writing with these influences, moving between Spanish and English as well as citing a diverse range of authors. By the conclusion of these two essays, Anzaldúa's identity is enmeshed and articulated within a broad cultural network from which and for which she is trying to speak. Write an essay in which you articulate your own identity as a writer within your own cultural network, making clear how this network's values both enable and charge you to take on specific types of work. Like Anzaldúa, write within the multiple voices that represent your heritage and actively blend these voices to demonstrate through writing how you see them

as interconnected. That is, don't approach this essay as an "academic paper"; instead, think of it as an essay in which you bring your full cultural knowledge into an academic classroom.

2. Anzaldúa's *La conciencia de la mestiza* begins by citing José Vasconcelos's vision of *una raza mestiza*, the "consciousness of the Borderlands" (para. 1 of the second selection). Write an essay in which you examine this "consciousness of the Borderlands" and how it differs from what Anzaldúa images to be more established ways of viewing the world. To what extent is her vision premised on reframing the meaning of our bodies? Of our consciousness? Does Anzaldúa see Vasconcelos's vision as a metaphor or as a necessary fact in the creation of this consciousness? How does Anzaldúa's vision of the new *mestizo* body also a call for a new body politic? Do you find her arguments for this new social vision compelling?

3. Anzaldúa writes that "the struggle of the *mestiza* is above all a feminist one" (para. 22 of the second selection). Do you agree or disagree with this assessment? Before deciding, however, you must first fully understand what Anzaldúa means by *feminism* and how it intersects with and emerges from other aspects of her work. Write an essay in which you articulate Anzaldúa's definition of *feminism*. How is it a product of her diverse cultural experiences? What goals does she imagine for feminism? How does it differ from other versions with which you might be familiar? Having done this work, discuss whether you believe the work of the *mestiza* is necessarily feminist. Are there other struggles you believe should take precedence? If so, which ones, and why?

Connecting

Anzaldúa makes many claims for the value of a *mestiza* consciousness, arguing for its value from the personal to the political. She attempts to enact this consciousness through her writing, particularly the style of her writing. Alexander (p. 403) argues that expanding students' cultural literacy, such as their sexual literacy, will expand their ability to use language. Write an essay in which you explore how Alexander might understand the value of a *mestiza* consciousness for students learning to write in the university. How might it relate to, expand, or build on his vision of sexual literacy? Do you agree with the importance of such literacy in a university writing classroom?

JONATHAN ALEXANDER

Queer Theory for Straight Students

Leigh Castelli Photography

Jonathan Alexander is a professor of English, education, and gender and sexuality studies at the University of California, Irvine. His work explores how emerging digital technologies are changing the meaning of writing for students, professors, and the general public. Within this context, Alexander explores how theories of sexuality, as a literacy practice, can be used to understand the possibilities of the current moment, both in terms of new conceptions of authorship as well as democratic literacy practices. In 2011, he was awarded the Charles Moran Award for Distinguished Contributions to the Field of Computers and Writing Studies.

In the following excerpt, Alexander discusses a moment when his students had to interpret a Web site called "StraightBoyz4NSync."

■　■　■

Henry Giroux has famously advocated for a "pedagogy of difference," which, in his words, "seeks to understand how difference is constructed in the intersection of the official cannon of the school and the various voices of students from subordinate groups, but also draws upon students' experience as both a narrative for agency and a referent for critique. . . . Such a pedagogy contributes to making possible a variety of human capacities which expand the range of social identities that students may become. It points to the importance of understanding in both pedagogical and political terms how subjectivities are produced within those social forms in which people move but of which they are often only partially conscious" (1992, 138).

Along such lines, some compositionists have taken advantage of the stories, essays, and articles by and about queer people included in first-year writing textbooks . . . to introduce their students to some of the "various voices of students from subordinate groups." Certainly, an aim of such inclusion has been to spark discussion about how certain groups, such as queers, narrate the story of their lives, coming to terms not only with their own self-awareness but understanding that self-awareness and their articulation of it as densely intertwined with the stories the greater society tells about sex and sexuality. As such, narrations by queers, such as "coming-out" stories, offer students and teachers an opportunity to see how a member of a "subordinate group" might attempt to make meaning out of the bits and pieces of information and narrative available to him or her in a culture whose dominant narratives about sexuality are heterocentric and frequently homophobic.

Curiously, my students at the University of Cincinnati, where I taught writing from 1998 to 2007, seemed increasingly "comfortable" with talking about sexual orientation; the "edge" is "off" our discussions of these once "touchy" topics. In many ways, this is good. I don't want the majority of my students to flinch when the topic of sexuality or sexual orientation comes up in conversation—or when I tell them that I am queer. And certainly, bringing in queer texts for study and analysis has probably made many students more comfortable with queer topics and issues—which, again, is good. At the same time, my students' seeming comfort may actually be complacency, or an unwillingness to think more *critically* about a topic that just *seems* passé. *So there are gay people. Big deal? What does that have to do with us? Gays have had a hard time in a homophobic culture and "coming out" is a big deal. Yes, that's terrible and it should change—but again, so what? We've all seen* Will & Grace. *What does that have to do with us?*

As such, I am left with a nagging question: as queerness "leaves the margins," are we losing a bit of that sharp vision a queer critique can offer? Put another way, is the actual work of *queer theory* getting done? For instance, are students questioning the naturalized structures of heteronormativity and heterosexism? Are they interrogating naturalized narrations of sexuality, identity, and normalcy? Beyond simply *including* queer voices into the rhetorical mix, I think that queer theories and scholarship offer us a chance to *critically* examine the ways in which gender and sexuality are constructed, narrated, and deployed in the creation of identities, modes of being, and community. Such analysis—intimately connected to the stories we tell about ourselves, the narrations we use to make sense of and question our ways of being—opens up possibilities of understanding how meaning is created and narrated for *all* lives, not just gay and lesbian ones. As such, the queer theoretical critique can help to underscore the intertwining of literacy and sexuality throughout our culture. More specifically, queer theory may offer us a chance to investigate some of the powerful "secondary discourses" of sexuality through which so much emotional, intimate, and even political energy is mobilized in the construction of and identification with categories of sexual identity—"gay" and "straight" being most dominant.

What I propose to do in this chapter, then, is explore what a queer critique   5
might mean for self-identified *heterosexual* students in first-year writing classes
and for their development of a critical sexual literacy. Specifically, I analyze in
some detail an in-class exercise in which I invited my students to write about an
online performance of heterosexuality. In the process of thinking about this activity with my students, I believe that we had a unique opportunity to explore the
constructedness of sexual orientation as an identity category and thus increase
both our critical thinking about the relationship between narration and identity
and our collective sense of sexual literacy. . . .

Disrupting the Narrative of Straightness, or Performing a Hoax

Inevitably, it is easier to say you're going to disrupt something than it is to actually disrupt it. But I am convinced that straightness can—and should—be "que-
ried." But how? Calvin Thomas suggests, "there can be nothing more terrifying
to what Monique Witting calls 'the straight mind' than being 'mistaken' for a
'queer'" (2000, 26). Since declarations of one's straightness seem most common
when that straightness is called into question or doubt, I have theorized that we
could "tease out" for examination a narration of straightness by playing with this
"soft spot" in the straight subjectivity—by poking at the point where straightness must maintain itself as an identity over and against queerness. . . . In other
words, performing a narration of straightness, inhabiting its story, might work
its weakness from the inside out. Just one problem. How can I, as a queer man,
"inhabit" or perform straightness? . . .

I took a clue from "hoax sites," such as *The Onion* online, and I postulated
that I might be able to create a Web site that did my theoretical poking for me.
For instance, one of the first hoax sites I ever used in a composition class was the
Senator Kelly Mutant Watch campaign site (www.mutantwatch.com), which is a
"hoax site" serving as an advertisement for the film *The X-Men*. The site *seems* like
a campaign site for Senator Kelly, the archconservative who wants to keep the
world—and your children—safe from the "evil" mutants. (Sound familiar, anyone?) What's wonderful about this site is how cleverly—and closely—the site
designers mimic both a campaign site and the rhetoric of an unthinking, knee-
jerk conservatism, and many writers and fans have noted how the antimutant
rhetoric deployed on the site is startlingly similar to that of antigay conservatives
such as former conservative senator Jesse Helms. Using such sites in class offers
an engaging way to examine how rhetoric is used to create, sustain, and prom-
ulgate various ideological stances, often based on misinformation, unfounded
assumptions and—frequently—the demonization of "others." As such, a hoax
site seemed a good vehicle to *queer* various rhetorics, to push at the soft spots in
certain ideological constructions.

I wondered: could the same medium be used to push at the soft spots in heterosexuality? And what would this look like? With such questions in mind, I

created a hoax site, a personal homepage, about a straightboy, Dax, who has a "secret." His site, Straightboyz4Nsync (http://www.geocities.com/straightboyz4n-sync), is about a college-aged male student who is trying to "come out of the closet," as it were, about his fascination with the boy band Nsync. His home-page is a "fan site," largely about his interest in the band, and it contains links to other Nsync fan sites and a developing short story (to which you can contrib-ute) about a straightboy's fascination with a boy band. Like many other fan sites, Straightboyz4Nsync also has pictures, a short bio, and even a link to a Yahoo! Group so that other straightboy fans of Nsync can communicate with one another.

My creation of such a site readily reveals my pedagogical—and personal—investments, which is *not* to say that I'm a fan of Nsync. I'm not. Really. And Straightboyz4Nsync is not just a revenge fantasy—virtually giving a straight guy a "shameful" secret he has to hide for fear of rejection or castigation. (Okay, maybe it's a little of that, but not much.) Rather, Straightboyz4Nsync is an attempt to provoke discussion: about the ways in which "straightness" is "per-formed," is narrated, is constructed and maintained as an identity. What would happen if students were confronted with a "straightboy" with a "secret"? How would they "read" his sexuality and his self-narration? What insights about the narration of straightness might be teased out with a site in which someone marks himself as "straight"? More generally, what thoughts, insights, or even defen-sive reactions about straightness might the site evoke, or disrupt? By giving a self-identified "straightboy" a secret—a secret that could homophobically bring his "straightness" into question—I hoped to prompt discussion about how one's "straightness" is constructed and maintained. In other words, I hoped to ask—and provisionally answer—the question, what is the "story" of "straight-ness"? Moreover, what might teasing out that story tell us about the politics—and rhetoric—of heterosexuality in our culture? . . .

Protesting a Little Too Much: Comments from Students

10   I used my hoax site in three separate sections. Two were fairly identical courses, both third-term (on the quarter system) first-year writing courses, which serve as "capstone" courses in which students write long, argumentative research papers. My focus in this course was on issues surrounding HIV/AIDS, personally, socially, and politically. Students participated in service-learning assignments, composing pamphlets, text for Web sites, and other projects for local AIDS service orga-nizations. The other course I used the exercise in was a "Web Literacies" course that I designed for our communications program; this course examined the Web in its sociocultural dimensions, as a tool for individual identity performance, community building, and even political organization and activism. In all three classes, we eventually discussed issues pertaining to homosexuality and homo-phobia, noting, in the writing classes, the continued association of AIDS with gayness and, in the communications class, the use of the Web by many queers to experiment with identity and find community. Since all three classes met in

computerized classrooms, I frequently had the opportunity to show students queer-themed homepages and sites for discussion, both face-to-face and electronically enabled. I began to think, though, that it was easy for many students to understand such sites as "other," as indicative of queer experience, and thus as having no connection to their own, avowedly straight lives. Straightboyz4Nsync was designed in part to "queery" that.

After viewing the Web site, students were asked to respond, comment, and discuss via a Blackboard discussion board. . . .

The majority of comments offered via the discussion board fall into two categories that, I think, invite and are willing to engage critical discussion of sexual orientation and its construction in our society—albeit in ways that are often surprising and in need of further interrogation. First, some students seemed to understand exactly what I had intended in posting the site for discussion, and they responded to the site critically, specifically pointing out the norms through which sexual orientation identities are maintained and the double binds in which they place men.

> I personally think ther is nothing wrong with a guy liking a boy band, however, it is just not the "norm" with society. Boy bands are seen as gay by society, so when a male likes a boy band they are seen as gay also.
>
> It [the site] might bring up the controversial "norms" of sexuality and why it is okay or not okay [for] one to stray away from these "norms."
>
> This is a typical example of what happens when somebody steps out of the "normal" boundaries: when guys like boy bands they are thought to be gay, why can't a guy just like a boy band?

Such responses served as useful "jumping-off" points for discussions of both how and why such "norms" are in place, as well as how difficult it is to "come out of the closet" as a transgressor of gender or sexuality norms. Indeed, we discussed Straightboyz4Nsync in terms of the "closet," suggesting that straight men's sense and performance of sexuality and gender are often carefully self-regulated to maintain the straight/gay and even masculine/feminine binaries. Again, such a discussion quickly leads to consideration of why such norms need regulation and policing, as well as to an examination of whose interests they serve. In the process, students think critically about how sexuality and gender are tied to our senses of identity. In particular, the following comment directly alludes to the connection between gender identities and sexuality, particularly as they apply to men:

> guys care too much if people think their gay. That's the real issue.
> I went to lilith fair, most people think of that as a lesbian thing.
> But I don't really care what people think, it's just good music. No lifestyle comes with it.

The student's comment is quick to dismiss the issues as seemingly trivial, but oral discussion in response to this comment revolved around our culture's careful policing of the boundaries of maleness as opposed to femaleness, the implied sexism of such policing, and the use of strict concepts of masculinity and femininity as a tool to maintain a delimiting division of labor as well as a marketing ploy to create distinct categories of consumers. The discussion was wide ranging and varied, and I was impressed that some students could use the Straightboyz4Nsync site as a launching pad, as it were, for making connections between gender, sexuality, economics, and politics. More significantly, in terms of queer theory's questioning of the normalization and naturalization of certain identity formations, students questioned why certain gender categories and expectations exist. A student asking a simple question—such as "why can't a guy just like a boy band?"—seems, well, simplistic, but it can introduce good discussion about the construction of social, gender, and sexual roles.

Such conversations were delightful, but the majority of students debated a very different aspect of the site—one that led to our most "disruptive" discussions about identity and sexuality. These students addressed the supposed *intent* of the site, questioning why Dax felt the need both to create the site and, more radically, to identify himself as "straight." The discussion began with several students who, seemingly sympathetic to Dax, were concerned that Dax might be a bit homophobic:

> it kind of seems that he has something against gay men, and he seems to speak of them pretty stereotypically

> This guy seems a little too homophobic. When people act like that, their heterosexuality is debatable. This kid's beliefs seem highly dubious.

> . . . he feels the need to defend his sexuality for some reason . . . maybe a little homophobic?? or a little unsure about himself??

> i think that the site is fine. although i am a little confused about why he had to make the point that he is straight. it's fine if you like n'sync . . . whether you are gay or not . . .

This last question sounds so ironic to my queer ears; how many times have we, as queer people, been asked why we have to "flaunt" our sexuality or "make the point" that we are gay? More curiously, though, I was pleased that the students seemed to respond negatively to homophobia, as though it isn't "cool" to be a homophobe; like what you like—and you should be fine.

The comments, though, also point in another direction: a questioning of Dax's sexuality and self-identification. Indeed, some students seemed particularly concerned that Dax had taken the time to construct a Web site about Nsync, as though that in and of itself raised a "red flag." For instance, one female student remarked that

> men who do enjoy insync and make [an] ELABORATE website about them, are not completely normal.

Or, as another student put it,

> i think it brings up gender isues bc it is very girly to like boy bands and for this guy to cross that boundary and actually admit he is a fan, is very unusual. i will give him credit, i do think that it takes a lot of courage to admit such an obsession! that is right, obsession, he actually cares so much as to make an entire website devoted to them.

One pair of comments, from a young female poster, is particularly telling along these lines, summarizing several points already made:

> Well . . . I mean Is this more of a personal webpage Im some what confused. The fact that he likes NSYNC is fine I dont think its that big of a deal. The only thing is that he has to say StraightGuys for NSYNC and if hes straight then why does he have to announce it. The same as if he was gay he would need not to say Gayfor NSYNC it just stirs unneeded contravercy and here say, from my opnion. It has nothing to do with a preference in music hes some what sterotying but then again Tis His Own!!:)
>
> I suppose some need to announce it b/c of what others think thats what it boils down to right? I mean at some time in his life he was probably called something derogitory and now he feels the need to stand up against it. Or he has fallen into the stereo-type that only gay guys would like boy bands and he feels the need to publiclly announce that he is not part of that. I dont know really b/c i dont know him so I dont want to pass judgment but thats what I got from what his site.

I appreciated this student's understanding of the "trap" of stereotyping, and we had a good discussion about how such stereotypes do not just demonize others (e.g., queers) but are used to support and maintain seemingly "normative" (e.g., straight) identities.

In many other ways, though, the concern that Dax is announcing he is "straight" is itself a problem, the gesture that calls his straightness into question: "if hes straight then why does he have to announce it." Indeed as Calvin Thomas reminds us, straights do not generally have to "come out of the closet"; they do not have to announce their sexuality since it is *normative* to be straight.

Conversely, marking one's *straight* sexuality is *not* without penalty. Some students stated directly their feeling that Dax is "protesting too much" on the site:

> I am going to have to say that the creator of the web-site is having some sexual identity crisis. I mean really, straightboyzforNsync or what ever. I don't know, I think it' a little fishy. I agree with his web site, but he needs to get real with himself.
>
> i thought the website was a little bizarre. the story was strange, the comments in every section were strange . . . i'm not a big fan. and as for the sexuality aspect, why does he feel the need to create something called "straighboyz" (dumb name anyway) but why cant he just create an n'sync website for all sorts of other people instead of limiting it to straight guys . . . seems a little questionable to me.
>
> UMMM . . . This website is WEIRD! I think this guy makes a point too many times to say that he's not gay, and that he likes the band, which to me seems like he really might be gay deep down, and is afraid to say something. I really don't think it's a big deal if a guy likes the band, I know a lot of guys who like them. ???????????

In a follow-up comment to this last posting, one student summarized many other students' general feeling:

> I don't know to me this guy isn't safe with his manhood? i think i read "I'm not gay" or "fag" in this website way to many times! If you like i n'sync great but why make a websit about it?

Interestingly, the word "fag" doesn't appear on the site, Dax never says specifically that he isn't gay, and he really doesn't mark his sexuality explicitly.

Such vociferous questioning of Dax's sexuality suggests a dynamic at play that deserves more attention. I *could* read such comments as questioning my ability to "perform" straightness! Rather, I think the comments serve as useful jumping-off points for provocative discussion. For instance, these self-identified straight kids largely seem to think that being homophobic is "not cool." And that's good. At the same time, many of these students are quick to identify even a hint of homophobia in someone else as potential *queerness*. And, contrary to what I had originally thought, it's not so much liking Nsync that is problematic; when we examine the comments and when I reconsider classroom discussion, it becomes clear that, for the most part, liking Nsync is *not* the issue; many students seem willing to accept Dax's interest in Nsync at face value, and I had a few young male students say—out loud and proud—that they were Nsync fans. At the same time, Dax's implicit self-identification as "straight"—a rhetorical gesture to forestall questioning of his sexual identity and affix his heterosexuality—actually calls that heterosexuality into question. One of my intentions in creating the Straightboyz4Nsync site was to prompt discussion of homophobia, but it seems that Dax's concern with being read as "gay" is itself read as insecurity about his straightness—perhaps a "questionable" inability to keep his story "straight."

How can we explain this dynamic? Perhaps just bringing up the topic of gayness—or straightness—is itself grounds for questioning one's straightness. But why? Queer theory offers one possible answer. In *Straight with a Twist: Queer Theory and the Subject of Heterosexuality*, Calvin Thomas, a self-proclaimed straight man, uses Judith Butler's notion of performativity to elaborate a queer understanding of "straightness," suggesting, "The terror of being mistaken for a queer dominates the straight mind because this terror *constitutes* the straight mind." More specifically, "according to some queer theorists, heteronormativity, 'straightness as such,' is less a function of other-sexual desire than of the disavowal or abjection of that imagined same-sex desire upon which straightness never ceases to depend" (2000, 27). In other words, heterosexuality as an identity is dependent upon gayness for its social, cultural, political, and personal legibility. Or, as Jonathan Ned Katz (1995) puts it, heterosexuality is an "invention" with a traceable history, dependent on its supposed opposite—queerness—for its very meaningfulness. More radically, heterosexuality must suppress knowledge of this dependence on queerness in order to situate itself as normative; after all, what kind of "norm" would heterosexuality be if it openly acknowledged the queer for its very meaningfulness? So, for a queer theorist such as Thomas, "to profess straightness is to claim an identity within an economy that assumes that one identification can only be purchased at the expense of another" (30). In terms of the Straightboyz4Nsync site, it seems that Dax's calling attention to his straightness simultaneously raised the specter of queerness—a queerness that is supposed to remain suppressed; and such raising of the repressed other rebounds into questioning, doubt.

In light of such theorizing, students' comments seem somewhat homophobic, perhaps a slightly more advanced game of "spot the queer." But they can also be used to introduce other possibilities of discussion, leading students to think about *why* straightness is "unmarked," un-*remark*-able. Indeed, as we talked and wrote about the site, it became apparent that students were not necessarily keen to accept the queer theoretical position that straightness is dependent on an unacknowledged queerness, but I think it was revelatory for all of us to consider that straightness *may* be dependent on not calling it into question. As such, straightness—and its privileges—remain unexamined, normative: it just feels so *normal* because we don't have to think about it.

Once we, as a class, saw how straightness depends in part on a silenced queerness for its existence as an identification, it became easier to see straightness as a "performance," and to spot the ways it is "performed." One final example from the discussion board underscored for students both this performative nature of a straight identity and the silences that surround such a performance. A young male student, perhaps a bit tongue-in-cheek, expressed his own liking of Nsync:

> Yes I must admit Justin Timberlake is the man. He had the sexiest girlfriend in the world. Now he can just do as he pleases and get with supermodels. I wish I lived the lifestyle of JT. The website is ok.

It's hard not to read this posting as simultaneously authentic and sarcastic, with the sarcasm acting as a rhetorical defense mechanism. Also, note that this student does not say he is straight, but rather he performs his straightness by commenting on Justin Timberlake's "sexiest girlfriend in the world." The Web site, though, is just "ok." Again, straightness lies in its performance, not in self-identification.

20   The student's girlfriend, however, *can* comment about his straightness, and she offered this follow-up post:

> in regards to the site . . . someone that i know . . . really looks up to justin timberlake. he like the clothes he wears, how he sings, as well as his curly hairstyle. He watches all of his videos and likes his ex-girlfriend. he is not at all ashamed of having justin as his idol and rolemodel.

Again, we could read this as playful, but its pedagogical value should not go unremarked. For instance, I questioned the class about this discussion, asking, if the male student is not ashamed of having Justin Timberlake as his "rolemodel," then why doesn't he say so explicitly in his own posting? Again, students here have the opportunity to see not only the rhetorical binds of straightness but also the ways in which one can—and cannot—perform straightness. . . .

Rereading Straightness

As I reflect on this exercise, a few critical observations come to mind. First, in many ways, the hoax site and discussion board helped me and my students turn a critical lens on "straightness," disrupting my own and my students' sense of the normal so we could question how identities are narrated, life stories constructed, and rhetorics of normalcy and the normative maintained. Specifically, we explored how "straightness" must be performed, and . . . it must be performed again and again to maintain its seeming "naturalness." As such, we saw how simply labeling or identifying something as "straight" becomes problematic in that the identification itself questions the naturalness of the category, rendering opaque what once was not seen as needing clarification or identification.

This critical awareness alone, I believe, powerfully demonstrated to me the need to develop a pedagogy of *sexual literacy* with students—or a more critical way to discuss how sexuality is constructed and performed rhetorically. Indeed, students began to develop a sense of how narrations of identity depend as much on certain silences as they do on certain annunciations. In this sense, I think students developed a crucial understanding of an important dimension of being literate; that is, what is *not* articulated shapes our perception of the meaningful as much as what *is* articulated. Specifically, that which passes as the norm is often "unremarked" and hence never brought up for discussion—until, that is, the performance of the norm reveals its own constructedness. In that case, *much* discussion often ensues, and we have the opportunity to see how intense conversation around the normative is designed in many ways to bolster or reassert a normative sense, a normative shared understanding.

Second, the use of follow-up discussions was crucial in interrogating student responses and interpretations. In "Queer Pedagogy and Its Strange Techniques," Deborah P. Britzman suggests that "the beginnings of a queer pedagogy" might lie in an "ethical concern for one's own reading practices and what these have to do with the imagining of sociality as more than an effect of the dominant conceptual order" (1998, 67). Did students learn to "read" with the "ethical concern" Britzman proposes—imagining "sociality as more than an effect of the dominant conceptual order"? That is, did they become aware of how their own perceptions, predispositions, and *assumptions of what is the norm* come under scrutiny? I believe so—but only in that *steady* and *sustained* examination of our combined online and in-class discussions revealed to all of us some surprising insights into the silences and oversights that bolster our sense of the "norm." . . .

Part of the project of becoming literate, then, is to understand the different ways in which the representations that surround us (in media, advertisements, etc.), and that we even create at times (of ourselves as we tell our own life stories) rest on certain assumptions—assumptions about intimate aspects of our lives, such as sex and sexuality, that have been given to us by our culture at large. Sinfield explains at length:

> The dominant ideology tends to constitute subjectivities that will find "natural" its view of the world (hence its dominance); this happens in subcultures also, but in ways that may validate dissident subjectivities. . . . "In acquiring one's conception of the world one belongs to a particular grouping which is that of all the social elements which share the same mode of thinking and acting," Antonio Gramsci observes. It is through such sharing— through interaction with others who are engaged with compatible preoccupations—that one may develop a plausible alternative subject position. To be sure, everyone is constructed by the dominant ideology through, we may say, the state apparatuses. But ideology, Althusser stresses, is lived in day-to-day interactions, and those

> socialize us also into subcultures of class, ethnicity, gender and
> sexuality, which may be in some respects oppositional; or at least
> negotiated (1994, 66).

From the perspective of critical sexuality studies, that "dominant ideology" is clearly heteronormative and heterosexist, suggesting—even demanding—that all of us align our intimate and personal lives along axes that value monogamous heterosexual reproductive sex and sexualities. Becoming aware of and being willing to [respond] critically to the narratives, stories, representations, legal codes, and ways of speaking that naturalize the heteronormative and bolster it is to become, in my view, sexually literate. It may also be life saving. For instance, as only one example among many possible, English professor Beth Loffreda's *Losing Matt Shepard* (2000) paints a complex portrait of how the town of Laramie dealt with the brutal, homophobically motivated murder of a young college student. Loffreda's work highlights the "real-world" dimensions not just of homophobia but also, I believe, of a failure of literacy, in that Shepard's murderers could articulate their discomfort with the homoerotic only through the torture and slaying of another human being.

25   In this sense, then, I believe the "Straightboyz" exercise contributed to students' development of sexual literacy in that, to borrow . . . from Brian Street, if we are to understand literacy as an "ideological practice [that] opens up a potentially rich field of inquiry into the nature of culture and power," then exploring how heterosexuality becomes "composed" as a norm is an important exercise in literacy development (2001, 437). As students read the "Straightboyz" site, they were beginning to question critically the narration of heterosexuality, of how someone comes to compose his straightness, and of how the narrative expectations for such "composure" are intimately tied to normative senses of what "straight" is—and is not. As such, this exercise was one of beginning to see the strong relationship between the stories we tell about ourselves sexually and the dominant, normalizing tropes of identity through which power circulates in our culture. Reading "Straightboyz" critically, then, offered a chance to develop greater sexual literacy, a more sophisticated way of understanding the relationship between the stories we tell about ourselves and their connection to knowledge and power, particularly as processed through sexuality.

Reading

1. How does Alexander define *sexual literacy*?

2. How does he argue students need to learn this literacy?

3. How did the StraightBoyz4NSync Web site demonstrate the sexual literacy of Alexander and his students?

4. How would this focus on sexual literacy change the work of the writing classroom?

Inquiring

1. A central part of Alexander's essay involves having his students explore StraightBoyz4NSync, a Web site he created to pose the question of gender identity. His students were unaware that he created the site, however. As a student, how do you respond to this strategy? Do you believe Alexander was justified in not telling his students the real nature of the site? Later, Alexander states that he learned something about his own ability to "perform" gender based on their comments. How might class discussions have changed if the students knew that Alexander was responsible for creating the site?

2. Alexander argues that sexual literacy should be a central component of the writing classroom. His argument seems to rest on the belief that sexual identity is a common element of human experience and, for that reason, needs to be researched and reflected upon as much as other issues, such as race or class. How do you respond to his argument? Do you see a connection between sexual literacy and language use? If so, how? How can such a literacy affect how you identity as a college writer? As a writer in your imagined future career?

3. Alexander uses the broad term *sexual literacy* in this essay, but in other parts of his work, he uses the term *transgender* to explain how he imagines a newly invigorated sense of "writerly identity." Why do you believe Alexander finds this concept so important for his goals as a teacher? How does his sense of the term *transgender* agree with or support more traditional definitions of transgender identity? Based on what you have read, how do you see this term relating to his belief about the value of exploring sexual literacy? How does he see this term altering the ways in which students write (and understand) the values informing the larger body politic?

Composing

1. One insight Alexander gains from StraightBoyz4NSync concerns the difficulty of performing straightness. Although he can capture broad strokes of such an identity, he also finds that his work lacks nuance, a point further confirmed by his students. The Web site and the reaction to it, however, only confirm his larger point: Gender is performed; it is a set of rhetorical and material actions designed to produce a certain effect. For this assignment, step into Alexander's role. Write an essay or create a Web page in which you attempt to perform a gender identity different from your own: male, female, transgender, cisgender, homosexual, heterosexual. In taking on this task, don't reduce this identity to simple stereotypical behavior; instead, articulate the nuance that would inform any person's actions. Then write a short essay in which you discuss not only the rationale for how you "performed" this identity but also your insights into the ways in which you enact your own gender identity.

2. A common scene in many movies is when two people of the same gender, often males, accidently hug for too long. After any such a moment, the individuals quickly move away from each other and do something "manly" to reestablish their heterosexuality. In teaching his class, Alexander recognized a similar fear among some of his students: a fear of their gender being misunderstood. Indeed, the failure to "perform" gender correctly was a central element of classroom discussion. Write an essay in which you try to understand why such a fear might be so prevalent among students. What does such a fear say about how students understand the larger culture expectations of gender performances? Do you believe such concerns are still warranted on your campus or within larger culture? What do you see as the larger forces working to maintain or alter gender expectations? Should a writing class be part of these efforts? Why or why not?

3. Alexander attempts to link the act of writing to discussions of sexuality, ultimately arguing that a more nuanced sense of literacy will result. In this way, he is attempting to expand the current conversation—our current terminology—about what it means to be "literate" in our culture. Indeed, our culture is dominated by such conversations about literacy, conversations that are often highly politicized and controversial. For this assignment, you will step into one such conversation: what literacy means in public schools. Research how your local public school defines its literacy goals. (These goals are often posted on the school district's Web page under curricular "outcomes" or "standards.") What type of literate citizen are these goals attempting to produce? Consider how Alexander's sense of literacy might expand or alter these goals. How might the local community respond to such an effort to revise what counts as literacy? That is, what would it mean for public schools to take on the task of teaching sexual literacy?

Connecting

Alexander claims that enhancing students' sexual literacy will improve their writing ability. They will, it seems, be able to use language in a way that can expand the scope and meaning of their identity. Waite's *Butch Geography* (p. 375) would seem to be an example of such sexual literacy. Write an essay in which you first explore Alexander's definition of *sexual literacy* and then discuss how Waite does (or does not) enact such literacy. Do you believe such literacy is useful in your own writing?

Projects for Chapter 10

The following are group and class projects. You should talk to your instructor about which projects you will complete in your course.

PROJECT 25 Bodily Encounters

Although each reading in this chapter discussed the need to respect the diversity of bodies that make up our public culture, few of them—with rare exception—actually described what it might mean for this idea of tolerance to be enacted. What might it look like in daily practice? This project is designed to demonstrate on your campus what a body politic based on tolerance might involve. For this project, you will develop an audio installation on campus that will allow students to hear personal testimony of how seemingly different perspectives can coexist. The project will be structured as follows:

1. Develop a broad theme through which individuals can tell stories of encounters that demonstrated an ethic of tolerance on campus. (You might look at the writing prompt "Strange Angels" that opens Chapter 1 as an extended example.)

2. Write a series of prompts that give individuals a variety of ways to respond to the theme. Keep the prompt questions as short as possible.

3. Choose important campus locations, especially places with a lot of foot traffic.

4. Break into groups to cover each location and ask individuals at that location to answer the prompt story.

5. Be sure to get each person's permission to use his or her recording. (See pp. 240–41.)

6. Once you have recorded the interviews, edit them and create a 15-second introduction to the project to be repeated across recordings. Be sure to give the project a name that will capture the interest of students.

7. Once you have multiple stories for each location, do one of the following:

    a. Create a bar code that, when scanned, accesses the story online.

    b. Create a Web link that, when accessed, plays the audio file.

    c. Write the story out, creating a series of posters to tell the story.

d. Write the story in chalk at the location. (Get permission from the owner of the location first.)

8. Provide an address where those encountering the story can upload their own experience.

9. On all materials, announce when the project begins and ends.

10. "Switch out" the recordings several times for each location during the project.

Once the project is complete, visit each location and ask students if they listened to the recordings; if so, ask them how they responded. Then, as a class, discuss how this project helped alter the public rhetoric—the body politic, as it were—of tolerance on campus. What else might need to be done to fully put in place a sense of tolerance on campus?

For strategies on prompts, see pages 199–202; and for publication permission see pages 240–41.

PROJECT 26 The Student Body

This chapter has implied a connection between definitions about bodies and the body politic. For many of the authors, such as Waite and Anzaldúa, how a body was defined represented the limitations or possibilities of equal treatment and justice. This project is designed to challenge existing representations of the student "body" on your campus, offering an alternative set of values, rules, and practices. In effect, you will choose a format to produce a new student publication, *The Student Body*, a publication designed to give voice to an underrepresented set of identities.

Although this project can be done by the whole class, it may work better to break into distinct groups of about five students each. Each group should:

1. Choose an underrepresented or marginalized identity on campus.

2. Research the needs of that population and contact any organizations focused on that issue.

3. Use this information to generate at least six possible stories.

4. Decide the language and format of your publication.

5. Write and then lay out the publication.

6. Publish enough copies for individuals in class to have one each.

Discuss how these publications approach the task of moving marginalized "bodies" into the "body politic."

As described, this project seems like a straightforward task. Before rushing to make decisions, however, consider the creative possibilities of the project.

Although the project asks you to consider an underrepresented group, how you define *underrepresented* is wide open. You might, as with some of the essays in this chapter, argue that LGBTQ identities are marginalized. Or, if you are at a liberal campus, you might argue that conservative voices need a stronger platform. Or, less politically, you might argue that fans of *Scandal* need their own publication to share their voices—and ditto for fans of the college's lacrosse team. Your publication will have to prove this position—make an argument that the reader finds believable—but at this point, almost any identity or group is fair game.

You might also use some of the diverse techniques of the authors in creating materials for your publication. Like Anzaldúa, you could choose to publish in multiple languages, highlighting the exclusionary nature of a single language context. Or you might, like Alexander, create a "fake" Web site, focusing on a particular identity and test if "real readers" would be fooled by your creation.

Finally, don't default to academic writing. Instead, for instance, choose to write about the situation of your selected group through the voices of those marginalizing them, satirizing their voices to the point of ridiculousness. (A classic example of this technique is Jonathan Swift's *A Modest Proposal*.) You might decide to write a series of ironic articles poking fun at the whole rhetoric used by these individuals (such as *The Onion* online). Or you might take an existing newspaper, one already published, and paste in your stories amid existing stories, using the insertion to show how such topics are typically ignored. (A group of activists known as the Barbie Liberation Organization once put a GI Joe voice box inside a Barbie to make a point about how women are represented.) As many of the authors, such as Anzaldúa or Waite, demonstrate, you too should think about how the very language and style of your publication can present your message.

Ultimately, as with how most individual and collective "bodies" are developed, this assignment is a creative exercise designed to let you express your collective values through the creation of a material artifact, a "student body" publication.

For strategies on publication design, see pages 242–43; and for print publishing considerations, see pages 244–46.

PROJECT 27 Beyond Singular Identity Politics

Many of the authors in this chapter argue that their cultural positions represent a new lens through which to understand society, making it more open to diversity and equality. Of course, not everyone would agree with these arguments. Individuals from other subject positions, Native American or Western European, might want to argue for a similar centrality for their culture, their historical heritage. Staking such a claim, it seems, only causes more strident conflict.

Here is where another important theme in this chapter emerges: the idea that we carry many identities in us at once. Think of Waite or Anzaldúa. The question becomes whether this concept, this theory, can generate a different type of conversation, one that might lead to alliances, new paths forward, and in some ways, a postidentity politics. It is this theory that will be put to test in this project.

As a class, create a list of either student or community groups that appear to approach their work through differing identity politics lenses. They can be based on religious, cultural, or ethnic heritages, for instance. Inform them that, as a class, you have been studying the importance of civic dialogue based on a person's heritage as well as how such heritages can be put in alliance for a specific cause and would like to invite them to your class to take part in this conversation. To make this project effective, at last five organizations should be involved.

Note: As discussed previously, such invitations work best after sufficient groundwork has been put in place or existing partnerships can be drawn upon. See pages 175–80.

As a class, create three scenarios around a campus or community initiative. These scenarios should be ones that will pull on common interests by those attending but offer challenges on how to proceed. For instance, here is one possible scenario:

> Recently, our university has decided to expand religious representation in our campus chapel. After much discussion, a decision has been made to hire a Wiccan Priestess to work for the chapel, offering services and counseling to students who find meaning in that religion. In hiring this individual, the chapel has stressed its long-standing tradition of representing a broad range of faith traditions—Christians, Muslims, and Buddhists, among others.
>
> Some students on campus are protesting this move, arguing it represents devil worship. Citing religious tolerance, the chapel has called together representatives of the faiths currently represented within the chapel and asked each to make a statement in support of this decision. To this end, the representatives have invited students from those faiths to take part in a closed-door meeting to decide whether to issue a statement and, if so, what it should say.

Implied in this question is whether the body politic of the campus will support the individual students who find comfort in this tradition—whether the self-professed identities of these students have the right to practice those beliefs. In addition, it is a question of whether there exists a sense of religious rights that requires a broader sense of religion than currently exists. These are profound questions about whether one set of beliefs has the ability to restrict the beliefs of others, including whether one set of values can determine that another set of ideas does not belong in the public sphere.

Having developed several questions, appoint one student to moderate the discussion. Invite your speakers to take up to 5 minutes to state their position on this issue and then open the floor for discussion. (You might want to set rules to ensure open participation: No one can speak for more than 3 minutes, a person cannot speak until two others have spoken, etc. See pp. 216–21 for additional strategies.)

At the following class, discuss whether the conversation ultimately rested on a singular sense of identity or on a sense that any one person contains a multitude of identities. Did the conversation remain within identity politics, or did it step beyond the topic? What does this discussion teach you about the difficulty of finding a rhetoric of collaboration, of a new space that would allow identities that cross over traditional categories and heritages to find a place in which to practice their beliefs?

For strategies on prompts, see pages 199–202; and for strategies on reaching out to local community and student groups for participation, see pages 175–86.

PROJECT 28 A Communal Body

There is a classic type of children's book where each page features a close-up of a particular type of person (pirate, chef, firefighter, etc.). The pages are cut horizontally into thirds, which allows the child to put the pirate's eyes with the chef's nose and the firefighter's chin. The idea is that the mixed-up faces are pretty funny (and if you are under the age of ten, it probably is quite funny).

This chapter has made a more serious argument about our bodies: that they inhabit many different identities all at once, that elements of them can cross over strict categories at any moment, and that our faces can be mixed and become part of many different traditions. It has been hard to express this point in a fashion that might make it clear to others, however. This project aims to provide such a tool by using the children's book structure.

Working with your community partner, choose ten individuals who represent important histories or identities in that community. It is important that these individuals represent the diversity of the community, however that is defined by the residents involved. Once selected, ask them to tell the story of their individual faces, beginning with the hair and eyes and leading down to their chin. In telling this story, be sure to prompt them to do the following:

1. Connect their features to their family (We all have prominent chins) and to their cultural heritage (All the women in my family have worn the hijab) as well as the meaning of that heritage. It will take time for individuals to make such connections, so plan accordingly.

2. Take a close-up picture of their face (be sure that all the individual photos are the same size and ratio within the frame).

3. Edit their stories so that they follow a similar narrative. Each section must also end with a sentence that would naturally lead to the next feature, such as "Now I'll move on and talk about my nose."

4. Embed the text on the appropriate feature of the person's face, which will take some design skill and discussion. Slice each photograph horizontally into equal thirds, with the faces aligning as much as possible.

5. Once the book is complete, develop a cover and an introduction describing the purpose of this book. You might also include information about how to contact your community organization.

6. Have the book printed, with spiral binding. Deciding collaboratively with your partner the number of copies to be produced.

7. Develop a list of offices that typically have magazines in their waiting rooms. Get permission from each office to leave a copy of the book there.

8. If possible, develop a Web site where individuals can submit their own photos and stories or offer to participate in the project.

For strategies on interviews, see pages 213–15; for publication permission, see pages 240–41; for publication design, see pages 242–43; for print publication considerations, see pages 244–46; and for strategies on reaching out to local businesses and campus offices for support of the project, see pages 239–40.

PROJECT 29 "This Is the Body of a . . ."

One theme within this chapter concerns the ways our bodies can simultaneously inhabit many different meanings—meanings as broad as our cultural heritage (such as Anzaldúa) and as intimate as our personal histories (such as Waite). It was difficult, however, for any of these writers to fully actualize how these diverse heritages and histories intersect within the diversity of an actual community. This project challenges you to consider how this might be done. In doing so, it relies on your knowledge of digital and social media.

For this project, you will develop a Web site that will allow residents of a particular community—usually the community with which your class is working—to disrupt or add nuance to how they are understood by the larger culture. You will do so by creating a Web site where, through residents telling different stories about how their bodies are perceived, alternative viewpoints are developed about their community. For instance, if a community is seen as being simply marked by one identity, your project will attempt to create a Web site where alternative identities are given voice.

For this project, you will need to do the following with your community partner:

1. Choose a community (or subset of a community) that would participate and benefit from having an alternative vision of the community told.

2. Develop a set of questions that highlight the stereotypical vision of that community and how residents themselves see the community.

3. Choose a set of people to interview, using their approved transcribed interviews as the base text for the project.

4. Work with your community partner to design a graphic interface that will guide the reader through the stories in a way that disrupts their understanding of the community.

5. Create mechanisms for community members to add their stories to the Web site.

6. Develop a campaign to advertise the Web site's existence.

Although this project would seem most applicable to communities for whom bodily identification is the object of violence, such as the transgender or LGBTQ community, the project can be applied to other identities as well. It might be possible to create sites that give more nuanced portrayals of Christians, Muslims, or environmentalists, for example. The strategy of this project is to use the stereotypical image of such a body or identity and have personal stories of individuals who can offer a more nuanced vision of that identity.

For strategies on interviews, see pages 213–15; for publication permission, see pages 240–41; and for publication design, see pages 242–43.

PROJECT 30 Coming Together

Many of the authors in this chapter speak about the connection between bullying and violence — think Waite or Alexander — as well as try to promote solutions, yet it is probably a truism that the most powerful stories and interventions occur at the local level, in our most immediate communities and networks. For this project, work with your community partner to identify at least ten individuals who are willing to speak out about (and against) the bullying they have received due to their sexual orientation, gender, race, or other aspect of their identities. Work with your community group to ensure that those selected represent the diversity of the community in which they live. Also be sure that they are comfortable with having their stories shared with a wider audience; this step is particularly important because you will be asking them to make public experiences that were most likely traumatic to them.

Once you have identified individuals willing to be interviewed, develop a set of questions that reflect the values and interests of the project with which you are working, questions that will explain the effect of bullying in a way that does not exploit the experiences of those bullied. These questions might include the following:

1. When did the bullying begin?
2. Do you have a reason why you believe it began?
3. Can you describe one moment that best represents your experience?
4. What resources helped (or might have helped) you during this experience?
5. How would the culture have to change to make such bullying be seen as completely unacceptable?

Remember, you do not want to ask too many questions; rather, your questions should be meant to spark the participants to share their experiences. See pages 213–15 for guidance. Once the interviews are complete, transcribe them. At this point, you will use these interviews as the basis for a performance piece on this issue. The following process illustrates one strategy for producing this piece:

1. You can work with the interviewed person, helping to refine his or her story and giving it a stronger narrative structure than is usually the case with interviews. Or you can choose to do this work as a class, sharing the edited version with the person interviewed. In any scenario, the interviewed person has to give official written permission to use the story. (Note: When read aloud, the edited interview should be no more than 5 to 10 minutes long.)

2. As a class or in partnership with those interviewed, decide in which order the edited interviews should be read. Work collaboratively to see if there is an overarching structure that will give the audience a sense of the deeper connection. (You might frame the pieces as occurring across time, or you might map them onto different parts of the community.) Once the piece is complete, the interviewees and community organization need to officially approve the final version. Be prepared to revise the piece based on their comments.

3. Once you have your final piece, decide who will read the script: those interviewed or members of the class? The decision will depend on whether an individual wants to publicly share his or her story (and name) or have the story read by someone else. Once you know who will read each script, make sure that each person practices.

4. Then, work with the community organization to plan a performance, seeking its guidance and material support to locate a venue and audience. If the class is being asked to do most of this work, see pages 205–15 for guidance.

5. Structure the performance with a short introduction about the goals of the piece. Be sure to allow time afterward the reading for discussion. For guidance on how to structure such events, see pages 233–37.

6. After the performance, a small event should be planned celebrating the work of all involved. Be sure to give copies of the script to each person interviewed as well as to the community partner.

For strategies on prompts, see pages 199–202; for publication permission (to perform the pieces), see pages 240–41; for event planning, see pages 233–37; and for strategies on reaching out to local businesses for support and performance space, see pages 239–40.

Notes to the Readings

Antonio Gramsci, "On Intellectuals" (pp. 49–55)

1. The Italian word here is *"ceti"* which does not carry quite the same connotations as "strata," but which we have been forced to translate in that way for lack of alternatives. It should be noted that Gramsci tends, for reasons of censorship, to avoid using the word *class* in contexts where its Marxist overtones would be apparent, preferring (as for example in this sentence) the more neutral "social group." The word *group*, however, is not always a euphemism for "class," and to avoid ambiguity Gramsci uses the phrase "fundamental social group" when he wishes to emphasize the fact that he is referring to one or other of the major social classes (bourgeoisie, proletariat) defined in strict Marxist terms by its position in the fundamental relations of production. Class groupings which do not have this fundamental role are often described as "castes" (aristocracy, etc.). The word "category," on the other hand, which also occurs on this page, Gramsci tends to use in the standard Italian sense of members of a trade or profession, though also more, generally. [Translator's note]
2. Heads of FIAT and Montecatini (Chemicals), respectively. [Translator's note]
3. Thus, because it can happen that everyone at some time fries a couple of eggs or sews up a tear in a jacket, we do not necessarily say that everyone is a cook or a tailor. [Translator's note]

David Bartholomae, "Inventing the University" (pp. 56–69)

1. Linda S. Flower, "Revising Writer-Based Prose," *Journal of Basic Writing* 3, no. 3 (1981): 63.
2. Linda Flower and John R. Hayes, "A Cognitive Process Theory of Writing," *College Composition and Communication* 32, no. 4 (1981): 365–87.
3. Ibid., 383.

Andrew Delbanco, "Who Went? Who Goes? Who Pays?" (pp. 70–79)

1. Max Weber, "The Chinese Literati" (1915), in *From Max Weber*, ed. H. H. Gerth and C. Wright Mills (New York: Oxford University Presss, 1958), 426. Weber's analysis was anticipated in some respects by Immanuel Kant, *The Conflict of the Faculties* (1798).
2. John McNees, "The Quest at Princeton for the Cocktail Soul," *Harvard Crimson*, February 21, 1958.
3. See Michael Rosenthal, *Nicholas Miraculous* (Columbia University Press, 2006), 332–52, and Diana Trilling, *The Beginning of the Journey* (Harcourt Brace, 1993), 269.
4. Jerome Karabel, *The Chosen: The Hidden History of Admission and Exclusion at Harvard, Yale, and Princeton* (Mariner Books, 2006), 51.
5. Alexis de Tocqueville, *Democracy in America* (1835–40), translated by Arthur Goldhammer (Library of America, 2004), 58.

6. Mitchell L. Stevens, *Creating a Class: College Admissions and the Education of Elites* (Cambridge: Harvard University Press, 2007), 58.
7. Donald E. Heller, quoted in *Does Higher Education for the Disadvantaged Pay Off across the Generations?*, ed. Paul Attewell and David E. Lavin (Russell Sage Foundation, 2007), 199; Brian K. Fitzgerald and Jennifer A. Delaney, "Educational Opportunity in America," in *Condition of Access: Higher Education for Lower Income Students*, ed. Donald E. Heller (Westport, CT: American Council of Education/Praeger, 2002).
8. See Clifford Adelman, *The Toolbox Revisited: Paths to Degree Completion from High School through College* (U.S. Department of Education, 2006).
9. Peter Sacks, *Tearing Down the Gates: Confronting the Class Divide in American Education* (University of California Press, 2007), 167.
10. Ibid., 169.
11. Between 2008–2009 and 2009–2010, need-based aid grew faster (by 4.6 percent) than merit-based aid (1.2 percent)—but it is too soon to tell if this marks a reversal of the long-term trend. "Mixed News on State Aid," *InsideHigherEd.com*, July 11, 2011.
12. Sacks, *Tearing Down the Gates*, 178.
13. Anthony T. Kronman, "Is Diversity a Value in American Higher Education?," *Florida Law Review* (December 2000), 40.
14. Roger Lehecka and Andrew Delbanco, "Ivy-League Let Down," *New York Times*, January 23, 2008; Theda Skocpol and Suzanne Mettler, "Back to School," *Democracy: A journal of Ideas* (Fall 2008), 8–18.
15. William Bowen, et al., *Equity and Excellence in American Education* (University of Virginia Press, 2005), 162.
16. "Despite Surging Endowments, High-Ranking Universities and Colleges Show Disappointing Results in Enrolling Low-Income Students," *Journal of Blacks in Higher Education,* January 6, 2008; David Leonhart, "Top Colleges, Largely for the Elite," *New York Times,* May 24, 2011.
17. Michaels, *The Trouble with Diversity: How We Learned to Love Identity and Ignore Inequality* (Metropolitan Books, 2006), 17.

Gerald Graff, "The Problem Problem and Other Oddities of Academic Discourse" (pp. 114–126)

1. Howard Gardner, *The Unschooled Mind: How Children Think and How Schools Should Teach* (New York: Basic Books, 1991), 172.
2. Wayne C. Booth, Gregory G. Colomb, and Joseph M. Williams, *The Craft of Research* (Chicago: University of Chicago Press, 1995), 59–63.
3. Ibid., 48–60.
4. Robert Scholes, *The Crafty Reader* (New Haven: Yale University Press, 2000), 22–24.
5. Ibid., 25.
6. Mina Shaughuessy, *Errors and Expectations: A Guide for the Teacher of Basic Writing* (New York: Oxford University Press, 1977), 240.
7. Booth, Colomb, and Williams, *The Craft of Research*, 95.
8. David Bartholomae, as quoted by Mike Rose in *Lives on the Boundary: A Moving Account of the Struggles and Achievements of America's Educational Underclass* (Penguin Books, 1989), 189. Bartholomae's comment is in "Inventing the University," *Cross-Talk in Comp Theory: A Reader*, ed. Victor Villanueva, Jr. (Urbana, IL: NCTH, 1997), 607. "Inventing the University" was first published in 1985. [See also p. 56 of this textbook. –Editor's note]
9. Rose, *Lives on the Boundary*, 189.

Carmen Kynard, "From Candy Girls to Cyber Sista-Cipher" (pp. 127–145)

1. Michelle Fine, *Framing Dropouts: Notes on the Politics of an Urban High School* (Albany: State University of New York Press, 1991); Michelle Fine and Lois Weiss, *Silenced Voices and Extraordinary Conversations . . . Re-Imagining Schools* (New York: Teachers College Press, 2003).
2. Adam Fairclough, *Race and Democracy: The Civil Rights Struggle in Louisiana, 1915–1972* (Athens: University of Georgia Press, 1995), 449; see also white teachers' responses in

David Gottlieb, "Teaching and Students: The Views of Negro and White Teachers," *Sociology of Education* 37, no. 4 (1964): 345–53.

3. Janet Duitsman Cornelius, *Slave Missions and the Black Church in the Antebellum South* (Columbia: University of South Carolina Press, 1999); Aldon Morris, "Centuries of Black Protest: Its Significance for America and the World," in *Race in America: The Struggle for Equality*, ed. Herbert Hill and James E. Jones (Madison: University of Wisconsin Press, 1992), 19–69; Vorris L. Nunley, *Keepin' It Hushed: Hush Harbor Rhetoric and African American Barbershops as Sites of Rhetorical Tradition, Education, and Knowledge*, unpublished doctoral dissertation (Pennsylvania State University, 2006).

4. I borrow the term *cipher* from Hip Hop Nation Language (H. Samy Alim, *Roc the Mic Right: The Language of Hip Hop Culture* [New York: Routledge, 2006]), a concept that often refers to the posse of folk who witnessed MC battles. The audience here is active and participatory in the call-and-respond tradition to encourage competition and community. If you get respect in the cipher with your story and style, then you have achieved the ultimate goal of being part of a living, dynamic system that spreads its knowledge, vision, and influence.

5. Gail E. Hawisher and Cynthia L. Selfe, "Becoming Literate in the Information Age: Cultural Ecologies and the Literacies of Technology," *College Composition and Communication* 55, no. 4 (2004): 642–92.

6. CSU has an undergraduate student enrollment of 6,600. Using the 2004 entering freshman group as an example, the cohort is comprised of 34 percent white students, 29 percent Asian students, 16 percent Latino/a students, 13 percent black students, 0.3 percent American Indian students; 0.9 percent are international students and 5 percent are considered "other." New dormitories mean that there is a growing residential community on the campus, but at least half of the students are commuters from various cities across the state. The majority of students are first-generation, working-class college students.

7. An idea reflected in Carmen Kynard and Robert Eddy, "Toward a New Critical Framework: Color-Conscious Political Morality and Pedagogy at Historically Black and Historically White Colleges and Universities," *College Composition and Communication* 61, no. 1 (2009), 261–96.

8. Vorris L. Nunley, "From the Harbor to Da Academic Hood: Hush Harbors and an African American Rhetorical Tradition," in *African American Rhetoric(s): Interdisciplinary Perspectives*, ed. Elaine B. Richardson and Ronald L. Jackson II (Carbondale: Southern Illinois University Press, 2004), 223.

9. Ibid., 226; Lawrence W. Levine, *Black Culture and Black Consciousness: Afro-American Folk Thought from Slavery to Freedom* (New York: Oxford University Press, 1977).

10. Nunley, "From the Harbor to Da Academic Hood," 222.

11. Ibid., 224.

12. Joanna C. Street and Brian V. Street, "The Schooling of Literacy," in *Writing in the Community*, ed. David Barton and Roz Ivanic (Newbury Park, CA: Sage, 1991), 106–31.

13. Glynda Hull and Katherine Schultz, eds., *School's Out! Bridging Out-of-School Literacies with Classroom Practice* (New York: Teachers College Press, 2002); Jabari Mahiri, ed., *What They Don't Learn in School: Literacy in the Lives of Urban Youth* (New York: Peter Lang, 2004).

14. Katherine Schultz and Glynda Hull, "Locating Literacy Theory in Out-of-School Contexts," in Hull and Schultz, *School's Out!*, 11–31.

15. Justin D. Baer, Andrea L. Cook, and Stephane Baldi, *The Literacy of America's College Students* (Denver, CO: American Institutes for Research, 2006); Tom Bradshaw and Bonnie Nichols, *Reading at Risk: A Survey of Literary Reading in America* (Washington, DC: National Endowment for the Arts, 2004).

16. Dana J. Wilber, "College Students and New Literacy Practices," in *The Handbook of Research on New Literacies*, ed. Julie Coiro, Michele Knobel, and Colin Lankshear (Mahwah, NJ: Erlbaum, 2008), 553–81.

17. See also Dana Cammack, "No Straight Line: Wrinkling Binaries in Literacy and Technology," *eLearning*, 2, no. 3 (2005): 153–68.

18. Wilber, "College Students and New Literacy Practices," 570.

19. Adam J. Banks, *Race, Rhetoric, and Technology: Searching for Higher Ground* (New York: Routledge, 2005).

20. Geneva Smitherman, *Word from the Mother* (New York: Routledge, 2006), 3.

21. Homi K. Bhabha, *The Location of Culture* (New York: Routledge, 1994).

22. Geneva Smitherman, *Talkin and Testifyin* (Detroit, MI: Wayne State University Press, 1977), 3.

23. Manuel Castells, *The Rise of the Network Society* (Malden, MA: Blackwell, 1996), *The Power of Identity* (Malden, MA: Blackwell, 1997), and *End of Millennium* (Malden, MA: Blackwell, 1997); Barbara B. Duffelmeyer, "Critical Computer Literacy: Computers in First-Year Composition as Topic and Entertainment," *Computers and Composition* 17, no. 3 (2000): 289–307; Stuart Selber, *Multiliteracies for a Digital Age* (Carbondale: Southern Illinois University Press, 2004).

24. Donna J. Harraway, *Simians, Cyborgs, and Women: The Reinvention of Nature* (New York: Routledge, 1991).

25. Anne Balsamo, *Technologies of the Gendered Body: Reading Cyborg Women* (Durham, NC: Duke University Press, 1996).

26. Harraway, *Simians, Cyborgs, and Women: The Reinvention of Nature*, 174.

27. Ibid., 175.

28. Signithia Fordham, "'Those Loud Black Girls': (Black) Women, Silence, and Gender 'Passing' in the Academy," *Anthropology and Education Quarterly* 24, no. 3 (1993): 3–32; Elaine Richardson, *African American Literacies* (New York: Routledge, 2003).

29. Michel Foucault, *The History of Sexuality* (New York: Vintage, 1990), 95–96.

30. James H. Jones, *Bad Blood: The Tuskegee Syphilis Experiment* (New York: Free Press, 1993).

31. Manning Marable, "The Political and Theoretical Contexts of the Changing Racial Terrain," *Souls* 4, no. 3 (2002): 1.

32. Heidi Lasley Barajas and Amy Ronnkvist, "Radicalized Space: Framing Latino and Latina Experience in Public Schools," *Teachers College Record* 109, no. 6 (2007): 1517–38.

33. Linda Darling-Hammond, *The Right to Learn: A Blueprint for Creating Schools That Work* (San Francisco: Jossey-Bass, 1997); Jeannie Oakes et al., *Becoming Good American Schools: The Struggle for Civic Virtue in Education Reform* (San Francisco: Jossey-Bass, 2002).

34. Jeannie Oakes, "Two Cities' Tracking and Within-School Segregation," *Teachers College Record* 96, no. 4 (1995): 681–90.

35. Kynard and Eddy, "Toward a New Critical Framework: Color-Conscious Political Morality and Pedagogy at Historically Black and Historically White Colleges and Universities."

36. Ira Shor, personal communication, November 1999.

37. Celia K. Rousseau, "Keeping It Real: Race and Education in Memphis," in *Critical Race Theory in Education: All God's Children Get a Song*, ed. Adrienne Dixson and Celia K. Rousseau (Routledge, 2006), 113–28.

38. Cornel West, "Black Culture and Postmodernism," in *Remaking History*, ed. Barbara Kruger and Phil Mariani (Seattle, WA: Bay Press, 1989), 93.

39. Maisha T. Fisher, *Black Literate Lives: Historical and Contemporary Perspectives* (New York: Routledge, 2009).

40. Cheryl I. Harris, "Whiteness as Property," *Harvard Law Review* 106, no. 8 (1993): 1707–91.

41. Elizabeth McHenry and Shirley Brice Heath, "The Literate and the Literary: African Americans as Writers and Readers—1830–1940," *Written Communication* 11, no. 4 (1994): 419–43.

42. Adrienne Dixson, "Extending the Metaphor: Notions of Jazz in Portraiture," *Qualitative Inquiry* 11, no. 1 (2005): 106–37; Jacqueline Jones Royster and Jean C. Williams, "History in the Spaces Left: African American Presence and Narratives of Composition Studies," *College Composition and Communication* 50, no. 4 (1999): 563–84; Jacqueline Jones Royster, *Traces of a Stream* (Pittsburgh: University of Pittsburgh Press, 2000).

43. Rochelle Brock, *Sista Talk: The Personal and the Political* (New York Peter Lang, 2005); Gwendolyn Etter-Lewis and Michele Foster, *Unrelated Kin: Race and Gender in Women's Personal Narratives* (New York: Routledge, 1996); Juanita Johnson-Bailey, "Enjoining Positionality and Power in Narrative Work: Balancing Contentious and Modulating Forces," in *Perspectives and Approaches for Research in Education and the Social Sciences*, ed. Kathleen deMarrais and Stephen Lapan (Mahwah, NJ: Erlbaum, 2003), 123–38.

44. Iris Marion Young, *Throwing Like a Girl and Other Essays in Feminist Philosophy and Social Theory* (Bloomington: Indiana University Press, 1990); "'Throwing Like a Girl': Twenty Years Later," in *Body and Flesh: A Philosophical Reader*, ed. Donn Welton (Oxford: Blackwell, 1998), 286–90.
45. Iris Marion Young., *On Female Body Experience: "Throwing Like a Girl" and Other Essays* (New York: Oxford University Press, 2005), 6, 11.
46. See Hawisher and Selfe, "Becoming Literate in the Information Age: Cultural Ecologies and the Literacies of Technology."
47. New Edition (1983).

Christopher Wilkey, "Engaging Community Literacy through the Rhetorical Work of a Social Movement" (pp. 146–163)

1. Paula Mathieu, *Tactics of Hope: The Public Turn in English Composition* (Portsmouth, NH: Boynton/Cook, 2005), 17. [See also p. 268 of this textbook. –Editor's note]
2. "Over-the-Rhine, Our Community," *Over-the-Rhine Community Housing*, May 10, 2009 http://www.otrch.org/otrcommunity.html.
3. "Fighting Hunger in Cincinnati," National Public Radio, *Weekend Edition Sunday*, podcast audio, December 24, 2006, http://www.npr.org/templates/rundowns/ rundown.php? prgId=10&prgDate=12-24-2006.
4. "Over-the-Rhine, Our Community."
5. "American Indian Special Issue," *Voices Over-the-Rhine Community Newspaper* 7, no. 2 (1975): 1–2.
6. Ibid.
7. The Dean of Cincinnati, "Walkability v. The Homeless," *The Cincinnati Beacon*, February 29, 2009, http://www.cincinnatibeacon.com/index.php/content/comments /walkability_v_the_homeless/.
8. Thomas A. Dutton, "Colony Over-the-Rhine," *Miami University Center for Community Engagement in Over-the-Rhine*, Miami University, August 1, 2007, http://arts.miamioh.edu /cce/papers/Colony%20Over%20the%20Rhine%202.pdf, 7.
9. Dan Horn, "The Trigger: Shooting 'Ignites Furious Response,'" *Cincinnati Enquirer,* December 30, 2001, http://www.enquirer.com/unrest2001/race2.html.
10. Dan Horn, "The Riots Explode: A City's Dark Week," *Cincinnati Enquirer*, December 30, 2001, http://www.enquirer.com/unrest2001/race3.html.
11. Dan Horn, "The Trigger."
12. Ibid.
13. "Photo Timeline," *Cincinnati Enquirer*, December 30, 2001, http://www.enquirer.com /unrest/unrestphotos.html.
14. Ibid.
15. James Darsey, *The Prophetic Tradition and Radical Rhetoric in America* (New York: New York University Press, 1997), 9.
16. Ibid., 5–6.
17. Richard Marback, "Corbett's Hand: A Rhetorical Figure for Composition Studies," *College Composition and Communication* 47, no. 2 (1996): 180–98.
18. Ibid., 189.
19. Quoted in Marback, 181.
20. Marback, 182.
21. Ibid., 184.
22. See Dutton, "Colony Over-the-Rhine."
23. "Private Firm Renovates 3 Sites in Over-the-Rhine," *Cincinnati Enquirer*, January 31, 2009, A4.
24. Marbeck, 191.
25. Christopher Wilkey, quoted in Donelle Dreese et al., "A People's History: Teaching an Urban Neighborhood as a Place of Social Empowerment," *Transformations: The Journal of Inclusive Scholarship and Pedagogy* 19, no. 1 (2008): 38–53.
26. Ibid.
27. Linda Flower, *Community Literacy and the Rhetoric of Public Engagement* (Carbondale: Southern Illinois University Press, 2008), 79.

Nedra Reynolds, "Reading Landscapes and Walking the Streets" and "Maps of the Everyday: Habitual Pathways and Contested Places" (pp. 253–267)

1. So what happens for those who cannot see? I'm intrigued by the tension in geography studies between 1) an expanding literature on geographies of disabilities; and 2) the continued persistence of the visual epistemology of geography. I cannot adequately address here the contributions that visually impaired people can make to geography and cultural studies, but "learning to see" is not entirely dependent on 20/20 vision; it draws on all the senses, on a type of embodiment or inhabitance. For example, Tom, the cultural geography lecturer mentioned "smellscapes" when introducing the streetwork project to students.

2. John Leighly, ed., *Land and Life: A Selection from the Writings of Carl Ortwin Sauer* (Berkeley: University of California Press, 1963), 3.

3. Ibid., 320–21.

4. Mike Crang, *Cultural Geography* (New York: Routledge, 1998), 15.

5. Ibid., 101.

6. Ibid., 5.

7. Linda McDowell, "The Transformation of Cultural Geography," in *Human Geography: Society, Space and Social Science,* ed. Derek Gregory, Don Martin, and Graham Smith (Minneapolis: University of Minnesota Press, 1994), 147.

8. Michael Keith and Steve Pile, eds., *Place and the Politics of Identity* (New York: Routledge, 1993), 7, their emphasis.

9. What would an abstract notion of culture be? The idea that culture is generally "good for people" or makes them civilized, or a dictionary definition not grounded in place.

10. Raymond Williams, *Marxism and Literature* (Oxford: Oxford University Press, 1977), 47.

11. Peter Jackson, *Maps of Meaning: An Introduction to Cultural Geography* (New York: Routledge, 1989), 39.

12. Williams, *Marxism and Literature*, 132.

13. Ibid., 132–33.

14. Ibid., 130.

15. Jackson, *Maps of Meaning: An Introduction to Cultural Geography*, 39.

16. Featherstone (Mike Featherstone, "The Flaneur, the City and Virtual Public Life," *Urban Studies* 35, no. 5–6 (1998): 909–25) says, though this is just one of many points, that flanerie is a method for reading texts, for reading the traces of the city. It is also a method of writing, of producing and constructing texts.

17. The use of the masculine pronoun is tough for me, or I'm very much aware of the "he," thus my use of forms of *flanerie*. Although I have no objection to *flaneuse* (Wilson's term), it's also important to recognize the sex and sexuality of the *flaneur,* who's often read as a dandy and coded as gay. Theoretical work on the *flaneur* tends to front this issue and tries to maintain levels of ambiguity or encourages foraging (see Munt on the lesbian *flaneur*).

18. Gunther Kress, "'English' at the Crossroads: Rethinking Curricula of Communication in the Context of the Turn to the Visual," in *Passions, Pedagogies, and Twenty-First Century Technologies*, ed. Gail E. Hawisher and Cynthia L. Selfe (Logan: Utah State University Press, 1999), 82.

19. William Morrish and Catherine Brown, *Planning to Stay: Learning to See the Physical Features of Your Neighborhood* (Minneapolis: Milkweed, 2000), 23.

20. Michel de Certeau, *The Practice of Everyday Life*, trans. Steven Rendall (Berkeley: University of California Press, 1984), 97.

21. Ibid.

22. Ibid., my emphasis.

23. Kevin Lynch, *The Image of the City* (Cambridge: MIT Press, 1960), 1. Readers of postmodern theory will recognize the term *cognitive mapping* as Fredric Jameson's. In an essay of the same name, he borrows Kevin Lynch's model from *The Image of the City* and tries to synthesize it with Althusser's formulation of ideology, which "has the great merit of stressing the gap between the local positioning of the individual subject and

the totality of class structures in which he or she is situated . . . this ideology, as such, attempts to span or coordinate, to map, by means of conscious and unconscious representations" (353).

24. Peter Gould and Rodney White, *Mental Maps*, 2nd ed. (Boston: Allen and Unwin, 1986).
25. Ibid., 17.
26. Edward W. Soja, *Thirdspace: Journeys to Los Angeles and Other Real-and-Imagined Places* (Malden, MA: Blackwell, 1996), 78–79.
27. Ibid., 79.
28. Derek Gregory, Don Martin, and Graham Smith, eds., *Human Geography: Society, Space and Social Science* (London: Macmillan, 1994), 10.
29. David Sibley, *Geographies of Exclusion: Society and Difference in the West* (New York: Routledge, 1995).
30. David Crouch, "The Street in the Making of Popular Geographical Knowledge," in *Images of the Street: Planning, Identity, and Control in Public Space*, ed. Nicholas R. Fyfe (New York: Routledge, 1998), 165.
31. Leeds City Council, *Site Map*, 27 August 27, 2001, http://www.leeds.gov.uk/sitemap/sitemap.html.
32. It's well known among students that Headingley is just a bit more posh than Hyde Park. Zoe notes: "I wouldn't be able to afford to live in Headingley though, because it's sort of popular to live there—the housing is just too expensive. The cheapest you can get is probably about £45 a week which is too much for me."
33. David Sibley, *Geographies of Exclusion: Society and Difference in the West* (New York: Routledge, 1995), 33.
34. Ibid., xiii.
35. Lynch, *The Image of the City*.
36. Alison Blunt and Gillian Rose, eds., *Writing Women and Space: Colonial and Postcolonial Geographies* (New York: Guilford, 1994), 10.

Paula Mathieu, "Writing in the Streets" (pp. 268–285)

1. Geoffrey Sirc, *English Composition as a Happening* (Logan, UT: Utah State Press, 2002), 8–9.
2. Patricia Harkin, "Game and Earnest in Curricular Reform," Conference on College Composition and Communication, Chicago, IL, 2002.
3. Writing teachers and theorists have responded to a desire for relevant pedagogy in many ways, including seeking to replace required composition courses with specialized electives (Crowley), creating expressivist pedagogies that ground inquiries in student-derived topics and ideas (see especially Elbow; Newkirk; Tobin), and prioritizing writing for peace (O'Reilly) and burning issues (Blitz and Hurlbert). See also Yagelski and Leonard.
4. See Isaacs and Jackson for a helpful overview of public writing in classrooms.
5. Susan Wells, "Rogue Cops and Health Care: What Do We Want from Public Writing?" *College Composition and Communication* 47, no. 3 (1996.): 328–29.
6. Ibid., 328.
7. Oskar Negt and Alexander Kluge, *The Public Sphere and Experience* (Minneapolis, MN: University of Minnesota Press, 1993), xlvii.
8. Wells, "Rogue Cops and Health Care: What Do We Want from Public Writing?" 334.
9. Louisa Stark, "Demographics and Stereotypes of Homeless People," in *Homelessness: A Prevention-Oriented Approach*, ed. Rene Jahiel (Baltimore, MD: Johns Hopkins Press, 1992), 27–39.
10. Michel de Certeau, *The Practice of Everyday Life*, trans. Steven Rendall (Berkeley: University of California Press, 1984), 38.
11. Ibid., 37.
12. Ibid., 15–18.
13. Ibid., 16.
14. Ibid., 17.
15. Caesrea Rumpf, "Vendors Take their Show on the Road," *Streetwise*, August 21, 2000, 14.

16. Heather Vogell, "Bus Tour Takes a Ride on the Gritty Side: Program Explores Life via Street Theater," *Chicago Tribune,* August 27, 2000, 4: 1+.
17. Gina Buccola, "Not Your Mama's Bus Tour: This Bus'll School Ya," review in *Big Shoulders,* 2000, http://www.sobs.org.
18. Rosa Eberly, "From *Writers, Audiences,* and *Communities* to *Publics:* Writing Classrooms as Protopublic Spaces," *Rhetoric Review* 18, no. 1 (1999): 165–78.
19. Sirc, *English Composition as a Happening,* 1.
20. Nancy Mack, "The Ins, Outs and In-Betweens of Multigenre Writing," *English Journal* 92, no. 2 (2002): 91-98.
21. Susie Lan Cassell, "Hunger for Memory: Oral History Recovery in Community Service Learning," *Reflections* 1, no. 2 (2000): 12–17.
22. Eli Goldblatt and Stephen Parks, "Writing Beyond the Curriculum: Fostering New Collaborations in Literacy," *College English* 62, no. 5 (2000): 584–606.
23. Paul Rogat Loeb, *Soul of a Citizen: Living with Conviction in a Cynical Time* (New York: St. Martin's Press, 1999), 5.
24. Mary Douglas, "Jokes," in *Rethinking Popular Culture,* ed. Chandra Mukerji and Michael Schudson (Los Angeles: University of California Press, 1991). 295.
25. Ibid.
26. There is not a clear dichotomy of transactional and nontransactional writing; rather the transactional ability of writing exists on a continuum. A law or other secure strategic edict operates with nearly direct performative power, in that its issuance creates material realty and names certain individuals as deviants. At the other extreme, a poem written by a homeless person, scribbled on the sidewalk, accomplishes nothing definite; if it affects a passerby at all, those effects are tactical. Much writing, however, falls somewhere in between. A grant proposal makes appeals to strategic power and might result in the transactional benefit of funding; but then again, it might not. A rhetorical appeal claims tactical power when its competent and timely completion does not guarantee any specific result. In a traditional writing class, competent and timely completion of work does guarantee a passing grade, which is why I characterize it as at least somewhat transactional.

Nicholas Christakis and James Fowler, "The Whole is Great" (pp. 305–317)

1. Genesis, 11:6 (King James Version).
2. Thomas Hobbes, *The Leviathan,* ed. Michael Oakeshott (Oxford: Oxford University Press, 1962), 100.
3. Bert Hölldobler and Edward O. Wilson, *The Superorganism: The Beauty, Elegance, and Strangeness of Insect Societies* (New York: W. W. Norton, 2009).
4. Martin A. Nowak, "Five Rules for the Evolution of Cooperation," *Science* 314, no. 5805 (2006): 1560–63.
5. Iain D. Couzin et al., "Effective Leadership and Decision-Making in Animal Groups on the Move," *Nature* 433, no. 3 (2005): 513–16; Iain D. Couzin et al., "Collective Memory and Spatial Sorting in Animal Groups," *Journal of Theoretical Biology* 218, no. 1 (2002): 1–11.
6. Daniel P. Bebber et al., "Biological Solutions to Transport Network Design," *Proceedings of the Royal Society B* 274, no. 1623 (2007): 2307–15; "Transport Efficiency and Resilience in Mycelial Networks," remarks by Mark Fricker at the Meeting of the German Physical Society, Dresden, March 27, 2009.
7. Toshiyuki Nakagaki, Hiroyasu Yamada, and Ágota Tóth, "Maze-Solving by an Amoeboid Organism," *Nature* 407, no. 6803 (2000): 470. G. Gergely Palla, Albert-László Barabási, and Tamás Vicsek, "Quantifying Social Group Evolution," *Nature* 446, no. 7136 (2007): 664–67.
9. Steve Crabtree and Brett Pelham, "Religion Provides Emotional Boost to World's Poor," Gallup, March 6, 2009, http://www.gallup.com/poll/116449/Religion-Provides-Emotional-Boost-World-Poor.aspx.
10. Edward L. Glaeser, Bruce Sacerdote, and Jose A. Scheinkman, "Crime and Social Interactions," *Quarterly Journal of Economics* 111, no. 2 (1996): 507–48.

11. Albert J. Reiss, "Understanding Changes in Crime Rates," in *Indicators of Crime and Criminal Justice: Quantitative Studies*, ed. Stephen E. Fienberg and Albert J. Reiss (Washington, DC: Bureau of Justice Statistics, 1980).

12. Francesco Gino, Shahar Ayal, and Dan Ariely, "Contagion and Differentiation in Unethical Behavior: The Effect of One Bad Apple on the Barrel," *Psychological Science* 20, no. 3 (2009): 393–98.

13. Independent Sector, "Giving and Volunteering in the United States—2001," http://www.independentsector.org.

14. Katherine Carman, "Social Influences and the Private Provision of Public Goods: Evidence from Charitable Contributions in the Workplace," Stanford Institute for Economic Policy Research Discussion Paper 02-13, January 2003.

15. Jacob K. Goeree et al., "The 1/d Law of Giving," *American Economic Journal: Microeconomics* 2, no. 1 (2010), 183–203.

16. Stephen Leider et al., "Directed Altruism and Enforced Reciprocity in Social Networks: How Much Is a Friend Worth?" NBER Working Paper No. w13135, May 2007, http://ssrn.com/abstract=989946.

James Paul Gee and Elisabeth R. Hayes, "New Kinds of People and Relationships" (pp. 318–328)

1. Penelope Brown and Stephen C. Levinson, *Politeness: Some Universals in Language Usage* (Cambridge: Cambridge University Press, 1987); Stephen C. Levinson, *Pragmatics* (Cambridge: Cambridge University Press, 1983); Nessa Wolfson, *Perspectives: Sociolinguistics and Tesol* (Cambridge: Newbury House, 1989).

2. Brown and Levinson, *Politeness: Some Universals in Language Usage.*

3. David Easley and Jon Kleinberg, *Networks, Crowds, and Markets: Reasoning about a Highly Connected World* (New York: Cambridge University Press, 2010); Granovetter 1973; Nan Lin 2001, *Social Capital: A Theory of Social Structure and Action* (New York: Cambridge University Press, 2001).

4. David Constant, Lee Sproull, and Sara Kiesler, "The Kindness of Strangers: The Usefulness of Electronic Weak Ties for Technical Advice," *Organization Science* 7 (1996): 119–35; Caroline Haythornwaite, "Building Social Networks via Computer Networks: Creating and Sustaining Distributed Learning Communities," in *Building Virtual Communities: Learning and Change in Cyberspace*, ed. K. Ann Renninger and Wesley Shumar (Cambridge: Cambridge University Press, 2002), 159–90.

5. Wagner James Au, *The Making of Second Life: Notes from the New World* (New York: HarperCollins, 2008).

6. Jonathan Rose, *The Intellectual Life of the British Working Classes* (New Haven, CT: Yale University Press, 2001), 45.

7. Kenneth Burke, *Rhetoric and Ideology* (New York: Routledge, 1993), 19.

8. Henry Jenkins, *Convergence Culture: Where Old and New Media Collide* (New York: New York University Press, 2006).

Matt Mason, "The Pirate's Dilemma" (pp. 329–348)

1. This was a little unfair, as every major European country was also heavily engaged in piracy and industrial espionage at some point in the eighteenth century. Piracy was the only way the United States could keep up.

2. For those unfamiliar with New York, the Canal Street area in Manhattan's Chinatown is one of piracy's main hubs, where vast numbers of knocked-off DVDs, handbags, and fragrances are traded daily.

3. That's not to say there isn't a rich, weird, and wonderful history of pirates in the United States. Stations that stand out include CSIC, which made a name for itself by mailing rubber chickens to its listeners, and Radio Cell, a pirate that exclusively broadcasts snippets of other people's telephone conversations (mostly of lovers and spouses arguing), eavesdropping on the people since 1996. Larger stations such as The Voice of Laryngitis

and Radio Free Harlem did attract many listeners, and pirate radio even upstaged Christian Slater in the 1990 brat- pack flick *Pump Up the Volume.*

4. Perhaps even more unusual than transmitting from France's most famous landmark was the fact that only three people ever wrote in to the station to say they had heard it.

5. There were worse repercussions than legislation. Radio Nordsee, a pirate transmitting to the Netherlands, was closed down by *air and sea attack* from the Dutch armed forces in 1964. Not to be discouraged, the pirate became TROS, now one of the Netherlands's largest broadcasting corporations.

6. Many major record labels, promoters, and legitimate blue- chip businesses advertise on pirate stations, looking to tap into their taste- making audience, even though it is illegal.

7. According to OFCOM estimates made in 2007, more than half of these pirates operate in London.

Gloria Anzaldúa, "Tlilli, Tlapalli/The Path of the Red and Black Ink" and "La Conciencia de la Mestiza/Towards a New Consciousness" (pp. 387–402)

1. R. Gordon Wasson, *The Wondrous Mushroom: Mycolatry in Mesoamerica* (New York: McGraw-Hill, 1980), 59, 103.

2. Robert Plant Armstrong, *The Powers of Presence: Consciousness, Myth, and Affecting Presence* (Philadelphia: University of Pennsylvania Press, 1981), 11, 20.

3. Armstrong, *The Powers of Presence*, 10.

4. Armstrong, *The Powers of Presence*, 4.

5. Miguel Leon-Portilla, *Los Antiguos Mexicanos: A través de sus crónicas y cantares* (México, DE: Fondo de Cultura Económica, 1961), 19, 22.

6. Ibid., 125.

7. In *Xóchitl* in *Cuícatl* is Nahuatl for flower and song, *flor y canto.*

8. Nietzsche, in *The Will to Power*, says that the artist lives under a curse of being vampirized by his talent.

9. This is my own "take off" on José Vasconcelos' idea. Jose Vasconcelos, *La Raza Cósmica: Misión de la Raza Ibero-Americana* (Mexico: Aguilar S.A. de Ediciones, 1961).

10. Vasconcelos.

11. Arthur Koestler termed this "bisociation." Albert Rothenberg, *Creative Process in Art, Science, and Other Fields* (Chicago: University of Chicago Press, 1979), 12.

12. In part, I derive my definitions for "convergent" and "divergent" thinking from Rothenberg, 12–13.

Key Terms

Academic discourse/academic writing (p. 22)   A term for the many different types of writing that exists and has have power within the university to share knowledge. More specifically, the writing done within an academic discourse community explores key terms of an existing argument occurring within scholarly journals and, in doing so, attempts to create new knowledge on the topic.

Annotating (p. 11)   The practice of underlining key sentences within a book or essay or writing notes in the margins to highlight key points.

Artifact (p. 15)   A material product such as an essay, art object, or sculpture that represents an abstract idea.

Audience (p. 32)   The group of individuals who are the intended readers, viewers, or participants of a piece of work (essay, film, theater performance).

Community partnership (pp. 25, 174)   An arrangement where a university (or one of its programs) agrees to work with a community partner (such as a neighborhood organization) on a specific project. The agreement typically includes having students enrolled in a class undertake a particular piece of work.

Drafting (p. 34)   A stage in the writing process where the author puts more emphasis on creating, exploring, and integrating a set of ideas on a topic than on being concerned with issues such as grammar or sentence structure.

Evidence (p. 22)   The information a writer uses to support her or his argument. Types of evidence can include articles from reliable authors and sources, historical or scientific facts, census data, theoretical models, and interviews.

Goal statement (p. 208)   A short paragraph which announces the specific goals for a project.

Limited involvement (p. 189)   A community partnership structure where student involvement occurs at the end of the semester and revolves around the production of a set of materials for a community partner.

Multimodal texts (p. 24)   A text that combines some mix of print, visual, and digital technologies, to make an argument.

Organic intellectual (p. 6)   An individual who bases her or his worldview on the experiences and insights of those sharing a similar lifestyle or economic position.

Prewriting (p. 34)   The initial stage of the writing process where the primary focus is on generating as many ideas as possible on a given topic.

Reading group (p. 12)   A group of individuals who meet to discuss a book or essay, with the goal of developing a common understanding of its meaning.

Reading journal (p. 12)   A notebook or Word document where you write down what you believe to be important quotes, interpretations, or connections within and among assigned readings.

Research community (pp. 33–34)   A set of individuals who are engaged in answering a common set of questions and who also typically also use common methods and strategies when looking for answers. Also called a discourse community.

Research focus (p. 31)   An approach to research that acknowledges the broad set of issues and voices already involved in the area of study. The *thesis* of an author's research is a sentence or set of sentences that state the research focus of a paper and the author's particular stance on that research.

Revising (p. 35)   A stage in the writing process where the author makes changes to the content, structure, or focus of her or his paper based on feedback from a teacher, community member, friend, or colleague.

Sustained involvement (p. 189)   A community partnership structure where student involvement occurs throughout the term, frequently interacting with the community partner, and producing such artifacts as publications or public forums

Traditional intellectual (p. 6)   An individual who bases her or his worldview on the experiences and insights of mainstream religious, educational, and political institutions.

Transformative involvement (p. 190)   A community partnership structure that exists beyond any particular course and allows students consistent long-term involvement in the creation of a new set of policies or programs designed to create fundamental, structural change in a neighborhood or community.

Work required plan (p. 233)   A document that details what tasks need to be accomplished as well as who is responsible for each specific task.

Index